Third Edition

The Politics of Education

Schools in Conflict

by

Frederick M. Wirt
University of Illinois,
Urbana

and

Michael W. Kirst
Stanford University

McCutchan Publishing Corporation
P.O. Box 774
Berkeley, California 94701

ISBN 0–8211–2270–3
Library of Congress Catalog Card Number 92–64196

Printed in the United States of America

To the pioneers in this field, Steve Bailey and David Minar

Contents

1

The Political Turbulence of American Schools

The purpose of this book is to trace the ways in which American schools are viewed as political. This perspective arises in part from the school's connection to such recognizable political systems as the state and national governments. It also arises from the way in which schools act as miniature political systems. Many school professional and lay participants, though, regard both these points as not only untrue but also misleading, if not actually pernicious. Their view is that the institution they know and operate is "apolitical," having nothing to do with politics—for, as everyone knows, politicians are vile folk, somewhat equivalent to used-car salesmen in status. The direct purposes of this volume are to reveal the extent to which politics and education do intersect and to demonstrate that "professional" tasks are highly political and that school professionals are also politicians.

The differences in interpretation stem from varying conceptions of what constitutes a political act. Schools have traditionally been characterized as apolitical. This meant that they had nothing to do with political parties, whose usual interactions with the citizenry have been regarded as "dirty"; schools were considered sanitized and outside the hands of party politics. For political scientists, though, parties represent only one facet of political life. From their perspective, the essence of a political act is the struggle of a group to secure

1

the authoritative support of government for its values. Within this definition of the term *political*, much of what schoolfolk regard as apolitical is highly political.

Let's be clear on our focus. We are not discussing *how* schools should be run nor *what* they should teach and *why*. Our focus is, instead, on *how the process of policymaking in schools has characteristics that can be termed political*. We will show how the policymaking process is becoming increasingly and more openly politicized as a result of major changes in the ways state and local governments and even citizens relate to the school system. New definitions of school purposes, new claims on school resources, new efforts to make the schools responsive to certain groups and their values are all giving rise to a larger, more weblike set of political relationships surrounding the local schools. Almost any and every element of school governance could get caught up in political controversy at present.

THE POLITICAL AGENDA IN THE 1990S

Public concern about education has remained at a high level ever since the early 1980s, after the release of numerous reports alleging the low quality of American education.[1] Recent policy has focused more on quality than equity. And President Bush made choice and federal aid to private schools a key part of his 1992 campaign, in order to spur market competition between public schools and private schools. Education was one of the four top issues in the 1992 presidential campaign, and was featured in numerous gubernatorial and legislative races as well. Typically, American politics does not permit such sustained attention to an issue.[2] Usually, the issue-attention cycle leads to periods of extreme interest in an issue followed by periods of disinterest.[3]

What is the cause of such unusual, decade-long political interest? The basic influence today is the same as in the early 1980s— widespread public concern that poor education was connected to slow U.S. economic growth and U.S. problems with international economic competition.[4] U.S. schools were blamed for producing workers who were not as productive, adaptive, or skilled as workers in other nations. By 1983, Toyota replaced Sputnik as the symbol of U.S. educational shortcomings. The 1991–92 recession generated the same criticisms and policy concerns as did the 1981–83 recession.[5] While middle-class support for public education is crucial, there are signs that the schools must make changes in addition to the intensification-type reforms of the 1980s if they are to keep middle-class support.[6] "Intensification" resulted in lower class sizes, high teacher salaries, and increased graduation or university entrance standards. During the 1980s, U.S. public education spent 30 percent more than inflation, but pupil outcomes increased only modestly.[7]

By 1992, the national debate stressed the urgent need for more radical reforms than 1980s' intensification; such reforms include national teacher certification, a national curriculum, nationwide subject matter exams, and break-the-mold experimental schools. Moreover, the genesis of new policies changed in the 1990s from the states and localities to nationwide organizations like the National Education Goals Panel and the National Governors' Association. Choice and vouchers were advocated as a way to break up political gridlock caused by the conflicting actors and forces described in this volume. The education interest groups resisted vouchers with all their resources, but may not be able to stave off market-oriented policies for all of the 1990s. This policy debate was embedded in education politics, with Republicans more enthusiastic about public aid to private schools than Democrats. Education employee interest groups are focusing their lobbying on preserving their financial gains from the 1980s in the face of a major economic recession. Political analyst William Boyd criticized recent reforms for their underlying "schizophrenia, amnesia, and ignorance in school politics." Such reforms, imposed from above—that is, "top down reforms"—ignore and even contradict research on organizational effectiveness, which means they have a high potential for failure, leading to further public disenchantment with the schools.

This current overview of education policy demonstrates the close and openly recognized linkages between education policy and politics. But this has not always been the case, as historical analysis of the roots of education policy will show.

THE MYTH OF APOLITICAL EDUCATION

By a mutual but unspoken long-standing agreement, American citizens and scholars have contended that the world of education is and should be separate from the world of politics. Although *elections* and *referenda* concerning school policies were viewed as political, these words did not connote "politics" in the usual sense when applied to educational policy. Two reasons existed for attempting to preserve the myth that "politics and education do not mix." The first was the risk to the school professionals who were overt players of politics when they were expected not to be. The second reason was the relative benefits to them—more legitimacy and money—if they preserved the image of the public schools as a uniquely nonpolitical function of government.[8]

At the turn of the century, a nationwide affiliation of "progressive" university presidents, school superintendents, and nonprofessional allies emerged from urban business and professional elites. One aim of these people was to free the schools from partisan politics and excessive decentralization. They saw political corruption as the prime cause of educational inefficiency in urban schools. And in fact, at that time many politicians did regard the schools as a support for their spoils systems and awarded school jobs and contracts as political favors.

Municipal corruption was everywhere, and the schools were as bad as any other city office. Muckrakers exposed textbook publishers, and contractors allied with corrupt school trustees for common boodle in the common school. Leaders concerned about these practices in urban education from 1890–1910 reported:

A superintendent in one of the Eastern States writes: "Nearly all the teachers in our schools get their positions by political 'pull.' If they secure a place and are not backed by political influence, they are likely to be turned out. Our drawing teacher recently lost her position for this reason." One writes from the South: "Most places depend on politics. The lowest motives are frequently used to influence ends." A faint wail comes from the far West: "Positions are secured and held by the lowest principles of corrupt politicians." "Politicians wage a war of extermination against all teachers who are not their vassals," comes from the Rocky Mountains.

In Boston, the teachership is still a spoil of office. It is more difficult, at the present time, for a Catholic than for a Protestant young woman to get a place, but nevertheless, some Catholics secure appointments, for "trading" may always be done, while each side has a wholesome fear of the other assailing it in the open board. A member said one day, in my hearing: "I must have my quota of teachers."

The worst kind of boss rule has prevailed in San Francisco, and the board of education gradually became a place sought by those who wished to use the position for political preferment or for personal ends. Once every six or eight years there would be an effort at reform, and a few good men were elected; but they were usually in a minority, and the majority, held together by "the cohesive force of plunder," ruled things with a high hand.[9]

This situation was vigorously reinforced by local control. A decentralized, ward-based committee system for administering the public schools provided opportunities for extensive political influence. In 1905, Philadelphia had forty-three elected district school boards consisting of 559 members. There were only 7 members on the Minneapolis board, while Hartford—with a third as many people— had 39 school visitors and committeepersons.[10] Despite such great variations, at the turn of the century, sixteen of twenty-eight cities with over one hundred thousand population had boards of 20 members or more.

Reformers maintained that board members elected by wards advanced their own parochial and special interests at the expense of the school district as a whole. What was needed to counter this atomization, they believed, was election at large. A good school system was good for everyone, not just for one segment of the community. Professional expertise rested on the assumption that scientific ways to administer schools did exist and were independent of any particular group's values. This unitary-community idea would help protect schools from local political processes. Reformers also charged that the executive authority of the larger school boards was splintered because they worked through many subcommittees. No topic was too trivial for one more subcommittee, ranging from how to teach reading to the purchase of doorknobs. At one time, Chicago had seventy-nine subcommittees, and Cincinnati had seventy-four.[11] The primary prerequisite for better management was thought to be centralization of power in a chief executive who would have considerable delegated authority from the school board. Only under such a system could someone make large-scale improvements and be held accountable.

By 1910, a conventional educational wisdom had evolved among the schoolfolk and leading business and professional men who had sought reforms. Sometimes only a very small group of patricians secured new charters from state legislatures and thereby reorganized the urban schools without any popular vote.[12] The watchwords of reform became *centralization, expertise, professionalism, nonpolitical control,* and *efficiency*—all of these would inspire "the one best system." The governance structure needed to be revised so that school boards would be small, elected at large, and freed from all connections with political parties and regular government officials such as mayors and councilmen.

The most attractive model for this organization and governance was the large-scale industrial bureaucracies that were rapidly emerging in the turn-of-the-century economy. Divorced from the city political leaders, a board elected by the city as a whole would be less susceptible to graft and job favoritism. The centralized power of the superintendent would overcome the bureaucratic tangle and inefficiency of board subcommittees. These reform concepts spread rapidly from the large to small cities and towns, and they found their major forum and vehicle in the National Education Association.

At the turn of the century, urban school reform was part of a broader pattern of elite municipal change. Public rhetoric then pitted the corrupt politician against the community-oriented citizen. The underlying motives of these reformers have since been questioned by several historians. Hays has emphasized that financial and professional leaders deplored the decentralized ward system largely because it empowered members of the lower and lower-middle classes (many of whom were recent immigrants). Reformers wanted "not simply to replace bad men with good; they proposed to change the occupational and class origins of decision makers."[13] Tyack expresses this viewpoint in stronger language:

> Underlying much of the reform movement was an elitist assumption that prosperous, native born Protestant Anglo-Saxons were superior to other groups and thus should determine the curriculum and the allocation of jobs. It was the mission of the schools to imbue children of the immigrants and the poor with uniformly WASP ideals.[14]

After reforms were enacted, membership on the governing agencies did change. Counts's classic study done in 1927 showed that upper-class professionals and business people made up the centralized boards of education.[15] For instance, in Saint Louis, after reforms in 1897, professionals on the board jumped from 4.8 percent to 58.3 percent and big businessmen from 9 percent to 25 percent; small businessmen dropped from 47.6 percent to 16.7 percent, and wage earners from 28.6 percent to none.[16] These board members then delegated many of their formal powers to professionals along with discretion to shape schools to meet the needs of industrial society— but only as defined by one segment of that society.

The no-politics ideal of public education has enjoyed impressive and lasting popularity with the general public. There have been hard-nosed advantages for the professional in nursing this folklore, as summarized by one school superintendent.

1. The higher social status and salary generally accorded school-people by the public is better maintained and somewhat dependent upon a situation in which the schools are seen as unique rather than as a mere extension of the same local government that provides dog catchers and sanitation departments.

2. In maintaining a tighter control over the public school system, the image of "unique function" allows greater leverage by the professional school administrator than an image acknowledging that schools are "ripe for the picking" by dilettante and professional politicians.

3. The "unique function"image also provides the schools with a stronger competitive position for tax funds wherever voters are allowed to express a choice of priorities among government agencies.[17]

The outcome of this nonpolitical ideology is a massive irony in our political system well characterized by Martin:

Thus is the circle closed and the paradox completed. Thus does the public school, heralded by its champions as the cornerstone of democracy, reject the political world in which democratic institutions operate. Thus is historical identification with local government accompanied by insistence on complete independence of any agency . . . of local government, lip service to general citizen activity attended by mortal fear of general politics, the logical and legitimate companion of citizen action.[18]

Political Turbulence and School Policy

More recently, several national trends have made the public schools more overtly political, strongly challenging the tenets of the turn-of-the-century reformers. The 1983–87 state reform legislation is only the latest example. In the 1960s a call was broadcast for "community participation" in all types of public agencies, and this was widely accepted by social critics and reformers. Proponents contended that citizens need to be more than "involved" or "consulted" if government is to gain their active consent. Instead they have to actually "participate" in democracy, even though this might sometimes involve social conflict, such as picketing and strikes. The federal school-aid legislation of the 1960s encouraged participation by creating a number of watchdog citizens' advisory commissions and requiring that school authorities consult with community groups.

This recent change in style highlights an ongoing basic problem in the governance of American schools; that is the tension between the community's need for school leadership that can lead and be trusted and the same community's desire to have its own will carried out by that leadership. Since its inception with Horace Mann's heresy, American public education has sought responsiveness to public needs for what Raymond Fosdick termed the extraordinary possibilities of ordinary people. The changing focus of American civic education over a century shows this.[19] So does the continuing search for ways to ensure public responsiveness—from party control of schools through the progressive model of corporate centralization to the contemporary call for "state leadership."[20] This brief history shows the truth of Paul's adjuration that there is nothing new under the sun, for an intriguing repetition of issues has occurred in schools over the last century: merit pay, school prayer, school closings, dropouts, and the gifted. In large part, we read both the repetition and variety as reflections of the classic political tension between the leaders and the led. In this case tension centers on having school policy work the way each wishes.

This tension between leader and led underlies current conflicts that were generated as new groups arose during the last three decades to challenge the former power pattern in the schools. New school "core constituencies" have emerged. (*Core* indicates that we have separated these groups for analytical purposes although they are not necessarily mutually exclusive in experience.) Each group creates special tensions for the school's political authority as exercised by the board and its administrators because each core constituency challenges the leadership in a special issue that involves reallocation of school resources.[21] These issues and their core constituencies are:

Parents—shared or community control, advisory input, decentralization, or whatever term is current.

Students—rights of governance, expression, dress, behavior, and so on.

Teachers—organization for collective bargaining (hereafter shortened to "teacher power").

Taxpayers—reform of local financing involving a larger assumption of costs by the state.

Minorities—the issues that encompass desegregation, dropouts, and equal employment.

Federal and state authorities—guidelines, mandates, court orders in matters of discrimination, curriculum, finances, and so forth.

Controversy over such issues may vary from locality to locality, but they move in response to certain forces. That is, local school conflict is shaped by forces both outside and inside an individual district. The absence of walls around the school districts opens them to public and private influences from the external, multiple centers of decision making that characterize American national life.[22] New concepts about how society should be conducted or life enjoyed, the episodic eruption of national events that crystallize local hopes and fears about school matters, and the immediate transmission by media of all these into every urban crevice are all major extracommunity stimuli of school conflict. When such local conflict mobilizes new groups, when national currents are at work locally, and when the rancor and clamor swells, we reach a level of conflict accurately termed *turbulence*.[23]

CURRENTS OF TURBULENCE

We develop a fuller treatment of these new power groups throughout this book, but it will help focus our analysis here to briefly review
their roles. Figure 1.1 provides an introduction to the concept of
turbulence and to these groups.

Parents and Shared Control

The turn-of-the-century triumph of the efficiency doctrine, achieved
through centralization and bureaucracy, weakened the ties between
school leadership and its constituents. That was acceptable in the
pre-World War II decades, when schooling laid minimal claims on
district resources, and professionals benefited from their own publicity about education as the key to success. In the two decades after
that war, this weakened linkage (as voting studies showed) continued
to be acceptable in the rush to obtain schooling for all.[24]
Sometime during the late 1950s, the professionals' aura began to
fade. In 1954 the *Brown* decision illustrated the disgraceful failure of
Southern educators with their black students for the first time. Other
complaints emerged that, regardless of race, Johnny could not read,
speak languages, or calculate in base ten and that the Russians were
somehow outperforming our school system. Our rivalry with the
Russians generated a vast injection of local and federal funds into
schools—the National Defense Education Act in the late 1950s,
university support in the early 1960s, and finally the Elementary and
Secondary Education Act in 1965.
The more voters contributed, though, the more they complained
that the educational bureaucracy was not sensitive to parental preferences in schooling their children. Social scientists joined with analyses
of the unresponsive nature of the schooling administration, with New
York City's central headquarters regarded as the prototype rather
than exception.[25] Suburbanites maintained that administrators were
insensitive to their demands either for richer or for plainer curricula,
whether in affluent Scarsdale, urban New York, or working-class
Maple Heights, Ohio. In the central cities—particularly the newly
mobilized black communities—central offices and site principals were
increasingly ridiculed for their insensitivity, which was easily labeled
"racism." From a surprisingly wide gamut of lifestyles, parents-as

Figure 1.1
Paradigm of Turbulent School Politics

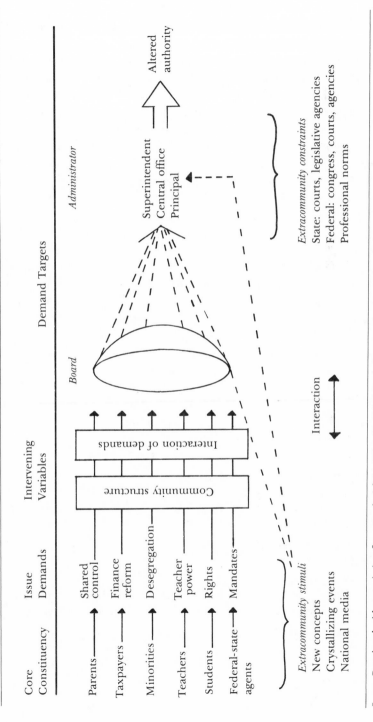

Core Constituency	Issue Demands	Intervening Variables	Demand Targets	

Core Constituency

Issue Demands

Intervening Variables

Demand Targets

Administrator

Board

Parents ——▶ Shared control

Taxpayers ——▶ Finance reform

Minorities ——▶ Desegregation

Teachers ——▶ Teacher power

Students ——▶ Rights

Federal-state agents ——▶ Mandates

Community structure

Interaction of demands

Interaction ↕

Superintendent
Central office
Principal

Altered authority

Extracommunity stimuli
New concepts
Crystallizing events
National media

Extracommunity constraints
State: courts, legislative agencies
Federal: congress, courts, agencies
Professional norms

Source: Reprinted with permission from Frederick M. Wirt, "Political Turbulence and Administrative Authority in the Schools," in Louis H. Masotti and Robert L. Lineberry, eds., *The New Urban Politics*, p. 63. Copyright 1976, Ballinger Publishing Company.

voters criticized their lack of connection with school district decision making.

Although reasons for this lack differed with locale and status, the old participatory impulse had clearly increased. Notions of shared control took on different forms during the 1970s. At times participation meant parents having structured input into school decisions. Thus, new structures were created for parental advisory committees at the school site level. In California, for example, community members joined the school principal and teachers to set a budget in tune with their own definition of good education. In Chicago, parent-dominated committees can hire or fire principals.

Parental input also focused on what was being taught in the classroom. The fear of teaching Communism during the 1950s became in the 1980s the anger at teaching about biological evolution or the anger about children reading fiction with harsh language or critical views of American society. Other parents rose to defend these same curriculum subjects, and battles were waged in street demonstrations, court suits, state legislative lobbies—accompanied by a steady vilification of professionals and board members. The worst example was in Kanawha County, West Virginia, in the mid-1970s, when the school district's central office was dynamited by someone opposed to the teaching of "Man: A Course of Study" (MACOS).

Parental input went even further to challenge the very quality of the school's results, namely, academic achievement. From the earlier concern with whether or not Johnny could read, growing claims—and some supporting data—suggest that schools were not teaching effectively. National news magazines featured articles on school "failures." Demands arose to hold teachers individually responsible for their pupils' progress, while professionals pointed to numerous factors more potent than teachers in influencing results. By the mid-1980s some states had moved to require examination of tenured teachers for their basic literacy.

In short, parents became much more than just the old PTA clique, which had loyally supported professionals prior to the mid-1960s. Parental energies and their agendas swelled along with their growing numbers. It no longer worked to keep them busy with a cake sale to raise money for a classroom projector. The traditionally unchallenged use of public authority once tendered to school professionals was being reexamined—and the professionals were widely regarded as failing.[26]

Taxpayers and Financial Reform

Demands for more control of schools have not been restricted to parents worried about what schools were doing to their children; over the last fifteen years, taxpayers have also challenged school financing.[27] A spate of litigation developed from the fusion of the Ford Foundation and university scholars in law and educational finance. It began in California with the famous *Serrano* decision, which found the principle of student expenditures based on district wealth unconstitutional. The United States Supreme Court's 1973 *Rodriguez* case narrowly prevented this from being elevated into a constitutional principle. Reform efforts continued though, focusing on state legislatures after the abortive attempts at change through the Supreme Court and statewide referenda.

Pressures to redistribute school financial resources are accompanied by pressures to have the state take on a higher share of local school costs. Since 1900 that state share has grown, stabilizing at around 40 percent after World War II (a figure concealing numerous small shifts up and down). By 1970 it was still at that level, but by 1981, it had jumped to over 50 percent due to recent reform movements and public disapproval of property taxes. Local financial support had also fallen off. The mid-1960s saw the peak for support of local bond and tax issues; thereafter the electorate became increasingly resistant.

A network of school finance reformers appeared amidst this current of protest. Public policy issues emerge on state political agendas for many reasons, but one of the most important and least understood is the role of interstate lobbying networks that sponsor and promote issues in a wide variety of forums. Elements of the network may be entrepreneurs, private nonprofit advocacy organizations, lawyers, interstate technical assistance groups, and often private foundations. Such networks spread ideas and create opportunities for state politicians to champion particular causes or programs. Many of the most interesting educational innovations, such as competency testing, have been promoted by such a lobby network.

By 1981 two of the largest networks—those for school finance reform and spending or tax limits—started clashing with each other. School finance reformers advocated large increases in state and local spending to meet "equity" criteria and special needs, such as those for bilingual, handicapped, or urban students. In contrast, members of the other reform group crusaded for tax limitation, seeking to stop or reverse the growth in state and local spending. Both networks were spawned by entrepreneurs who generated activity and structure rewards; both unified members from diverse organizations.

The 1983–92 reform era has focused more on instructional policy than finance equity. But expenditures increased by about 30 percent after inflation during 1980–1990 as politicians voted to fund higher salaries and academic standards. More science and mathematics teachers were hired, and teachers received more dollars as they moved up their new "career ladders." By 1992, there was a new spate of lawsuits challenging the equity of state school finance formulas.

Racial Minorities and Desegregation

The core constituency of racial minorities, so intimately involved in school desegregation, has two purposes. First members seek a status goal, recognition that the Constitution's commitment to equal protection of the law applies to them as well, despite centuries of prejudice and discrimination. As such, desegregation is only one aspect of the "politics of deference," the central struggle of American ethnic politics to gain respect for one's importance and value as individuals and as a group.[28] The second goal of minorities in school desegregation is material, namely, the reallocation of school resources to improve life opportunities for their children. Desegregation is thus one aspect of the concern for redistributive justice sparked in the recent decades by challenges to the standards of urban service provided to America's poor of whatever race.

In this effort, almost nothing has been achieved without external pressure on the local district. Everywhere the forces of court orders—and in the South before the Nixon administration, the threat of fund cutoffs to segregated schools—have accounted for any progress. Despite nationwide publicity, local protests brought little change in encrusted racial conditions.

Against local racial barriers, a coalition of national and local interest groups, scholars, legal studies centers, and national media interacted with the federal courts to dramatically alter the face of Southern education. Between 1962 and 1972, the South dismantled its de jure segregated schools under the combined attack of private groups and federal action. Year after year, the number of all-white schools shrank abruptly to amaze many who thought these changes would take decades. By 1981, Southern desegregation had gone well beyond the publicized stage of parental protest over busing or white supremacists's fears of racial mixing. School problems were now more educational than political; that is, they involved improving the educational services and enhancing the life chances of the poor regardless of race.

The situation in the North during the 1970s looked a lot like that of the South during the 1950s, with actual segregation increasing. The federal thrust had diminished over the years because of presidents with little political will for the issues, Congresses under great pressure from those who saw busing as the special evil of desegregation, and the lack of support from Northern whites for a range of special programs that originated in President Johnson's Great Society program. Enormous movements of whites out of central cities, recalcitrant local school boards, aroused local political organizations, and hesitant local press all combined at the district level to slow or block a movement that was simultaneously changing dramatically in the South. But litigation continued in the North, and a rash of federal district judges ordered desegregation planning and busing. Every fall during the 1970s, the opening of Northern schools witnessed some big city in turmoil over beginning this task; in 1980 it was Los Angeles and Saint Louis. Yet much desegregation did take place without publicity, especially in middle-sized places. But for many Americans, the street fighting in Boston was what they associated with such change, although Denver desegregated quietly that same fall. Wherever such turbulence occurs, there is a formal, almost inescapable, drama that must unfold, with each stage set regardless of locale. By 1981, however, an impressive number of districts existed where desegregation at least extended to the stage at which the outcry dies down, the buses roll regularly, and education begins. Since then very few court orders have been issued, and Northern cities are now even more segregated. Minorities have turned to educational quality and a share of school jobs.

Students and Their Rights

Core constituencies sketched to this point are based outside the school walls, but two groups that operate on the inside are students and teachers. Both have known the same remarkably brief and recent period during which novel concepts have suddenly flowered to offer them new powers formerly controlled by administrators. Considering their position of relative weakness, students have made strides that contrast dramatically with the background of the law's long indifference to them.[29]

For most of our history, the authority of the school administrator over the student's life at school has been almost complete. Legislatures gave state departments of education broad authority that they in turn passed on to the school professional. The federal Constitution and statutes had no sway here, for the idea of student rights rooted in these sources did not yet exist. During this era, an administrator's response to any student even politely questioning why he or she had to dress, walk, eat, speak, and otherwise act in the prescribed manner was much like that of writer Ring Lardner when his children questioned him: "'Shut up,' I explained."

The seminal United States Court decision in this field, which typified subsequent thinking by other courts, was another of those abrupt changes in the power context of schools—the 1969 decision of *Tinker* v. *the Des Moines School District*. Here, Des Moines students wearing black armbands to protest the Vietnam War had been suspended even though they had created no disruption. The Court's opinion noted that when a basic constitutional right, such as free speech under the First Amendment, was being exercised, and no evidence showed that the student action interfered with school purposes or disrupted schooling, no punishment could be levied. As later cases demonstrated, such an exercise *could* create disruptions and so be prohibited. Thus, Southern schools could not restrict the wearing of civil rights buttons if the results were nondisruptive, but they could do so if they caused disturbances.

In only a few years, this principle and those of due process and equal protection of the laws have permeated many traditional school practices. Only a brief listing of judicial restraints on once-conventional disciplinary rules and management decisions is possible here, but recall that these have all emerged since 1969. They include rulings in: use of athletic symbols, Confederate flags, and schools names; regulating hair length; lack of procedures for suspension and expulsion; corporal punishment; use of bulletin boards; use of achievement or aptitude tests; rules for athletic eligibility; preference for male rather than female sports programs, and so on.

As a result, school authorities everywhere drew up lengthy statements of student rights and school authority. Professional associations helped with model statements relating to different fields. None of this meant that students could not be expelled or suspended, their publications controlled, or their expressions banned. They could, but now only according to set procedures and over a longer period of time. All of this constituted an additional challenge to the once unchallengeable school authority, adding another eddy to school turbulence. But students' rights have not advanced significantly in the 1980s as the courts have retreated slightly from the due process concerns of the 1970s. Principals now can check lockers without search warrants and censor the student newspaper.

Teachers and Organizational Power

The other core constituency challenging traditional authority from inside the school is teachers—once widely viewed as submissive. A city superintendent or principal who would regard teachers so today would be hard to find. A change has transpired among teachers in the past twenty years. In part this stems from changes in American education itself and in part from teachers' perceptions of themselves. As with other education groups, things will never be the same here again.

Teachers achieved a potential for power as education became big business.[30] When more parents wanted their children to have more schooling after World War II, and more children were there to educate, Americans spent more on education. This in turn meant that the schools needed more teachers. As a proportion of the gross national product, school expenditures rose during the period 1949 to 1970 from about 3.5 to 8 percent. Where we spent only $2 billion in 1940, we spent $50 billion in 1970 and over $220 billion in 1992. Riding this massive injection of funds into the schools, teachers grew in numbers from just over 1 million in 1940 to almost 3 million in 1971 and to about 3.3 million in 1980. By the mid-1970s teachers were 1 million fewer in number than farmers but substantially more than teamsters, auto workers, steelworkers, and doctors. Not surprisingly, their income rose too. Between 1952 and 1968 teachers' incomes increased by over 125 percent, while personal income and employee average earnings rose nationally by about 94 percent. Their salaries passed the average earnings of industrial workers some time back, and the gap increased even more during the 1960s. By the middle 1970s, however, teachers' wage increases lagged behind inflation and private industry only to regain their momentum after the 1983 reform era.

Concern about wages helped teachers' increasingly conscious efforts to organize for collective bargaining on salary and other matters. The cause-and-effect relationship is ambiguous, however. Did bargaining legislation and subsequent organization precede or follow teachers' dissatisfactions? Were boards and legislatures frightened into voluntary improvements in reaction against successful teacher strikes elsewhere? Did the advent of collective bargaining increase teacher salaries?

There is no question about the growth of teachers' affiliations that have become more insistent on improving working conditions. This insistence was seen in the toughening up of the larger National Education Association (NEA), once passive on these issues, and in the rise of the smaller but more militant American Federation of Teachers. These groups both became more active in party politics as well. For the first time, the NEA endorsed a presidential candidate, Carter, in 1976 and 1980.

The growth of powerful teachers' organizations has been paralleled by the rise of the strike. Despite widely prevalent state laws against public employees using this tactic, some form of strike—"withholding of labor"—has developed as the main instrument used to secure teachers' benefits in recent years. Between 1955 and 1965 there were only 35 strikes in all, but during the one year of 1967–1968 there were 114, and 131 the next year. Coincidental or not, during this first period of strike action, 1966–1968, the number of signed contracts increased by almost one-half. By 1985, the strike threat of teachers was as much a part of autumn as the new football season.

Their success has not been without its problems for teachers. As teachers participate more and more in the reallocation of resources at the local, state, and national political level, they lose the aura of being apolitical, with all the opprobrium the term signifies in American culture. It was this mythical quality that helped them claim a large share of resources for so long without having to contend with other claimants. Now, in the state legislatures and city councils, where school budgets are sometimes reviewed, teachers are only one more pressure group whose claim to special treatment must be balanced against others' claims. It follows that other pressure groups will increasingly combine against the teachers' claims and so draw teachers even more into open political conflict. Whatever their form, however, these trends change the traditional interaction between teacher and administrator, adding yet another constraint to the broad authority school officials once had.

Federal and State Authorities

From the perspective of school boards and professionals who watch this turbulence breaking against their walls, probably the most noticed—certainly the most complained of—has been the force of external governments. The movement of core constituencies—demanding new definitions of how schools should be structured, financed, and their services delivered—has often been frustrated by local authorities. The protests have then escalated to higher levels of government within the federal system. This second stage of the conflict resulted in some groups securing state and federal statutes, administrative rulings, or court orders in their favor that then impinged on the local power structure. This has meant great limitations on local authorities' control of the school program.[31]

Each of the constituencies referred to has generated many such external requirements. These cross the desk of local authorities in the forms of mandates, guidelines, orders, suggestions, and reporting forms. Sometimes the source is a funded program to enhance educational services, but it can also come in the form of a court injunction not to do something or a court mandate to do something else. These can all become enormously detailed in their requirements. In some cases regulations or suggestions come without the finances necessary to administer them. And always multiple forms must be filed to show a state or federal authority that what was required has in fact been achieved. These add enormously to the volume of services and standards the schools must maintain.

Some standards work their way into the regular procedures of the district, where they constitute a new force from a new constituency working against the previous professional dominance of schools. The general rule, supported by research, is that what the district favors in this flow of external demands becomes what is most implemented. But where the district neither asks for nor rejects the demands, then adaptation of the law becomes the norm. It would be a rare district among the sixteen thousand in the nation where this response did not take place, but bit by bit, across two decades, this extramural force has challenged and gradually altered traditional local control to become another current in the contemporary turbulence of American schools.

Political Forces Outside the Locality

No constituency acts independently; the turbulence of school politics is also affected by extracommunity stimuli. The outside forces noted in Figure 1.1 may be the most important factor in all current local politics, whether dealing with schools, high-rise buildings, welfare, ethnic conflict, roads, or other public policies.[32]

Three broad stimuli affect school constituencies today. First the *state of the economy* greatly influences the amount of resources available and their allocation. Many administrators, particularly older superintendents, have witnessed the two extremes of bust and boom. The Great Depression of the 1930s shrank all school budgets, preventing new programs and cutting old ones. Under such intense constraints from a public sorely pressed, the school boards could listen to few if any claims from core constituencies except the taxpayers.

More recently, an enormous prosperity and then subsequent recession affected every school district in the nation. In the resurgence of public support for schools beginning in 1983, booming expenditures characterized local politics. With ever-expanding resources seemingly available, claimants for new programs and benefits could be satisfied by boards and administrators. By 1983, the growth in imports and the loss of jobs in autos, steel, and other basic industries made international economic competitiveness a key issue. This concern spawned a massive movement to increase educational standards.

Another extracommunity stimulus is *the power of new concepts*, particularly those centered on social change. Every change mentioned for a core constituency illustrates this process. In addition, education seems particularly subject to faddishness in curricular matters, such as new math, critical thinking, merit pay, and so on. Certainly the concept of "evaluation," given a powerful push by Title I of the 1965 Elementary and Secondary Education Act, has penetrated school activity wherever federal monies are deposited.

Spawned by some scholarly "scribbler," funded by foundations, transmitted by educators' meetings and journals, researched and certified by schools of education, reform ideas sweep through the American school system in recurring tides. Some are transitory, for example, Nixon's Right to Read Program, but others leave a permanent mark on schools, such as desegregation in the South. Behind them all, however small or large, is someone's notion of the preferable, the efficient, the humane, the inexpensive, and the just in matters of schooling.

Another class of extramural stimuli is those highly publicized *crystallizing events* that capture core constituencies and dramatically generate new demands on local school authorities, adding even more turbulence to school politics. The death of a prominent athlete due to cocaine; the spread of AIDS; precedent-shattering judicial decisions in the *Tinker, Brown,* and *Serrano* cases; a clash over community control in New York City—these all illustrate the singular event that no one can ignore.

We cannot separate these extramural events from extramural concepts, for each of them emerged from a new full-blown conception about the schools' allocation of resources and values. Yet a concept that is only circulated among scholars lacks both life and influence until an event embodying it grabs national attention. But a concept can also have an effect without the crystallizing event—for example, the spread of the doctorate as a requirement for the school superintendency. The combination of concept and event, though, creates an intensely powerful stimulus for change among the core constituencies that make local school politics so turbulent today.

THE IMPACT OF TURBULENCE ON SCHOOL GOVERNANCE: NOBODY IS IN CHARGE

The Growth of State and Federal Influence

One impact of school turbulence is that the local superintendent has lost his once-preeminent position in setting the district agenda and controlling decision outcomes. The superintendent and school board have become more of a reactive force, trying to juggle diverse and changing coalitions across different issues. Many school reforms such as new math have disappeared, but some left structural changes that could be easily monitored and that created a constituency. Consequently, a partial legacy from the 1960–1980 era was tremendous growth in the specialized functions of the school, including administrative specialists in career education, bilingual education, nutrition, health, remedial reading, and so on. Many of these new structural layers diluted the superintendent's influence because the specialists were paid separately by federal or state categorical programs. Hence they were insulated from the superintendent's influence by separate financing and the requirements of higher levels of government.

One element that today is very different for local authorities is the intensity and scope of recent state policy actions. The most striking feature of state-local relations in the last twenty years has been this growth in state control over education. Today organizations of professional educators and local school boards are making suggestions for only marginal changes in proposed new state policies. And under the Reagan administration, new federal initiatives were restricted to rhetoric, data collecting, and sponsoring small pilot programs.

These trends cede considerably more control of education to the states. However, there will be enormous variation in how states take control—from the highly aggressive states, such as California and Texas, to the more passive, such as New Hampshire and Colorado. Dangers attend aggressive, broad-based state education policy. States change policy through statutes and regulations, which have a standardizing effect. Also, the focus of state policymaking is no longer on categorical groups, such as handicapped or minority students. Instead it is aimed at the central core of instructional policy, including what should be taught, how it should be taught, and who should teach it. State-level political actors leading the current wave of reform are legislators, governors, and business interests. The traditional education interest groups—teachers, administrators, and school boards—have been used primarily in pro forma consultative roles.

Also noteworthy is that increasing state control has not been limited to such traditionally high-control states as California and Florida. The high tide of state intervention in local instructional policy is washing over Virginia and Connecticut—longtime bastions of local control. National movements and widespread media coverage have played a crucial role in the current reform wave, just as they did with the 1970s issues of school finance reform and minimum competency testing. Some state initiatives, such as high school graduation standards, moved through the states without any federal mandate or organized interest-group lobbying.

The Squeeze from the Bottom

As a result of these changing internal and external forces, the discretionary zone of local superintendents and boards has been progressively squeezed into a smaller and smaller area. The superintendent's discretion is squeezed from the top by increasing regulations from the legislative, administrative, and judicial arms of the federal and state governments, as noted. In addition, there has been the expanding influence of private interest groups and professional reformers, such as the Ford Foundation and the Council for Basic Education. Moreover, interstate groups, such as the Education Commission of the States, increased their influence, as did nationally oriented organizations, such as the Council for Exceptional Children. All over the nation, networks of individuals and groups sprang up to spread school finance reform, competency testing, increased academic standards, and other programs.

Superintendents and local boards also found their decision-making powers squeezed from the bottom by forces such as the growth of local collective bargaining contracts reinforced by national teacher organizations. A national study documents the incursion of these organizations into educational policy.[33] And, as noted, the last three decades have been a growth period for local interest groups often resulting from national social movements, as our thesis on turbulence here proposes and as shown in Figure 1.2. A yet-unstudied question is whether these constraints and forces external to the local settings have been more influential and effective than those of the 1920–1950 era, for example, the Progressives and professional societies.

The social movements of this period differ from those of the nineteenth century, exemplified by Horace Mann, which were interested in building up institutions like the schools. Today social movements are interested in challenging public institutions and trying to

Figure 1.2
Trends in Educational Governance—1950–1992

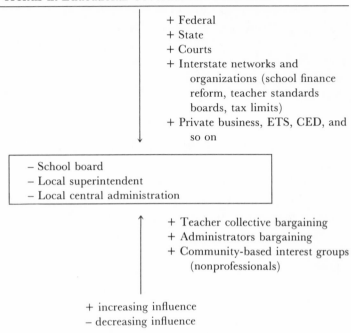

+ Federal
+ State
+ Courts
+ Interstate networks and
    organizations (school finance
    reform, teacher standards
    boards, tax limits)
+ Private business, ETS, CED, and
    so on

— School board
— Local superintendent
— Local central administration

+ Teacher collective bargaining
+ Administrators bargaining
+ Community-based interest groups
    (nonprofessionals)

+ increasing influence
— decreasing influence

make them more responsive to forces outside the local administrative structure. Some would even assert that these movements help fragment school decision making so that schools cannot function effectively. The litany of the media portrays violence, vandalism, and declining test scores as the predominant condition of public education.

In California, for example, this situation has become so serious that the schools increasingly suffer from shock and overload characterized by loss of morale and too few resources to operate all the programs the society expects schools to offer. The issue then becomes how much change and agitation a public institution can take and still continue to function effectively. Californians are confronted with numerous successive initiatives such as Proposition 13, vouchers, spending limits, and an extreme version of all the other forces sketched above. Citizens there and elsewhere go to their local school board and superintendent expecting redress of their problems only to find that the decision-making power is at the state or some other nonlocal level. The impression grows that no one is "in charge" of public education.

All of this does not mean that local school authorities are helpless. Rather it means that they cannot control their agenda or shape decision outcomes as they could in the past. The superintendent must deal with shifting and ephemeral coalitions that might yield him some temporary marginal advantages. But many of the policy items on the local agenda arise from external forces, such as state and federal governments, or from the pressures of established local interest groups, including teachers.

The earlier 1920-1960 era of the "administrative chief" has passed with profound consequences; the new school politics is much more complex and less malleable. How can we understand as political the seeming confusion of actors and events, emotion and rationality, conflict and conformity described in this chapter? That is the purpose of this book—to provide an analytical framework for understanding the politics of education.

NOTES

1. Among these reports are: National Commission on Excellence in Education, *A Nation at Risk* (Washington, D.C.: U.S. Government Printing Office, 1983); Mortimer J. Adler, *The Paideia Proposal* (New York: Macmillan, 1982); John I. Goodlad, *A Place Called School: Prospects for the Future* (New York: McGraw-Hill, 1983); Twentieth Century Fund Task Force on Federal Elementary and Secondary Education Policy, *Making the Grade* (New York: Twentieth Century Fund, 1983); Ernest L. Boyer, *High Schools* (New York: Harper & Row, 1983); College Board Educational Equality Project, *Academic Preparation for College: What Students Need to Know and Be Able to Do* (New York: College Board, 1983); Theodore R. Sizer, *Horace's Compromise: The Dilemma of the American High School* (Boston: Houghton Mifflin, 1984); Task Force on Education for Economic Growth, *Action for Excellence* (Denver: Educational Commission of the States, 1983); and National Science Board Commission on Precollege Education in Mathematics, Science, and Technology, *Educating Americans for the 21st Century* (Washington, D.C.: U.S. Government Printing Office, 1983).

2. Anthony Downs, "Up and Down With Ecology — The Issue-Attention Cycle," *Public Interest* 28 (Summer 1972): 38–50.

3. Thomas James and David Tyack, "Learning from Past Efforts to Reform the High School," *Phi Delta Kappan* (February 1983): 400–6.

4. Information supplied by Chris Pipho, Education Commission of the States, July 1986, via phone interview.

5. William Boyd, "Public Education's Last Hurrah: Schizophrenia, Amnesia, and Ignorance in School Politics," *Educational Evaluation and Policy Analysis* 9, no. 2 (Summer 1987): 85—100.

6. Paul Peterson, *The Politics of School Reform, 1870–1940* (Chicago: University of Chicago Press, 1985), and "Economic and Political Trends Affecting Education." Unpublished paper (Washington, D.C.: Brookings Institution, 1985).

7. Field poll reported in David Broder column, *Washington Post National Weekly Edition*, 21 September 1987, p. 6.

8. The theme was introduced by Thomas H. Eliot, "Toward an Understanding of Public School Politics," *American Political Science Review* 52 (1959): 1032–51.

9. David Tyack, "Needed: The Reform of a Reform," in *New Dimensions of School Board Leadership*, National School Boards Association (Evanston, Ill.: NSBA, 1969), pp. 29–51.

10. Ibid., p. 32.

11. Ibid.

12. Raymond E. Callahan, *Education and the Cult of Efficiency* (Chicago: University of Chicago Press, 1962); David Tyack, *The One Best System* (Cambridge, Mass.: Harvard University Press, 1974).

13. Samuel P. Hays, "The Politics of Reform in Municipal Government in the Progressive Era," *Pacific Northwest Quarterly* 55 (1963): 163.

14. Tyack, "Needed: The Reform," p. 35.

15. George S. Counts, *The Social Composition of Boards of Education* (Chicago: University of Chicago Press, 1927).

16. Elinor M. Gersman, "Progressive Reform of the St. Louis School Board, 1897," *History of Education Quarterly* 10 (1970): 8–15.

17. Lesley H. Browder, "A Suburban School Superintendent Plays Politics," in *The Politics of Education at the Local, State and Federal Levels*, edited by Michael W. Kirst (Berkeley: McCutchan, 1970), pp. 191–94.

18. Roscoe C. Martin, *Government and the Suburban School* (Syracuse, N.Y.: Syracuse University Press, 1962), p. 89.

19. Gladys A. Wiggin, *Education and Nationalism* (New York: McGraw-Hill, 1962).

20. Michael B. Katz, ed., *School Reform: Past and Present* (Boston: Little, Brown & Co., 1971).

21. For an overview of how this affects the superintendent, see William Lowe Boyd and Robert L. Crowson, "The Changing Conception and Practice of Educational Administration," in *Review of Research in Education*, edited by David C. Berliner, Vol. 9 (Washington, D.C.: American Educational Research Association, 1981), pp. 311–73.

22. See Michael W. Kirst, *Who Controls Our Schools* (New York: W.H. Freeman, 1984).

23. Norton Long, *The Unwalled City* (New York: Basic Books, 1972); Frederick M. Wirt, *Power in the City* (Berkeley: University of California Press, 1974).

24. See the survey data in Richard F. Carter and John Sutthoff, *Communities and Their Schools* (Stanford: Institute for Communication Research, 1960).

25. David Rogers, *110 Livingston Street* (New York: Random House, 1968).

26. For a broader perspective on current professional challenge, see Frederick M. Wirt, "Professionalism and Political Conflict: A Development Model," *Journal of Public Policy* 1 (1981).

27. The fullest analysis of the following material is found in Walter Garms, James Guthrie, and Lawrence Pierce, *School Finance: The Economics and Politics of Federalism* (Englewood Cliffs, N.J.: Prentice-Hall, 1987).

28. The ethnic factor is set out in Wirt, *Power in the City*, Pt. V. The fullest analysis of events in this section is found in Gary Orfield, *Must We Bus? Segregated Schools and National Policy* (Washington, D.C.: Brookings Institution, 1978).

29. The following material draws upon John C. Hogan, *The Schools, the Courts, and the Public Interest* (Lexington, Mass.: Lexington Books, 1974). See also David Kirp and Mark Yudof, *Education Policy and the Law* (Berkeley: McCutchan, 1987).

30. Following data are drawn from James W. Guthrie and Patricia A. Craig, *Teachers and Politics* (Bloomington, Ind.: Phi Delta Kappa Educational Foundation, 1973).

31. The fullest review of this current is Tyll van Geel, *Authority to Control the School Program* (Lexington, Mass.: Lexington Books, 1976).

32. Frederick M. Wirt, "The Dependent City?: External Influences Upon Local Control," *Journal of Politics* 47 (1985): 85–112.

33. Lorraine McDonnell and Anthony Pascal, "National Trends in Teacher Collective Bargaining," *Education and Urban Society* (1979): 129–51.

2

Systems Analysis: A Guide to Political Turbulence

Given the turbulence described in Chapter 1, it would seem hard to find patterns in the turmoil, in what Henry James called the "buzzing, booming confusion of reality." The currents discussed operate in roughly sixteen thousand school districts, a truly indecipherable mosaic without some guide for classifying and explaining what transpires. What analytical scheme can make sense of the diversity and similarity in American education? What political framework of analysis enables us to understand the political nature of school turbulence?

METHODS OF EDUCATION SYSTEM ANALYSIS

Some of the explanation that follows has been provided by scholars with different purposes and methods in mind. Educational journals are filled with *descriptions* of the operations of school systems and subsystems, their agents and participants, and their laws and regulations. Description is invariably accompanied by normative *evaluations*, that is, value judgments about whether the object described is worthwhile or workable. Description and evaluation further merge into

29

prescription—recommendations for changing the reality to achieve the normative objectives, to close the gap between real and ideal. What has been least common is *explanation*—suppositions and supporting evidence about the causes, consequences, and interrelationships of objects in reality. Causal theory of this kind is frequently found in the psychology of education and sometimes in the sociology of education but seldom in educational administration before the 1970s.[1]

When we look for causal theory in the study of the politics of education today, we find very much where once there was little. The reasons lie in the myth of apolitical schools and the lack of a theory to direct and channel research. This became less true after 1970 as the myth was discarded and the theory sought. So long as school policy was regarded as "above" politics, its study via political, analytic frameworks was regarded as misguided. As a consequence, theoretical statements of explanatory power were unlikely to develop. Accepted theories of one sort make it difficult to entertain opposing explanations. If the stork is said to bring babies, there is not much room for sex education.

Iannaccone has explained how the profession had earlier incorporated this orientation by asserting that education was a "closed system," isolated from politics, and its leaders, therefore, free from external control. Also, by controlling what comes in from the outside environment, educators could reduce change within their system. Such effort was clearly useful for professional educators, freeing them from many external constraints and from the unsettling demands for internal change that characterize other social and "more political" institutions.[2] In the past educators were so skilled that they moved the community to adopt the apolitical myth. As Eliot, a pioneer politics-of-education analyst, wryly noted thirty years ago, a successful superintendent was one adept in "community relations," but "why not say frankly that he must be a good politician?"[3] Yet most political scientists accepted the educators' closed-system definition unquestioningly, and almost none studied it. Only recently—seeing similarities in education to other policies—have they recalled that "Rosy O'Grady and the Colonel's lady are sisters under the skin."

The most significant reason, however, for the once-meager scholarly analysis of educational politics is probably the lack of an applicable theoretical orientation and methodology. As political scientists pointed out twenty years ago, no single theory, simple or complex, guided such research, nor was there agreement on the appropriate methodology.[4] Political scientists, then and now, are severely divided between traditional studies of institutional or legal analysis and quantitative studies of political behavior. Among the behavioralists are a number of partial theories of political behavior, which is another complication. In short, despite the flood of "politics of education" work done in the 1970s noted in the preface, no overarching general theory generated any hypotheses that could be tested by acceptable methods in the crucible of political experiences. Instead there was a grab bag of partial theories and contrasting methods. That this is typical of the early stages in any scholarship is nonetheless frustrating for those who want to create order amidst confusion. The politics of education is certainly not for those who prefer scholarship that explicates established truths, but it is exciting for those who prefer to innovate in the development of theory and hypothesis.

How can we proceed, then, in the absence of an established theory for organizing knowledge? First, we need some definitions. *Theory in its traditional sense is directed toward explanation and prediction* by means of "a set of . . . related propositions which include among them some lawlike generalizations, and which can be assigned specific truth value via empirical tests."[5] Because scholarship, like life, is always imperfect and because all research involves some compromise with ideal requirements, we turn instead to another form of theory— heuristic. *Heuristic theory is not so much a predictive scheme as a method of analytically separating and categorizing items in experience.* Much of what parades in political science as theory of the first type—predictive—is actually heuristic, at best providing a "framework for political analysis." We agree with Easton that "the appropriate question to ask about a theoretical analysis today is not: does this fully explain the functioning . . . or does it offer a fireproof set of concepts toward the end? . . . The appropriate question is: does this approach help us to take a small step in the right direction?"[6]

Easton's comment is appropriate, for it is his heuristic scheme or "framework for political analysis" that we employ in organizing the concepts and data of this book. This framework is termed *systems analysis*. Easton deemphasizes theory in the classical sense and prefers instead to discuss a "conceptual framework" or "categories for the systems analysis of politics."[7] The utility of systems theory is that, like all heuristic schemes, it enables us at least to order our information or hunches about reality. We can thereby determine what portions of the scheme are clearly untenable in reality, which have some support there, and which need to be further studied. The use of systems analysis has limits, noted later, but presenting the current state of knowledge in the politics of education is our major purpose; for this, systems analysis provides an organizing principle to deal with the current turbulence in school politics. In this fashion only, we can "take a small step in the right direction."

COMPONENTS OF SYSTEMS ANALYSIS

Easton's framework contains the familiar perspective of a society composed of major institutions or "subsystems"—the economy, the school, the church, and so on. Individuals interact with one another and with these institutions in patterned ways that constitute a distinctive culture. One of these institutions is the *political system*. It differs from the others because it alone is the source of, in Easton's classic statements, "authoritative allocation of values, [i.e.,] those interactions through which values are authoritatively allocated for society." This is the subsystem whose decisions—about how individuals and groups will be allocated the valued but limited objects—are generally accepted as authoritative, that is, *legitimate*. The values this system allocates may be *material*—a textbook, defense contract, free land for constructing railroads, or dropout schools. Values allocated may also be *symbolic*, conferring status and deference on favored groups—for example, making Christmas or Martin Luther King's birthday a school holiday. Such an allocative system exists in every society, although its exact forms, inherent values, and public politics differ with place and time.

The link between the political system and other subsystems is a key element in this analysis because Easton is reaching for a general statement about the conditions under which other subsystems reciprocally interact with the political system. This interrelationship is one in which *stress* in other subsystems of the social environment generates *inputs* of *demands* on and *supports* of the *political system*. The political system then reduces or *converts* these inputs into public decisions or *outputs*, which in turn *feed back* allocated values and resources into the society where the process began. Figure 2.1 is a

Figure 2.1
A Simplified Model of a Political System

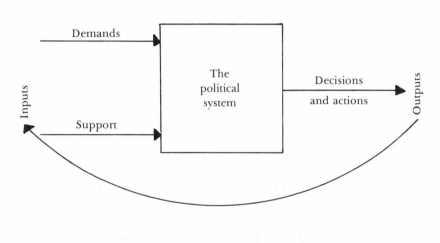

Environment   Environment

Environment   Environment

Source: Reprinted from *A Systems Analysis of Political Life* by David Easton by permission of the University of Chicago Press. © 1965 by the University of Chicago Press.

sketch of this set of interactions.[8] These concepts seek to describe components of a dynamic, interactive, political system that may or may not *persist* in the society in which it is embedded. Easton's concern is not merely with how the political system operates, but with how it persists through time by adapting itself to the host of demands made on it.

The Model Illustrated for Schools

What does all this have to do with schools? The rest of this book will answer this question, but we can briefly illustrate our theme now. Schools allocate *resources*—revenues, programs, professionals—and they also allocate *values*—teaching Americanism or the importance of learning for intrinsic or occupational purposes. If so, then schools are as much political systems as are Congress or the presidency, the state legislature or executive. School systems do this in a society in which other institutions—economic, religious, family, and so on—seek certain valued resources from the schools. This interaction can take two forms. The most obvious are *demands*, such as those set out in the preceding chapter, that characterize today's political turbulence. For example, a group wants a special curriculum, more parental authority, or more teacher power, and these wants are *articulated* and *mobilized* toward the school authorities. A second form of interaction with the schools is *support*; that is, certain groups provide the school with taxes or with intangibles, such as a favorable attitude toward education.

The political system of the school that receives such demands must deal with them selectively because it lacks resources to meet them all. In short, a gap exists between what all groups want and the resources to meet those demands. This gap is a powerful generator of social and political conflict in all times and places. So school systems must act politically because they must choose which demands to favor and which not. The result is an *output*, for example, a state or federal law, a school board resolution, or a superintendent's program. An output could even be a principal's memo to the faculty on how the library budget will be allocated between the science and social studies departments. This may not seem to be choosing among resources and values on a major scale—unless you are the science teacher. Whatever form an output takes, all are alike in containing a statement of "who gets what, when, and how," the classic definition of politics by political scientist Harold Lasswell. More formally stated, all these outputs are alike in that they authoritatively allocate values and resources.

After this act, as the arrow at the bottom of Figure 2.1 implies, the output must be implemented in order to cope with the inputs that originally gave rise to it. For example, demand for bilingual education generates a district program, which is implemented by organizing the resources of personnel and material that constitute the program. In another example, the lack of popular support for a school program because it is unproductive or biased can generate new pressures on the school authorities to alter it. In short, schools can be viewed as miniature political systems because they share certain qualities with large-scale political systems. And, as discussed later, the school professional must operate within this system in a way that shares much with the classical position of the politician. That is, he or she mediates among competing demands from school constituencies that have been organized to seek their share of valued allocations from the school system.

The Concepts Defined

A fuller statement of systems analysis is appropriate here, beginning with the environment of subsystems outside the political system.[9] This environment is of two parts. The first is the environment that exists within a nation (the economy, culture, social structure, and personalities), which represents potential sources of inputs for the political system. The second part is the environment that exists outside the nation; this is the international world, a "suprasystem of which any single society is part." This includes the international, political, economic, and cultural systems of the world.

Within either part of the environment—internal or external— disturbances arise from changes in existing interactions. Some disturbances are in the form of *stress*, which critically impinges on the basic capacity of a political system, that is, its ability to allocate values for society and to induce most members to accept such decisions as binding. This stress could be a world war, a major depression, an energy crisis, or a new consciousness of ethnic frustration within a school district. Failure of the political system to cope with stress can be severe. The Greek city-states and the Roman and Aztec empires, as well as various tribal clusters, illustrate political systems that failed to reduce stress and consequently disappeared. However, so long as the stress is maintained within a limited range, the system persists.

At some point, a stress can move from the external environment in the form of *exchanges* or *transactions* that penetrate the political system's *boundaries*. These stress-generated influences, *outputs* of the environment and hence *inputs* to the political system, "concentrate and mirror everything in the environment that is relevant to political stress." The inputs, whether *demands* or *supports*, are "key indicators of the way in which environmental influences and conditions modify and shape the operations of the political system."

Demands are pressures on the government, that is, requests for justice or help, reward or recognition. Behind these demands lies the common problem of wants, the human condition of longing for something in short supply. In all societies these wants are never plentiful enough to satisfy all claims—a phenomenon of tremendous importance to all aspects of our society. This is particularly the case with the political system, for without such wants there would be no demands; without demands (not all of which can be met), society would not need to authorize an agent to meet them—that is, "authoritatively allocate resources and values."

Supports, on the other hand, are a willingness to accept the decisions of the system or the system itself. A steady flow of supports is necessary if any political system is to sustain its legitimacy (i.e., the accepted sense that the system has the right to do what it is doing). So vital is this input that all societies indoctrinate their young to support their particular system, a task that is part of the school's work but is shared with family and peers.

The whole process of demands and supports can be illustrated in the issue of Southern school desegregation. Demands for desegregation arose from a racially based stress, long endured—but later unendurable—by blacks. Moving from private rancor across the political boundary to create a public challenge, blacks mobilized their resources, first in demands upon courts and later upon Congress but continually upon local school boards. The segregationists' counterdemands mobilized other resources to block and delay this challenge. During this process, both those seeing too much change and those seeing too little began to decrease support for the Supreme Court's authority to allocate values generally.

The political system *converts* such inputs, sometimes combining or reducing them, sometimes absorbing them without any reaction, but at other times converting them into public policies or outputs. Clearly not all demands are converted into policy, for the political system is more responsive to certain values, those dominant in the conversion process and its personnel and in the larger society. What inputs get through depends upon which values the conversion process reinforces and which it frustrates and upon the values of the political authorities operating within this flow of inputs.

For example, some educators insist that maintaining discipline is a prime value of classwork, while others prefer to achieve intellectual excitement that often looks undisciplined. Which of these values gets reinforced by state authority is the end result of a political struggle. That is, one method will eventually be "authorized," and the school system and its personnel will allocate their resources toward that value. This struggle to have resources allocated authoritatively for one's own educational value is political, much like the process in other policy fields.

The authorities responsible for running the political system constantly interact in the conversion process with either those outside or those inside the political system. The pattern of their interactions often stems in part from role definitions imposed by the political system itself. Such interactions generate certain pressures inside the political system—or *withinputs*—which in turn shape the conversion process and its products.

For example, desegregation demands were ignored much longer by Congress and some presidents than by the Supreme Court and other presidents. Border states in the 1950s and 1960s desegregated more quickly than Southern states, and Mississippi school boards resisted most of all. These differing reactions reflected various combinations of power and values in each political subsystem, as well as the varied role definitions of political authorities. The role definition of a member of Congress or a school board member from Atlanta, Georgia, or Holmes County, Mississippi, was different from the role definition of one from Kentucky. Each used his or her resources in the political system to advance or impede these demands, and the resulting conflicts generated the conversion process—which still continues.

The outputs of the political subsystem once achieved then become inputs to the other social subsystems that had first generated stresses. The implementation of outputs in the larger community, however, always has a differential impact. Policy implementation can enhance the safety, income, and status of some persons or groups while it also detracts from those of others. A resulting profile of public policy, while varying with the culture and times, will mirror the structure of power and privilege and tells us much about what values currently dominate the political system.

Moreover, the authorized purpose of the output will find meaning in reality only through the process of *feedback*. This is the interaction of output with its administration, which becomes in time an established behavior—an *outcome*. For example, the Supreme Court required desegregation at "all deliberate speed," but federal district courts defined that output differently for school districts. In 1965 Congress authorized school aid for schools with *poor* children, but the outcome in the U.S. Office of Education's implementation of that law was aid for *all* schools.

Clearly, the gap between output and outcome becomes a major stimulus to future policymaking. That is, the action of the political system may not result in outcomes. Rather, because outputs can influence society, they generate a subsequent set of inputs to the political system through a *feedback loop*. That is, dealing with stress causes a response in the system, the response creates new stress, and the new stress is communicated to the political authorities, and so a new round begins.

The Concepts Illustrated

The preceding concepts are incorporated in Figure 2.2, educational examples of Easton's system analysis. Stresses affect the schools from events as far away as Saudi Arabia or Japan, or as close as meetings of local ministers or teachers. These events emerge in the school's political system as group demands, for example, to cut school costs or institute school prayers. All such demands, whatever their content, are seeking to reallocate school values or resources. Those in the school political system authorized to decide on such reallocations— whether formal agencies or the voters—can reject some of these demands or convert others into formal outputs. The latter can be an act of Congress or a local referendum. The resulting educational policy is then implemented as an administrative decision—for example, busing plans—which in time has outcomes for particular groups, say academic gains for blacks. And the latter group generated the environmental stresses in the first place.

Note that this framework presents the political system as something other than just an allocative process. After all, this structure is an attempt to address the larger question of how any allocative process persists. As Easton notes:

> Persistence . . . is intricately connected with the capacity of a political system, as an open, self-regulating, and goal-setting system, to change itself. The puzzle of how a system manages to persist, through change if necessary, forms a central problem of the analysis of political life.[10]

Figure 2.2
The Flow of Influences and Policy Consequences in the School's Political System

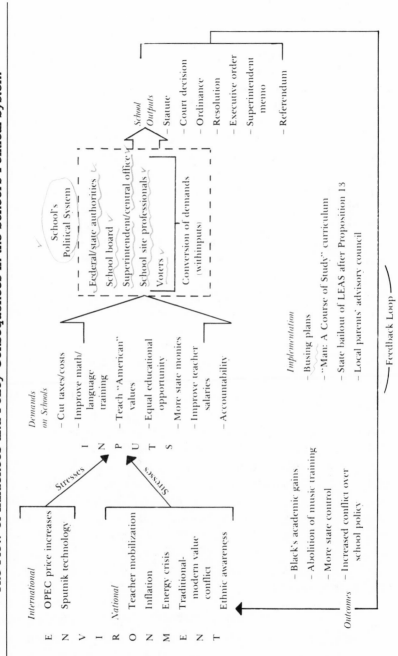

The belief that schools are embedded in society and responsive to its demands is a truism, perhaps the oldest in the study of education. We believe systems analysis can help illuminate this relationship more clearly through such specific concepts as *wants*, *demands*, and *supports*. We believe that observing the school systems as converting inputs from subsystems of society in response to group-defined stresses can lead to considerable explanation. Further, it seems to us that schools act out conversion processes like those in other subsystems that are more clearly recognized as political. That political authorities in schools do seek to maximize support through use of appropriate outputs also seems clear. Certainly a central question to be explored in this book is the degree to which the feedback loop operates between schools and society.

In exploring similarities between schools and larger, more recognized political systems, we say with Easton that we are seeking to "elaborate a conceptual structure and suggest, where possible, some theoretical propositions. . . . In the outcome, we shall not have a theory in the full-blown sense of the term [but] a conceptual structure which . . . is the most that we can expect in the area of general theory today."[11]

In this work we seek something more. We want to know how valid such a general concept is in explaining the structure and processes of American public education in this time of stress. As the first chapter noted, old forms and ideas in education are everywhere challenged, and not only by new interest groups seeking a reallocation of resources. Widespread and increasing resistance to school tax referenda in recent years (about one in three failed during 1969, three in four in 1979) as well as to the states' quality reforms of the 1980s, suggest disappointment, frustration, or malaise about our schools. Stress, then, is not an abstract academic concern. Rather, it is a characteristic of contemporary education that affects school boards, classrooms, administrators' offices, and professionals' conventions, as well as the decision-making forums at state and national levels. And, as polls show, the public's disenchantment with schools creates a nationwide condition of stress that has motivated recent reforms.

Systems analysis offers a contour map designed to stimulate thinking and research by scholar and administrator alike. We will explore knowledge based on existing research and also provide some of our own. We will also explore major national educational policies, not only because systems analysis seems to explain them well but also because they suggest how stress adaptation is important to all those interested in schools.

The precise labels used for these concepts are not the important thing, of course. What matters is whether the concepts provide insight into what is happening and some guide to action. If so, then our contribution, too, must ironically be classified as feedback, which Wiener once defined as "the property of being able to adjust future conduct by past performances."[12]

Uses of Systems Analysis

The links between politics and education are clearly not new, as Chapter 3 will explain. However, two disagreements arise over this tie. How are politics and education to be viewed, in empirical or value terms? In other words, how *do* schools and politics relate to one another as a matter of fact and how *should* they relate as a matter of value? In many respects, this book focuses only on the empirical question. However, putting an empirical question to reality is no simple matter, for we can make errors in framing the question—as well as in verifying it and estimating the significance of the facts unearthed.[13] Nor do we stand mute on the value questions that lie at the heart of turbulent issues. But to do this, we will use the systems analysis framework to organize this wealth of data and values.

We must point out, though, that this framework has been criticized, for basically two sets of reasons. One set argues that such analysis is ineffective; that is, it does not or cannot do what it claims to do analytically. The second set argues that even if it does meet its claims, it is an undesirable way of thinking about schools—or any other segment of social experience. That is, because of what it implies about the values of humans in society, individuals are ignored in such a global concept. Also it is a conservative concept for its emphasis on how political systems cope with stress (a perspective of importance only to the power holders). We have countered these criticisms in detail in the first edition of this book. Documenting the rich pool of research and ideas from the 1970s and 1980s seems a better use of limited space than repeating this evaluation. We still believe that these two criticisms are not valid because they see only part of the schema.

We continue to find this concept useful in organizing the complex reality that constitutes the politics of education. For this reason, systems analysis frames the rest of this book in which we attempt to make sense out of new actors, issues, and resources swirling about the schoolhouse door.

NOTES

1. Fred N. Kerlinger, "The Mythology of Educational Research: The Descriptive Approach," *School and Society* 93 (1965): 222–25.

2. Laurence Iannaccone, *Politics in Education* (New York: Center for Applied Research in Education, 1967).

3. Thomas H. Eliot, "Toward an Understanding of Public School Politics," *American Political Science Review* 52 (1959): 1032–51.

4. Michael W. Kirst and Edith K. Mosher, "The Politics of Public Education: A Research Review," *Review of Educational Research* 39 (1969); Frederick M. Wirt, "American Schools as a Political System: A Bibliographic Essay," in *State, School and Politics: Research Directions*, edited by Michael W. Kirst (Lexington, Mass.: Lexington Books, 1972), pp. 247–81.

5. A. James Gregor, "Political Science and the Uses of Functional Analysis," *American Political Science Review* 62 (1968): 425.

6. David Easton, *A Systems Analysis of Political Life* (New York: Wiley, 1965), p. 490; hereafter referred to as Easton, *Systems Analysis*.

7. David Easton, *A Framework for Political Analysis* (Englewood Cliffs, N.J.: Prentice-Hall, 1965).

8. Easton, *Systems Analysis*, p. 30.

9. Citations for following unnoted quotations are ibid., pp. 22, 26, 27.

10. Ibid., p. 479.

11. Ibid., pp. vii-viii.

12. Cited in ibid., p. 368.

13. For the problems involved, see David H. Fischer, *Historians' Fallacies: Toward a Logic of Historical Thought* (New York: Harper & Row, 1970).

3

Schools
and System Support

We view as political both the larger system, over all of society, and the smaller one of the schools. In this chapter, for clarity we shall use a shorthand term for each of these political systems: *State* and *School*. We focus on one of the links between these two—the child to be educated as a civilized and political person. Other factors link State and School, particularly programs of finance and regulation; these will concern us in later chapters. But before we focus on the child at the intersection of the two systems, we must clarify some theoretical problems.

STATE-SCHOOL LINKS IN DEMOCRATIC THOUGHT

The previous delineation of the apolitical myth of the schools needs to be recast from a broader perspective on the State-School relationship. Three views of this interlinking are found in classical political theory, democratic theory, and systems analysis.

The Classical Question: Which Is the Independent Variable?

As Eulau has noted, Western political philosophy concerning the State-School relationship centers around a basic question: Should the

State shape the School's function and purpose, or should the School shape and guide the State's?[1] During any period of history, much of the controversy over schooling has been rooted in how one answers this.

The Greek tradition was explicit on the matter. The two were one, both concerned with producing the good political community (*polis*). Schooling should shape citizens to fulfill themselves in the interests of the *polis*, which in turn ensured that the school did its job well. There is about this notion what Eulau termed "the utopian scent— education can create the perfect political order." More important, this orientation assumed that education was subordinate to, indeed the servant of, the political order.

While Plato and Aristotle wrote about a culture now twenty-five centuries dead in which a good society was sought by the integration of all institutions and values, their insistence on the State-School relationship has echoes in our own day. We hear it from School critics on the right who insist that teacher, student, and curriculum should uphold the purposes of the national government. They demand an uncritical acceptance of a patriotic, generalized presentation of history. In short, individuals must be subordinated to the State and School in order to shape their values. Only by having School support State and State support School can society be preserved. On the left, meanwhile, one hears another version of the same viewpoint, namely, that the School creates and reinforces the "establishment" that dominates and controls American life. These charges are followed by demands that the School be reformed because its submission to false values is producing a conformist population.

These opposing views are alike in many ways, however. Both want subordination of School to State. Both agree that the State can be upheld only by the School's instruction in a moral life, though they disagree about what that is. Both believe that the State can be only what the School supports. Thus, the potential independent effect that the School can have on the State makes schools the potentially dominant institution in society—and therefore they must be controlled. In such a formulation, the collectivity, or society as a whole, is more important than the individual, and so the individual must be shaped to the larger end. Athenians would agree.

So do Americans. The harnessing of education to shape the political and religious order was a dominant feature of states until quite recently. Education for the pursuit of only the approved ends, political and religious, was accepted. Indeed, the development of private education in this country, with its independence from state dictates, originated in the desire to be free—free to inculcate the right religion. Not even that development was allowed to be unpatriotic or politically heretical, though.

In the last century, however, another possibility has emerged from this State-School union. After all, it would be hard to find, as Eulau has observed, a "political order in the real world which, even if we could agree on its being close to perfection, has been created out of or by an educational system." Might not the reverse be the case, that the political order has shaped the educational system, that the State is the independent variable? If so, political problems are basically traceable not to the School but to the State.

The argument here is something more than that schools have to teach patriotism so as not to undermine the State. Rather, it is that from society to society the basic School philosophy, practices, and structures are shaped by the State more often than the reverse. Note two examples. First, conceive of a State whose political premise is exclusive, unchallengeable, and immutable. There, School philosophy takes as its first duty shaping the child to understand, accept, and glorify that premise. Behind this duty is the belief that when the Truth is known, it is foolish at best, and sinful at worst, to permit the malleable young to have equal access to Error. This thinking influenced Plato's classic advice of a strict curriculum to produce different classes of society. All authoritarian societies since have followed the Platonic syllabus.

However, the case is different if the premise of the State is that political Truth is either not known or not knowable, that there is not a Truth but many truths. Then the School may be more open to instruction admitting of plural truths—from which individuals choose as befits their own values.

The second example of the State shaping the School underlies the rise of the liberal democratic state in the Western world. Its pluralist premise doubts a Truth and so rejects the absolutism of those who believe a Truth exists. These are familiar elements of English and American thinking in the nineteenth and twentieth centuries. John Stuart Mill's essay *On Liberty* is an expression of this philosophy, just as Plato's *Republic* expresses the other. Writing before universal

education, Mill argued against "State education" and for "enforcement of education by the State" in a statement that urges breaking the
State-School pattern from its traditional mold. "A general State
education is a mere contrivance for moulding people to be exactly like
one another . . . [I]n proportion as it is efficient and successful, it
establishes a despotism over the mind, leading by natural tendency to
one over body."

The possibility that school systems might vary with political systems suggests the independent quality of the latter. A major research
question would be to determine whether new School concepts actually
do change old State programs or whether State changes School. This
question is not only academic. The importance that education plays
in the development of new states has been closely studied in the
post-World War II era. Yet, until the 1970s, there had not been
enough comparative research to determine whether or how school
systems are shaped by distinctive elements in new and old political
systems.*

In the United States, which of the two institutions is independent
and which dependent? Is the union a closed one, wherein Truth is
known and each system reinforces the other in its impact on the
young? Or is the union an open one, where doubt prompts a search by
School and State for answers to fit a varied population? Our necessarily ambiguous answers point directly to the fact that education is
caught in a conflict of values that are rooted in traditional political
thought.

Problems of Education in a Democracy

An additional conflict arises because our study focuses on a democratic system in which the School must manage tensions between
opposing values. Two paradoxes underlie these tensions. First, the
School must teach not only support of the State but also the virtues of
individualism. However, individualism can result in opposition to the
State, as our history of civil rights protests and violence attests. This

---

*Until recently comparative education as a subdiscipline consisted primarily of
country-by-country analyses, in which the potential power of diverse influences in the
political order was not completely assessed. However, the late 1970s saw a shift to
comparing a number of states' school systems or policies within a comparative
framework guided by theory. The *Comparative Education Review* led in this change.

all means that the line between support and opposition gets easily blurred. This is the current and yet historic dilemma that has haunted the sensitive intellect from *Antigone* to today's conscientious objector: How far can the State go in commanding my obedience?

A second paradox about democratic values arises when the range of values is narrowed by State and School in order to control the environment where they exercise authority. An example is the School that praises the American ideal of freedom but also seeks to regulate every aspect of the student's life. The familiar ringing of bells in American high schools is a reflection of the drive of organizations toward standardization and regularity. We discuss this paradox more fully below.

These conflicting norms of freedom and regulation created a major crisis in the 1960s among American youth, who challenged rote learning, denied reality perceptions that were at odds with their own, and rejected the widespread effort to impose uniformity upon them in the name of national security.[2] Here the School shared a common problem with the State. Liberty has never been total, for individuals' pursuits of their diverse definitions of freedom have always created social conflicts. This result has caused authoritative institutions to define freedom in order to avoid disorder and injustice. However, each definition becomes a constraint for some who do not share it but a shield for others. Against this narrowing of freedom, some people will always rebel, decrying the hypocrisy of an institution that says one thing but does another.

These paradoxes of democracy are of course related. The very breadth of democratic values is a convenient justification for any narrowing act by the State and School. For example, local control of the School has been a dominant value in our history, but so has the concept of equal educational opportunity. These two values collided over the segregation issue since 1954, as the federal government's actions in the name of equality have restricted the school district's actions. In short, the potential for value conflict exists due to our value pluralism, and the reality of these conflicts exists due to selective emphasis on some values by those who hold authority.[3]

In a totalitarian State, such value disunity rarely exists, as all values and institutions are designed to achieve monolithic results.[4] In a democracy, though, values are diverse and value conflict is frequent, all to be worked out within the system by majority decision making. In both systems, the School is assigned prime responsibility for instructing the young in civic virtue. When such virtue is defined under totalitarianism as obedience to the State, all other civic values can be aligned to this central command. In democracies, where individualism is stressed as a central virtue, and where individuals differ about what civic virtue means, the lack of consensus on values places an inordinate and perhaps impossible burden on the School.

We can illustrate these tensions by looking at the value of equality in American society.[5] One norm of citizenship in our society is egalitarianism, and national surveys of thirteen- and seventeen-year olds at our bicentennial celebration found the belief to be deeply rooted. Huge proportions of those surveyed opposed racial (96 percent), religious (97 percent), political (82 versus 92 percent of the two groups), and sexual (87 percent) discrimination in the job market.[6] Yet we live in a hierarchical system of unequal social statuses, opportunities, and rewards.

The paradox is that the School acts not only to socialize norms such as equality but also to select those who will get the most and least of society's rewards. In important ways, to be "educated" is to be sorted into groups that vary widely in skills, self-esteem, influence, and social status. Schools are selective in distributing rewards or allocating values, whether grading on the curve or applying admission requirements. School structures thus provide an important means of legitimating a whole system of inequalities for students, as well as for business and governmental leaders. By the end of high school, grades and other performance records will largely determine whether a student goes on to a prestige college or begins low-skilled work. Meanwhile, the School has been propounding a vague "equality" as desirable behavior expected of apprentice citizens. Against this teaching it also implicitly teaches the inequalities of society, even if only offered as something to be corrected. This conflict produces a parallel conflict in the perceptions of young people, a form of cognitive dissonance that has to be resolved, when they are called to act upon contradictory notions of equality.[7] The School, then, leaves the young to sort out the contradictions.

Political Socialization and Systems Analysis

Systems analysis provides an additional theoretical perspective on School and State. Whether writers use systems terms or not, all agree that School and State are close in every nation. Further, while the School is everywhere subordinate to the State, it engages in a trade-off of needs and advantages. Thus, the School supports the state by instilling obedience to the law and the legitimacy of the State, while the State supports the School with funds, some protection from outsiders, and a near monopoly in educating the young.[8]

This broadly stated interrelationship is familiar in systems terms. The School is one of the agents that provide the State with *diffuse support*, defined by Easton as "broad political good will that a system generates through various means over the years . . . that helps members to accept or tolerate outputs to which they are opposed or the effect of which they see as damaging to their wants."[9] The securing of such support takes place as a result of *political socialization*, "those developmental processes through which persons acquire political orientations and patterns of behavior."[10] Political socialization is designed to orient the young to appropriate political values, attitudes, and behaviors.[11] To Easton, diffuse support is a theoretical explanation for the political system's ability to handle stress when its specific outputs fail to meet demands.

Political socialization affects not only what happens to the system's outputs, but it also has consequences for input. The young are taught what demands can be properly presented and what roles can be properly performed by citizens in policymaking. First, such instruction helps limit demands to those the system can normally and usefully handle. For example, the fact that political authorities were never a resource in bank crises before 1900 was clearly accepted then. But by the 1930s, government intervention had become marginally proper and in our own time unquestionably appropriate—indeed, expected. During the earlier era, lesser demands upon the political system eased the task of political authorities, but in later periods an expanded view of their responsibilities overwhelmed them. Second, political socialization also defines proper role behavior for citizens. Instilling the view that voting is a proper way to effect School change, whereas bomb throwing is not, helps reduce the number of schoolhouses the political authorities must rebuild. Such role instruction also helps recruit and train political leaders who are attracted to political power and its uses.

In this fashion, the political system's persistence is enhanced by the School's political socialization. System-citizen interactions are regularized, citizen expectations about outputs made realistic for the system, their input demands shaped, and leaders attracted.[12] Although school operations in different states will show considerable uniformity in such political socialization, its specific content—such as role expectations—can vary with time and society. As Litt asked:

> Is this model student to be a member of a mass who does not question the rule of a superior and ordained elite, an industrial worker who needs the skill and understanding to know his role in modern society, or a child of the Englightenment expected to participate in the voluntary mosaic of parties, interest groups, and informal circles of political opinion-formation?[13]

The variation and uniformity that exist in the practice of political socialization, and the forces that account for them, are basic research topics for which as yet few state and national cross-analyses exist.[14]

THE STAGES OF LEARNING POLITICAL MAPS

We know a lot about how political socialization takes place among youngsters; this knowledge stems from extensive research from after 1960. Basically, the young learn a kind of political map that they then carry in their heads, with few additions or changes throughout their later life. That map shows the citizen how to behave and what to believe in the political system. The map usually has few details about the system's actual operations, for most citizens know little of this. Polls in the bicentennial year of the signing of the U.S. Constitution repeatedly found many who believed incorrect statements about it. The political map is important because it moves one to support or condemn the political system, to participate fully or not at all in its workings, and to like or dislike certain political groups. We now know much about how that map is learned formally (as in a civics class) or informally (by imitating parents' views), about what is learned, and how alterations in the map occur over time.[15] We will summarize much of that research by posing the model of the young pliable mind that gains a map over several life stages.

As Table 3.1 sketches these stages, young citizens find maps of the political world shaped for them from their earliest years. This map-making begins with adopting a general acceptance, or "support," of

Table 3.1
Stages of Political Learning

Primary Model: Early to Late Childhood	General Action Model: Late Childhood–Early Adolescence	Specific Action Model: Late Adolescence–Adulthood
Learns basic political *loyalty* to country, national symbols, and heroes.	Understands conceptually the meaning and significance of participation, e.g., the duty and right of voting.	Adopts stands on *specific issues* of the day, e.g., abortion.
Has first vague attachment to *ideology* of country, e.g., democracy, free enterprise.	Learns about political *participation skills*, communication skills, social manipulation.	Makes *distinctions between candidates* for office, e.g., voting choices.
Receives first, widely held *facts* about political system, e.g., there was wide colonial support for the American Revolution.	Has *involvement* in adult political behavior, e.g., discussing issues or campaigning.	Learns *effects* of policy decisions on one's life, e.g., budget-cutting means cutting services one desires.
	Acquires *general political information*, i.e., fleshes out knowledge of policymakers as persons rather than as official positions.	Obtains more exposure to *political events*, e.g., follows closely United States policy in the Middle East.
	Realizes *legal relationship* between officials and the uses of law to regulate them.	
	Political preferences harden, party identification, stands on political values.	

Source: Abstracted from Robert Weissberg, *Political Learning, Political Choice, and Democratic Citizenship.* Englewood Cliffs, N.J.: Prentice-Hall, 1974, pp. 25–31.

our national political *community*—the psychological sense that we all belong to one group. Once learned, this attitude creates a foundation—emotional and uncritical—for judging details of the political system that come later. The second stage brings learning about, and support for, the political *regime*—the accepted rules of formal governing. In later stages of life comes support for and learning about the actions or policies of political *authorities*—those in charge of running the political system.[16] We will expand on these stages to show their complexity.

In earliest childhood, the school stresses loyalty to country. The classroom flies the flag, the teacher has the class pledge allegiance, and students celebrate political authorities' birthdays. Teachers introduce and endorse basic political values with terms like *democracy* and *free enterprise*. A few facts of the political world also appear, widely shared but often misconstrued or incorrect. From about ten years on, added generalized concepts about the regime are layered over this primary learning. Concepts that earlier would have been so much fog become clearer. Now a rough picture of the regime and one's participation in it appears; some rudimentary political skills can be taught; and the child sees adults engaged in politics (even if only discussing it). Also, the student is getting more specific information about how the political system operates ("Why are arrested people read their rights"?); for the first time political judgments may emerge ("Which political party do I support?").

The third stage of political learning brings even more specific information about how to operate (or not) politically and what world events mean (if anything). Such learning may impel the young not to act, as well as to act, in the political world. The level of learning emerges from the effects political and economic events have upon one's values and interests. The young now get more exposure to events in the political regime; the once-shadowy stage of politics comes more into focus via headlines and television ("Why are they shooting one another in the Middle East?"). Moreover, specific issues in the public arena become important to perceive, discuss, and decide about ("Do I believe in abortion laws?"). Candidates for public office are sorted out, and young people make decisions about them ("Why does that candidate act like a wimp?"). In short, a connection emerges between what political actors can do and the possible effects of those acts on the individual.

Some cautions are in order, however. Not everyone fits every stage in Table 3.1; no neatness typifies this learning process. For example, many families teach nothing about politics, and schools can do an incomplete job of instruction. Also, political events must compete for other far more important things going on at these stages—dating, mating, schooling. Another caution is that life events can cause changes in these maps, sometimes massive changes. For example, parents with schoolchildren may stop voting for school referenda once their children graduate. A third caution is that political learning differs sharply among Americans; it is much higher among the few who lead or support organizations that lead American life. These "elites," understanding that knowledge is one form of power, obtain and use it to their advantage. The "masses," however, have extremely little political knowledge, reject learning it, and consequently exercise at best few limits on what political authorities do.

It should be clear, then, that this learning process does not dictate everything that the adult will later do; this is not a process for stamping out cookies. In the words of Weissberg, whose ideas we have followed:

> We are not arguing that these early orientations remain forever unchanged. Any political identity, loyalty, evaluation, or myth can undergo radical change at any point in a person's lifetime. Rather we claim that this early learning acts as a filter and sets broad limits on subsequent learning.[17]

MODELS OF POLITICAL SOCIALIZATION

We now want to bring together these various perspectives as they relate to American political socialization. Two basic queries arise. What is attempted and what results in efforts to socialize American young people to the political system? Little empirical analysis bearing on these questions existed prior to the 1930s, but studies of earlier periods would probably not show patterns much different than today. When scholars did turn to study political socialization, they found highly similar values transmitted by the instruments of curriculum, textbook, and teacher.

There is no one necessary way these instruments must interact. Indeed, one can argue, as Litt has, that two distinctive models of civic learning have operated at different stages in our history, that a third may be emerging now, and that these models reflect social changes and produce political learning changes.[18] A "rational citizen" model of political action dominated the nineteenth century. It emphasized a citizen's "mastery of the political environment [through] reasoned, voluntary effort" and the search for "harmony and political compromise." Instruction in this period emphasized one's "rights, duties, and obligations"; that is, a citizen was to participate out of a sense of moral duty and be responsible for his or her use of power. Policymaking was conceived of as a town meeting, based on "rational deliberation . . . an open exchange of opinion in face-to-face meetings, and strong confidence in the ability of self-governing men to decide for the good of the community." The preparatory schools and strong liberal arts colleges generated these norms and infused them into public civic instruction through secondary textbooks and teacher training.

However, Litt argues, changes in society produced a new concept of civic education, that of the "allegiant American" model. The new urban immigrant masses had threatened national consensus with their passionately different views about the nature of the State and its uses of power. Consequently, civic education took the form of "Americanization" textbooks and of courses to mold aliens into a loyal consensus. The immigrant was to be swayed from "dirty" parties, patronage, and ethnic group conflict in order to accept nonpartisanship, the merit system, and "a harmony of community interests." A conventional wisdom about our history and institutions was taught and a common set of values about our politics and economics given. These portrayed a nation working smoothly for the benefit of all, with no room for conflict, only for allegiance.

Litt suggests that a third, more recent alternative, not widespread in civic instruction, could be termed "analytical." This seeks to develop skills of technical intellectual analysis that are highly abstract and impersonal—such as "models." The generating institution for such analytical thinking is the research group, which transmits its ideas to the large public universities. Indeed, an introductory college course in political science is invariably of this kind. These collegiate emphases are then transmitted into public schools by teacher trainees taking such a course. The purpose of such civic instruction is to help the young analyze the actual—as against the ideological—operations of political systems. Its emphasis is on how citizens, pressure groups, and political authorities actually conduct themselves, what values these behaviors reflect, and what comprehensive social science theory can incorporate behavior and values.

THE INSTRUMENTS OF POLITICAL SOCIALIZATION

We can weave the methods of political socialization into three instructional models. One emphasizes civic duties and obligations, rational deliberation, and compromise in policymaking. A second emphasizes allegiance to a common culture, social harmony, and distaste for political agencies that threaten this harmony with conflict. The third emphasizes the technical ability to understand the nature of the political world so that one can manage it. Which model best describes what is currently taught in American schools by the curriculum, textbooks, and teachers, as the School seeks to support the State?

Curriculum Content

What, for example, do we know about the actual content of the curriculum? A major answer is "Not much," because in the 1980s only half of the fifty states even required a course about government and politics in their public schools. As for the actual course offerings in curriculum design, the answer can be brief, as the findings generally agree. The curriculum is descriptive, weakly linked to reality, devoid of analytical concepts except legalistic ones, highly prescriptive in tone and—as a direct consequence of all this—noncontroversial. Few changes occurred over a half century of social studies offerings: civics in the ninth grade, world history in the tenth, American history in the eleventh, and some government or social problems in the senior year.[19] This means that most of this curriculum contains little of the recent behavioral developments, comparative analysis, or international studies, and almost no sociology, anthropology, or psychology.[20] A rare review by the American Bar Association of what state laws mandate found that their laws require either nothing or else a vague "citizenship" or morality class. Table 3.2 provides a summary. The absence of mandates to teach about the government itself is striking, although teachers often give such classes. Many states list doctrines that are to be taught (e.g., "evils of Communism" in Alabama or "free enterprise" in Arizona). Wirt found that state controls in curriculum and textbook policies in this field differed sharply by regions, reflecting contrasting political cultures. Controls were much greater and more specific in the Southern states, fewer in New England, and intermediate in the West and Midwest.[21]

From the elementary to the secondary schools, instruction proceeds from indirect and symbolic patriotism to selective facts about American history and government. In the elementary schoolchild's world,

Table 3.2
State Mandates for Political Socialization, 1979

N States[1]	Subject	Example
16	Nothing	Colorado
15	Morality	Maine
11	Patriotism	Kansas
8	Citizenship	Iowa
7	Obedience to law	Oklahoma
5	Legal rights and duties	Michigan
4	Justice	Massachusetts
4	Bill of Rights	Virginia
3	Loyalty	Nevada
3	Importance of voting	Pennsylvania

[1]Totals exceed fifty because more than one mandate exists in some states.

Source: Abstracted from Joel Henning et al., *Mandate for Change* (Chicago: American Bar Association, 1979), Table 9.

Hess and Torney found widespread use of classroom symbols and rituals, for example, pledging allegiance, showing the flag or pictures of important events or people, singing patriotic songs. With the child's increasing interest in institutions, teachers give more attention in succeeding years to specific political structures. This curriculum has special empirical and normative perspectives. Empirically, it ignores events and conditions that contradict the ideal descriptions of the political system. The normative content emphasizes compliance with rules and authority, while skimping information on citizens' rights to participate in their government. This in turn leads to a deemphasis on parties, interest groups, and partisan behavior.[22]

At the secondary level, teachers provide more information to the student, but this bears little relation to the world social scientists portray.[23] What dramatically distinguishes the perceptions of the latter is the absence of controversy in the teacher's world. The clamor of issues over which contemporary Americans are sharply divided rarely enters the classroom; even issues that divided our ancestors may still be handled gingerly. American history courses characteristically leave little time for current politics; often the course conveniently fuzzes away somewhere after World War II.

This blandness is attributable to a lack of teacher competence at handling controversy and to pressures on teachers, textbook publishers, and school boards by special interest groups. We will note the pressure of "curriculum evangelism" that is used to assure a neutral, if not favorable, treatment for certain groups and values.[24]

Textbook Content

Textbooks are an obvious major instrument for political socialization. They played a powerful role in the decades after the Civil War, training citizens in history and patriotism when, in Wiggin's phrase, the textbook was "teacher to America."[25] Indeed, the Southern white viewpoint saturated the national perspective of Reconstruction due to the dominance of Southern historians' ideas in secondary textbooks. More recently, as Table 3.2 showed, the historical task of citizenship training still fills our textbooks.[26]

Again, the findings here are much like those for the total curriculum—textbooks are just as bland as the curriculum they serve. Noncontroversial, offering few conceptual and analytical tools for understanding political reality, jingoistic, and narrowly moralistic (only the rare book mentions any mistake the United States has ever made in domestic policy and none in foreign affairs), naive in describing the political process, overly optimistic about the system's ability to handle problems—the criticisms of these books are repetitive and insistent. The instructional methods used are not much more attractive. At a chapter's end are often questions for review that stress formal facts. The question of what the individual student might do about all these facts is never raised. The "naturalist fallacy"—that by assembling enough empirical facts, one can make value judgments—pervades such instruction.

These critiques from decades ago do not improve in recent years. Katz's 1984 review of the ten leading American government and history textbooks for secondary school reached the familiar conclusion:

> The ten are essentially alike and, with one possible exception, are dry institutional descriptions. . . . The government texts especially provide almost no consideration of theory, very little attention to the dynamics of the political process, and almost no discussion of issues — a view shared by other observers.[27]

A vivid illustration of this blandness is in the treatment of minorities. Our society has always depended on many minorities, what Walt Whitman called, "A Nation of nations." But until very recently, whatever students could learn about this social fact from their books would be scant and stereotyped. Jews, blacks, and other immigrants, as well as American Indians, were often not presented at all or only as picturesque, human-interest facets of history. They were never shown as having an impact on our history. The "melting pot" thesis of such books is the implicit reason for avoiding the historical evidence; somehow, the immigrant stepped off the boat into a giant social fondue. Often made explicit was the viewpoint that there was a social harmony in which all groups were said to live, except for the regrettable aberration of the Civil War. Blacks disappeared from history textbooks after that war, except for an occasional patronizing reference to George Washington Carver—rarely to Frederick Douglass and never to William DuBois. Indians were presented as quaint natives who sometimes caused trouble that was quickly put down. America was "discovered" by an Italian or a Viking, never by Indians. It is hard to adequately parody such a narrow view of the pluralistic basis of American history; the actual presentations do so on their face.

Then, sometime in the 1960s, minorities began getting more realistic treatment of their roles in history as a result of political and educational protest. A comparison of textbooks from 1949 to 1960 found some improvement for Jews but little for blacks and immigrants of other races. By 1980s, however, a fuller exposition of the blacks' historical role—including changing terminology from Negro to black—and removal of offensive characterizations were widely evident in textbooks. Pressure from the urban centers by the increasingly politicized blacks was a major force in this change.[28] The rate of adopting these modified textbooks, however, was still influenced if not set by statewide decisions, as in California, where special interest groups could affect an entire state.

The Role of the Teacher

Intervening among curriculum, textbook, and student, the teacher has been regarded as a potentially powerful instrument for political socialization since the days of Athens. And, as Socrates learned when the Athenians executed him for his teachings, societies have always placed constraints upon this power. A review of teacher preparation provides important clues to the direction of such constraints. Despite some acceptance of social science courses, teacher training continues to emphasize history. Strikingly, no state requires teachers to be certified in political science, so no uniform training exists among the states for this subject. That is significant given that a five-state study recently found how important the teacher's role is in civic education. Teachers in this study claimed they were the ones most responsible for choosing any topic and selecting instructional materials in such courses. Some states may require a specific course, such as the state or federal Constitution or U.S. history; only four states require even one course in civics, government, or public administration.[29]

The outlook, training, and methodology of the historian is not that of the social scientist. As a consequence, "the student comes to think of human activity in a descriptive, sequential, and narrative fashion rather than in an analytical and predictive way. History and historians do not address themselves to the problem of systematically developing theories of human conduct."[30] Also, such training implants a past rather than present orientation in teachers themselves that inhibits them from directing students' attention to the social world around them. All this makes it easier for teachers to instill allegiant, passive attitudes about the political and social world—and also makes it safer for them.

Under the spur of program reforms of the 1980s, social science courses were increasingly added to secondary school curriculum; the gap between the teacher's competence and the potential quality of the offering may grow. Despite great student interest in government in the 1960s, for example, few teachers were trained to offer the new thinking in political science as analytical tools. Many only had an introductory course in college, often years behind them, and some had none. In Kansas, "14.6 percent of the government teachers and 25.5 percent of the citizenship instructors had never had a college course in government." Better preparation should come with upgrading high school curricula by the professions and recent federal projects.[31]

Certain characteristics of civics teachers can be important in their work of socialization. In the early 1960s, lack of controversy in textbooks was matched by teacher avoidance of controversy. The safer the topic, the less reluctance there was to express views. Those who were younger, more liberal, and more politically active, though, consistently expressed themselves more openly. Avoidance by teachers sampled was partly a function of what one taught; those in social studies, English, and languages were more expressive and liberal than their colleagues in art and music. Issue avoidance in class did not carry outside the classroom, however, as most teachers agreed they would express themselves in their role as citizens. Yet "even for the expressive teachers the closing of the classroom door means goodbye to the world of politics."[32] In a later chapter, we shall note some changes in this behavior, however.

Timidity—or lack of competence—in the face of controversy is not new. Thirty-five years ago Beale asked, "Are American teachers free?" and in his classic study found that they were not.[33] Countless other studies show that teachers are urged not to get involved in controversy, an insistence backed by sanctions of disapproval or dismissal.[34]

Efforts to constrain teachers are not the monopoly of any particular group but rather a recognition of their purported power as socializing agents. We have mentioned minority pressures that recently moved textbook publishers to present a more complete and honest treatment. Teachers have also been charged with racism and bias by these same groups, while, from the other side, right-wing elements charge subversion if teachers do change. Unsafe because controversial, particular issues consistently appear in accounts of these conflicts. Favorable—or even any—reference to evolution, the United Nations, the right to dissent, civil rights, current politics, the role of blacks in our history, the Soviet Union, sex education, family life, class and status conflict—again and again the same curriculum items appear at the hub of local community conflict with an embattled teacher.[35]

One curious feature of the teacher-as-socializing-agent is the wide evidence that teacher adherence to values normally defined as democratic is not very strong. Teachers' responses to attitude scales on civil rights raise questions about their knowledge of and attachment to civil rights values. If prevalent, this presents a picture of a socializing agent who is not particularly well trained for her or his task, noncombative, sensitive to community pressure, and uncertain about if not antipathetic to at least part of the democratic credo she or he is supposed to transmit.[36]

Summary

Upon review, these three instruments of political socialization—curriculum, textbooks, and teachers—share common features. They are uncritical of the political system, unconcerned with contemporary social conflict, and undemanding of the student. Formal exposure to politics—if any—is concentrated during the latter part of the curriculum, and much of that focuses in a selective way on the past. Any window opened to the student on this nation reveals a social monochrome, not a kaleidoscope, of people. Groups are characteristically portrayed as interacting by accommodation not competition. The political system is presented as an arrangement of dust-dry institutions, and its presentation is formalistic; no live or lively people fill these positions of power. Our system's values are offered as an unchallengeable heritage of the past, to be accepted as fact, not opinion, whose content is given and whose clarity is obvious.

In short, if diffuse support for a political system is best created by exposing the young to a uniform set of stimuli in a structured way, then the instruments of American socialization surveyed are just the thing. The allegiant American model prevails, offering students "one nation, under God, indivisible, with liberty and justice for all." The instructional design, explicit or not, prompts students to see their oneness and ignore their distinctness, with similar treatment for their allegiance and dissent, their cooperation and conflict. In our terms, then, all of this, if successful, looks like diffuse support.

Even though the reality of the political world is passion and maneuver, cut and thrust, ambition and ideals, devasting losses and high rewards, what emerges, however, is an extremely bland picture of political socialization. The politics of curriculum policymaking, as Boyd has pointed out, has great potential for hurting those who provide civic education. Accordingly, Wirt has argued that the resulting blandness of the civics curriculum has many uses. It deflates the interest of high school students at a time of much questioning; it angers no parents who could challenge school authorities in public arenas; it disturbs no local power group active in politics; it provides a marketplace for publishers in which calmness fosters sales; and it promotes a community view of school professionals as nondeviant. Politically, then, blandness prevents threats to teachers' and administrators' control of classroom and education. Could this be why the National Assessment of Educational Progress reported several years ago that high school students judged their civics courses to be the most boring in the entire curriculum?[37]

Yet it remains to be seen what the result is upon the young. When we ask how effective such socialization has been, we raise a more significant query than asking what the instruments are like. The answer here leads us into a more dynamic study of the citizen at the intersection of State and School.

THE EFFECTS OF POLITICAL SOCIALIZATION

The flood of research on this issue must necessarily be summarized here,[38] but we can draw several conclusions. First, institutions other than the School also work as socializing agents—family and peer groups, as well as reality signals (feedback) stimulated by distinctive events. Second, the School instruments we described are found to have *little* effect for white middle-class Americans but substantially more for black Americans. Third, the psychology of the socialization process is highly complex. And fourth, enough is systematically known about these psychological aspects to allow valid generalizations about the socialization process. These comments should not be taken as overly critical, for only recently has anyone focused on this complex process. However, just enough is known to conclude that current School theory of curriculum and instruction is misplaced and ineffective.

Causes and Effects of Socialization

The scholarly disregard, until quite recently, of the School as a political socializer is seen in the fact that Hyman's seminal volume in 1959 emphasized family influence but totally ignored that of the School.[39] The primacy of family influence on the political socialization of children has been challenged recently by Hess and Torney's study of over twelve thousand elementary children, confirmed in other details by a smaller national sample in the work of Jennings and Niemi. From these studies the family emerges as important in creating early gross but deep attitudes of support for country and government and in shaping the child's party identification.[40] For other aspects of attitude, value, and cognition about the political world, other agents—such as the School, peers, and communications media—operate.

Clearly an elaborate theory is needed to explain why the child is not the mirror image of the parent. Such a theory may be something like Dennis's suggestion: "The views of the socialized are likely to follow the socializers who most often interact with him, present more explicit political content to him, and have higher salience, prestige, and capacity to influence him generally." And yet, as he concludes,

> The comparative assessment of these forces and the extent to which they operate in concert or disharmony has only begun. There are still remarkably few published findings comparing different agency inputs with their ostensible socialization outputs, or relating both to the properties of learner and teacher as intervening variables.[41]

Keep in mind that the School's socializing stimuli are probably not the same everywhere in America. Hence, variation in curriculum, textbook, and teaching quality, as well as in the local community's demands upon such instruction, is probably associated with variations in what is transmitted. Thus, Litt showed that of three Boston suburbs with different statuses, each emphasized a different model. Even within the school site, Morgan showed that tracking will produce greater differences within schools than between them in the lessons about democracy that the students obtained.[42]

Yet repeated research finds that the impact of high school civics courses is minimal for white middle-class American youth, the large majority in all schools. In a large national sample of high school students in civic courses, Langton and Jennings found that little change in knowledge or attitudes took place over the course of a class, which is ostensibly the behavioral objective of such courses. Blacks, on the other hand—particularly those of lower- and middle-class origins—did show significant increases in political knowledge, toleration, efficacy, and the desire to participate in politics. For them at least, the course content was new information; for whites it was redundant. The implication is that other agents, such as peer groups and family, can socialize whites before such courses enter their lives. But how and with what comparative effect this occurs, we do not know.

Such insignificant findings lead one to question much of what is now offered as civic instruction in high schools. So much effort with so little results suggests either the need for change in the instruction at this level or a shift to instruction in earlier years where effects are more likely.[43] Many major questions on the means and results of political socialization remain,[44] though by the late 1970s scholarly interest in them had lagged.

What can be said about the School's effect on political socialization is complex but fairly consistent.

> Taking any single dimension of school life, its reverberations on adolescent political orientations are customarily modest. When these dimensions are combined, however, they suggest that the school has significant although not overwhelming importance.[45]

What we do not know about this process suggests some research directions never explored. For example, the once-common assumption by psychologists that little political learning occurs in childhood has been the basis for curriculum theory requiring civics only in secondary schools. But this assumption proved doubtful when scholars first searched for specifically political aspects of socialization during early life. They found that as early as the second grade, children possessed images of government and political leaders and held an extraordinarily and unsuspectedly benign attitude toward both political objects. That finding suggests that the School could be more influential than the family in many of these respects.

Also, it was once believed that attitudes toward authority within the family were transferred to political authorities, first via personalized attraction to idealized presidents and then to political institutions, eventually accounting for citizen acceptance of the political system's legitimacy. This purported tie evaporates, though, as soon as children learn that families and government act differently and that responsibilities within each are different. The psychological analysis of socialization has its critics, but at least the questions raised have relevance for other aspects of political studies.[46]

The "Hidden Curriculum" Possibility

Another strong perspective on civics learning emerged in the 1970s. Some interpreted the political socialization research to mean that the

School did not teach civic values—or anything civic—very well. Critics charged that instead the School transmitted other values from the structure of education and the organizational imperatives of the profession. In short, there was a "hidden curriculum" being imposed on students, a case of "what we do is so loud you can't hear what we say."

This concept has several dimensions:

> a set of common practices which, by teaching quite different behavior and power relationships, supposedly prevents the transmission of democratic values in the school. . . . It is alleged that the school teaches hierarchy, not democracy. Instead of student power in the school, we find teacher control over curriculum and administrator control over the school building. Instead of genuine equality among students, we find invidious ability groupings. . . . Instead of liberty for students we encounter constant surveillance. Instead of the "personal interest in social relationships" envisaged by Dewey, we observe egotistic competition for grades, for status, and ultimately, for admission to "appropriate" colleges and universities. Instead of the democratic citizen's enjoyment of choice and spontaneity, we discover the dead hand of delay and queing. . . of teacher dictates, of a fixed, externally prescribed, stultifying curriculum. Behind the pretence of "democratic" socialization lurks the reality of closely supervised, standardized training where students fight each other in order to please those in power. In sum, students cannot learn democracy in the school because the school is not a democratic place.[47]

The idea of a hidden curriculum fit well into the swelling disenchantment with American schooling in the 1970s and 1980s, when the school was widely condemned for not teaching much of anything to anybody. But as Merelman charges of the "hidden curriculum" thesis, it claims more than it can substantiate. For example, conformist and alienated students are both offered as evidence of the same thesis, but how can one system produce such contrasting results?

Describing teachers, curriculum, and administrators as everywhere repressive is also inaccurate. After all, students do find areas of freedom for their own activities within the school, and teachers who emphasize student assertiveness in pursuit of academic goals cannot also be teaching submissiveness. Some authoritarian school practices have come under successful legal attack; in addition, little of this thesis accounts for the ties between students' backgrounds (which may also be highly authoritarian) and the values that the school teaches. Finally, students find ways to avoid being dependent upon the system and surrendering to the hidden curriculum they experience—it is not all that "hidden," it seems. Nor is the evidence strong that students alienated from school are also alienated from the larger political system, as a study of over eighteen hundred high school leaders revealed.

An alternative explanation for the order, discipline, and hierarchy that underlie the hidden curriculum, Merelman urges, may not be political but rather stem from the nature of large organizations. Like other professionals, teachers are granted authority by the community to provide services deemed highly valuable to all, services that require special training. That authority has been strongly challenged in the last decade in all professions, here and abroad.[48] But normally the grant of authority has presumed that professionals, like educators, have special knowledge, both in substance and in methods of transmitting it. However, teachers are called upon to provide not only learning but order as well. To achieve both goals, educators claim that ordered ways of learning are necessary because they must handle large numbers of students. In short, at the heart of the hidden curriculum is the need for professional control over the dissemination of knowledge and the maintenance of order within the organization.

Note, though, the special problem that accompanies teaching political values. Given the pluralism of our political choices and values, the civics classroom is not a place where the teacher can impose a singular ideal with which all agree. Hence the student finds value relativism, not just the usual conventional wisdom, transmitted by professionals whose pursuit of order rests on that wisdom base. However, if the teacher tries to impose a single set of values in the traditional fashion of professionals, he or she must face those in the community advocating other values—a most threatening situation.[49]

For example, how can one deal with the key democratic values of popular sovereignty and political equality within the education structure when both challenge the very concept of that structure? Merelman suggests that to deal with the problem of popular sovereignty, the School hires civics teachers who are not that much more knowledgeable than the students so that the latter will feel closer to their teachers and come to think that intellectual authority is not to be feared. As for the problem of political equality, the School has grading practices and curriculum adjusted in every course so that a large majority of students neither fail nor excel; the result is that the majority shares roughly the same knowledge as a community of equals. All this is facilitated if, as is often the case, these values are taught as "facts." That way few students learn the crucial intellectual distinction between fact and value. By treating values as facts, the potential danger of someone inquiring into them can be avoided, and the necessary order of the school enhanced.

All of these suggest why few strong links have been found between schools and political socialization. Students cannot take seriously what they regard as "softness" in the school's text, teacher, content, and grading in civics instruction. The ostensibly democratic values being taught therefore remain poorly conceptualized and difficult to apply to specifics, as almost all studies of students and adults demonstrate. For example, many believe in "freedom of speech" in the abstract but also wish to restrict it in practice. Sadly enough, it may be the brightest students who see through the softness most easily and become disillusioned with political schooling.

Like all larger-scale critiques of social institutions, the notion of the hidden curriculum has been challenged for its conceptualization, methodology, and interpretation.[50] There should be little doubt, however, that schools do teach these values. Critical of the assumption that schools do not teach political values, Jennings assembled the results of twenty years of major studies in 1981; he found a strong relationship between the amount of education and the amount of political knowledge. In short, debate no longer need focus on whether the School has effects on the values of the State. It is the "how" of the effect that is little understood, a major research topic for the years ahead.

POLITICAL THEORY AND POLITICAL LEARNING

What we do know about the political values that the School teaches should be understood, for its teachings clearly shows the "political" quality of education. Research is in agreement about the content of this instruction, the map of politics that is taught the young. Such learning emphasizes: prescription but not analysis; the positive qualities of our history and social life but not the problem areas; the harmony and the unity of the political process but not its divisions;

and the past far more than the present. We see here many features of the allegiant American model with its impersonal, abstract institutions of governing.

Most scholars summarized here are appalled at their findings, mainly because they judge from the analytical model. Their criticisms are that current civic instruction provides few political skills, develops no techniques of analysis and inquiry to help citizens understand political reality, and presents little knowledge of our conflictual pluralistic political world—including knowledge of who wins and who loses in that conflict. Critics complain of textbooks and teachers pressured by representatives of our society into concealing the complex reality of the world they represent. Increasingly, there is growing challenge to the conventional wisdom that more education means greater support for racial tolerance.[51]

Just as people get the government they deserve, so their civic instruction reflects their dominant educational demands. After all, the civic instruction portrayed here is useful for many people in the world of education. And, in terms of the larger political system, those socialized to be nothing but allegiant are less likely to be very active politically. They are unlikely to assert a right to participate more fully, to strive for more resources from government, and, if disappointed in that effort, to challenge the political authorities, if not the political regime itself.

Apathy by many, therefore, is highly useful to the few powerful whose political muscle is made stronger by the absence of the many. A curriculum that tells students that politics is not hard to understand thus encourages their belief that it is also not important and so should not claim their time and energy. However, learning that emphasizes inquiry or that asks the students to look closely at reality is not useful to political elites, who cooperate in limiting such inquiry. Socrates, it will be recalled, felt the consequences of his urgings that "the unexamined life is not worth living." Few are like Socrates in the world of American civics teaching today.

A further conclusion is that the socialization content described here illuminates the theoretical perspective of the chapter opening. The tensions among the plural, democratic values noted there can be soothed by the allegiant American model that stresses acceptance of a consensual society. On the other hand, these tensions are aggravated if students are taught an analytical model that stresses a conflictual society. The School reduces challenge to a consensual ideal through several means. Most important is a curriculum that avoids current politics or issues and postpones consideration of that political scene to the last years of schooling.

Note the implications of this for systems analysis. The School's assertion that all is well and its avoidance of conflict will create more emotional diffuse support of the State than do other means. Further, School support will flow from its instruction that presents the political system as free from error in the past; as a set of impersonal institutions, not human beings among whom passions rage; and as vaguely embodying a creed that ties all Americans together but ignores their conflicts. This homogenized view thereby generates support for the authorities, regime, and community of the political system.

But there may be a penalty that the School pays for providing this diffuse support; students move from a benign attitude toward government in their elementary years to one of cynicism in their high school years.[52] The School is certainly not teaching such cynicism directly; rather, additional learning is coming from elsewhere—parents, peers, the media, reality. These influences inevitably set up a perspective that clashes with what the School offers. The political events of the last quarter century have thrust upon the students' attention a world of unending rancorous conflict, bumbling leaders, and group divisions. Against this, the School offers only the allegiant American world, which students see does not conform to reality. Little research has dealt with what students learn about politics without civics,[53] when they are directly caught up in an aspect of reality such as the draft, desegregation, teacher strikes, and other characteristics of recent political school turbulence. We believe that the School's instruction—with its emphasis on the harmony, unity, and perfection of American politics—must turn off many students, certainly the most aware. In sum, the short-term benefit of avoiding conflict via civics instruction may well be exceeded by the long-term costs of contributing to the general disenchantment with American institutions, political or other. If so, this strategy of achieving diffuse support for the political system costs more than it is worth.

In the chapters that follow we deal directly with *specific* support for the political system resulting from satisfaction with system outputs. What we see when we turn to the political conversion of demands into outputs is not the simple "clean" process the Schools present but a divisive, difficult, and often messy struggle among conflicting groups. It is in fact a world of political turbulence, not a utopia.

NOTES

1. This section has been informed by reflections on this question by Heinz Eulau, "Political Science and Education: The Long View and the Short," in *State, School, and Politics: Research Directions*, Michael W. Kirst, ed. (Lexington, Mass.: Heath, 1972).

2. Charles Silberman, *Crisis in the Classroom* (New York: Random House, 1970), documents much of this contradiction and dissent.

3. These reflections are elaborated upon in T. Bentley Edwards and Frederick M. Wirt, eds., *School Desegregation in the North*, Chaps. 1, 13; Frederick M. Wirt and Willis D. Hawley, eds., *New Dimensions of Freedom in America* (San Francisco: Chandler, 1967, 1969).

4. For comparison with the USSR, see George Z. F. Bereday and Jaan Pennar, eds., *The Politics of Soviet Education* (New York: Praeger, 1960), esp. Chaps. 3–4; George Z. F. Bereday and Bonnie B. Stretch, "Political Education in the U.S.A. and the U.S.S.R.," *Comparative Education Review* 7 (1963): 1–16; and Jeremy R. Azrael, "Patterns of Polity-Directed Educational Development: The Soviet Union," in *Education and Political Development*, James S. Coleman, ed. (Princeton: Princeton University Press, 1965), pp. 233–71.

5. The following was suggested by Kenneth Prewitt, "Social Selection and Social Citizenship," in *State, School and Politics*, Kirst, ed. Prewitt leans on two earlier essays: Talcott Parsons, "The School Class as a Social System: Some of Its Function in American Society," in *Social Structure and Personality* (New York: Free Press, 1964), pp. 129–54; and T.H. Marshall, "Citizenship and Social Class," in *Class, Citizenship and Social Development* (New York: Doubleday, Anchor, 1964).

6. National Assessment of Educational Progress, *Education for Citizenship: A Bicentennial Survey* (Denver: National Assessment of Educational Progress, 1976), Chap. 3.

7. For a classic statement of these notions and their origins in the clash between class realities and the American creed, see H. Lloyd Warner, *Democracy in Jonesville* (New York: Harper & Row, 1949); and A.B. Hollingshead, *Elmtown's Youth: The Impact of Social Classes on Adolescents* (New York: Wiley, 1949).

8. On these interrelationships, see David Easton, "The Function of Formal Education," *School Review* 65 (1957): 304–16; Byron G. Massialas, *Education and the Political System* (Reading, Mass.: Addison-Wesley, 1969), Chap. 1; and Dean Jaros and Bradley C. Canon, "Transmitting Basic Political Values: The Role of the Educational System," *School Review* 77 (1969): 94–107.

9. David Easton, *A System Analysis of Political Life* (New York: Wiley, 1965), p. 273.

10. David Easton and Jack Dennis, *Children in the Political System* (New York: MaGraw-Hill, 1969), p. 7. The definition is not so simple as it looks; see Fred I. Greenstein, "A Note on the Ambiguity of 'Political Socialization': Definitions, Criticism and Strategies on Inquiry," *Journal of Politics* 32 (1970): 969–78.

11. The contents of these orientations are usually conceptualized broadly as values, affect, and cognition, but role behaviors may be taught without such prior understanding. For a summary of scholars' agreement on this orientation content, see Jack Dennis, "Major Problems of Political Socialization Research," *Midwest Journal of Political Science* 12 (1968): 91–98; Richard Dawson, Kenneth Prewitt, and Karen S. Dawson, *Political Socialization*, 2d ed. (Boston: Little, Brown & Co., 1977).

12. A fuller explanation of the theoretical and conceptual elements here is developed in Easton and Dennis, *Children in the Political System*, Part 1, esp. Chap. 3. Easton reminds us in private correspondence, however, that schools are not always successful in bolstering a system. In Quebec, he notes, many teachers are accused of fostering "separatist" sentiment among their students.

13. Edgar Litt, "Education and Political Enlightenment in America," *Annals of the American Academy of Political and Social Sciences* 361 (1965): 35.

14. The first systematic examination of civic education was an eight-country study directed in the late 1920s by Charles E. Merriam; see his *The Making of Citizens: A Comparative Study of Methods of Civic Training* (Chicago: University of Chicago Press, 1931). Political science concern on the subject was dropped for another quarter century until Easton's writing in the 1950s and Herbert H. Hyman's *Political Socialization* (New York: Free Press, 1959), although this study ignored schools as a socializing agent in its focus upon the family. The first fully cross-national studies in the mode indicated in the text were Gabriel A. Almond and Sidney Verba, *The Civic Culture: Political Attitudes and Democracy in Five Nations* (Princeton: Princeton University Press, 1963); Almond and Verba, *The Civic Culture Revisited* (Boston: Little, Brown & Co., 1980).

15. Dawson et al., *Political Socialization*.

16. These terms are fully defined in Easton, *A System Analysis*, Part 3.

17. Weissberg, *Political Learning, Political Choice, and Democratic Citizenship*, p. 28.

18. The following quotations are drawn from Litt, "Education and Political Enlightenment." The model labels are those of the present authors.

19. Frederick R. Smith, "The Curriculum," in *New Challenges in the Social Studies*, Byron G. Massialas and Frederick R. Smith, eds. (Belmont, Calif.: Wadsworth, 1965).

20. M. Kent Jennings, "Correlates of the Social Studies Curriculum," in *Social Studies in the United States*, C. Benjamin Cox and Byron G. Massialas, eds. (New York: Harcourt Brace Jovanovich, 1967), pp. 289–309.

21. Frederick Wirt, "The Uses of Blandness: State, Local, and Professional Roles in Citizenship Education," in *Teaching About American Federal Democracy*, S. Schecter, ed. (Philadelphia: Center for the Study of Federalism, Temple University, 1984), pp. 79–89.

22. Robert D. Hess and Judith V. Torney, *The Development of Political Attitudes in Children* (Chicago: Aldine, 1967), pp. 105–15. For an extended analysis, see Hess and Torney, *The Development of Basic Attitudes and Values Toward Government and Citizenship During the Elementary School Years, Part I* (Chicago: University of Chicago, Cooperative Research Project no. 1078, 1965).

23. For specific content analysis, see Franklin Patterson, "Citizenship and the High School: Representative Current Practices," in *The Adolescent Citizen*, Franklin Patterson et al. (New York: Free Press, 1960), pp. 100–75; Frederick R. Smith and

John J. Patrick, "Civics: Relating Social Study to Social Reality," in *Social Studies*, Cox and Massialas, eds., pp. 105–27; Byron G. Massialas, "American Government," in ibid., pp. 167–95.

24. John P. Lunstrum,"The Treatment of Controversial Issues in Social Studies Instruction," *High School Journal* 49 (1965): 13–21; for a fuller picture, see G. Massialas and C. Benjamin Cox, *Inquiry in Social Studies* (New York: McGraw-Hill, 1966), esp. pp. 158–60. A detailed study of right-wing pressures upon textbooks and curriculum is Jack Nelson and Gene Roberts, Jr., *The Censors and the Schools* (Boston: Little, Brown & Co., 1963).

25. For a thorough historical study of these instruments in calculating nationalism, see Gladys A. Wiggin, *Education and Nationalism* (New York: McGraw-Hill, 1962); the role of the textbook is examined in Chap. 9. On the Southern perspective, see Bernard A. Weisberger, "Dark and Bloody Ground of Reconstruction Historiography," *Journal of Southern History* 25 (1959): 427–47.

26. The earliest such analysis may have been Bessie L. Pierce, *Civic Attitudes in American Schools* (Chicago: University of Chicago Press, 1930). The study covering the most texts (ninety-three) is James P. Shaver, "Reflective Thinking Values and Social Studies Textbooks," *School Review* 73 (1960): 226–57. See also Mark M. Krug, "'Safe' Textbooks and Citizenship Education," ibid., 68 (1960): 463–80; Edgar Litt, "Civic Education, Community Norms, and Political Indoctrination," *American Sociological Review* 28 (1963): 71–72; Byron G. Massialas, "American Government: 'We Are the Greatest,' " in *Social Studies*, Cox and Massialas, eds., pp. 167–95; Smith and Patrick, "Civics"; Stanley E. Ballinger, "The Social Studies and Social Controversy," *School Review* 71 (1963): 97–111. For studies of alternatives, see Massialas and Cox, *Inquiry in Social Studies*, Chap. 9.

27. Ellis Katz, "Federalism in Secondary American History and Government Textbooks," in *Teaching about American Federal Democracy*, S. Schecter, ed., p. 91. See similar findings reported here. Noteworthy is the exception, Judith Gillespie and Stuart Lazarus, *American Government: Comparing Political Experiences* (Englewood Cliffs, N.J.: Prentice-Hall, 1979).

28. Content analysis of the earlier omissions are found in sources cited in n. 26. For specialized studies, see United States Congress, House Committee on Education and Labor, Ad Hoc Subcommittee on De Facto School Segregation, *Books for Schools and the Treatment of Minorities* (1966); the foregoing is popularized in John Brademas, "Don't Censor Textbooks—But Let's Keep Out Biased or Inaccurate Information," *Nations' Schools* 79 (1967): 38–52; for a study of a special distortion, see Virgil J. Vogel, "The Indian in American History," *Integrated Education* 6 (1968): 16–32; for studies of changing content, see Lloyd Marcus, *The Treatment of Minorities in Secondary School Textbooks* (New York: Anti-Defamation League of B'nai B'rith, 1961) and Sol M. Elkin, "Minorities in Textbooks: The Latest Chapter," *Teachers College Record* 66 (1965): 502–08.

29. The study is Joel Henning et al., *Mandate for Change* (Chicago: American Bar Association, 1979), Chap. 6. For a full review of this training, see Mary Turner, "Civic Education in the United States," in *Political Education in Flux*, D. Heater and J. Gillespie, eds. (Beverly Hills, Calif.: Sage, 1981).

30. For elaboration see John R. Palmer, "The Problem of Historical Explanation," *Social Education* 27 (1963).

31. The Kansas figure is cited in Harlan Hahn, "Teacher Preparation in Political Science," *Social Education* 29 (1965): 86–89. Symptomatic of professional social scientist interest is the development in the American Political Science Association in 1970 of a Pre-Collegiate Education Committee and earlier the work of the center mentioned in n. 23, to develop a model curriculum. New thinking on such preparation is reviewed in Turner, "Civic Education in the United States." It is striking how often this course is taught by an athletic coach.

32. Harmon Ziegler, *The Political Life of American Teachers* (Englewood Cliffs, N.J.: Prentice-Hall, 1967), Chap. 4, quotation at p. 113; Hillel Black, *The American Schoolbook* (New York: Morrow, 1967), pp. 91–92.

33. Howard K. Beale, *Are American Teachers Free?* (New York: Scribner's, 1936).

34. Reviewed in Wirt, "The Uses of Blandness."

35. For case studies, see Joseph F. Maloney, *"The Lonesome Train" in Levittown* (University, Ala.: Inter-University Case Program, No. 39, 1958); Donald W. Robinson, "The Teachers Take a Birching," *Phi Delta Kappan* (1962): 182–88. For more systematic analysis of teacher constraints and sanctions, see Ziegler, *Political Life*, Chap 5; and Howard S. Becker, "The Teacher in the Authority System of the Public School," *Journal of Educational Sociology* 27 (1953).

36. For a review of research on this attitudinal dimension, see Merlyn M. Gubser, "Anti-Democratic Attitudes of American Educators," *School and Community* 54 (1967): 14–16; see also John C. Weiser and James E. Hayes, "Democratic Attitudes of Teachers and Prospective Teachers," *Phi Delta Kappan* 47 (1966): 476–81.

37. William Boyd, "The Changing Politics of Education," *Review of Educational Research* 48 (1978): 577–628; Wirt, "The Uses of Blandness." A full review of such issues are found in Jon Schaffarzick and Gary Sykes, eds., *Value Conflict and Curriculum Issues* (Berkley, Calif.: McCutchan, 1979).

38. A full review is found in Dawson et al., *Political Socialization*, and M. Kent Jennings and Richard G. Niemi, *The Political Character of Adolescence: The Influence of Families and Schools* (Princeton, N.J.: Princeton University Press, 1974), pp. 327–28; see also William R. Schonfeld, "The Focus of Political Socialization Research: An Evaluation," *World Politics* 23 (April, 1971): 544–78.

39. Hyman, *Political Socialization*.

40. Hess and Torney, *The Development of Political Attitudes in Children*, Chap. 5; M. Kent Jennings and Richard G. Niemi, "The Transmission of Political Values from Parent to Child," *American Science Review* 62 (1968): 169–84, involving a national sample of 1,669 seniors. Another study of these data shows that it is the mother rather than the father who is more influential in shaping partisan affiliation and attitudes on some public issues; see M. Kent Jennings and Kenneth P. Langton, "Mothers vs. Fathers: The Formation of Political Orientations Among Young Americans," *Journal of Politics* 31 (1969): 329–58.

41. Dennis "Major Problems," p. 109. For a similar judgment drawn from a review of the literature, see Vernon M. Goetcheus and Harvey C. Mansfield, "Innovations and Trends in the Study of American Politics," *Annals of the American*

Academy of Political and Social Science 391 (1970): 178–81; and Dawson et al., *Political Socialization*, pp. 215–18.

42. See Litt, "Education and Political Enlightenment," n. 26; Edward P. Morgan, *Inequality in Classroom Learning: Schooling and Democratic Citizenship* (New York: Praeger, 1977) shows in three high schools the great variety of factors working in the teaching of civics.

43. Earlier research with null findings includes Roy A. Price, "Citizenship Studies in Syracuse," *Phi Delta Kappan* 33 (1951): 179–81; Earl E. Edgar, "Kansas Study of Education for Citizenship," ibid.: 175–78; Roy E. Horton, Jr., "American Freedom and the Values of Youth," in *Anti-Democratic Attitudes in American Schools*, H. M. Remmers, ed. (Evanston: Northwestern University Press, 1963), pp. 18–60; Litt, "Education and Political Enlightenment"; Patterson, "Citizenship and High School," pp. 71–73.

For similar results in college, see Albert Somit et al., "The Effect of the Introductory Political Science Course on Student Attitudes Toward Political Participation," *American Political Science Review* 52 (1958): 1129–32; James A. Robinson et al., "Teaching with Inter-Nation Simulation and Case Studies," *American Political Science Review* 60 (1966): 53–65.

The Langton-Jennings study is "Political Socialization and the High School Civics Curriculum in the United States," *American Political Science Review* 62 (1968): 852–67, with exchange following at *American Political Science Review* 63 (1969): 172–73. Curriculum revisions flowing from such findings have been suggested by idem and by Patrick.

44. Dennis, "Major Problems"; see also Dawson et al., *Political Socialization*.

45. Jennings and Niemi, *The Political Character of Adolescence*, pp. 327–28.

46. The findings grossly simplified here are drawn from Hess and Torney, *Development of Political Attitudes*; Easton and Dennis, *Children in the Political System*; Fred I. Greenstein, *Children and Politics* (New Haven: Yale University Press, 1965). For some criticisms, see Goetcheus and Mansfield, "Innovations and Trends"; Sheilah R. Koppen, "Children and Compliance: A Comparative Study of Socialization Studies," *Law and Society Review* 4 (1970): 545–64; Dean Jaros et al., "The Malevolent Leader: Political Socialization in an American Sub-Culture," *American Political Science Review* 62 (1968): 564–75; Schonfeld, "The Focus of Political Socialization Research"; R. W. Connell, *The Child's Construction of Politics* (Carleton, Victoria: Melbourne University Press, 1971).

47. Richard M. Merelman, "Democratic Politics and the Culture of American Education," *American Political Science Review* 74 (1980): 320; the following paragraphs, unless noted otherwise, are drawn from this source, 319–32. See the extensive bibliography on the hidden curriculum concept at this source for support of propositions in the following paragraphs.

48. Frederick M. Wirt, "Professionalism and Political Conflict," *Journal of Public Policy* 1 (1981): 61–93.

49. This threat from community pressure appears in all studies of the civics teacher; see Zeigler, *Political Life of American Teachers*, passim; Massialas, *Education and the Political System*, Chap. 6; Wirt, "The Use of Blandness."

50. The following is drawn from: Kent Jennings, "Comment," *American Political*

Science Review 74 (1980): 333–37; Merelman, "A Reply to Richard M. Jennings," ibid.: 338–41; and Jennings, "Communication," *American Political Science Review* 75 (1981).

51. Mary Jackman, "General and Applied Tolerance: Does Education Increase Commitment to Racial Integration," *American Journal of Political Science* 23 (1978): 303–25; challenged by Michael Corbett, "Education and Political Tolerance: Group-Relatedness and Consistency Reconsidered," *American Politics Quarterly* 8 (1980): 345–60.

52. Greenstein, "Note on the Ambiguity." Although this work draws data from before the turbulent national events of the last two decades, this finding has been confirmed by all later longitudinal studies; see Dawson et al., *Political Socialization*, passim.

53. Frederick M. Wirt, "Politics without Civics," *Society* 14 (1977): 46–48.

4

The Origins and Agents of Demand Inputs

The political system is not subject to the input of support alone; it is demands that provide the more contentious stuff of governance. We turn in this section to the exchange, across boundaries, of wants arising from unsatisfied values. Such dissatisfaction promotes stress in the social environment, which can produce demands on the political system. This chapter investigates how stress arises through value conflicts and what agents transfer the resulting demands across the system's boundary.

VALUES AND THE ORIGIN OF CONFLICT

Individualism and Majoritarianism

The first—and perhaps still best—commentator on American political life noted a curious contradiction in its fundamental values. Alexis de Tocqueville pointed to the individualistic and the collectivist impulses whose clash provided a vital dynamism to the America that he knew in the 1830s. Being a good aristocrat, he feared that the collectivist impulse with its adoration of the majoritarian principle would triumph. The stresses at work in our society today still stem from the confrontation between individual and group pressures to shape politics or governmental policy.

The fundamental value of our political system may well be individualism, with its roots in Greek and Christian beliefs. This is reflected in our economic processes, our records of violence, and the restless spirit characterizing the westward migration in the 1800s and the migration to the cities in the 1900s. We see political reflections of this value in the bills of rights in national and state constitutions. These documents draw lines around the individual that, for governments to cross, constitute tyranny. Such declarations are also designed to guard any minority against possible tyranny by popular majorities. Yet the problem remains that majorities hold special authority in a democracy, so the conflict of a minority right and majority rule has been endemic in our history.

The interaction of these two principles is mediated by our political system. If all persons are regarded as important, their wishes must be responded to by that system. But people's wishes are many and often conflicting. If government is to persist, it must regulate these conflicts to keep them within tolerable levels. The operating principle of such regulation is that any given policy will take the direction the majority prefers. Of course, this simplifies a highly complex body of theory; "majority rule" is a concept whose ambiguity is exceeded only by its sister concept of "majority will."[1]

If our history shows conflict between individualism and majority rule, our political practices and institutions do the same. For example, minority rights are protected by numerous devices, including the two-thirds requirement to pass school tax levies. We see majority rule in the American concern to *elect* everyone in sight, including members of fourteen thousand school boards. Many constitutional principles are barriers erected against temporary majorities; for example, separation of power, checks and balances, federalism, and civil rights. For instance, school boards may issue policies, but they are subject to taxpayer suit, popular referendum, and even recall of officials. The national will may call for outlawing school segregation, but the power of Southern congressmen can long thwart that will in their region, and Northern whites can do so by suburban flight.

If not checked, individualism operating in political channels might tear the society apart. To an uncertain degree, diffuse support for the political organization—the accepted basic rules of governance—has contributed to the creation of a political community, the sense that Americans want to exist together. Diffuse support, though, is neither absolute nor deeply entrenched among Americans due to the divisive effect of individualism.[2]

The centrifugal pull of individualism has been checked by our tendency to live and socialize mostly with people who agree with us. In much of our past, American society consisted of islands of conformity, each oriented to different values and indifferent to or unaware of the other islands. The Bible Belt schools ignored evolution while urban Northern schools treated it fully; rural Protestant schools might require prayers while urban liberal enclaves ignored them. This cultural insolationism broke down when outside forces disrupted the civil serenity—the issues of slavery and union 125 years ago, the movement from farm to the city 100 years ago, and the impact of suburbanization and the communications media in the last half century. Along the way, a surprising amount of violence took place.[3] In all these matters, however, these changes created new stresses and demands on the political system; one arose over conflicting claims on the nature of schools.

The variety of region, policy, and community life reflects the basic individualism in American life.[4] Not for us the French school system, where at a given hour every child of a certain age in every school is learning the same thing. The idea is unthinkable for us; our philosophic individualism reinforces social differentiation and is reflected in our political system.[5] The rate of exchanges between the environment and the political system is highly influenced by a value system that emphasizes an obligation to translate private preference and need into public policy. Such exchanges are then augmented by an environment of great social diversity that necessarily generates more wants and demands than a homogeneous environment.

Pragmatism and School Policy

Another basic American value also influences this series of boundaries exchanges—pragmatism.[6] While the political system began with all its subsystems relatively uninvolved in citizens' lives, that condition continued only so long as private action worked to meet wants. When that failed, Americans did not hesitate to turn to the political system and public policy. First we turned to local political authorities, but if this proved inadequate, then to state authorities and, in time, to federal authorities. This political pragmatism has certain special aspects. Americans will use collective action in the name of individualism and blithely ignore the "states rights" doctrine if national action will get us what we want.[7]

In seeking authoritative allocation of resources, individuals let no single doctrine stand in their way, because many doctrines are at work among our states and regions.[8] One general cultural value—individualism—promotes inputs into the political system that another value—majority rule—authorizes as legitimate. In addition, pragmatism—undeterred by bonds of the past, stimulated by the challenge of a new society, and mobilizing collective, mutual interests—provides a crystallizing value. Combined with the other two, pragmatism generates numerous exchanges across that vague boundary between private and public systems.

We can see this value complex in school policies. The desire for education has *not* been a major value from the founding of this republic in the sense that everyone wanted it. Indeed, many reasons existed for opposing the early establishment of public schools, echoes of which we still hear today.[9] Yet along the way, many Americans *did* accept this value. We see signs of this in:

1. The *national* commitment to use land sales to finance schools and colleges, for example, the Northwest Ordinance of 1787 and the Morrill Land Acts of 1862 and 1890;[10]
2. The *states'* commitment, beginning in the 1850s, to provide a free public education at least to the grammar school level, then to high school, and now to some college;
3. Local *communities'* efforts at private support to reinforce state efforts in the private academies and colleges of the nineteenth century, and the community college effort after World War II.
4. The constant shaping of the curriculum to meet the special concerns of Americans, for example, in farm, industrial, and military training classes.[11]

Government action alone did not accomplish this; the nationalizing force of professionalism has been of greater consequence over a shorter period. Growing professional standards for administration, teaching, curriculum, testing, and other elements of education were all a phenomenon of the last century. Before this force emerged, the fabric of American schools was plaid, and a rather ragged plaid at that. It was experience drawn from testing ideas and transmitted through new journals and new training for the new profession that did far more than the political system to impose striking uniformity on American instructional practices. Pragmatism shows everywhere in the early history of this profession, for what worked well in one site was soon used elsewhere.

Despite this powerful nationalizing force, the belief in local control of schools never wavered, nor does it today even when the existence of local control seems in doubt. Yet those favoring local control in earlier times were just as busy adopting the innovations that professional administrators and teachers proclaimed as the "one best system."[12] In this way, most American schools accepted a standard set of graduation requirements (thus the Carnegie-unit concept), learning theories and their instructional practices, teacher- and administrator-training standards, and so on. So it was that the local adoption of nationwide professional standards eroded local control.

If the political system's relationship to education has varied over time, so has the citizen's. The belief that "education is a good thing" has had various meanings in the pluralist perspectives of our society. Early on, education was considered important for religious training. In colonial Massachusetts, in "the Bible Commonwealth," the first schooling law was known as the "Old Deluder Satan Act"; a favorite early textbook was John Cotton's *Spiritual Milk for Babes Drawn Out of the Breasts of Both Testaments*; and the enormously popular *New England Primer* featured a biblical alphabet, *A* being "In Adam's fall/We sinned all."[13]

In later centuries, schooling was endorsed for pragmatic goals: transmission of basic literacy. This included: the three Rs, provision of trained labor (i.e., vocational training for farmers and industrial workers), molding the diverse cultures of our immigrants into one culture (i.e., "Americanization"), and the absorption of "culture" in the popular sense (i.e., humanist and liberal education). Then, across time, education has been supported by many citizens—but not all— for the boost it provides children in the economic and status struggle.

BASIC VALUES IN EDUCATION POLICY

Key Variables Defined

We have noted that groups use political power to satisfy their values, that politics is indeed, in Easton's terms, "the authoritative allocation of values and resources." Now we wish to specify these values as they appear in educational policy. A recent study of such policy in six states by Mitchell and colleagues focuses that examination as they posit four values that are subsumed in school policy.[14]

1. *Quality:* "A substantial net improvement in the well-being of those affected by policy," best seen in states mandating standards of school performance and then providing resources and regulations to ensure their use. Typical are requirements for staff training, use of instructional resources, or performance by staff and students. This value is instrumental, a means to another value goal, namely, the fulfillment of diverse human purposes, thereby making life worth living and individuals worthwhile.

2. *Efficiency:* takes two forms, economic (minimizing costs while maximizing gains) and accountability (oversight and control of the local exercise of power). The first is regularly seen in such state mandates as pupil-teacher ratios or the minimum needed for kindergarten schools. The second is familiar in the details of procedures that local school authorities must follow (e.g., the budgetary process). This value is also instrumental, serving the end of responsibility for the exercise of public authority—the central operating premise of a democratic nation.

3. *Equity:* "the use of political authority to redistribute critical resources required for the satisfaction of human needs." Two steps in policymaking are required in equity matters—the perception of a gap between human needs and the availability of resources and allocation of resources to close that gap. This value is seen most often in federal compensatory, handicapped, or bilingual programs over the last three decades; but much earlier policy was moved by equity concerns to redress the imbalance in local school finances (e.g., the familiar foundation programs).

4. *Choice:* "the opportunity to make policy decisions or reject them" by local school authorities. Such policies are often mandated but can exist even when no state law does (i.e., what is not prohibited may be done). Law can mandate selecting among alternative allocations of resources (textbook selection), can permit local authorities to use authority or not (program choice by parental advisory boards), and can leave it to special groups to exercise authority (voting for or against bond issues). This value is also instrumental, serving the sovereignty of citizens in a democracy—the most fundamental of all American political views.

Attributes of Values in Operation

Manifest in statutes, these four values generate political conflict because they are not a nicely integrated schema or ideology. Rather, they may oppose, as well as reinforce, one another. These values emerge in a particular sequence during policy conflict.

Choice can inherently oppose all values because nothing in the other values compels one to select them. The exercise of choice can—and has—rejected quality programs and equity programs in education; the South's de jure segregation is a classic example. Efficiency, on the other hand, reinforces all values except choice because efficiency is designed to realize quality and equity goals. Clear illustrations are the "state regs"—heavily oriented to efficiency—that seek compliance with state policy goals. Finally, the quality value opposes all but efficiency; the latter usually reinforces quality, as noted, but quality is unrelated to questions of what should be equitable and what should be chosen. The clash between redistribution policies after 1965 and the quality ("excellence") policies of the Reagan administration is well known.

This brief argument makes a larger point, namely each value is always pursued in policy in relationship to other values. Also, a tension arises among them because different policy actors back different values. Broadly expressed, professionals have historically left their mark on quality and efficiency values in education, as the modern school system that emerged over the last century demonstrates. They usually defined the quality goals as well as the efficient means to achieve them. The participatory thrust of democracy can get in the way of this activity at times—but not always. This depends on how the force of choice and the search for equity emerges either directly from citizens or from professionals who share these values.

Another attribute of these policy values is the way they are sequenced into law. The history of American education shows that the first efforts to build this service were based on a belief in quality. The movement stems from Horace Mann and other reformers' moral objection to an illiterate population. Decades later it was stimulated further by public reaction against party machine control that had resulted in poor education. Efficiency values in policy would come second in this historical sequence because quality goals are not self-executing. Like all good aims in life, they must be worked at to be realized. That necessity prompted considerations of what it would take to administer quality goals and how to ensure compliance. Later, because of the maldistribution of educational services, equity values would be stimulated. The classic example is how the local property tax—a rational means of raising funds—had made the quality of a child's education a function of district wealth; equity-driven funding reforms in the 1920s and 1970s testify to that maldistribution. It is in the effort to redress these imbalances in the distribution of rewards that equity policy arises. Finally, choice values in policy do not follow this sequence; instead they pervade it at every step. Citizens chose the idea of free public education, voters supported elected school boards or tax levies to hold power accountable, and today, professionals must work within what Boyd terms a "zone of tolerance," constraints implicitly imposed by local citizens' preferences.[15]

The Infusion of Values in State Education Law

We see the reality of these values when we search state laws. Mitchell and his colleagues subjected state codes to content analysis within the framework of values. Table 4.1 summarizes their findings for their four values in seven areas of state policy mechanisms, or policy domains, and in two states of differing political cultures, Illinois and Wisconsin. Across the first row, we can see the proportion of each value in the finance laws of each state. The table reports that finance and governance policies are dominated by the efficiency value, although Wisconsin offers more equity-based law. Personnel policy is dominated by different values in the two states, and other policies

Table 4.1
Distribution of Values by State Policy Mechanisms in Illinois and Wisconsin

SPM	Quality		Equity		Efficiency		Choice	
	Ill.	*Wis.*	*Ill.*	*Wis.*	*Ill.*	*Wis.*	*Ill.*	*Wis.*
Finance	6	10	9	36	68	36	16	19 = 100%
Personnel	47	29	22	29	25	39	7	3
Testing and assessment	45	–	45	50	–	50	10	–
Program definition	34	27	28	30	17	23	21	20
Organization and governance	10	9	17	18	64	53	9	20
Curriculum materials	23	33	39	–	23	–	16	67
Buildings and facilities	26	27	21	27	29	31	24	15

Source: Frederick Wirt, Douglas Mitchell, and Catherine Marshall, "Analyzing Values in State Policy Systems," *Educational Evaluation and Policy Analysis*, Fall, 1988.

show more diffuse values. The results challenge any simple notion that a given policy domain is dominated by a single value.

Social Context and Educational Policy

Let us put the preceding discussion of values within the system analysis framework of the preceding chapter. How do values and a political system interact to produce educational policy?

Filtered through the pluralist prism of our society, general values take on specific definitions. At times the private pursuit of these definitions produces cooperation and accommodation among groups. Yet other groups come into conflict because insufficient resources for satisfying their values exist in private subsystems. As a result, some groups are rewarded and others are not. The resulting stress can mobilize the group that went unrewarded to drive for additional resources. This drive can transfer the resource struggle from the private to the political system. That system, in turn, seeks to maintain support for its political objectives by finding different ways of adjusting to such demands for value satisfaction.

Each school district reflects locally prevailing values to some degree. The guardians of community values, for whom schools are important instruments for keeping the faith, operate here. We have seen in Chapter 3 how the indoctrination function dominates schools when they teach about our government. When insulated from outside forces, local guardians of orthodoxy can exist without challenge. But in this century, as mentioned, obstacles to local autonomy abound. Local control over school policy has been weakened by those groups increasingly unwilling to accept the dominance of localism. A centralization to the state level of demands for quality and equity has resulted from this.

This centralization, though, is far from the bland homogeneity of the French school system. Certain American schools still hold the theory of evolution suspect, while others teach evolution, calculus, or Asian history. The decentralization impulse of pluralism wars with centralizing national forces, such as professionalism and state and federal laws. In this process, education is not unique but merely reflects the tensions that emerge in many other policy areas of a federal system as well. But whatever the balance among these conflicting values before, it has been tipped by new nationalizing forces in recent decades.

Within this general framework of values and demands pursuing policy, we need to know more specifics about this exchange and conversion process. Who are the agents that transfer demand inputs into the political system from their position on its boundaries? We need some flesh-and-blood referents for these abstract "transfer agents." For our purposes, we focus on the transfer roles that interest groups, electoral mechanisms, and local power structures play. Latently, each is involved in boundary transfer activities that affect the ability of the political system—in this case the school—to persist as it seeks to cope with stress-generated demands. Manifestly, each speaks for or transmits the variety of American individualism living in the swirl and clamor of local school politics. Both functions tell us much about how Americans give educational values a political form when they seek to transfer private preference into public policy.

INTEREST GROUPS AS TRANSFER AGENTS

Interest groups, working between citizens and educational authorities, are involved in the full spectrum of private demands on the school as a political system: claims for justice, help, reward, or recognition—all in the pursuit of quality, efficiency, equity, and choice. They do more, however, than just transmit political desires from citizens to officials. As transfer agents for the political system, interest groups often reformulate demands so that they differ somewhat from citizens' desires. Also, interest groups do not confine their activities to just the input and conversion phases of the political system; they provide feedback on the implementation of school policy as well. Competing claims for scarce educational budget resources often mobilize them. Despite such political activities, the tradition that overt politics and schools should be separate has shaped the nature of school interest groups.

Many reasons move individuals to join interest groups and engage in collective action. Most get something for it. Other potential members do not join because they can, without cost, benefit from gains the group may make—the "free rider" syndrome. Leaders mobilize groups for the diverse benefits that group activity can render. Not surprisingly, past decades have witnessed an impressive growth in the numbers and types of educational interest groups. This complex array is part of the greater political turbulence with which educational policymakers must contend. The emergence of a wide spectrum of narrow-based interest groups reflects a weakening national consensus about educational goals over the last three decades and the diminishing influence of broad-based groups, such as school boards and PTAs. Moreover, reforms such as compensatory, bilingual, and special education have created their own separate constituencies to preserve these new school functions. In addition, such programs spawn cohorts whose prime allegiance is to the program rather than to the broad concept of a common school. Categorical programs from Washington and the state have generated a jumble of interest groups that includes local project directors, parent groups, and federal and state categorical administrators.

Educational interest groups also grow as spin-offs of broader social movements, including women's liberation in the 1960s and the Moral Majority in the 1980s. These movements form political action groups with sections devoted to educational policies. For example, the National Organization of Women (NOW) may urge a state board of education to include a broader variety of female occupations in textbooks, or the Moral Majority will appear before local boards advocating that the story of creation be taught alongside evolution.

Another type of interest group includes networks of interstate experts and advocates who focus on particular policies, such as school finance reform or competency education. These "policy issue networks," not so broadly based as social movements, emphasize technical expertise and assistance in their lobbying strategy. All of these newer interest groups are added to the collective action groups that have been around for years, including the Council for Basic Education and the school administration association. We will turn to these shortly.

This complex and shifting kaleidoscope confronts educational administration with a much broader range of demands than faced even a few years ago. There is a political saying that any contest changes in nature when the number of participants changes. Two tenth-graders engaged in a schoolyard fight, one black and one white, are most likely working out their budding masculinity in a fashion characteristic of that age. But if a hundred students of each color are involved, it is not merely a melee; there are likely to be racial overtones to the fighting. Increasing the number of participants facing the administrator means that he or she is in a different kind of contest than before, a contest in which one's role definition will change. Cuban has noted how role definitions have altered through this century as a result of new social environments affecting big-city superintendents.[16] A later chapter will explore these role changes in depth. In one sense, the current period is the most exciting since reformers started pulling schools out from under political bosses and machines a century ago, but in another, it is unpleasant for those involved.

One of the major changes is that the administrator must work with these new interest groups. Sometimes NOW will join forces with a local PTA, but at other time it will oppose local preferences and align with a state organization made up of compensatory education parents. Because education has lost its diffuse support, appeals for loyalty to general public education will be insufficient to mobilize interest-group support for many things, including increases in local taxes. Splintered interest groups want a specific "payoff," such as access ramps for handicapped children. As Cuban notes, the role of the local school superintendent as an administrative chief has long since changed to that of a chief political negotiator and coalition builder. The objective of the next section is to categorize the interest groups that confront policymakers at all levels, to explain their formation and growth, and to underline the necessity for coalition formulation of public school policy.

The Role of Interest Group Entrepreneurs

If the social and structural forces at work in our society create interest groups, why do so many individuals join and contribute to them? The initial simple answer was that people join a group because they agree with the group's goals. Mancur Olson, in his *The Logic of Collective Action,* changed this straightforward emphasis on motivations.[17] As an economist, he stressed that individuals will *not* contribute to interest groups if they receive the same benefits through nonparticipation—as a "free rider." Why join the local teachers' organization if everyone receives wage increases through the efforts of those who give time and money? Olson answered this puzzle by focusing on the other benefits an organization can extend to or withhold from individuals. Anything of tangible value—group insurance programs, newsletters, tire discounts—can be contingent upon individual contributions. Interest groups thus attract members and resources by supplying benefits only partly related to politics or specific public policies. Yet interest group political activities are possible because the people who join want private benefits, not because they share common values or goals.

Olson's thesis has gone through several adaptations, which help explain the broad array of motives for individual contributions to groups. Salisbury has demonstrated that ideology, moral principles, and social pressures can generate collective action.[18] In an analogy to the marketplace, lobbyists form groups because, like entrepreneurs, the benefits they can obtain exceed the costs they must invest in mobilizing others. Members of a group also join because the cost-benefit ratio is favorable. Benefits are not merely material, such as good teacher contracts. They can also be "solidarity," the intangible psychological reward that comes from belonging—the pleasure of sharing the company of like-minded others—as in a group of mothers protecting the neighborhood school against dangerous drugs. Benefits can also be "expressive," so that one's personal goals are incorporated into and expressed by group action. An example would be a belief in the value of education manifested by work in the PTA. Common Cause is a classic example of all these. Other analysts have emphasized the motive of "imperfect information," as when individuals underestimate their ability to become a free rider or overestimate the importance of proposed education legislation for their job performance. Moe broadens individual motives for collective action by positing that people join interest groups because they like to go to meetings or have feelings of responsibility.[19]

Due to this variety of motivations, we cannot predict what inducements will make people join a group. Politics need not be a by-product of membership gained through discounts for auto rentals or tax shelter annuities. Interest group entrepreneurs can attract members through ideological appeal, emphasis on fairness, social pressure, and the structuring of meetings. We lack empirical studies on the perceptual and value characteristics that motivate membership in education lobby groups. We do know, however, that numerous motivations exist and that the interest group leader is well advised to develop diverse appeals. At the core of this exchange, though, one trades off group dues for individual benefits.

A recent key change in education politics has been the decline of loyalty as a motivation for supporting education interest groups. The PTA, American Association of University Women, and National

Committee for the Support of Public Schools have all lost ground in membership to such groups as state Chapter I ESEA coordinators, the Ford Foundation, and parents of limited-English-speaking children. Selective benefits are increasingly organized around categorical programs or professional specialties. Also, loyalty to the harmony of the education profession no longer inspires the membership it did when National Education Association headquarters included administrators, professors, and schoolteachers under one roof.

Reflecting all this activity is the fact that expenditures for group action have grown dramatically since 1960. A state-local "arms race" results in creating Washington or state capitol lobby offices for cities, categorical groups, low-wealth school districts, and women's organizations. Two examples illustrate this point. Table 4.2 is a listing of groups on one side of a current school issue; they are opposed to federal tax credits for private school tuition in Washington, D.C. This staggering variety illustrates two qualities of current school politics. Education policy touches on a mosaic of American values—religious, ethnic, professional, social, economic—that often clash in politics. Table 4.2 also illustrates the shifting quality of coalitional policymaking; this amalgam will rearrange itself for other school issues. Some groups will drop out, for example, if the issue does not involve federal aid to private schools.

Another perspective on the recent proliferation of interest groups is shown in Table 4.3, a statewide collective that supports increased state aid in California. Note how many separate school employee and support groups are represented in Sacramento. Although rarely studied, much the same situation probably exists in most if not all the states.[20]

A CLASSIFICATION OF SCHOOL INTEREST GROUPS

Differences existing among these educational groups parallel those found in interest groups of other areas, for example, in whether they possess temporary versus permanent organization, special versus broad interests, and larger versus limited resources. The National Education Association (NEA) illustrates the qualities of permanent organization, broad interests, and large resources; however, taxpayer-revolt groups exemplify the temporary, narrow, and limited-resource type of group. A major distinction of all such groups

Table 4.2

*Groups in Washington, D.C., Officially Opposing Private School
Tuition Tax Credits—1986*

American Association of Colleges for Teacher Education
American Association for Health, Physical Education, and Recreation
American Association of School Administrators
American Civil Liberties Union
American Ethical Union
American Federation of State, County and Municipal Employees
American Federation of Teachers, AFL-CIO
American Humanist Association
American Jewish Congress
Americans for Democratic Action
Americans United for Separation of Church and State
A. Philip Randolph Institute
Association for International Childhood Education
Baptist Joint Committee on Public Affairs
Coalition of Labor Union Women
Council for Education Development and Research
Council for Exceptional Children
Council of Chief State School Officers
Council of Great City Schools
Division of Homeland Ministries, Christian Church (Disciples of Christ)
Federal Education Project of the Lawyers Committee for Civil Rights under the Law
Horace Mann League
Labor Council for Latin American Advancement
League of Women Voters
National Association for the Advancement of Colored People
National Association of Elementary School Principals
National Association for Hearing and Speech Action
National Association of Secondary School Principals
National Association of State Boards of Education
National Coalition for Public Education and Religious Liberty
National Committee for Citizens in Education
National Congress of Parents and Teachers
National Council of Churches
National Council of Jewish Women
National Council of Senior Citizens
National Education Association
National School Boards Association
National Student Association
National Student Lobby
National Urban Coalition
National Urban League
Student National Education Association

Union of American Hebrew Congregations
Unitarian Universalist Association
United Auto Workers
United Methodist Church
United States Student Association

Table 4.3
A California Collective Education Interest Group—1986

Education Congress of California

American Association of University Women—California Division
Association of California School Administrators
Association of California School Districts
Association of Low Wealth Schools
Association of Mexican-American Educators, Inc.
California Association of School Business Officials
California Congress of Parents and Teachers, Inc.
California Federation of Teachers, AFL-CIO
California Personnel and Guidance Association
California School Boards Association
California School Employees Association
California School Nurses Organization
California Teachers Association—NEA
The Delta Kappa Gamma Society—Chi State—California
League of Women Voters of California
Los Angeles Unified School District
Schools for Sound Finance
United Teachers of Los Angeles

centers on how broad their interest is in the many facets of education. Thus, we divide groups into those for whom education is an end and those for whom it is a means to other ends. The first consists of professional educators or those professionally oriented, and the second of those wishing to use the school to serve other values, such as reducing taxes, protecting moral or patriotic values, and so on. In Chapter 10 we analyze policy issue networks that are in some ways an interest group but do not fit any of the conventional definitions. Networks can encompass interest groups but will focus on a *single* issue such as creation science or a national standards board for teacher certification. In contrast, interest groups are concerned with numerous issues.

Professional Interest Groups

For many years the most numerous interest group—teachers—
exerted only minimal political influence. Schoolteachers had traditionally hesitated in using collective action for transmitting demands
to political authorities either within or outside school systems. The
doctrine of the school administrator also played down the usefulness
of teachers' collective organizations, stressing instead negotiations by
individual professionals. This doctrine also emphasized the authority
of the superintendent and played down democracy and participation,
as those terms are used in the current popular sense. Later, an altered
conception of administration favored teacher participation, but only
for its effects on morale building and consequent improved performance. Not surprisingly, until recently the views of teacher representatives differed only slightly from the administrators' tenets.

A review of the history of the NEA will help to illuminate the norms
of the professional educator.[21] This group wanted a unified profession
that would not split into opposing interest groups competing for
scarce educational resources and would not engage in public conflict
over competing educational values. As the leading national organization, the NEA concentrated its efforts at the national and state levels.
It gave scant attention either to local teachers' interest groups or to
collective pressure to change local school policy. Educators were
inculcated with the "professional" need for a harmony of interests and
thus agreement on educational goals for children. Group activity,
when reinforced by formal arrangements such as interest groups,
would only lead to unnecessary and harmful conflict. With that
perspective until 1960, the NEA focused its concern on standards and
ethics and lobbied for general federal aid for buildings and salaries,
conduct and dissemination of research, and technical assistance for
state affiliates.[22]

This national group's resources are not minor. In 1992, it had over
1,650,000 members, representing about 60 percent of our public
schoolteachers. It has an extensive bureaucracy and hierarchy, although the executive staff usually makes policy with the concurrence
of a board of ninety-two directors and an executive committee of
eleven.[23] Every state has its own teacher's association, which is
frequently a powerful interest group at the state level. Over eighty-five

hundred dues-paying local school affiliates filter their money through the state affiliates.[24]

At the national level, the NEA functions as an umbrella for major segments of the profession. Within the national organization are over seventy-five departments, divisions, commissions, and committees. Separate professional organizations within NEA exist even for audio-visual specialists, as well as for home economics and speech teachers. The Political Action Council of NEA planned to spend $1.6 million in 1981-82 supporting political candidates at the state and national levels. In one building the NEA houses groups with specialized orientations and values that increasingly compete with each other in the political system. Principals and counselors feel they are not well represented by either teachers or administrators, that they get lost in an intermediary position. These divisions over priorities for money and values within the profession have spawned professional competitors who argued their cases before school boards and legislatures.

The most noticeable NEA competition comes from within the teaching profession itself. The American Federation of Teachers (AFT) restricts membership to teachers and administrators who have no direct authority over teachers. The AFT has affiliates in one-half of the states and a 580,000 membership concentrated in large cities or nearby. It has not been able to take significant numbers of members away from the NEA in the last decade. While the two teachers' groups take common positions on some policy issues, for example, increased state aid for teacher salaries, they have differences on others.

The AFT grew rapidly between 1960 and 1975 by contending that professional unity is a myth because value conflicts are inevitable between teachers and their managers who administer the school.[25] AFT rhetoric was replete with *we* and *they*, terms that reflect an adversorial relationship between an aggressive labor union and its employer. The AFT's willingness to resort to a strike proved attractive to urban teachers but shattered the professional ethic of low-profile interest group activity. However, the organizing success of the AFT in the 1960s led to the NEA taking a more militant stance in stressing collective bargaining.

The differences between the two unions are clear in their organization of political efforts. If the AFT has succeeded more in big cities, the NEA has been more effective at the state level, where its affiliates—one of the largest organized interest groups in the states—spend much time dealing with state politicians.[26] The AFT, on the other hand, has few effective state federations, concentrating its efforts at the local level. Both have Washington offices, but until 1968 neither had been very successful in getting political demands approved by the president and Congress.[27] This changed dramatically during the 1970s when the NEA endorsed Jimmy Carter and became a major factor in both his campaign structure and Walter Mondale's in 1984. NEA support of Carter led to his support for a cabinet-level Department of Education.

Major administrative groups of superintendents and principals now frequently make their own distinctive demands on the political system and maintain their own offices at the state and federal levels. The National Association of School Boards (NASB) has traditionally joined forces with the administrator-teacher groups at the state and federal levels but not when these groups cannot agree. The NASB has overcome its early reluctance to lobby in Washington and is now the most aggressive of the lay groups in Washington, D.C.

These divisions among professional educators should not be overestimated, for other forces work toward their unity. The tradition of a unified profession and the common training and experience of professional educators have led them to agree on many fundamental values, a factor that tends to restrict the range of interest group activity. For example, most administrators move up through the teaching ranks, and accrediting associations are usually staffed by professional educators. Indeed, the faith that the public has in accreditation makes regional accrediting agencies a professional interest group of considerable importance, often bringing irresistable pressure to achieve their standards of faculty, budget, facilities, and curriculum.

Professionally Oriented Interest Groups

Other groups, although not composed of professionals, are also interested in educational policy as an end in itself. Like educators, they provide schools with diffuse support, but they also differ as educators do on some aspects of school governance and so present their own demand inputs. These demands may represent their own purpose or be only of secondary interest.

The National Congress of Parents and Teachers is not only the largest group in this category, it is also the largest volunteer organization in the nation, with 5.3 million members. The PTA is a loose confederation of about twenty-five thousand local units concerned primarily with specific problems facing *specific* schools. It is most influential and active at the local or district level, where its heterogeneous membership precludes agreement on controversial issues.[28] Although the membership is now one-third men, the organization is still dominated by women.[29]

Analysts of PTA history stress the generally dependent and close relationship it has to school administrators. In 1968 Koerner expressed it this way:

> The American PTA is rarely anything more than a coffee and cookies organization based on vague goodwill and gullibility. It is chiefly useful to the administration for raising money for special projects and persuading parents who are interested enough to attend meetings that the local schools are in the front ranks of American education.[30]

But as we shall see in the next chapter, such participation can have important positive social and psychological benefits for individuals. Moreover, in the last two decades, the PTA has become more aggressive, asserting that it is a consumer advocate organization. Major PTA issues include reading improvement and opposition to tuition tax credits and TV violence. A 1974 national study found the PTA was the group most frequently named by board of education members as seeking to influence school policy.[31]

The PTA's local role is amplified at the national and state levels. However, it does not provide an independent source of demand inputs into school policy; rather it proceeds as an instrument of educators who use it to reinforce or implement *their* policy inputs. Indeed, the national PTA is a resolute member of the "Big Six"—a coalition of three professional groups and three lay groups in education: American Association of School Administrators, NEA, Council of Chief State School Officers, National School Boards Association, National Association of State School Boards, and National Congress of Parents and Teachers. At another level, a study of three states in the Midwest concluded that legislators view the PTA as a useful friend but not a very bothersome enemy. In effect, the values of the PTA leadership and the school professionals are similar; as a consequence, the PTA does not sponsor many conflict-oriented demands with school policymakers. However, it can produce many letters to legislators on major education issues.

The PTA is not, however, the only professionally oriented lay interest group. The Council for Basic Education (CBE) is an organization that has emphasized different values from those of the PTA and has become known as a "critic of public education." The CBE believes that the schools have neglected the fundamental intellectual disciplines in their purported overemphasis on social adjustment. Its intentions are to increase the amount of academic versus vocational content in the curriculum. The CBE tries to influence school authorities primarily through publications, conferences, and other uses of the media. It does not have local chapters but has provided material to local groups who express an interest. It opposes cutbacks of traditional academic subjects for electives like driver training or photography.

Professionally oriented interest groups also exist among numerous organizations that embrace education as a secondary concern, for example, the League of Women Voters and the American Association of University Women. These groups promote general social improvements, some of which touch on school programs and processes. They usually try to influence the political conversion process for education only when the members are deeply and widely concerned about a particular aspect of school policy. This condition occurs rarely, however, such as when the state constitution for education is revised. Like the PTA, these are non-issue-specific groups that provide support for the ongoing system and so inject little conflict into it. They also constitute a resource for decision makers in times of crisis. They are losing active members as more women are working full or part time, leaving less time for community activity.

Transcendental Groups

Several kinds of interest groups see the schools as a means to ends that transcend the schools, such as reducing the tax burden, eradicating Communism, and so on. Around the turn of the century, taxpayer organizations began to mold support for the elimination of "wasteful" public spending. Of particular interest is the finding that taxpayer organizations have been *supporters*, as well as opponents, of increased tax support—depending on the tax source. They are strongly opposed to local property taxes but on occasion will support increases in state sales or income taxes.

Distinct from those whose main interest is material are those whose concern is the moral instruction in schools; the overlap of the two, however, needs study. The educational function of moral indoctrination dating from our schools' colonial origins did not disappear with the *New England Primer*. Concern for religious instruction has not disappeared either, as seen in the continuing outcry against, and disobedience of, Supreme Court decisions banning Bible reading and school prayers.

The main focus of these groups is to guard orthodox values. Their support of the schools is secondary to their concern for maintaining certain community norms. The school is only one of many institutions whose moral sanctity must be protected against subversion or direct challenge. Constituting what LaPiere has called "societies for the prevention of change," they maintain a protective surveillance over teachers' drinking and dating in small rural towns, over students' music, dancing, and clothing in suburbia, and over teachers' and administrators' "Americanism" everywhere. Few such groups have more than a local organizational basis, although their frequent church associations might imply otherwise. Their tactics lean heavily on direct contact with suspected deviants who are challenged to prove their moral worth. These tactics can escalate into board confrontations or, in small towns, into whispering campaigns. In smaller communities that are more homogeneous and have fewer independent bases for the defense of the challenged, educators have little recourse. They walk a narrow line, not only in their individual morality but also in what they transmit to students.[32]

Crisis Interest Groups

Despite the broad variety of interest groups in public education, not all interests or values show up in organized groups. Also, existing groups may choose not to carry certain demands to school officials. Subsystem stress over value concerns can, however, activate people who share attitudes and values but as yet have no interest group to reflect those values. Feeling the urge to impress their values on school policies, they create temporary new organizations.

A typical illustration of this occurred in a northeastern suburb, where two interest groups developed in one year and then dissolved after the school board elections.[33] One was a "taxpayers association," formed to defeat three board members and cut back school expenditures. The superintendent countered with a group called Save Our Schools in order to reelect the incumbent board members and pass the budget. Both groups played important roles in conveying their special values and demands in a political system where local groups had not traditionally been important.

More broadly, integration crises across the country frequently spawn "Parents to Preserve Neighborhood Schools" as a counterweight to civil rights groups advocating integration. Such groups disband after the integration crisis passes. Aside from such case studies, however, no systematic examination of crisis interest groups has yet been made.

Testing Agencies and Foundations

Several groups that do not fit the usual idea of an interest group nevertheless do influence the political system of American schools. Although this country does not have a system of national exams, we do have several national testing agencies. The most important is the Educational Testing Service in Princeton, New Jersey. Most American schools do not have a choice in whether to provide their best students with courses in most of the subjects covered by College Board Achievement Exams. Because high school administrators want their students to score well on these exams, they do not have absolute flexibility to teach what they want. Such external constraints reflect value judgments on quality, that is, what should and should not be taught, urged in the interest of professionalism. This is the force of professionalism that we earlier argued may be a more powerful external constraint on local school policy than are local demands or federal laws.

Further, while private philanthropic foundations are not thought of as interest groups, they exercise a major influence on such school issues as curriculum reform, teacher training, testing, finance, facility design, educational television, and so on. Foundations have also used their grants to generate stress over value concerns. For example, in the 1960s foundations financed the development of instruments to assess national achievement in education; this helped create a political issue that pitted those who opposed national testing against those wanting increased accountability by professional educators. As a result, conversion systems at all levels—local school boards, state departments of education, and the United States Congress—had to make a decision on whether to permit national assessment. Consequently, the questions and approaches in the approved assessment represented many compromises, including a decision *not* to include interstate test comparisons.[34]

A foundation does not act like a conventional interest group by seeking access to public policymakers and then advocating its case for public support. But, by using grants to start experiments and demonstration projects (often reflecting certain value orientations), foundations may make value conflicts more visible. Then this can create a new demand that provides an existing or new interest group with an issue. These interest groups may modify the content of the demand as they transmit it to the school board or state legislator, but the foundations need interest groups in order to reach the political authorities through collective pressure. The weight of this policy influence is suggested by one fact alone: Foundations give twice as much money to education as does any other category of interest group.[35] They have played a major role in recent debates about the quality of education. In the mid-1980s the Carnegie Foundation for Advancement of Teaching funded Ernest Boyer's major book, *High School*. The Carnegie Corporation also funded a major report calling for a national standards board to certify outstanding teachers. Carnegie then provided money to the National Governors Association to promote this concept. Indeed, most major reports outside of government sponsorship involve foundation subsidies.

CURRICULUM POLICY: AN EXAMPLE OF NEW FACTORS IN SCHOOL GOVERNANCE

The external factors that currently penetrate the local school district affect the traditional mode of local governance dramatically. As a consistently general finding, the more that the channels to the board and administrator are swept by regular floods of aroused school constituents, the more the board becomes responsive. The more that the board challenges traditional professional definitions of educational service, the less autonomy such professionals have. This weakening of local professional control has been ongoing in the political study of education, although it has proven impossible to define the concept of local control precisely. Curriculum decisions will illustrate this political process of group pressures.

Curriculum Conflict

While strong demands for local control on some traditional matters such as the curriculum still exist,[36] political conflict about curriculum has escalated in the past decade. Many literary classics spark local political debates, ranging from the Idaho Falls banning of *One Flew Over the Cuckoo's Nest* to Anaheim, California, proscribing Richard Wright's *Black Boy*. After the Warsaw, Indiana, school board banned copies of *Values Clarifications*, the school board president posed the essential political question, "Who shall control the minds of the students?"[37]

A federal attempt by the National Science Foundation to take a role in influencing local curriculum was rebuffed in 1981 by the Reagan administration but then resumed in 1984 after national concern about overseas economic competition became intense. Congress reduced the federal curriculum development role in large part because of a 1975 debate on the National Science Foundation's proposed social curriculum, "Man: A Course of Study" (MACOS). Typical of this pressure was the charge of Congressman John Conlan (Rep., Arizona) that MACOS was a federal attempt to "use classrooms for conditioning, to mold a new generation of Americans toward a repudiation of traditional values, behavior, and patriotic beliefs."[38] Yet twenty years ago, after Sputnik, the federal government rushed into the curriculum and text development field when critics alleged that schoolbooks were outdated, inaccurate, dull, and lacking diversity. In 1984, Congress forced the Reagan administration to start another effort to upgrade science textbooks through funds to the National Science Foundation. The value conflict over school curriculum intensified during this decade, however. Boyd explains that the scholars and experts whom the federal and state governments rely on for curricular improvement have been criticized for trying to impose their own cosmopolitan and secular values. Curriculum reform itself has been professionalized through government and foundation grants. No longer are such perceived crises as Sputnik required to generate curriculum change; it now has a self-starting ability.[39]

Curricular conflict stems from many roots. Military threats or changes in public sentiment such as the women's movement generate value conflict about curriculum, even though this is not why they were initiated. Other forces, such as court decisions favoring bilingual education or statements from influential individuals, can change the curriculum orientation without the direct development of new materials. To incorporate all these influences, textbook creation is now "managed" in a new process that has a writing team preparing a series of texts. The actual author is frequently the publisher's internal editor, not the authors listed on the title page. Teachers are also contributors to textbook content through their instructional preferences.[40]

When educators say they regard the curriculum as a "professional" matter, this does not mean they remain unaffected by the society at large. In the course of American history, curriculum has related closely to major concerns in the larger society—religious training, literacy, Americanization, occupational training, and so on. When left to themselves, the criteria that professionals use for deciding such matters will vary—appeals to tradition, scientific testing, common social values, or individual judgment. No broadly accepted criteria for curricular judgments have existed, although there has been rough agreement to teach English, history, science, mathematics, health, and somewhat less agreement on social studies and foreign languages. With their varied citizenry and value orientations, however, no agreement exists among the diverse states and LEAs on the required content and intellectual level of these accepted curricula.

Supporters and critics of existing curricula transmit conflicting signals to the education policymaking system of any state. Traditional actors have included:

1. School accrediting and testing agencies, which are private groups with public overtones.
2. Schools of education, often slow to change because of the insulation of professors from the pressures of local school politics.
3. State boards of education and state departments of education discussed earlier, which must by law oversee a host of earlier policy decisions.

Those seeking curricula changes have blossomed in recent years. Publishers invest a lot in maintaining their existing textbooks, so on the one hand they are not agents of change. But they also invest in new instructional materials, which they try to sell to LEAs or states. They are also swayed by intense pressure group activity, so they cannot impose just any values in their materials. The federal government has been another source of curriculum change. By the early 1970s, half of the schools were using a new physics course instigated with federal research funding, and about two-thirds were using a new biology course, likewise funded. The next section highlights the more aggressive role that state governments play in curricular alignment. Private foundations also stimulate research that can eventuate in new curricula and teaching materials. Professional associations of scientists and other scholarly, business, and professional groups engage in such research as well. And always, university professors generate ideas about curriculum change. To further complicate how we understand the matrix of private groups, we need also to realize that none of these speaks with a single voice.

This picture of curriculum decision making grows even fuzzier when we consider what happens at the local level. LEAs, teachers, administrators, boards, and parents may feel strongly about changing some part of the curriculum to fit prevailing local values. Despite central control of curriculum in some states (particularly the Southeast), LEAs can blunt these outside forces. Frequent emotional episodes of local opposition to teaching about evolution, the United Nations, the role of racial minorities, and the social nature of humankind have erupted. In each case, local people wanted to block either state directives or professionally accepted norms of "good" curriculum.

New ideas about instruction and its materials are part of the more general questioning of the once-unchallenged professional's dominance of school policy. For example, parents have demanded more homework and dress codes for their children or have lobbied for alternative schools with more curricular electives. Despite such dramatic incidents, the larger picture is one of LEAs slowly adapting to what the professionals decide from their positions at the state or national level. Nonetheless, powerful local forces, such as advocates of the creation story, can always intrude on this policymaking system.[41]

CONCLUSION

This chapter has introduced major components of the conversion process by examining only the input side. We have suggested some of the basic values in the social environment that influence the conversion process and have indicated how interest groups act as transfer agents for these values.[42] The energizing force that impels the input process is environmental stress arising from unsatisfied values.[43] This process reflects felt needs, and groups or individuals pursue satisfaction by turning to the political system. When such a force is set in motion, it crosses the boundary between private and public systems in distinctive ways. The presentation of demands by interest groups is not restricted to education policy alone, as interest articulation is widespread for most policies.

NOTES

1. For analysis, see Willmoore Kendall, *John Locke and the Doctrine of Majority-Rule* (Urbana: University of Illinois Press, 1941); Henry Steele Commager, *Majority Rule and Minority Rights* (New York: Oxford University Press, 1943); Herbert McClosky, "The Fallacy of Absolute Majority Rule," *Journal of Politics* 11 (1949): 637–54; J. Roland Pennock, "Responsiveness, Responsibility, and Majority Rule," *American Political Science Review* 46 (1952): 791–96.

2. Evidence is found is Samuel A. Stouffer, *Communism, Conformity, and Civil Liberties* (New York: Doubleday, 1955); James W. Prothro and Charles M. Grigg, "Fundamental Principles of Democracy: Bases of Agreement and Disagreement," *Journal of Politics* 22 (1960): 276–94; Herbert McClosky, "Consensus and Ideology in American Politics," *American Political Science Review* 58 (1964): 361–82. For similar evidence about teachers, Merlyn Gubser, "Anti-Democratic Attitudes of American Educators," *School and Community* 54 (1967): 14–16, and John Weiser and James Hayes, "Democratic Attitudes of Teachers and Prospective Teachers," *Phi Delta Kappan* 47 (1966): 476–81.

3. Hugh D. Graham and Robert Gurr, *The History of Violence in America* (New York: Bantam Books, 1969).

4. On the impact of regionalism, compare Norval D. Glenn and J. L. Simmons, "Are Regional Cultural Differences Diminishing?" *Public Opinion Quarterly* 31 (1967): 176–93; Samuel C. Patterson, "The Political Cultures of the American States," *Journal of Politics* 30 (1968): 187–209; Daniel J. Elazar, *American Federalism: A View from the States* (New York: Crowell, 1982); and Ira Sharkansky, *Regionalism in American Politics* (Indianapolis: Bobbs-Merrill, 1969). On sex and income differentiation, see

Lester W. Milbrath, *Political Participation* (Chicago: Rand McNally, 1965), Chap. 5; V. O. Key, Jr., *Public Opinion and American Democracy* (New York: Knopf, 1961), Chap. 6.

5. These combinations are explored in Oliver P. Williams et al., *Suburban Differences and Metropolitan Policies: A Philadelphia Story* (Philadelphia: University of Pennsylvania Press, 1965).

6. The following relies upon Currin Shields, "The American Tradition of Empirical Collectivism," *American Political Science Review* 46 (1952): 104–20.

7. Louis Hartz, *The Liberal Tradition in America* (Chicago: University of Chicago Press, 1955).

8. Elazar, *American Federalism*.

9. H. G. Good, *A History of American Education* (New York: Macmillan, 1956), Chap. 4.

10. A historical catalog of this national expansion includes Ordinance of 1785; Ordinance of 1787; 1862, First Morrill Act; 1887, Hatch Act; 1890, Second Morrill Act; 1914, Smith-Lever Agricultural Extension Act; 1917, Smith-Hughes Vocational Act; 1918, Vocational Rehabilitation Act; 1933, School Lunch Program; 1935, Bankhead Jones Act (amended Smith-Lever); 1936, George Dean Act (amended Smith-Hughes); 1937, First Public Health Fellowships granted; 1940, Vocational Education for National Defense Act; 1944, GI Bill of Rights; 1950, National Science Foundation Act; 1954, Cooperative Research Program; 1958, National Defense Education Act; 1963, Higher Educational Facilities Act; 1963, Manpower Defense Training Act; 1964, Economic Opportunities Act; 1965, Elementary and Secondary Education Act and subsequent amendments. For a review, see *Congressional Quarterly, Federal Role in Education*, 2d ed. (Washington: Congressional Quarterly Service, 1967).

11. Ibid., Chap. 5.

12. David Tyack, *One Best System* (Cambridge, Mass.: Harvard University Press, 1974). For a detailed study of this process, see Lawrence A. Cremin, *The Transformation of the School: Progressivism in American Education, 1876–1957* (New York: Vintage Books, 1964).

13. Adolphe E. Meyer, *An Educational History of the American People*, 2d ed. (New York: McGraw-Hill, 1967), Chap. 2.

14. See writings by Douglas Mitchell, Frederick Wirt, and Catherine Marshall in *Culture and Education Policy in the American State* (New York: Falmer, 1989); a symposium on "State Politics of Education," in *Peabody Journal of Education* 62–4 (1985): 7–115; and *Alternative State Policy Mechanisms for Pursuing Educational Quality, Equity, Efficiency, and Choice Goals* (Washington, D.C.: Office of Instructional Research and Improvement, U.S. Department of Education, 1986), Chap. V; following quotations are from this source.

15. William Boyd, "The Public, the Professionals, and Education Policy Making: Who Governs?" *Teachers College Record* 77 (1976): 539–77.

16. Larry Cuban, *Urban School Chiefs Under Fire* (Chicago: University of Chicago Press, 1976).

17. Mancur Olson, *The Logic of Collective Action* (New York: Schocken, 1965).

18. Robert Salisbury, "An Exchange Theory of Interest Groups," *Midwest Journal of Political Science* 13 (1969): 1–32.

19. Terry Moe, *The Organization of Interests* (Chicago: University of Chicago Press, 1980). For a market theory analysis, see Michael Hayes, *Lobbyists and Legislators* (New Brunswick, N.J.: Rutgers, 1981).

20. See Roald Campbell and Tim Mazzoni, *State Policy Making for the Public Schools* (Berkeley: McCutchan, 1976). For an update, see Mitchell, Wirt, and Marshall, *Alternative State Policy.*

21. Alan Rosenthal, *Pedagogues and Power* (Syracuse, N.Y.: Syracuse University Press, 1969), pp. 6–10. For a full current history, see G. Howard Goold and Arvid J. Burke, "The Organized Teaching Profession," in *Educational in the States: Nationwide Development Since 1900*, Edgar Fuller and Jim B. Pearson, eds. (Washington, D.C.: National Education Association, 1969), Chap. 14.

22. James Koerner, *Who Controls American Education?* (Boston: Beacon Press, 1968), p. 26.

23. See Roald F. Campbell et al., *Organization and Control of American Schools* (Columbus, Ohio: Charles E. Merrill, 1985), pp. 253–57.

24. Anthony Cresswell and Michael Murphy, *Teachers, Unions, and Collective Bargaining* (Berkeley: McCutchan, 1980).

25. For a general background on the American Federation of Teachers, see Patrick W. Carlton and Harold I. Goodwin, *The Collective Dilemma: Negotiations in Education* (Columbus, Ohio: Jones, 1969). AFT publishes a monthly newspaper, *American Teacher*, which provides current information on AFT policy directions.

26. See Mitchell, Wirt, and Marshall, *Alternative State Policy.*

27. James Sundquist, *Politics and Policy* (Washington, D.C.: Brookings Institution, 1968), pp. 155–200. However, in 1969, the National Education Association was a crucial part of the Emergency Committee for Full Funding. This committee was able to persuade Congress to increase the president's education budget by over $500 million.

28. For an elaboration on this view, see Koerner, *Who Controls American Education?* pp. 32–33.

29. Campbell et al., *The Organization and Control of American Schools*, pp. 293–297; William T. Kvareceus, "PTA: The Irrelevant Giant," *The Nation*, 5 October 1963, pp. 200–1.

30. Koerner, *Who Controls American Education?* pp. 147–48.

31. L. Harmon Ziegler et al., *Governing American Schools* (North Scituate, Mass.: Duxbury, 1974), pp. 31–32.

32. See Richard LaPiere, *Social Change* (New York: McGraw-Hill, 1965), p. 197; Mary A. Raywid, *The Axe-Grinders* (New York: Macmillan, 1962); Jack Nelson and Gene Roberts, Jr., *The Censors and the Schools* (Boston: Little, Brown & Co., 1963). The distinction offered here borders on that of the "sacred and secular communities" analyzed in Laurence Iannaccone and Frank W. Lutz, *Politics, Powers and Policy: The Governing of Local School Districts* (Columbus, Ohio: Charles E. Merrill, 1970).

33. Lesley H. Browder, "A Suburban School Superintendent Plays Politics," in *The Politics of Education at the Local, State, and Federal Level*, Michael W. Kirst, ed. (Berkeley: McCutchan, 1970).

34. Ralph Tyler, "National Assessment: A History and Sociology," in *New Models for American Education*, James Guthrie and Edward Wynne, eds. (Englewood Cliffs, N.J.: Prentice-Hall, 1971), Chap. 2.

35. For a good overview, see Robert J. Havighurst, "Philanthropic Foundations as Interest Groups," in *Education and Urban Society* 13 (1981): 193–218.

36. For an analysis of the curriculum area, see Jon Schaffarzick and Gary Sykes, *Value Conflicts and Curriculum Issues* (Berkeley: McCutchan, 1979).

37. *Time*, 9 January 1981.

38. Schaffarzick and Sykes, *Value Conflicts*, p. 3.

39. William L. Boyd, "The Changing Politics of Curriculum Policy Making," in Schaffarzick and Sykes, *Value Conflicts*, pp. 73–138.

40. Paul Goldstein, *Changing the American Schoolbook* (Lexington, Mass.: Lexington Books, 1978).

41. See Tyll van Geel, *Authority to Control the School Program* (Lexington Mass.: Lexington Books, 1975).

42. See James Hottois and Neal Milner, *The Sex Education Controversy* (Lexington, Mass.: Lexington Books, 1975).

43. Larry Cuban, "Determinants of Curriculum Change and Stability," in Schaffarzick and Sykes, *Value Conflicts*, pp. 179–90.

5

Access Channels to School Policymaking

MODES OF CITIZEN POLITICAL CONTROL

The political turbulence of the school system today finds many groups getting into policymaking. The preceding chapter described how a vast array of pressure groups have sought access. But more direct access occurs when citizens directly participate through elections. A systems analysis viewpoint on how their demands are treated can be stated simply. Although many demands originate outside the political system, some enter it when they "are voiced as proposals for decision and action on the part of the authorities."[1] Some demands do not enter the political system, however, for at least two reasons. They may not be valued highly by society (e.g., a Mafia interest) or they lack sufficient resources to move the system to act adequately (e.g., the poor).

Public preferences have concerned school professionals long before recent turbulent times. Given that citizens vote on school governors and some programs, it is not surprising that these school officials have long sought to detect and defend themselves against such political control. At the turn of this century, reformers tried to depoliticize education by substituting nonpartisan for partisan elections and election at large for election by ward. But citizens still possessed the means to control those given authority over school matters. For

109

decades, professionals tried to deflect popular control by mobilizing citizen support, as research shows.[2]

Popular participation in school policymaking has traditionally taken two forms—election of officials and referendums on issues. We treat the referendum process in a later chapter because it partakes more directly of demand conversion than elections do. *Local* school elections operate independently of political parties. Contrary to popular impression, political parties at the *national* level have sought unsuccessfully to serve as a link between citizens and school policy. For almost a century of national party platforms, education has been among "the predominant forces in operation during election years."[3]

Yet schools have not escaped citizen control by avoiding the clutches of national parties, for direct and indirect popular control still exists. Directly, there is the widespread practice of electing school boards at the local level and boards and superintendents at the state level.[4] Indirectly, control exists in the election of state legislators, executives, and judges, whose broad responsibilities include authority over many aspects of public education. In both local and state elections, then, policymakers must operate within popularly derived limits. This is a vague limit, true, but elected officials know it exists.

THE ARROYOS OF SCHOOL BOARD ELECTIONS

Although 85 percent of local school boards in this country are elective, the politics of these elections was a great unknown until recently.[5] We know that these officials, five to seven on a board, almost always seek their three- or four-year terms on a nonpartisan ballot. We also know that the board appoints a superintendent, usually professionally trained, who operates under its general policy guides and who may also be removed by it. The exception to this pattern is the appointment method often used in our biggest cities. In the usual community, the theory of democratic control makes the board member a pivot between community demands and school operations. We examine how that role is performed in the next chapter, but first we must see whether the election of board members is itself a major channel for popular inputs to the school political system. Some widespread general impressions about this citizen-elected official interaction existed when the first edition of this book was written a decade ago. Recent studies have provided a more highly complex picture of school board representation, though.

The "Dark Continent" of Board Elections

What was once known raised more questions than it settled. One clear point remains, that school board elections have little voter turnout, even less than that for other government offices. The reasons for this are not clear. Is it because of the nonpartisan myth of school politics or because school board elections are held in off years and at primary dates when turnout is low for all contests? If there is variation in the degree of citizen participation in different states or cities, what accounts for it? Does the mere requirement of nonpartisanship preclude political parties from playing a direct role, as they do in Detroit, or do voters' party identifications influence their choices, as they do in some city council races? Does low turnout benefit some groups but not others? That is, might board elections more often represent the weight of Republicans—who go to the polls more than Democrats—and consequently more often represent the viewpoint of groups attracted to the GOP?

A partial test of such queries has been provided recently in the case of Florida, where the nonpartisan system was *not* adopted.[6] For many board elections during 1964–1974, participation was higher than for other partisan contests for state office, including those for the U.S. Senate; participation was strongly affected by population size. A similar result was found for the degree of competition. It is clear, though, that campaigning in school contests is limited, candidate visibility low, and the contest rarely based on specific policies. It this again attributable to the nonpartisan myth, which requires participants to act as if they were not engaging in political acts? Or is it due to the lack of highly visible issues that might stimulate popular interest? Under what conditions do election contests become visible and the public highly participant? Further, although most boards are elected, a minority in significant American cities are appointed. What difference does this make in representative roles? Is there any difference in policy orientation under the two methods; if so, can we trace such differences directly to the methods? A clue that this difference has policy consequences is suggested by the finding that boards immune from elections were somewhat more able to move toward school desegregation than elected boards.[7]

Recruitment: Few Are Called, Fewer Chosen

Given knowledge of school politics that became available in the 1970s, a better conceptual picture developed of how board members are recruited to that office. In any political system, leaders must be recruited to fill the constitutional positions, but this process is not random. Rather, the qualities of this process are in harmony with the dominant values of the larger system, just as the selection of kings and presidents tells us much about the values of their respective societies.[8] Also, the process by which a mass of citizens provides few decision makers involves winnowing away those who do not meet the dominant values. Successful recruitment must be followed by effective role learning in the new position of authority and that in turn by successful role performance before a political system produces its leadership.

The relevance of this conceptual understanding to actual local politics was promoted in the work of Cistone during the 1970s.[9] Recruitment in North American school elections is a process of many being excluded, few being called to office, and even fewer becoming leaders. Being recruited comes from possessing political opportunities, some formal, some practical. There is always an unequal distribution of these opportunities, a fact that provides a first screening of the total population. Formally, the legal code may set down minimum requirements—being a qualified voter, a district representative—but clearly these only screen out from the enormous numbers those who do not qualify to vote. Practically, eligibility is screened by social status, political resources (the more eligible have more of these), age, and gender (men get elected disproportionately in government). The fact that such opportunities are structured in society, some having many and many having few, means that most citizens are filtered out of the recruitment process.

Note the results of this process in the social composition of school boards. When the Progressive reforms of nonpartisanship in school matters finally settled into place across the nation, the large working-class membership had almost disappeared from school boards, and white middle-class members dominated everywhere. Moreover, most of these members were male, married with children in the public schools, and active in the community. From the landmark study by Counts in 1924 to a replication by the National School Boards Association almost fifty years later, all the research substantiates this finding.[10] A test of the link between representation and the possession of resources appears with blacks.[11] Their representation on 168 big-city boards was smaller than their resources (i.e., numbers, money, organization); at-large systems effectively widened the gap between resources and board seats.

High social status alone does not give entry to the school board, but community activity—whether civic, business, political, or educational—joined with high social status provides training for office that few of the well-off actually use. We consider whether or not this affects representativeness in policy decisions in the next chapter. Clearly, though, in the recruitment stages, the eligibility processes of our democratic system leave out a vast majority of Americans who cannot or will not seek entry or who simply don't care for the game.

Selection: Democratic Reality and Theory

Given even the small number who are eligible, the selection process further pares the list. The major in-depth study of this process among a national sample of board members by Zeigler, Jennings, and Peak labels the factors that moved some of the eligible to run for office "precipitating conditions."[12] Although most credited encouragement from others, 23 percent were self-starters whom no one had encouraged. These stand as a corrective to a view of school boards as "closed systems" that outsiders cannot penetrate. Most members, however, pointed to a supportive network of significant others who induced—or pushed—them to run, such as other board members (29 percent), citizen groups (21 percent), friends and neighbors (21 percent), and the remainder, who were split between school professionals and political figures. The number of these sources of support may be misleading, for in most districts sampled either members were sponsored by previous board members or were initially appointed to fill an unexpired term or both. Tendencies toward a closed decision-making system were reinforced by the lack of competition for these seats in about one-quarter of this sample. Significantly enough, a high degree of sponsorship was closely associated with lack of competition $(r=-.40)$.

Using elections to select unrepresentative school boards always generates questions about the validity of those elections. Thus the continuing criticism of the unrepresentational nature of board membership just noted has implied that without such "virtual representation" the people cannot be well served. This then implies a theory of democracy in which only those with like characteristics can speak for like-minded constituents. On historical grounds alone this is simplistic, for leaders in expanding civil liberties or social policy for the less favored have largely been drawn from higher social status groups. Franklin D. Roosevelt and John F. Kennedy were far removed in status from the millions of poor and ill favored who saw them as their leaders.

Board members, individually or collectively, have been studied within the context of more complex theories of democracy and representation than this. Theories of popular democracy have been applied to studies of school referenda.[13] Theories of federalism illuminate the school policy programs emerging from among "the family of governments."[14] In all this the natural sequence of how knowledge is built becomes visible. That is, knowledge moves from the particular case study—heavily descriptive, bound to time and place—to preliminary theories, which seek to generalize across such particulars and to generate testable propositions about social behavior. These, in turn, can build to an established theory. Several such efforts are applicable in the study of elections to school boards. Each springs from a model of democracy that links citizens to policymakers through the electoral process.

Probably the largest scale effort was drawn from the eighty-eight-district national sample Zeigler et al. analyzed. While some have criticized this work for its design and its conclusions on the superintendent's responsiveness to the board,[15] almost no one challenges its findings on the model of citizen-board linkage through elections.

The authors deduced the major aspects of a popularly held democratic model, including beliefs

that the opportunity to seek office should not be restricted unduly, that a choice of candidates is ordinarily preferable to only one, that public attention should be engaged, that elections should be fair, and that the losers should step out in favor of the winners. Such elements lie at the heart of democratic selection procedures.[16]

Subsequent analysis of board elections demonstrated, in the authors' words, that reality "scarcely meets the stiff requirements of the democratic ideal."

We can summarize the quantitative analysis of this study broadly.[17] Only half the board members faced any competition in their election bid. Also, democratic theory assumes that officeholders have *ambition* to remain or to move to higher positions; ambition is what should make officials responsive to voter demands. But this research finds that board members have little ambition, and they rarely move on to high state or national office (President Jimmy Carter was an exception). Indeed, four of five explicitly ruled out any interest in higher office, a finding parallel to those found among city council members in a large California study.[18] In this tepid electoral climate, few signs indicate that board members are bound to heed public demands because of their ambition.

Are these elections contentious, with candidates taking opposing stands on school issues as the democratic model assumes? This study found that in only 58 percent of the contests did members report that their ideas about schools differed much from other candidates'. When the opposition included incumbents, however, candidates reported more differences than when there were no incumbents; in short, incumbency offers a visible target for challenging policy ideas. The data of the Zeigler study support the democratic proposition that opposition is useful if voters are to choose among policy ideas, but this opposition does not occur often.

Few of the differences that did exist were over educational programs and personnel, which one would expect to be central to electoral school conflict. The issue content of voters' choices more often dealt with the board—its role and operations, composition, or community relationship. Physical and fiscal problems or civil rights issues were somewhat less evident in election competition. These concerns are much more visible to the community than are educational issues, particularly when the latter are obscured by professionals' claims. Thus when incumbents are among a candidate's opposition, that board's role will more likely be an issue than when no incumbent is in the lists.

The portion of democratic theory that calls for voter turnout also lacks support in real life. Public involvement in board elections is low, as any voting study will show. Another form of involvement, the formation of citizen support for particular candidates, does occur but again only among the minority of citizens that votes at all. About half the candidates in the Zeigler study reported no public group support. The presence of incumbents will change the electoral context; there was more public support than when no incumbents faced the voter. So the incumbent's record seems to encourage group mobilization, providing a personal focus to school issues of considerable complexity.

Time and again what emerges from studies of board elections is that they are little-used channels to the political system. Like arroyos in the Southwest, only rarely does intense turmoil surge through these channels. Certain occasions can, however, have the effect of flash floods through desert courses—enormous conflict followed by altered features in the immediate environment. Much more often, however, these election campaigns offer only slight variations in ideology or policy orientation. And, as noted earlier, the structure of voting, dominated by nonpartisanship, depresses turnout. These conditions make the democratic model of informed choice between significant policy options by a sizable electorate more a pleasant fiction than a hard fact. Neal Peirce, reviewing a 1986 study of school boards, summarized the issue this way:

> I found it compelling to read how much the public believes in the need for school boards, how much it remains attached to the concept of grassroots educational self-governance. But it was equally disturbing to note, from this report, that the same public evidences essential illiteracy about the actual role and activities of school boards. Moreover, the public turns out in appallingly thin numbers to vote for the school boards it otherwise believes to be so essential. We are left with the disturbing question: If the school boards' popular constituency misperceives their role and doesn't care enough to exercise its franchise in their selection, how fully or forcefully will the boards *ever* be able to function?[19]

Competition and Responsiveness

This pervasive condition is greatly affected by the past—the nonpartisan reforms begun a century ago and now commonplace in American local government. Many scholars report that such reforms as nonpartisan ballots and at-large elections lower electoral school conflict, particularly in metropolitan areas. This is true whether conflict is measured by the degree of competition, office turnover, or incumbent defeat. Very little difference is explained by district size, frequency of elections, or the timing of board elections.

Rather, nonpartisanship has a more qualitative effect on the nature of school elections in both city and rural districts. The nonpartisan approach and at-large elections affect the degree of competition, however one measures it. Is competition measured by whether candidates are fighting over a major change in school policy, by the degree of differences among candidates over a range of policy issues, or by whether they differ about the board's role? None of these attributes of competition increases if there are nonpartisan ballots or at-large elections involved. Quite the contrary, the reforms reduce such measures of competition, and the same reduction of competition occurs in metropolitan and nonmetropolitan districts. Partisanship, on the other hand, can increase turnout and competition.[20]

In short, political scientists have found that what applies to nonpartisanship in other aspects of the local political scene holds true for school politics. Such reforms increase the cost of citizen participation, make the bridge between representative and citizen more tenuous, and consequently muffle expression of the full range of political interests within a community. Those constrained citizens tend to be of lower socioeconomic status, so governing structures are not value free. Rather, these reforms actually encourage the access and satisfaction of another group, middle-class and higher-status people. The rhetoric of Progressivism proclaimed the expansion of democracy—"the cure for the evils of democracy is more democracy" was their standard. The reality has been otherwise, deflecting those who cannot use the cue of political party to decide among complicated public issues, including those of schooling. Such reforms ensure that—until recently at any rate—the game of school politics was played by few, and mostly by those whom fortune favored.

The popularly accepted democratic theory of responsiveness and responsibility was in the past known as a poor explanation of school elections. Today, we still see a tepid political environment, rarely upset by a raging electoral storm. We still need to know how the linkage operates when we move from a normally consensual electoral condition to a normally conflictual one. Conditions of political turbulence in the 1970s already outlined suggest a changed and charged electoral climate. Storms brewed from the discontent of lay and professional groups filled political arroyos with raging torrents that swept away the old and deposited new forms on the landscape of school governance.

A clear illustration of this metaphor is the desegregation conflict. In a ten-year review of this issue in several score Northern cities, Rossell demonstrated that desegregation generated a truly conflictual electoral politics for school boards.[21] Thus she found that the issue generated much higher voter turnout. This surge of interest led to increased defeat of incumbents, usually those identified with support of the issue, especially in higher-status school districts. Her findings also support propositions not discussed before in this research. For example:

1. Low turnout does not necessarily mean the absence of conflict, and high turnout is not a consistent measure of electoral conflict in local elections dealing with single issues. Other measures of electoral dissent than high turnout exist.
2. The stage of the issue affects the participation rate; general controversy in the early stages increases turnout more than implementing a specific desegregation policy in later stages does. But implementation generates more electoral dissent if local officials must work with something forced on them rather than something they adopt.
3. Citizen perceptions of when to use the ballot to "throw the rascals out" is quite discriminating; incumbents are more likely to be defeated when they try to implement desegregation than when a general controversy over citizen demands occurs.

The results of all these electoral forces are summarized in Table 5.1 reporting board member characteristics.

OTHER PLACES, OTHER MANNERS

Such research findings agree that the citizen-board linkage in elections is not simple; it must be differentiated for different issues, times, and communities. The issue that enters the election, whether in a period of high or low conflict, and the constituency characteristics

Table 5.1
National Demographics of School Board Members, 1991

Sex	Male	65.3%
	Female	34.7

Race	Black	2.2
	White	96.5
	Hispanic	0.8
	American Indian	0.3
	Oriental	0.1

Age	Under 25	0.4
	26–35	5.6
	36–40	15.8
	41–50	45.6
	15–60	18.8
	Over 60	13.3

Family income	Under $20,000	1.7
	$20,000–$29,999	6.4
	$30,000–$39,999	11.6
	$40,000–$49,999	14.9
	$50,000–$59,999	13.7
	$60,000–$69,999	10.9
	$70,000–$79,999	9.4
	$80,000–$89,999	7.7
	$90,000–$99,999	4.6
	$100,000–$149,999	9.6
	$150,000 or higher	6.6

Base: Random sample of 4,841 school board members who subscribe to *The American School Board Journal*, of whom 1,306—or 27 percent—responded.

Note: Includes fifty states, the District of Columbia, and the Virgin Islands. Some percentages do not total 100 because of rounding.

Source: *School Board*-Virginia Tech Survey, 1991

seem to affect the electoral connection. The Zeigler-Jennings study alluded to such distinctions occurring even in a period of consensual school politics; the city or rural context makes a difference in many matters, as do distinctions in how the election is structured. Several research efforts in the last decade have sought to show the effect of these differences.

Community Status and Electoral Turnout

Implicit in much analysis of competition's role in democracy is an assumption that greater social variety in a community leads to greater competition. Clearly, researchers can contrast the variety of city lifestyles with the conformity of nonurban life. The first generates more political conflict because more opposing social and economic bases exist for making demands on the local political system. Hence an urban setting generates greater competition and greater turnout in elections. On the other hand, the rural setting provides only a limited basis for either. The same is reported for the 1940s, the 1950s, and the 1970s.[22]

While this thesis may be correct for city-rural differences in a social context, the evidence for different electoral behavior is much less certain. Outside the South, rural turnout rates in general elections are quite high, certainly more so than in the city. The figures for board elections are less studied, yet research shows that the urban population's greater social complexity generates a greater concentration or intensity of organizational life. Measures of the latter in the eighty-eight-school-district study found them closely associated with metropolitan or nonmetropolitan status (beta=.44) and with population size (.35). This is not simply a matter of the absence or presence of political parties that can mobilize school concerns. There might well be an argument that boards should be partisan, but the best evidence finds that party influence appears only where other pressure groups are highly active.[23]

Another way to look at the influence of community context is to compare the status differences of districts. Some scholars had proposed that people with the same distinctive status, class, or occupation would generate the same kind of demands on political systems. But the evidence has told different stories at different times after World War II. Conventional wisdom prior to the 1960s found the politics of working-class schools to be associated with low intensity and low election turnouts; upper middle-class politics were the reverse.[24] It seemed that workers were less interested in school politics and that interest grew as one moved up the social scale. Then comparative studies of working-class and middle-class suburbs around Chicago, based on data gathered around 1960, found the reverse.[25] There, competition varied inversely with status; working-class school politics turned out to be highly contentious with high election turnout and frequent challenge to the superintendent. Conversely, middle-class suburban school politics was low keyed and hardly visible, with few voters and limited challenge to the professionals. Minar argued that the difference resulted from the workers' propensities to challenge school decision making by professionals of higher status and from middle-class voters' tendencies to leave such matters to the "experts," a status they often shared.

Almost a decade later, the Zeigler-Jennings research came to a third conclusion—status showed minor impact on the electoral competition for these boards.[26] Status does, however, help explain how certain electoral arrangements affect competition. The differences among the studies may lie, the authors noted, in a broader measure of what constitutes competition and in the greater variation in lifestyles found in the larger sample of districts they used.

Another national sample about the same time composed of Northern cities facing desegregation did not reach the same result. Rather, Rossell found what the first researchers had: High-status groups participated more in elections in which desegregation was central. Rossell suggests that her differences with Minar lie in the fact that his high-status citizens let professionals handle elections because their decisions were not threatening, whereas the decision to desegregate generated greater concern about racial and other threats.[27]

These recent studies provide a much richer perspective on what citizens are doing when they vote in board elections than previous research did. The turbulence of the last decade or so has clearly generated a new electoral process. Where few issues agitate the local political system—which could be most of them in the small suburban districts—the old pattern may prevail. Such elections have low visibility and little heat, with low turnout facilitating school support by middle-class voters. But one hotly contested issue will change all this, for then the arroyo becomes a gullywasher. High-visibility, high-turnout elections, with the social strata sharply opposed to one another and professional educators dodging strong criticism, yield a boiling electoral process.

The exact nature of the status alignments in voting may depend on the particular issue. No one has yet tried to classify board elections in such terms, a modification of the Lowi concept that different policies generate different kinds of politics.[28] Rossell's work on desegregation suggests that it rearranges electoral coalitions. At the other extreme, and during the same time period as desegregation, sex education has been an area in which professionals have changed the curriculum without much controversy.[29] Education about American society, however, seems to generate fierce status conflicts between ideologues, who also come into conflict over science; for example, the current evolution–creationism dispute.[30] But financial reform conflict seems to unite all status levels, as in the Proposition 13 mood of the late 1970s. A theoretical analysis of various policy effects has yet to be done, but a rich diversity is available to study and draw from in the recent turbulence of school politics.

Policy Dissatisfactions and Community Conflict

The most recent theoretical framework that helps us understand the citizen role in local school policymaking turns away from a static view of community context as an explanation. The "dissatisfaction theory" of Iannacconne and Lutz seeks to explain both quiescence and turbulence as a set of sociopolitical sequences in community life.[31] At one point in a community's life, rough agreement will exist among citizens, board, and superintendent on the course of school policy. Citizens are satisfied with what they have, and their participation in such access channels as elections is quite limited.

This satisfaction can suddenly break down with growth in the local population that brings newcomers whose policy demands differ from what prevails, and then these are rejected by the oldtimers. The result is dissatisfaction with existing school policy. A new protest then ensues before the school board, which is now less a reflective council than an arena where spokespersons for old and new policy views clash with much rancor. Another outlet for dissatisfaction is the channel of elections. Its use by newcomers in time will produce new board members; a new majority then fires the superintendent, and finally the new policymakers act in congruence with newcomers' policy preferences. At that time, citizen participation falls off due to satisfaction with the new policy.

Table 5.2
Policy Dissatisfaction and Political Reactions

Likelihood of:	Focus of Dissatisfaction:		
	School Board	Board and Superintendent	Superintendent
Increased rate of school board member turnover	High	High	Low
Shift to arena-like council behavior	High	High	Moderate
Involuntary superintendent turnover	Low	High	High

Source: Roger Rada, "Community Dissatisfaction and School Governance," Planning and Changing 15: 246.

The advantage of this theoretical approach is that possessed by all longitudinal analyses; it captures shifts or sequences that researchers explore further. The theory is dynamic, as the time quality is central to explaining what occurs. The cross-sectional approach, on the other hand, only permits analysis at one point in time. Dissatisfaction theory generated qualitative research in a few communities. A study of Santa Barbara from 1930 to 1980 found that the theory did explain what happened, but it needed to be specified more clearly. That is, all old board members had to be replaced, the new superintendent had to understand the new mandate, and he or she must be able to express and implement it. Those conditions flow from a realigning election and end with the voting public's influence evident on valued school programs.[32] Similarly, a three-district study over two years, using the same exhaustive search of records and interviews, found that dissatisfaction varied with the object or focus of the feelings. Dissatisfaction with board, superintendent, or both created different likelihoods of citizen protest, as Table 5.2 summarizes. For example, if board and superintendent are a common focus of dissatisfaction, a high chance of arena-like council behavior and subsequent board and superintendent turnover existed. Table 5.2 predicts that the superintendent will be thrown to the wolves if the focus of dissatisfaction is on that person.[33]

Why Citizen Participation?

During the period after the mid-1960s, many people called for more participation in school decision making. This ran beyond calling for greater voter turnout in board and referenda elections. Rather, this movement sought a qualitative change in the process of policymaking by expanding the number who sit on the boards. This could be done directly, as in the New York City decentralization movement of the 1970s, which created thirty-three neighborhood school boards in place of one. Or it could be arranged by attaching "citizen advisory councils" to existing boards or local school sites. This movement was not restricted to the United States, as it recently surfaced in France, Italy, England, Sweden, West Germany, and China.[34]

Several purposes motivated these changes. Some wanted increased participation for instrumental reasons, for example, to increase the chances of specific policy changes. Thus, if more black or Hispanic parents were put on such councils, they could influence the system to be less racist via more sensitive teachers and administrators, a multicultural curriculum, and so on. A second purpose for greater participation was psychological, that is, the process itself would improve the participant's sense of value as a person. There might not be much policy change, but participation would stimulate others and so permit the emergence of a "community will."

Salisbury has recently traced the origins of these different purposes for participation (rooted in classical political theory) as a way of understanding why citizens participate today.[35] His subjects were citizen participants in the schools of six St. Louis suburbs during the middle and late 1970s. Different kinds of communities were studied to determine the effects of social differences on participation. The findings are complex, but a few suggest how the simple act of participation is altered by social context.

Social context is everywhere important in defining who participates and what participation means. Mothers with children, those deeply rooted in the community, the upper social strata—not all in these categories participate, but those with these characteristics are more predisposed to participate than not. The amount of participation does not seem to be highly influenced by family background and socialization, but having children in school is important, and participation itself leads to more intensive participation. Participation has traceable but highly complex effects on one's personal development, level of information, social interaction, and subsequent civic involvement.[36]

Participants in school politics are more distinguished by *what* they do rather than *how much* they do. Some only go to meetings, some specialize in contacting public officials, others talk to fellow citizens about school matters, and still others work primarily in school elections. Three types of participants work through different institutions—family and neighbors, political parties, voluntary organizations, the elections system, and school officials. Those who participate remain positive in their support of public education, with trust in the honesty and effectiveness of its administrators; they are also sanguine about their own ability to influence local school policy. As Salisbury notes:

> There is broad support in these findings for the ancient view that the active citizen would also be the confident and effective citizen. And there is broad support also for the view that suburban school-centered participation bears little relationship to the larger and more cynical world of national politics. . . . The central finding is that . . . the more people participate, the greater will be the impact on them, and the greater the impact, the more likely it will take the form of enhanced personal growth and development.[37]

All this unfolds in a school politics that is dynamic—constantly changing actors, participants, issues, and conflicts. The changes that accrue from such participation are not dramatically large or abrupt; rather they are small and incremental. But over time, as Lindblom and others have noted, these subtle shifts add up to massive changes in the amount and quality of a policy service like education.[38] Those entering the policy world expecting fast big changes are doomed to disappointment. No system, by definition, changes in this way short of violent revolution—and not even then, as the Soviet system illustrates. However, those entering the school policy world with a sense of developing their capabilities and generating pressures for some change are much more likely to have effects, though small. Over time, as the American experience has shown, these people can transform an institution and thus benefit their children.

NONLOCAL PARTICIPATION

To this point, we have focused only on the channel of input demands to the school board's authority on the local level. Yet partisan elections for state and federal office can certainly impact local schools because of the resources those levels transmit to schools. Increasingly, the budget fight in the state legislature over the amount spent for local schools becomes an annual drama in every state. Governors and legislators thus have a direct bearing on school quality, equity, efficiency, and choice. As we will see in a later chapter, this state role makes "local control" more imaginary than real. Further, what the legislature says about the taxing authority of local units is vital to the operation of the schools and the pocketbooks of most citizens. In 1983 public opinion showed dramatic increases in concern about education quality, so that state governments were galvanized to enact numerous reforms.

One other nonlocal channel for popular participation exists, the elections of Congress members and the president. When the range of issues facing political authorities is extensive at the state level, the reach becomes enormous nationally. This should mean that the importance of school issues goes down when most persons vote for higher governmental offices. That is, concern over school taxes or curriculum is less than issues of war and peace or the national economy. However, citizens follow national affairs more closely than local affairs, but state affairs least—when they pay any attention to public affairs at all.[39] As yet we have little research on citizen use of resources to affect national authorities on school policy. Citizens may have *opinions* on Washington's policies, as we shall see, but the gap between popular opinion and action on many issues rivals the Grand Canyon. And even then, citizen demands or even attitudes on federal policy may be so diffuse as to be nonexistent.

Some input is provided, however, through party channels in the form of issue stands. Rather consistently in the past, those identifying with the Democratic Party have been stronger supporters of federal aid to education than have Republican identifiers. Professional politicians of either party were even more widely separated on these issues than average party members.[40] After 1965, as federal funds became increasingly available to local school budgets already straining under an overloaded property tax, this partisan difference began to disappear. It reemerged in the Carter administration over creation of the Department of Education. In 1980 Ronald Reagan campaigned for its abolition and sought that end after his election, including abolishing federal funds for schooling. Forceful opposition frustrated both efforts; by 1987, the department still stood, and school funds had been cut from a high of 8 percent down to 6 percent.

Diffuse attitudes on federal school policy can crystallize under certain circumstances. For example, there was intense support for the GI Bill after World War II; to oppose this was to oppose our soldiers' efforts in that war. In another example of crisis-based opinion, during the later 1960s national attitudes coalesced in profound opposition to school busing during the desegregation controversy. However, citizen attitudinal input into national arenas deals little with educational policy, and little evidence shows that it flavors the decisions of voters in federal elections. Yet, if a perceived threat existed to a closely held value, opinions can have electoral impact. After all, some of the support for Ronald Reagan was from foes of busing.

In summary, then, although elections in the United States serve as potential channels for citizens to have school inputs in a way that is rare among nations, they seem little used. Board elections are barometers, normally reflecting little dissatisfaction in the environment, but subject to sudden change. Additional examination of changes that produce dissatisfaction or "rancorous conflict" would be immensely valuable.[41]

Such analyses would have several uses. Practically, they would describe the conditions under which school administration can trigger public concerns. Theoretically, they would help develop an understanding of the links between private wants and public outputs under stress conditions. These practical and theoretical concerns generate interesting questions. Practically, how much can the superintendent support external demands for quality from the profession when community standards reject or resist them? Does the frequency of superintendent turnover—chronic in the profession and especially so in larger cities—inhibit or enhance this executive's efforts at financing, curriculum and staff improvement, or desegregation?[42] We will return to the superintendent's situation in a later chapter.

Any theoretical questions we posed are in contrast to the available evidence that American schools receive a minimum of significant input through the direct channel of elections. Yet from this one must *not* conclude that the political authorities of School or State ignore the wants of citizens. The possibility always remains that a school issue which agitates the community or the nation deeply enough could suddenly focus on the channel of elections, suddenly displacing the old with the new. Dissatisfaction theory research substantiates this possibility. In the satisfied stage, school officials are confined by a "zone of tolerance," that is, public expectations. But in the dissatisfied stage, voters use elections to focus their demands and restructure the local policy system. In either case, school officials must keep tuned for public signals, no matter how muted.

COMMUNITY POWER STRUCTURE AND SCHOOL POLICY

Another exchange mechanism, less visible and formal than elections, is community groups with special influence on school policy. In the last several decades, researchers have studied how power is organized in communities to make public decisions. Many "community power studies" have appeared, and often the research matches sociologists against political scientists, who debate whether local power is hierarchical ("elitist") or segmented ("pluralist"). This literature is in part theoretical, methodological, and normative, although the distinctions among these modes of knowledge have not always been clear. That research faded in the 1970s, but its products still appear in training programs for school administrators. We propose only to summarize the contours of this search for community power as a preface to noting its relationship to schools.[43]

Four Queries in Community Power Studies

We suggest that the complex intellectual debate on this subject centers around four questions: What is meant by power? How is its presence and arrangement discovered in the community? What accounts for the differences in power arrangements that exist among American communities? What differences in terms of community life stem from these different power arrangements?[44]

Despite their enormous fascination with power, social scientists share little agreement on its meaning, except to say that power involves the capacity tò cause or inhibit change in behavior impossible to effect without it. This modest consensus fails as a theoretical statement that can help explain and predict the outcome of social conflict. As March's survey of the term's meanings concluded, "On the whole, however, power is a disappointing concept. It gives us surprisingly little purchase in reasonable models of complex systems of social choice."[45] Much of the conflict in the field could stem from this vagueness at the heart of the inquiry.

Given the indefinite meaning of the term, the measurements of power have been equally varied. Most research has dealt with the problem of how to detect community power and, once certain methods were justified, with what was found. It may be too strong to say that much of this work was trivial compared to the larger scholarly questions in this list; perhaps the problem of method had to be tested in research before we could arrive at the present situation. However, for a decade after the publication of Hunter's *Community Power Structure* in 1953, the pages of the journals of sociology and political science were the forum for a strong, even bitter, clash over methods—positional, reputational, decisional, combinational. Part of this may have reflected a bias stemming from disciplinary training for such research.[46] By the mid-1960s, it was clear that no one method was sufficient; combinations were needed to trace the dimensions of community decision making accurately.

The third query—what accounts for differences among community power arrangements—required collecting a pool of comparable data. That goal has been slow to accomplish. One approach was to compare a small number of communities within the same methodological framework; thus, in the mid-1960s Agger et al. developed a theoretical and conceptual framework for studying four communities. Another approach was to compare what was known about existing case studies, in order to test hypotheses about different power arrangements arising under varied conditions. But the limited-sample approach was not a sample, so generalizations were limited; at best they were a modest advance over the host of independent case studies. On the other hand, analysis of pooled case studies faced the problem of the varying methods and research questions used in each study. By the end of the 1960s, the third approach was getting under way; this involved working with a large number of communities to which unified theory, concept, and hypothesis were applied. The announcement of a "permanent community sample" of fifty-one American towns with resident community analysts opened a new possibility; here was a more established data base for testing research questions about policy outcomes and decisional arrangements.[47]

The final query is one that has often been implicit in all this research: What difference does it make for the community whether power arrangements are elitist, pluralist, amorphous, and so on? Far too often, of course, each analyst dealt with only a single town in answering that question, hardly the basis for meaningful generalization. Nevertheless, the first major works on community power, the Lynds' *Middletown* and *Middletown in Transition*, were critical of the quality of life they found in a community dominated by one family. Many later writers never quite abandoned this normative approach. Much research has had an implicit criticism of the arrangements found (particularly the elitist) for what these meant to democratic values and the way people lived. For the researchers, even the somewhat broader power arrangements found in pluralist studies were criticized for seeming to justify a status quo that defeated the democratic promise.[48] The emergence of new federal programs and resources for those without resources attracted the attention of scholars concerned about whether this development might rearrange power at the local level.[49] With this development, it was thought in the 1960s that elite power structures could be overcome and power returned to the people. And in fact, by the 1980s, blacks and Hispanics in ten California cities could report increased representation and incorporation in the local power system as a result of such programs.[50]

A fuller picture of the ties between school and community enables teachers and administrators to carry out their professional tasks better. Another utility is more practical. As a leading school administration textbook asks: "For example, does the administrator become subservient to the power structure when elements of it are known to him? Or is he then in the position to become a manipulator? Or in a better position to provide constructive leadership?"[51]

We can illustrate some of what is implied here. If the community is dominated by one small group that shares the same values, (i.e., is elite), then school professionals wanting new educational programs must know the group whose support they must enlist. Educational innovation that proceeds with no notion of community values or the guardians of these values, the zone of tolerance, and elite resources is an empty exercise. If, however, the community has a number of groups, each important in shaping policy in one domain, or has shifting coalitions that form temporary majorities on each issue area, another strategy is called for. In this case, one has a better chance of finding bases of support in the community by seeking coalitions of power. In sum, given that the school is part of the community, power research provides information about that relationship and suggests strategies for working with it.

Oddly, before 1970, the scholarly debate on community power research did not deal much with the schools. Four works that mark the major developments of this controversy—by the Lynds, Hunter, and Agger et al.—illustrate this neglect.[52] A review of the hundreds of research studies in this field further supports this finding; not even the aggregate, comparative studies carried out prior to 1970 showed interest in this policy area.[53] An exception was Alford's study of the political cultures of four Wisconsin cities.[54] Among these four, no evidence of elitist control emerged—other than the educational interest group of administrators and PTAs. In this work, schools are clearly seen as a proper policy concern for the analyst due to the size of the resources they expend and the occasional flash flood of citizen concern about school actions.

The relevance for schools of studying community power structures has primarily been drawn by a few educational administration scholars who have provided a bridge to other disciplines. Little such scholarship exists, however, and less of it is comparative, even after 1970. In 1967 only 10 of 310 studies were clearly related to educational policy; 2 of these had the same author, and 4 were unpublished dissertations.[55] The theoretical perspective in these earlier studies was limited, most found elitist arrangements, and all urged their results enabled superintendents to fulfill their jobs better.[56]

It must be emphasized that such utility is possible only with findings drawn from *comparative* study. The comparative phase began with a little-noted 1956 study of three small towns in Wyoming, one with the delightful name of Wideroad.[57] Using reputational techniques and opinion surveys from samples in each town, Webb discovered that community control rested in the hands of a few people who were mostly unknown to the average citizen and to superintendents. The comparative aspects of this study are a considerable advance. The years that followed showed that case studies still prevailed in the limited research on schools and power structures, and few were comparative.[58] But then in 1963–1964, a freshet of publications appeared whose quality was much improved. These emphasized the comparative method; their theory and concepts were well developed; and the consequent hypotheses and empirical grounding pushed the research to a substantially higher level.[59]

What Difference for School Policy?

Remaining to be answered was the question, What differences did a specific form of local power make for school outputs? This research orientation guided the 1960 Syracuse studies of "values, influence, and tax effort" in New York suburbs.[60] Although the power arrangements in these suburbs were quite similar, they "displayed major differences in their levels of relative expenditure and tax effort." That is, power arrangements were irrelevant to financial differences. A year later, though, Kimbrough found that finances did control many school matters in four Southern counties.[61] The two studies contrast sharply because the Southern communities were so alike, but the Syracuse suburbs were not. The Kimbrough work has been widely cited as showing the intervention effect that covert groups can have on determining inputs before the school board.[62] One way that such groups can have an effect is on the superintendent's tenure, as McCarty found in the 1960s.[63]

The theoretical complexities of school and power arrangements increased in the mid-1960s. A collection of essays edited by Cahill and Hencley contained a wealth of research strategies, questions, typologies, hypotheses, and interactional analyses.[64] The theoretical and practical usefulness of comparative study is also evident in Crain's examination of school desegregation, first in nine major cities and later in over ninety.[65] These studies reported complex findings that challenged the popular belief in the power of a "civic elite," at least in the desegregation process. Such an elite did, however, seem to set the "political style" of each city; it indirectly influenced the appointments to school boards and was more likely to exist in the South than the North. In another of those ironies that our conflicting basic values occasionally generate, desegregation proceeded more smoothly if the board was more independent of the general public, that is, more elite.

A major comparative study by Johns and Kimbrough on the ties between power structure and school policy, still the largest of its kind, appeared in 1968.[66] They focused on the community effort to reform school finances over a seventeen-year period after World War II in 122 school districts in Illinois, Kentucky, Georgia, and Florida. In 24 of these communities, in-depth studies of their power structures developed two "open" and two "closed" types (i.e., nonelite vs. elite systems). As hypothesized, closed systems were associated much more often with less financial efforts for schools.

One set of findings is particularly meaningful. If a system is closed and noncompetitive, we would expect to find citizens less participative, but then more participative if the system extended them more opportunities. This was indeed the case, no matter how participation was measured. Citizens tended to misperceive the power arrangement in their communities drastically, seeing more competition than actually existed. But if they perceived that they lived in a competitive system, they also felt more effective politically. Also, the type of power structure showed little relationship to the civic, economic, and educational beliefs of major community influentials, teachers, and voters. The best explanation for a district's pattern of financial effort or expenditure was whether it had employed that pattern in the past.[67] In addition, the independent effect of the power structure, the superintendent's role or influence, and citizens' values was very limited. Note that the taxpayer revolt that came later would tend to confirm the lack of relationship between the type of power structure and financial effort. With districts everywhere swept up in the fervor of this revolt, few qualities of community life seem to make a difference in tax cutting.

Finance is not the only issue studied in relationship to local power. McCarty and Ramsey's study of fifty-one cities of varying size showed that local power structures can also have relevance for school governance.[68] Again, no single pattern emerges, such as an elite that controls local power. Often an association existed between the kind of power structure in the community and on the school board, which had important consequences for the superintendent's role. Thus, if the power structure in the community and on the board was elite, the superintendent was limited to being a "functionary." If the structure in both was bifactional, the superintendent was a "strategist" maneuvering between the two. But if the context in both places was pluralistic—power varying with school issue—the school official worked as a "professional advisor," serving all factions equally and fairly. If, however, a community and board lacked any structure of power or was unpatterned, the superintendent defined her or his role as "decision maker."

This is a far cry from how this professional is usually described as dominating the board across a range of school matters; certainly the subsequent national study by Zeigler and Jennings argued emphatically for this popular view. Boyd has also pointed out certain limitations of the McCarty-Ramsey findings, challenging the degree of pluralism they thought they found and, by implication, the impact of power structures on school policymaking.[69] In the next chapter we will review this debate over whether the board or the superintendent controls school policymaking.

From such works, the concept of community power study and its relevance to school decisions slowly made its way into the training of educational administrators.[70] That they should relate to their communities is not a new idea, of course. But now the emphasis has shifted to the usefulness of knowing that a few influential people can shape community outputs by controlling demands to the school system. Similarly, this training more explicitly adopted the pressure-group approach to policymaking. Whether these forces were valuable or not for the administrator's tasks was not clear, for some writers rejected the impact of lay pressures, while others insisted they were a necessary and inescapable part of the job.[71]

These scholarly concerns could be belated; the findings of most studies in a society that is changing rapidly are time bound. A reanalysis over time of power structures in 166 communities shows that political processes are tending to become more pluralistic: "power . . . . is less and less in the hands of a privileged few and is increasingly dependent upon the broker, be he elected official or not, who can bring together (to the extent he can bring together) the various elements in the community."[72] The strong possibility also exists that the intervention of major forces from outside into local communities may be rearranging power all over the nation.[73] We have mentioned the recent nationalizing force of federal school laws following the older nationalizing forces of professionalism. Such intrusion into the school scene could not only diminish the weight of any local elite in decision making, but it could also narrow the options for decisions by *any* power form.

The Vertical Axis of Local Control

These changes suggest the metaphor of a "vertical axis of power" that now orients all school districts, namely, influences from outside their boundaries. School boards are faced with extramural pressures they cannot control that determine what they can do. Thus, changes in the shape of the national economy—a time of boom or a bust—can drastically affect the local school budget. The oil crisis after 1973 seriously redirected school budgets away from strictly educational purposes to cover rising energy costs. In the boom time for the Sunbelt states in the 1980s, school programs expanded under the pressure of greater resources.[74] Similarly, the expansion of the control over school boards by state and federal laws brought a storm of complaints during the 1970s, as Cronin's widely circulated declaration notes.[75] Perhaps an even greater outside influence stemmed from the state itself, as it expanded its constitutional powers under political pressures. The rise of strong teacher organizations also represents a local sign of what is in essence a national development. This group's influence in one big city's schools has led an analyst to label it "union rule in Chicago."[76] If the state continues to extend its control and take up its share of local costs into the 1990s, teacher groups may well escalate their pressure on state legislatures to reach decisions that are binding on local districts.[77] We know how teachers, under fiscal stress, favor instructional and personnel costs or resist merit pay schemes suddenly popular in the 1980s.[78]

These influences on the school scene are only part of national forces that show up in the total urban setting. Changes in the economy, the growth of state and federal controls, the emergence of national professional groups—all afflict mayors and city councils as well as schools. Just as schools face desegregation problems, city halls face affirmative action orders. When schools have to budget a third or more of their financial resources for fuel oil, urban bureaucracies must do the same. If the state capitol mandates drug abuse curricula in the local school, it also mandates more training courses for city service employees—and both local authorities face increased reporting requirements. When local teachers strike for higher pay, police or fireworkers could be out on the line just down the street. As Long's persuasive book points out, urban Americans live in an "unwalled city." A close examination by Wirt of a major city like San Francisco shows just how these centralizing influences work on city and school governance.[79]

The result of all this has been an increase in the number of groups seeking to influence local school governance, in the issues that get on the school agenda, and in the resources brought to bear upon the school board. As recently as 1960—in some cases 1970—the agenda before almost all school boards did *not* include: slashing budgets, organized teacher demands, desegregation, congruence with federal guidelines on a range of program services, court requirements about treatment of minorities and students, cutting energy uses and costs, laws on accountability, incorporating parents into decision making, and so on. In 1980 some or all of these external influences appear on all school board agendas in all districts across the nation. That is why Cistone, editing a series of studies on school board problems in the mid-1970s, characterized the present

> as a time when the external environment of the school board, as of virtually all social organizations, has been undergoing rapid and profound transformation. . . . The insularity, the selective responsiveness, that once characterized school board decision-making is being eroded under the powerful impact of social, economic, cultural, and political pressures. . . . The need to respond and adapt to the external situation is precipitating changes in the personality and character of the school board itself.[80]

Just as recent research upsets any simplistic notion of school boards as dominated by narrow local elites, so this phenomenon of the vertical power axis counters the notion of the great influence of local structures. That would be the case if basic decisions are being made for local power structures at other power centers, public and private, outside the district. What the local people can do, though, is work with the residue of decisions left them by others. Peterson's influential 1974 review of the literature concluded that pursuit of the question, Who controls? in local schools was empty of meaning, despite the voluminous writing, when evidence of *any* local control was absent.[81] Wirt has pointed out that external influences may indeed weaken local control; a "sandbox model" of depleted power may result, where much of the local activity is actually bounded severely by mandates, economic constraints, and professionalism. But external influences can also empower local groups with resources they did not have before—a "shopping mall" model of additive power for the community.[82]

Even if local control exists only for marginal matters, preoccupation with marginal matters has its value; Salisbury has shown how citizens working with such margins are enhanced in spirit and mind. Also, marginality does not mean no independent courses are left for administrators or boards. For example, when the blizzard of 1977 struck Columbus and Cincinnati with the same fearful blows, each school system reacted differently in response to its own organizational ethos.[83]

What all this does mean, as van Geel documents in detail, is that the authority to control school programs has always been altering due to our numerous and sometimes conflicting principles of school and society.[84] The newest model of local control clearly emphasizes extensive sharing—not autonomy—in school board authority. Given that, the independent power of even the most elite local power structure is quite limited.

DEMOCRACY AND SCHOOL POLICY

In these last two chapters, we have tried to trace the various access channels for transmitting demands to the schools. One finding seems consistent: Relatively few citizens use the channels available to them to register their educational needs. Popular participation is episodic at best, providing spasms rather than a flow of demands. When finally aroused, these demands do not focus on broad policies but rather on specifics. Of late, this involvement has taken the form of an increasing failure to pass local school levies, from almost two-thirds passing in the mid-1960s to only one-third by 1980. Alongside this flood of dissatisfaction with public schools by an apathetic public are occasional waves of protest generated by a sex education course, a too-liberal textbook, student dress regulations, or some other specific causes.

Interest groups may thus be the most common form of participation, but few citizens belong to them; the difficulties PTAs have in getting members enrolled and turned out are well known. Even groups seeking wide popular authority over local schools through "community control" programs have found it hard to get "the community" to participate. And board elections are rarely enticing enough to attract more than a small minority; they are dominated by the success of incumbents in getting reelected, and the competition is negligible. The potential exists for sweeping the "school rascals" out of office and replacing them with members who have different ideas. Elections certainly can operate in this fashion—but usually they do not.

Yet to say that relatively few participate is not to say that this frees the school authorities to do whatever they wish. The power of one parent with a complaint raised against a perceived injustice is enough to agitate administrators and can, if not met, escalate into a flood of community energy. After all, in the late 1970s, only a few objected to the MACOS* curriculum in the Charlestown, West Virginia, schools, but those few disrupted schools greatly. The bombing of the district's central office symbolizes the potency of this frustrated minority. While the day-to-day life of school officials or teachers is filled with simply administering past directives from the public and profession, the potential exists for new waves of citizen inputs. At any moment, the schools can be caught between the forces of popular participation and bureaucratization, as Alford has noted.[85] Over time, the latter prevails, but also through time the influence of citizen participation becomes a zone of tolerance within which school authorities must act. This does not mean that they live in ongoing hypersensitivity to community and group demands—far from it, if one accepts the continuous criticism of school bureaucracy. Nor does this mean that the authorities are so inert that they cannot change their course—the history of educational reform belies that charge.

Under some conditions, then, demands do enter the political system of the school and do make their way through to policy outputs. The conditions under which this takes place at the local and state levels are the subjects of the next chapters.

---

* "Man: A Course of Study" is a social science curriculum package scholars developed with U.S. Office of Education funding support.

NOTES

1. David Easton, *A Framework for Political Analysis* (Engelwood Cliffs, N.J.: Prentice-Hall, 1965), p. 122.

2. H. M. Hamlin, "Organized Citizen Participation in the Public Schools," *Review of Educational Research* 23 (1953): 346–52. Compare this with the study fifteen years later by Otis A. Crosby, "How to Prepare Winning Bond Issues," *Nation's Schools* 81 (1968): 81–84.

3. Richard J. Brown, "Party Platforms and Public Education," *Social Studies* (1961): 206–10.

4. Roald F. Campbell et al., *The Organization and Control of American Schools* (Columbus, Ohio: Charles E. Merrill, 1965); Peter J. Cistone, ed., *Understanding School Boards: Problems and Prospects* (Lexington, Mass.: Lexington Books, 1975); Tyll van Geel, *Authority to Control the School Program* (Lexington, Mass.: Lexington Books, 1976).

5. Charles R. Adrian and Charles Press, *Governing Urban America*, 3d ed. (New York: McGraw–Hill, 1968), p. 434.

6. Sande Milton, "Participation in Local School Board Elections: A Reappraisal," *Social Science Quarterly* 64: 646–54; Sande Milton and Robert Bickel, "Competition in Local School Board Elections: Findings in a Partisan Political Environment," *Planning and Changing* 13: 148–57.

7. Robert L. Crain et al., *The Politics of School Desegregation* (Garden City, N.Y.: Doubleday-Anchor, 1969), and David Kirby et al., *Political Strategies in Northern School Desegregation* (Lexington, Mass.: Lexington Books, 1973).

8. Lester G. Seligman, *Political Recruitment* (Boston: Little, Brown & Co., 1972).

9. Peter J. Cistone, "The Recruitment and Socialization of School Board Members," in Cistone, *Understanding School Boards*, Chap. 3, and Cistone, "The Ecological Basis of School Board Member Recruitment," *Education and Urban Society* 4 (1974): 428–50.

10. George S. Counts, *The Social Composition of Boards of Education* (Chicago: University of Chicago, 1927), Supplementary Educational Monographs, No. 33; National School Boards Association, *Women on School Boards* (Evanston, Ill.: NSBA, 1974).

11. Ted Robinson, Robert England, and Kenneth Meier, "Black Resources and Black School Board Representation: Does Political Structure Matter?" *Social Science Quarterly* 66: 976–82.

12. L. Harmon Zeigler, M. Kent Jennings, and G. Wayne Peak, *Governing American Schools: Political Interaction in Local School Districts* (North Scituate, Mass.: Duxbury, 1974). Chapter 2 provides the following information.

13. Howard D. Hamilton and Sylvan H. Cohen, *Policy Making by Plebiscite: School Referenda* (Lexington, Mass.: Lexington Books, 1974).

14. This felicitous phrase is from Edith K. Mosher, "The School Board in the Family of Governments," in Cistone, *Understanding School Boards*, Chap. 5.

15. William Boyd, "The Public, the Professionals, and Educational Policy-Making: Who Governs?" *Teachers College Record* 77 (1976): 539–77.

16. This and subsequent quote from Zeigler et al., *Governing American Schools*, p. 25.

17. Ibid., Chap. 3.

18. Hawley, *Nonpartisan Urban Politics*, analyzes this outcome throughout California.

19. Neal Peirce, Preface in *School Boards: A Strengthening Grass Roots Leadership*, by Lila N. Carol et al. (Washington, D.C.: Institute for Educational Leadership, 1986).

20. Milton, "Participation"; Milton and Bickel, "Competition."

21. Christine H. Rossell, "School Desegregation and Electoral Conflict," in *The Polity of the School*, Frederick M. Wirt, ed. (Lexington, Mass.: Lexington Books, 1975), Chap. 4.

22. H. Lloyd Warner et al., *Democracy in Jonesville* (New York: Harper & Row, 1949); Arthur J. Vidich and Joseph Bensman, *Small Town in Mass Society* (Princeton: Princeton University Press, 1958); and Alan Peshkin, *Growing Up American* (Chicago: University of Chicago Press, 1979).

23. On the association between complexity and social organizations, see Zeigler et al., *Governing American Schools*, p. 100; on party and pressure groups, see ibid., pp. 104–5; on an argument for boards to be a matter for political parties, see Michael D. McCaffrey, "Politics in the School: A Case for Partisan School Boards," *Education Administration Quarterly* 7, no. 3 (1971): 51–63. Where these elections occur in a partisan context, turnout in board elections is as high as for other offices; see Milton, "Participation," and Milton and Bickel, "Competition."

24. Richard F. Carter, *Voters and Their Schools* (Stanford: Institute for Communications Research, 1962).

25. David W. Minar, "The Community Basis of Conflict in School System Politics," *American Sociological Review* 31 (1966): 822–34. Enhancement of this work is found in William L. Boyd, *Community Status and Conflict in Suburban School Politics* (Beverly Hills, Calif.: Sage, 1975).

26. Zeigler et al., *Governing American Schools*, pp. 60–62.

27. See Rossell, "School Desegregation." Note that she used yet another measure of competition—dissent—based on the defeat of incumbents.

28. Theodore Lowi, "American Business, Public Policy, Case Studies and Political Theory," *World Politics* 16 (1964): 677–715.

29. James Hottois and Neal A. Milner, *The Sex Education Controversy: A Study of Politics, Education, and Morality* (Lexington, Mass.: Lexington Books, 1974).

30. Paul Goldstein, *Changing the American Schoolbook* (Lexington, Mass.: Lexington Books, 1978).

31. Frank Lutz and Laurence Iannaccone, eds., *Public Participation in School Decision Making* (Lexington, Mass.: Lexington, 1978).

32. Ruth Danis, "Policy Changes in Local Schools," *Urban Education* 19: 125–44.

33. Roger Rada, "Community Dissatisfaction and School Governance," *Planning and Changing* 15: 234–47.

34. Fred S. Coombs and Richard L. Merritt, "The Public's Role in Educational Policy Making: An International View," *Education and Urban Society* 9 (1977): 169–96.

35. The following paragraphs rely upon Robert H. Salisbury, *Citizen Participation in the Public Schools* (Lexington, Mass.: Lexington Books, 1980).

36. For reviews of the literature on the impact of participation on the participant, see David H. Smith and Richard D. Reddy, "The Impact of Voluntary Action upon

the Voluntary Participant," in *Voluntary Action Research, 1973*, David H. Smith, ed. (Lexington, Mass.: Lexington Books, 1973), pp. 169–239; and Dale Mann, *The Politics of Administrative Representation* (Lexington, Mass.: Lexington Books, 1976), Chap. 5.

37. Salisbury, *Citizen Participation*, pp. 177, 199.

38. Charles E. Lindblom, *The Policy-Making Process*. (Englewood Cliffs, N.J.: Prentice-Hall, 1968). For particular evidence of the proposition as it applies to changes in education, see Diane Ravitch, *The Revisionists Revised: A Critique of the Radical Attack on Schools* (New York: Basic Books, 1978); and Frederick M. Wirt, "Neoconservatism and National School Policy," *Educational Evalution and Policy Analysis* 2, no. 6 (1980): 5–18.

39. M. Kent Jennings and Harmon Zeigler, "The Salience of American State Politics," *American Political Science Review* 64 (1970): 524–27.

40. Herbert McClosky et al., "Issue Conflict and Consensus Among Party Leaders and Followers," *American Political Science Review* 54 (1960): 413; Thomas A. Flinn and Frederick M. Wirt, "Local Party Leaders: Groups of Like Minded Men," *Midwest Journal of Political Science* 9 (1965): 82.

41. William Gamson, *Power and Discontent* (Homewood, Ill.: Dorsey Press, 1968), although the focus here is not upon school issues.

42. Joseph M. Cronin, *The Control of Urban Schools* (New York: Free Press, 1972); and Larry Cuban, *Urban School Chiefs Under Fire* (Chicago: University of Chicago Press, 1976).

43. For a review of this debate, see Willis D. Hawley and Frederick M. Wirt, eds., *The Search for Community Power*, 2d ed. (Englewood Cliffs, N.J.: Prentice-Hall, 1974). For illustrations of the level of analytical thinking, see Terry N. Clark, ed., *Community Structure and Decision-Making: Comparative Analysis* (San Francisco: Chandler, 1968); for an illustration of comparative research, see Terry N. Clark, "Community Structure, Decision-Making, Budget Expenditures, and Urban Renewal in 51 American Communities," *American Sociological Review* 33 (1968): 576–93.

44. We have been informed on these queries by Willis D. Hawley from an unpublished paper. For a bibliography, see Hawley and Wirt, *Search for Community Power*, 1st ed., pp. 367–79; and Willis D. Hawley and James H. Svara, *The Study of Community Power—A Bibliographic Review* (Santa Barbara, Calif.: ABC-Clio, 1972).

45. James G. March, "The Power of Power," in *Varieties of Political Theory*, David Easton, ed. (Englewood Cliffs, N.J.: Prentice-Hall, 1966), pp. 39–70.

46. See the articles by John Walton, "Discipline, Method and Community Power: A Note on the Sociology of Knowledge," *American Sociological Review* 31 (1966): 684–89; and "Substance and Artifact: The Current Status of Research on Community Power Structure," *American Journal of Sociology* 71 (1966): 430–38; Terry Clark et al., "Discipline, Method, Community Structure, and Decision-Making: The Role and Limitations of the Sociology of Knowledge," *American Sociologist* 3 (1968): 214–17.

47. The first approach is illustrated in Robert E. Agger et al., *The Rulers and the Ruled* (New York: Wiley, 1964); and William V. D'Antonio and William H. Form, *Influentials in Two Border Cities* (South Bend, Ind.: University of Notre Dame Press, 1965). The second is illustrated in Walton, "Discipline, Method" and "Substance

and Artifact" and in Claire W. Gilbert, "Some Trends in Community Politics: A Secondary Analysis of Power Structure Data from 166 Communities," *Southwestern Social Science Quarterly* (1967): 373–81. The third approach is seen in T. Clark, *Community Structure and Decision Making.* The "sample" is reported in Peter H. Rossi and Robert Crain, "The NORC Permanent Community Sample," *Public Opinion Quarterly* 32 (1968): 261–72.

48. Peter Bachrach, *The Theory of Democratic Elitism* (Boston: Little, Brown & Co., 1967).

49. Nicholas Masters et al., *Politics, Poverty and Education: An Analysis of Decision-Making Structures* (Washington, D.C.: Office of Economic Opportunity, 1968); Roland W. Warren, ed., *Politics and the Ghettos* (New York: Atherton, 1969); and Paul E. Peterson, "Forms of Representation: Participation of the Poor in the Community Action Program," *American Political Science Review* 64 (1970): 491–507.

50. Rufus Browning, Dale Marshall, and David Tabb, *Protest Is Not Enough* (Berkeley: University of California Press, 1984).

51. Edgar L. Morphet, Roe L. Johns, and Theodore L. Reller, *Educational Organization and Administration*, 2d ed. (Englewood Cliffs, N.J.: Prentice-Hall, 1967), p. 194.

52. Robert S. and Helen M. Lynd, *Middletown*, Part 2 (New York: Harcourt Brace Jovanovich, 1929); and *Middletown in Transition* (New York: Harcourt Brace Jovanovich, 1937), Chap. 6. For a more thorough critique of the Lynds for imputing power to this family, see Nelson W. Polsby, *Community Power and Political Theory* (New Haven: Yale University Press, 1963), pp. 14–24; Floyd Hunter, *Community Power Structure* (Chapel Hill: University of North Carolina Press, 1953), pp. 214–15, 223; Robert A. Dahl, *Who Governs?* (New Haven: Yale University Press, 1960), Chap. 11; Agger et al., *Rulers and Ruled*, Chap. 4.

53. For articles on this power and the policies of transportation, defense, contracts, poverty programs, and Japanese communities—but none on schools—see the entire issue of *Southwestern Social Science Quarterly* 48 no. 3 (December, 1967). An aggregate study omitting this is Clark, "Community Structure, Decision-Making, Budget Expenditures."

54. Robert R. Alford, *Bureaucracy and Participation: Political Culture in Four Wisconsin Cities* (Chicago: Rand McNally, 1969).

55. See the Pellegrin bibliography in *Southwestern Social Science Quarterly* 48 (1967), and especially the reference to Agger, Bloomberg et al.

56. See Leland C. Wilson, "Community Power Controls Related to the Administration of Education" (Ph.D. diss., Peabody College, 1952); Theodore J. Jensen, "Identification and Utilization of Opinion Leaders in School District Reorganization" (Ph.D. diss., University of Wisconsin, 1952); Keith Goldhammer, "The Roles of School District Officials in Policy Determination in an Oregon Community" (Ph.D. diss., University of Oregon, 1954); Keith Goldhammer, "Community Power Structure and School Board Membership," *American School Board Journal* 130 (1955): 23–25; Donald E. Tope, "Northwest C.P.E.A.—Aims and Results," *The School Executive* 74 (1955): 74–76; Vincent Ostrom, "Who Forms School Policy?" *The School Executive* 74 (1955): 77–79.

57. Harold V. Webb, *Community Power Structure Related to School Administration* (Laramie: Curriculum and Research Center, College of Education, University of Wyoming, 1956).

58. John M. Foskett, "A Comparative Study of Community Influence," in *The Social Sciences View School Administration*, Donald Tope et al., ed. (Englewood Cliffs, N.J.: Prentice-Hall, 1965), pp. 115–30.

59. Reviewed in Hawley and Wirt, eds., *The Search for Community Power*, Part 3.

60. Warner Bloomberg et al., *Suburban Power Structures and Public Education* (Syracuse: Syracuse University Press, 1963), pp. 88 ff., 168; In a related study from the same series, see Jesse Burkhead, *Public School Finance: Economics and Politics*.

61. Ralph B. Kimbrough, *Political Power and Educational Decision-Making* (Chicago: Rand McNally, 1964), esp. Chaps. 4–5, 10–11.

62. This interest has stimulated a number of dissertations at the University of Florida. Compare Kimbrough, *Political Power*; Kimbrough, "Development of a Concept of Social Power," in *The Politics of Education in the Local Community*, Robert S. Cahill and Stephen P. Hencley, eds. (Danville, Ill.: Interstate Printers & Publishers, 1964), Chap. 5; and Appendix H in n. 58.

63. Donald J. McCarty, "How Community Power Structures Influence Administrative Tenure," *American School Board Journal* 148 (1964): 11–13, offers some hypotheses in a highly researchable area.

64. Cahill and Hencley, *Politics of Education*, p. 75.

65. See sources in note 7.

66. Roe L. Johns and Ralph B. Kimbrough, *The Relationship of Socio-economic Factors, Educational Leadership Patterns, and Elements of Community Power Structure to Local School Fiscal Policy* (Washington, D.C.: Bureau of Research, Office of Education, HEW, 1968). The first edition of our book has a more detailed analysis of this study.

67. This phenomenon has been reported for many other kinds of expenditures; that is, what has been spent in the past determines current expenditures more than other potential explanatory variables. See Ira Sharkansky, "Economic and Political Correlates of State Government Expenditures: General Tendencies and Deviant Cases," *Midwest Journal of Political Science* 11 (1967): 173–92; and Ira Sharkansky, *Spending in the American States* (Chicago: Rand McNally, 1968). This research found that this explanation was most true for general government and next for education among state expenditures. The data for education are found in Frederick M. Wirt, "Education Politics and Policies," in *Politics in the American States: A Comparative Analysis*, 3d ed. (Boston: Little, Brown & Co., 1976), pp. 326–330.

68. Donald J. McCarty and Charles E. Ramsey, *The School Managers* (Westport, Conn.: Greenwood, 1971).

69. William L. Boyd, "The Public, the Professionals, and Educational Policy-Making."

70. A clear signal in an important training journal is Russell T. Gregg, "Political Dimensions of Educational Leadership," *Teachers College Record* 67 (1965): 118–28. Illustrative of texts' use of the concept is Morphet et al., *Educational Organization*, pp. 75–76; and Thomas J. Sergiovanni et al., *Educational Governance and Administration* (Englewood Cliffs, N.J.: Prentice-Hall, 1980), pp. 112–14.

71. John H. Bunzel, "Pressure Groups in Politics and Education," *National Elementary Principal* 43 (1964): 12–16, is typical of the political science approval, while Neal Gross, *Who Runs Our Schools?* (New York: Wiley, 1958), typifies the educational scholar's disapproval.

72. Gilbert, "Trends in Community Politics," p. 381.

73. John Walton, "The Vertical Axis of Community Organization and the Structure of Power," *Southwestern Social Science Quarterly* 48 (1967): 353–68, and Roland L. Warren, *The Community in America* (Chicago: Rand McNally, 1963).

74. The energy crunch affected most nations. See the account for the United States in James Guthrie, "The United States of America: The Educational Policy Consequences of an Economically Uncertain Future," in *Education, Recession and the World Village*, Frederick Wirt and G. Haxman-Harmon, eds. (Philadelphia: Falmer, 1986); the impact of seven other nations is analyzed in this source.

75. Jospeh M. Cronin, "Federal Takeover: Should the Junior Partner Run the Firm?" *Phi Delta Kappan* 57 (1976): 499–501.

76. William J. Grimshaw, *Union Rule in the Schools: Big City Politics in Transition* (Lexington, Mass.: Lexington Books, 1979).

77. See the possibility in James W. Guthrie and Patricia A. Craig, *Teachers and Politics* (Bloomington, Ind.: Phi Delta Kappa Educational Foundation, 1973). For evolution of teacher power, see Jack Culbertson et al., *Preparing Educational Leaders for the Seventies* (Columbus, Ohio: University Council for Educational Administration, 1969), Chap. 7.

78. William Hartman and Jon Rivenburg, "Budget Allocation Patterns," *Journal of Educational Finances* 11 (1985) 219–35; Gail Schneider, "Schools and Merit," *Planning and Changing* 15 (1984): 89–105.

79. Norton Long, *The Unwalled City* (New York: Basic Books, 1972); Frederick M. Wirt, *Power in the City: Decision Making in San Francisco* (Berkeley: University of California Press, 1974). For a set of case studies showing extramual influences on schools from government, see Mary F. Williams, ed., *Government in the Classroom: Dollars and Power in Education* (New York: The Academy of Political Science, 1978).

80. Cistone, ed., *Understanding School Boards*, pp. xii–xiv.

81. Paul Peterson, "The Politics of American Education," in *Review of Research in Education II*, Fred Kerlinger and John Carroll, eds. (Itasca, Ill.: Peacock, 1974), pp. 348–89.

82. Frederick Wirt, "The Dependent City? External Influences upon Local Autonomy," *Journal of Politics* 47 (1985): 83–112.

83. David K. Wiles, *Energy, Winter, and Schools: Crisis and Decision Theory* (Lexington, Mass.: Lexington Books, 1979).

84. These developments are treated in detail in van Geel, *Authority to Control*.

85. Alford, *Bureaucracy and Participation*.

6

The Local Conversion Process: School Boards, Politics, and the Community

A superintendent in Cleveland commits suicide over the pressures of his job, average tenure in this office everywhere declines, and principals talk up the problem of "burnout." The central office of a school system in West Virginia is dynamited over a dispute about a "humanistic" social science curriculum. Once-placid school board meetings become shouting matches over single-issue matters, most recently on whether to keep children with AIDS in school or provide birth control information. Teachers strike by the thousands late every summer, and the public criticizes them for lack of competence and lowered achievement scores. Whites leave schools when black children appear, creating a new apartheid of black inner cities and white suburbs. In many localities, the superintendent is beseiged, the board bombarded, the teacher berated. From the 1960s on, the authoritative agencies of local school government have been held in ever lower regard; a public "feeding frenzy" of attack affects even the most remote school systems.

This political turbulence that we explored in the first chapter focuses on the chief agents of public education. Elected school boards

145

and appointed professionals alike are criticized, removed from office, and are, in general, as distrusted as all institutions of American life have been in the last two decades. These views are captured in the poll data of Table 6.1, where the contrasting rankings of school problems are exhibited by the board, superintendents, and principals, on the one hand, and by the general public on the other. What is near the top of eighteen problems for school authorities is near the bottom for citizens; note the first, second, and third rankings in each column. Incidentally, the ranking of school board presidents parallels those for superintendents and principals.

These anecdotal and poll data indicate an important recent challenge to how school officials operate that is unlike the usual dry arroyo of school politics set out in the preceding chapter. To understand this turbulence, we need to know more about how the school system operated when stress arose in the environment and fastened on school governance. In the next two chapters, we will explain what the behavior of boards, superintendents, and teachers has been and how they have adapted to the crisis of their challenged authority.

We can understand these events within the systems analysis framework set out in earlier chapters. To review those concepts, through the channels and agents already described environmental demands move into the political system of the schools. Some are rejected, but others are converted into outputs—laws, ordinances, court decisions, guidelines, and so forth. This conversion process involves interaction with state and national political authorities, but it is acted out primarily among forces within the local community—the school board, superintendent, bureaucracy, teachers, voters, and so on. These contribute to what Easton terms *withinputs*: "The effect that events and conditions both within and without a system may have upon its persistence [whose study] sensitizes us to the value of looking within the system as well as the environment to find the major influences that may lead to stress."[1] This set of interactions at the local level is what concerns us in the next two chapters.

The term *withinputs* may be new, but the concept is already familiar. Scholarly interest in the internal dynamics of policymaking is not new; what is new is the broadening intellectual perspective that relates internal to external factors in that process. Our focus here will be on the formal subsystems of the school system—board, superintendent, and principals—where most conversion activity takes place on a

Table 6.1
School Board Presidents' Attitudes About Public Schools (in percentages)

	All School Board Presidents	Superintendents	General Public
What grade would you give public schools in the nation as a whole—A, B, C, D, or Fail?			
A	2%	5%	3%
B	31	66	20
C	51	25	48
D	9	1	13
Fail	2	*	3
Don't know	5	3	13
What grade would you give the public schools in your community—A, B, C, D, or Fail?			
A	23	32	9
B	56	58	31
C	18	8	34
D	1	1	10
Fail	0	*	4
Don't know	1	*	12

Base: Random survey conducted by the National Center for Education Information from November 15, 1988, to February 10, 1989, of school board presidents in 2,197 school districts, of whom 1,217 responded.

Note: *=less than 0.5 percent. Figures for superintendents are from a National Center for Education Information survey of 1,704 superintendents, 1,349 public school principals, and 524 private school principals conducted between October 20 and December 20, 1987. Figures for the general public are from a Gallup Organization poll of 2,118 adults (18 years of age and older) conducted on April 8–10, 1988, for the Phi Delta Kappa/Gallup Poll of the Public's Attitudes Toward the Public Schools.

Source: Profile of School Board Presidents in the U.S., National Center for Education Information, 1989.

day-to-day basis. As with people in any organization, their work is to routinize activity in order to rationalize objectives and economize resources. The consequence of such efforts is inherently to maximize system persistence. But such decision making also has varied consequences for different groups. A second major local force—voter influence—provides episodic inputs to the school system, as described in the preceeding chapter. The best way to think of that force is as generating a set of potential limits on school authorities—a relationship that is unclear. In this chapter, we move from the outside to inside the political system of American schools.

COMPOSITION AND HISTORY

The school board and professional educators authoritatively allocate values in creating and administering public policy for the schools. Service on the board was once an extremely low-profile, low-conflict position, but in the last two decades, board members have been thrust into the middle of all those politically turbulent issues already described. In the process their roles changed; some became champions of lay groups, but others supported professional groups. A board member now needs to know and judge issues in finance, discrimination, textbook values, teacher demands, and so on—a lengthy list of crucial and excruciating claims on school resources. Board membership has become exciting in terms of the ancient Chinese *curse* we mentioned, "May you live in exciting times."

But, whether meeting or blocking a demand, the board is not static nor are its members value free. They modify, regulate, innovate, or refuse political demands in response to a variety of value preferences. On the one hand, they are somewhat controlled in this conversion function; local groups may conflict within the system, higher system levels can constrain, and voters may disrupt. In short, board members and administrators are not "passive transmitters of things taken into the system, digesting them in some sluggish way, and sending them along as output."[2] Rather they reflect a highly personal element in the interplay of school politics. Policy output, then, partly depends on the feelings and values, failures and successes of human beings. Consequently, it is important to know something about what school board members are like.

Their social characteristics have changed little since the famous Counts survey of 1927.[3] Most are still owners, officials, and managers of businesses, or else they are professionals. Their income is well above average. Only a fraction are women, and even fewer are workers. The reforms that began over a century ago resulted in the replacement of one class—workers—by others—middle class and professionals—who had generated those reforms. Their motives are a mix of orientations to self, group, and community. As stated, however, few rarely do show much interest in higher office,[4] and rarely do any move up politically. Only as an exception does a President Jimmy Carter or Senator Richard Lugar (Rep., Ind.) launch a national career from such boards.

We cannot understand the meaning of the social qualities of this governing agency without some sense of its political function. A historical sketch will help set the framework for understanding the school board's current role.[5]

The Local Conversion Process

When public schools began, no administrators intervened between teachers and board; the board itself was an administrative body. Each member undertook responsibility for a special school task, much as the commission form of local government operates today. The growing details of the board's administrative job, which accompanied growing enrollments, and the growth expertise of the new professionals transformed the board into a legislative body. Its major function altered to set broad policy guidelines and act as watchdogs over these. Yet even that function was transformed in this century with the increased control over local schools that state and national laws and the increased power of professional administrators and teachers' unions exercised.

Prior to the mid-1960s, a description of the board's function would be something like this: School boards most often mediated major policy conflicts, leaving determination of important policy issues to the professional staff or to higher external levels if no evidence of community concern showed up—and even in mediating, they might do little. In the process, they legitimated the proposals of the professional staff—making only marginal changes—rather than represented citizens. Board members spent the bulk of their time on details but established a policy zone of consent for the administration.

Beginning in the 1960s, the board found that this picture of low conflict was disrupted, but many believe the school board still cannot do much.[6] This picture of a weakened board is partially true. Missing is an explanation of how the board usually operates in its relationship to the community and to the professionals. It must represent both; yet it must control both. A pivot between community notions of schooling and professional standards of service, the board must be seen in some larger perspective than leading an exciting, cursed life.

BOARD SUPPORT FROM THE COMMUNITY

We need an understanding of boards as small political systems, reflecting the ever-present tension in a democracy among the demands of quality, equity, efficiency, and choice. Mann's analysis indicates that we expect education to be decided by and responsive to people's choice in general but also, and simultaneously, to be technically advanced and determined by standards of quality.[7] Despite fervent wishes to the contrary, the two expectations do not always coincide. More, as Mann demonstrates, the board is caught up in an ideology of an informed citizenry participating in democratic decision making.

In fact, citizens are poorly informed on such matters and seemingly disinterested in acquiring such information; hence they participate little. But even if this is does describe citizen inattention and inactivity, this does not mean that citizens do not affect schools. For, some argue, this lack of citizen information and participation has generated a massive public loss of support for schools that is potentially devastating. Actually, the evidence can support both the pessimist and the optimist on this matter.[8] Pessimists can point to: Gallup polls that show declines in the high rating of schools, especially on the coasts and in their big cities; decreasing votes for tax and bond referenda; and evidence from other nations of criticism, disenchantment, and loss of funding for some public schools. Optimists can point to: the failure to evaluate confidence in schools or achievement records over long enough periods of time; growing funding for most schools; education's relative vote of confidence compared to other American institutions (in 1986, much better than for big business, news media, Congress, organized labor, and a bit better than for the Supreme Court); high support for maintaining or increasing current service levels by those also voting to limit taxes and expenditures; and movement of blacks into college and of more people into adult education.

One must understand the school board's role partly in terms of this system support for education as a whole. By 1980, the signals being transmitted to all boards were charges of failure, inefficiency, inequity, and the rest of the pessimist perspective. Media fastened on evidence of "failure" or "crisis" and accentuated—maybe even stimulated—this perception of breakdown. This signal did not jibe with many boards' perceptions of their problems, though.[9] Consequently, serious problems of support exist for some aspects of schools, particularly in an era when the public is far more critical about everything in public life and uninterested in looking for success in that area.

Strong evidence suggests that our schools may have done a better job with more people, compared to earlier eras and other nations.[10] But in politics what is important is what citizens *think* is reality—not reality. The 1980s has been, as the 1970s was, a period of skeptical challenge to boards and professional educators for the job they are doing. What occurred was that the usually dry arroyos of community-board linkage became flooded by protests over a disparity between expectations and reality in school services.

What are the consequences of this gap for the school board, the system's authoritative local agency? There is evidence of what Lutz and Iannaccone have termed "the dissatisfaction theory of democracy." Their study is unusual for its effort to modify theory by testing it in successive analyses in different contexts and locales.[11] It asserts that voters' dissatisfaction rises as the gap between their values and demands and those of board members and superintendent increases. In districts characterized by rapid population shifts—either expanding or contracting in size—dissatisfaction is particularly strong. Newcomers' values, expectations, and demands differ sharply from those of older residents. At some point, the dissidents become strong enough to defeat board incumbents, and a new board replaces the superintendent.

Rare in its use of longitudinal research, this study presents convincing evidence from over fifteen years of testing, leading to a strong affirmation that school boards are indeed democratic. As Lutz has argued, it depends on the question put to the system. Such an affirmation is not possible from answers to the research question, Who governs? or Do administrator actions coincide with citizen preferences?

Rather, the critical question may be, Who has access to modify the governance, under what conditions, and how?[12] If that is the critical question, it seems likely that once the public knows, it can redirect governance to meet certain conditions, one of which is to redefine the needs they want the school system to meet. It is much clearer that continued dissatisfaction with board efforts to meet these new needs produced not simply changes in board membership but also new agendas, new constituents, new resources, and in time even new structures of governance.

THE BOARD AND STATUS POLITICS

Another conceptualization of the community-board linkage stems from status differences in the former that affect the latter. If a community were homogeneous in status, board member's tasks would be simple—just consult one's own preferences, which would largely reflect the community's. Studies of small town school politics show such congruence between citizens and their boards. This also shows up in the pervasive role of the high school within the black community, where the school embodies most aspects of the latter; among whites, the school is only one aspect of institutional community life.[13]

American community life is becoming much more varied than this, so boards face competing demands arising from needs that reflect diverse community statuses. The historical record of such a process is clear, although there is debate about which groups were favored or not as a result. We already noted the shift from working class to middle class and business domination in board composition. For some scholars, this was evidence of industrialists controlling schools in order to provide a trained labor pool; for others, this was evidence of capitalists foisting education on a proletariat in order to control them. But Peterson's current historical analysis of this shift in board role demonstrates something else. The spread of professionalization in the schools was actually encouraged by trade unions; it attracted the middle class to the schools; and at least in the case of three major regional cities, it was welcomed, not resisted, by the middle class.[14] In the past, this status context underlay the control of schools in our cities. Reformers focused on changing the structures of power, for these are never value free but rather dispense varying rewards to different groups. Certainly this was what the business groups who supported such reform believed.[15]

In the contemporary period, this status orientation to understanding school conflict undergirds the work of Minar and Boyd, among others.[16] The role behaviors of superintendents differ in working-class, as opposed to middle-class, suburbs and are associated with different political turbulence. With qualifications, findings show that before the 1970s higher-status districts had fewer political conflicts (that is, votes for losing candidates), lower electoral participation in board elections, and less challenge to superintendents' administrative decisions than did lower-status districts. Associated with these differences were dissimilar cultural norms about citizen involvement with schools and school professionals. A similar tie in between status and school politics was found in a national sample of districts analyzed in the late 1960s.[17] A strong correlation showed between high interest-group activity among districts within the metropolis (a heterogeneous set), but much lower interest-group intensity in districts outside the metropolis.

Set in less turbulent days than described in the Introduction, these findings were qualified by later events. Thus, when an issue becomes significant to the traditionally low-conflict, higher-status community, its members can actively challenge boards and school professionals. This has been the case in Northern cities in the matter of desegregation, where higher-status elements became just as vocal as South Boston working-class citizens.[18] Both status groups were protecting their social neighborhoods, on racial grounds in this case, although it could have been for other matters such as freeways, low-income housing, or heavy-industry location.[19]

Further, some evidence suggests that the status of the district affects the "board culture" of that school.[20] Homogeneous districts develop a board style of "elite" councils—small in size, seeing themselves as guardians of the public but separate from it, making decisions privately, consensually, and in limited range, and exhibiting administrative, judicial, and legislative functions. On the other hand, "arena" councils exhibit the opposite qualities, many of which reflect a heterogeneous community. This elite cultural system has usually prevailed, modifying inputs from different ethnic, religious, and status groups so as to subordinate them.

The Special Stimulus of Consolidation

Consolidation is a factor that has increased not only the volume but also the conflict of status demands on boards enormously. What was once an archipelago of districts in America, each island homogeneous with board and community in harmony, has been fused into larger, more varied districts. The 89,000 districts of 1948 became 55,000 five years later, 31,000 by 1961, and 14,000 by 1987. During the 1970s, on any given day, three districts disappeared forever between breakfast and dinner. But earlier in the 1960s, that many had evaporated between breakfast and the morning coffee break, with another seven gone by dinner.[21] Not only are there now more diverse values and status bases confronting board members, but there are also fewer board members to handle this increased input. By the early 1970s, as Guthrie calculated, "Where a school board member once represented about 200 people, today each . . . must speak for approximately 3,000 constituents."[22]

This problem in accommodating increasingly diverse views under-lies the Lutz-Iannaccone dissatisfaction theory of democracy noted earlier. Evidence of this mixing of districts is suggested by the finding that a greater rate of interest groups is coming to board attention in metropolitan areas and a lesser rate in nonmetropolitan districts.[23] We will return to this shortly.

The Mosaic of Status Politics

No consensus about what the board's link is to the community appears from the preceding mainly because the literature spans different periods and issues. However, the view that a board's open-ness to its community is a variable does emerge. That is, the linkage should be different under conditions of low versus high community dissent over school policies. We could expect, and a national sample study validates,[24] that when little conflict exists, boards are less receptive to community input. When more intense community con-flict exists, however, the board becomes more receptive to challenging established policies. This linkage appeared in four possible styles of board politics, illustrated in Table 6.2.

Like all typologies, this is a still life that covers many communities, but it hints at a dynamic process. That is, the four board styles shown

Table 6.2
Styles of School Board Politics

Numbers in Conflict

Skills of Opposition	High	Low
High	I. Reform ideal of citizen democracy	II. Challenge by takeover group
Low	III. All-out battle	IV. Continuity under traditional ruling group

Source: Leigh Stelzer, "Institutionalizing Conflict Response: The Case of Schoolboards," *Social Science Quarterly* 55 (1974), reprinted in *The Polity of the School*, Frederick Wirt, ed. (Lexington, Mass.: Lexington Books, D.C. Heath and Company. Copyright, 1975, D.C. Heath and Company), p. 81. Reprinted by permission of the publishers.

represent different stages of the Lutz-Iannaccone model of longitudinal school conflict. Both typology and model have their respective uses, but the more dynamic model is capable of generating more powerful hypotheses. However, a proposition about school politics that should not be overlooked exists in both constructs. That is, boards do not merely transmit what the community says, for often it says very little; nor do boards dictatorially block off any signals not on their wave lengths. Rather, when issues heat up the local environment, considerable evidence shows that boards become much more receptive to citizen inputs and more willing to oppose the traditional direction of school policy. There is a particularly political quality to this response of school boards, best caught in the aphorism of V. O. Key: "Public opinion is that opinion which politicians find it prudent to pay attention to." In this and other respects, board members are true politicians.

THE BOARD AS A DECISION-MAKING AGENCY

A question that is analytically separate from the role of community inputs is how boards make decisions, although the two merge in reality. Several older models of this process were characterized by their naivete. One was that the school board necessarily reflected the social composition of its members. As we have just seen, that does not work as an explanation of who governs and, as we will soon see, it does not answer the further question, How does it govern? Another naive model was found in education administration literature for a long time. This described the board as the maker of school policy and the superintendent as the administrator of that policy, with a clear separation of function. Empirically, that has not been the case, for the two stimulate and affect each other. Thus, when Wirt and Christovich recently asked a national sample of superintendents to indicate whether their policy involvement had recently become greater or lesser, two-thirds answered that it was greater, and one-half reported that their professional judgments were increasingly accepted by their boards. Similar results were found for city managers and planning directors.[25]

Multiple Currents of Decision Making

Another, more sophisticated way of viewing board decision making is to see it as different processes for different kinds of issues. In Figure 6.1, we see that any naive model of decision making is confounded by a more varied reality. In the null response model, we are looking at what happens to most environmental demands made upon a political agency—the agency does not respond. The blocked arrow symbolizes this process, and extensive evidence validates this model. Thus only a small fraction of proposed bills ever become laws in legislatures at any level of American government, and only a fraction of appellate court appeals are ever accepted for hearing and decision. As for the school board, its time is primarily spent elsewhere, as noted below.

Under special conditions, the negotiated model of Figure 6.1 describes other board decision making. The several arrows here indicate the flow of competing demands into the political system over an emerging issue; in time these become narrowed as alternatives are formulated and a decision is authorized in the form of board policy (output). Here, the board member's role is that of negotiator among competing community groups, "working out things" over time, seeking compromises that create a coalition majority. Such action, though, is episodic, an occasional pressured decision making rather than a regular agenda.

Figure 6.1
Models of Decision Making in a Political System

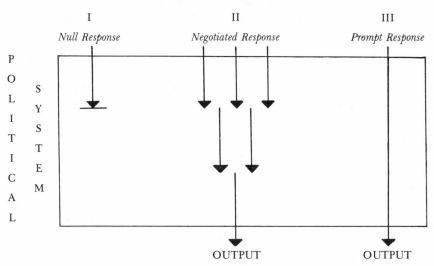

The third model, prompt response, moves us to two quite different occasions when the political system responds that way to community demands. One of these occasions occurs during a *crisis*, a sudden combination of threats either to the school system or its constituents. The crisis might arise from physical causes—buildings burned, flooded, or blown away—or from social causes that generate conflict over values the schools serve and the resources they distribute. A crisis has a curious quality in that most political actors must agree that a crisis exists or else the third model does not describe what happens. The danger must be clear to those helped or those helping, and the remedy must be relatively simple, understood, and accepted by all. If not, then some group or board member will question the necessity of taking fast action. Much of the conflict in local school politics arises from some claims that a "crisis" exists while opponents deny it and then redefine the situation in terms that agree with their own interests.

There is a second and quite different aspect to the prompt response model that involves *routines*. These include filling in the details of major policy decisions and are found in reports received and acted on, procedures for implementing a given policy, budgetary support for accepted programs, and so on. The unusual aspect of this context is that there are so many outputs of this kind. Indeed, much political decision making, including board actions, consists of routines as measured by the volume of personnel, funds, paperwork, and so forth issuing from a political agency. A 1964 study of board members found that they spent over 80 percent of their time on managerial details, not on deciding broad issues of general importance, but we have no current data.[26]

As noted earlier, in every typology a longitudinal model is crying to get out, and so it is with Figure 6.1. If these three models are seen as a sequence, they form a rough chronology of policy evolution. That is, many demands begin as the unthinkable of the first model, supported by only a few "crackpots" and ignored by the political system. An illustration would be blacks seeking equal resources for their segregated schools decades ago in the South. Then, later, the second model starts to work. New combinations of societal events generate more support for the now "reasonable" idea so that its opponents must exert large energies to block it; over time, however, opposing sides move toward resolutions that yield a new output. For example, under Supreme Court threat Southern school systems first moved to deny discrimination, then to equalize resources for black education without desegregating, and then reluctantly and under pressure to accommodate external pressures by desegregating. A nationwide example is the pattern of invasion of city folk into rural areas where they succeeded in developing new suburban school systems after World War II.[27] Given enough time, resolution of conflict results in opinion closure, in which what was unthinkable is now conventional, so that schools in the South and suburbia show few signs of formerly raging conflicts. At this stage, the third model dominates decision making—routines.

RATIONAL AND OTHER DECISION MAKING

Another conceptual framework exists for analyzing the decision making of school boards; this focuses on the degree to which officials use "rational" versus other methods of arriving at decisions.[28] During the 1970s, this became a major inquiry about public policy, but only

Table 6.3
Models of School Board Decision Making

Pluralist

Theme: Decisions are the result of a contest among groups lacking much common interests.

1. *Pluralist:* decision the result of a contest among board members representing narrow-purpose groups and designed to defend and enhance as many group interests as possible, for example, budgetary contests among curriculum interests.

2. *Ideological:* decision the result of a contest among board members representing broad-purpose groups designed to defend and enhance interests of a class or a race, for example, affirmative action policy on teacher promotions or principal appointments.

Unitary

Theme: Decisions are the result of interactions among groups that share some qualities which presume an overreaching unity among them.

1. *Organizational:* decision the result of board members motivated by desires to promote objectives of the school organization, for example, maintenance of professional standards against challenges by laypersons.

2. *Rational:* decision the result of board members agreed on a set of educational objectives, which are referred to in decisional debate and which are consistent with the decision itself.

Source: Abstracted from Paul E. Peterson, *School Politics Chicago Style* (Chicago: University of Chicago Press, 1976).

one scholarly study of school boards has been done from this analytical base.

Peterson's powerful analysis of three major decisions by the Chicago school board over several decades uses alternative perspectives, set out in Table 6.3. Depending on the issue, decision making could take the form of bargaining among members. This could be of two kinds, protecting or promoting relatively narrow organizational or electoral interests ("pluralist bargaining") or involving broader interests rooted in protection of race, class, or a regime ("ideological bargaining"). Alternatively, decision making could take different forms within a policymaking body with a presumed unity, that is, a "unitary" model, as found in organizational theory or in assuming rationality in decision making. In this last, Peterson made a highly useful adaptation to an intense debate over the possibility of "rational" policy. He modified the definition of rationality to be more realistic. That is, it meant that "board members agreed on certain objectives, that reference to these objectives was made during the course of policymaking, and that policy outcomes were consistent with these objectives."[29] Prior to this, any discussion of rationality was so bounded by unrealistic empirical requirements that no decision could be termed rational; yet thousands of board members thought they were, in fact, acting rationally.

Such models of decision making provide alternative perspectives of a complex process without dictating which is "correct."[30] They also provide the means for testing competing causal theories. Such variety, laid across preceding typologies of board actions provides a rich pool of analytical constructs to research amid the mosaic of school boards.

School Boards and Education Reform

Why is there more concern about the effectiveness of school boards at this time in our history? One major reason is the lack of attention to school boards in virtually all the major national and state reports on education from 1983–86. For example, rather than not discussing school boards, the reform reports could have said that the school board is the crucial agent for school improvement and that state reforms should be directed at strengthening the local school board's capacity to bring about and monitor change. Instead, the unstated implication of many reports is that school boards are part of the problem and have not exercised leadership and their authority to improve education.[31] This message further implies that boards need to be circumvented, if not through direct state regulation, then certainly through vastly increased state prescriptions and monitoring. Many state reformers felt that the school board agenda, as they understood it, did not match state policy priorities. That is, mismatched priorities exist in curriculum content, years required in academic subjects in high school, review of student academic standards, teacher evaluation, and standardized rigorous testing of students' advancement through elementary and secondary schooling.

This suspicion about the inability of school boards to provide academic leadership was exacerbated by the predominant research emphasis of these reports, which was on effective schools (in contrast to effective school districts).[32] It was the school site that was the crucial focus for improvement, and the principal was the key catalyst. Where did school board stimulus and assistance fit into this view? The answer was unclear and vague compared to the checklists and criteria for effective schools. This relative lack of emphasis in the reports on school district policies is surprising, given the findings from research on successful school improvement.[33]

Thus, an apparent paradox characterizes the education reform movement. On the one hand, reformers have felt free or obliged to circumvent local boards; on the other hand, reformers focus on improvement at the school site that is governed by a school board. To this point, local school boards in most states have seemed to be either ignored or cast in a passive role as weak reactors or even deterrents, rather than as partners in shaping educational improvement. Many school boards contend, however, that they initiated and enacted most of the reforms in local districts prior to state action.

SCHOOL BOARD EFFECTIVENESS

Where does the school board stand in the public's view of education? In 1986 the Institute of Educational Leadership conducted surveys and case studies in eight metropolitan areas across the United States to answer this question.[34] Surveys were sent to each school board president within a metropolitan area, and one district was used for a case study. Additional surveys were sent to a sample of rural districts.

The Public Judges Its Boards

The study found strong support among the public for maintaining the basic institutional role and structure of school boards. The public saw school boards as the governance mechanism to keep schools close to the people and to avoid excessive control by professional educators or state authorities. But a basic paradox exists here, too. This support of the concept is coupled with widespread public ignorance of boards' role and functions. Deep public apathy and indifference are common, as reflected in difficulties with attracting quality candidates to serve

on boards, or the tiny turnout for board elections in many communities. This civic ignorance bodes even greater trouble for the future
when student populations become more diverse and creative leadership more needed.

The apathy and ignorance about school boards is made worse by
another finding. Local boards and board members interact with
general government only occasionally and seem to be isolated (in
boards' and civic leaders' perceptions) from mainstream community
political structures. Very little systematic communication takes place
between school boards and general government, despite the fact that
ever more students have learning problems associated with nonschool
factors such as poor housing, lack of family support and resources,
and drug dependencies. When such interaction does exist on a regular
basis, it often is only through the superintendent. Fiscally dependent
boards that must interact with municipal governments are frequently
mired in adversarial relationships. Some urban community leaders
believe it may be time to rethink the nonpartisan nature of school
board elections (the majority of boards in the United States are
nonpartisan) and to operate board elections through mainstream
political party structures.

The public seems to have different expectations, because the political behavior, degree of sophistication, and level of general learning
school board members have stood in contrast to other political
officeholders. This is a complex phenomenon that expresses itself in a
variety of ways, from statements that "these people aren't real leaders" to state legislative mandates for school board "training." Imagine a state legislature mandating training for city council members or
for state legislators. Such altered expectations may stem from the fact
that at some level in the public's mind there is a mystique about
education.

Differences in Boards and Communities

Differences among various types of communities exist in their views
of board leadership capacity and whether "real" leaders serve on
boards. In suburban communities that are middle to upper-middle
class, board membership is sought more frequently by persons perceived as traditional community leaders—professionals, business
leaders, ministers, or wives of any of the former, League of Women
Voters members, and so on. In large urban communities, boards deal

with enormous diversity, majority-minority school enrollments, highly politicized and thus volatile educational issues, and loss of the middle class in the schools. Their boards suffer most from negative community perceptions about the quality of individual members and leadership. To some extent these perceptions are unfortunately based on the reality of less-than statesmanlike behavior by some board members that influences the board's leadership capacity.

These perceptions arise because many members of urban boards are apt to come from, and to have been leaders in, distinct areas of the community or are concerned with single issues. Frequently, these members are more tied to specific constituencies to which they owe their election or appointment. Such "new leaders" have not achieved recognition or acceptance, as have other leaders from the spectrum of traditional community leadership and power structures. On the other hand, the Institute of Educational Leadership (IEL) found that school boards, particularly urban ones, are more representative of the diversity of their communities and often include leaders from different constituencies. In several districts, this was due to board elections from separate electoral districts, with only a minority of board members being elected districtwide.

A corollary to the above finding is the increasing perception that the number of board members who represent special interests or particular ideological positions is growing. This finding cuts across types of communities, but again is strongly related to communities with volatile political and social issues and to communities in transition, for example, from suburb to aging, urbanized to suburb, and so on. Board members, educators, and the various publics in these places believe that divisiveness and building a board from disparate members—many with single constituencies or issues—are major factors shaping effectiveness and community perceptions of its leadership. The IEL study observed that the trusteeship notion of service, in which board members represent the entire community and govern the school system through consensus about priorities, has been less prominent recently.

Board Members View Their Problems

Data from the study survey and the case studies also support the finding that more commonalities than differences challenge the effectiveness of these boards in all locations. These issues include:

Lack of public understanding of the role of boards.

Poor relationships with state policymakers.

Improving teaching in the framework of collective bargaining.

Amount of time boards invest in their work versus satisfaction with accomplishments and ability to determine their own priorities.

Board members report they do not spend enough time on any important issue.

Problems in becoming a board rather than a collection of individuals.

Need for board strategies and a framework to assess and communicate board effectiveness.

Boards are perceived (and see themselves) as operating, in the main, on the basis of administrative or individual members' agendas and behaving in a reactive rather than deliberative and action-oriented way. One aspect of the school board's leadership for education is the continuing challenge of sorting the gray areas between its policymaking and leadership roles from the superintendent's administrative role. Sorting these areas affects not only the management of the system and relations with staff below the superintendent, but it also affects the question of who is the leader for education in the community. In districts where board-superintendent relationships are good and processes exist for dealing with natural tensions in the gray areas, little attention is paid to this dichotomy. For some school boards, though, particularly larger heterogeneous districts, lay governance and administrative relationships degenerate into a "we-they" situation. In many such districts, a school board has its own staff responsible only to the board in order to buttress its political and substantive role on the issues.

Two additional major findings from the study are not surprising, given all the above. Sixty percent of boards in the IEL sample do not assess their own performance and so are frustrated in assessing their effectiveness and in communicating this to the public and the school system. Only one-third of the boards had any process for "evaluating" itself. Further, although the need for school board development to improve effectiveness is generally recognized, activities and strategies by board members directed toward this goal are generally episodic and usually consist only of briefings on current events, rather than such real skill-building exercises as budget analysis. Board members generally agreed they lacked preparation for board service.

Many felt totally unprepared for their new responsibilities and had little experience in building the consensus leadership needed for effective policymaking. The study clearly revealed that far too little attention is given to developing working relationships among board members and to developing boards as corporate governing bodies.

Bigfoot: The Weight of State Policy Initiatives

Board members are worried about growing state intrusiveness as the reform movement evolves. Their concerns are not just about who controls but also reflect uneasiness about the boards' ability to respond to their very real local needs and to differences within local goals and expectations. A very different element faces boards today, and dangers do attend aggressive, broad-based, state education policy. States change policy through statutes and regulations, which have a standardizing effect. Also, the new focus of state policymaking is aimed at the core of instructional policy—not at categorical groups. In several states, school board members complained that state mandates help improve low-quality districts but are not helpful, and may even be deleterious, to the better districts.

The assertion that stronger state government results in weaker school boards is questionable, though. New state activities do reduce local autonomy and create interrelationships that constrain independent action. But power and autonomy are not the same. New state initiatives also often create more local school board influence because there are more issues to decide and programs to be influenced locally. State initiatives provide added forums for bargaining, added resources, and a broader scope of local activity. School boards, for example, are now much more involved in curriculum policy in California following state reforms. Yet board members view most state initiatives as a zero-sum game. State reforms may be viewed as adding to local authority's influence, but many board members view them as depleting that influence. This additive versus depletive view of external power echoes the "sand box" and "shopping mall" model of community power discussed in Chapter 5.

These overall trends in state policy show up clearly in the IEL field study and questionnaire. A growing sense of alarm among local school boards about state intrusion was expressed. For example, 85 percent of local boards responded that they believe their state is becoming more directive overall. When asked if their boards in the last two years have devoted time on their agendas to education reform issues, 55 percent responded that they had. Forty percent or more listed these issues: increased graduation requirements, revised curricula, teacher evaluation/competency testing, and student testing. Asked if the national reform movement has encouraged the board or community to initiate change, 44 percent had. A majority reported that the state is becoming more directive and creates more local board agenda items.

Despite wide historical differences in state control traditions among the areas of the study, state influence is growing in each. Every school board is concerned about it, even though recognizing some substantial benefits (e.g., more money and public support for quality in education). Increased state influence is evident in terms of new policy areas (e.g., curriculum and teacher evaluation). Nevertheless, every one of the states in the IEL sample drastically increased the scope and intensity of mandated testing.

What can be said about all this? First, it is part of a long-term trend. So far, the trend has not "crippled" local school boards, but in California and Texas, for example, board ability to respond to local conditions has deteriorated. Also, the trend has produced many major agenda items—and more paperwork. Local boards cannot take the policy initiatives they could take twenty years ago. Moreover, state policy is not significantly determined by local school board considerations. State policymakers perceive school board associations as defensive and reactive to recent state initiatives, rather than as actors in setting the state agenda.

State school board associations (particularly in the smaller states) are reconsidering their capacity for state policy leadership. These associations in states with several million people often have only an executive secretary, an assistant, and a secretary. This provides some capacity for reactive lobbying but not the ability to be proactive. Moreover, they are dominated by smaller districts simply because many more small districts exist in any state. This can result in a certain inattentiveness to the issues of the urban districts, where the vast majority of schoolchildren reside. These are the districts whose educational deficiencies and politically volatile school district governance have generated much of the steam for the state reform engine.

In sum, the IEL analysis of school boards highlights the changing balance of control between state and local authorities. What *should* the proper balance be? We now turn to this issue.

Justifications for a Strong Local Policy Role

Why should the local role in education policy be maintained and even strengthened in certain states where it has declined precipitously? Coombs gives a vigorous explanation:[35]

1. Public opinion still supports more local influence and less influence for higher governments.
2. Local school politics tend to be more democratic in several important ways than are decisions made at higher levels.
3. While there will be tension between state and local policymakers, the result is policy that is better adapted to diverse local contexts.
4. Further erosion of the local role risks diminishing public support for the public schools.

In support of the first point, Coombs cites in Table 6.4 relevant 1986 Gallup poll data:

Table 6.4
Public Views About Who Should Control Schools

Should have:	Federal Government	State Government	Local School Board
More influence	26%	45%	57%
Less influence	53	32	17
Same as now	12	16	17
Don't know	9	7	9
	100%	100%	100%

Source: Gallup Poll, 1986.

The biggest loser in this public referendum is the federal government, but note that local school board influence is preferred much more often than state government. Attitudes on the property tax and local control are also important to understand. Other data in the 1986 Gallup poll suggest that the public is no less reluctant to increase local property taxes than any other broad-based taxes. Public dissatisfaction with the property tax peaked in the late 1970s and has now dissipated. Odden analyzed the dramatic 25 percent real increase in spending for education from 1983 to 1986 and concluded that one "secret" of education reform funding has been the significant role played by the property tax.

> The big news at the local level is this large overall [property tax] increase that nationwide nearly matches the rise in state revenues and actually exceeds big state rises in several reform states, such as Florida, Texas, and Virginia, where the state rise has received national attention. Despite national swings in sources of funding for schools, the property tax remains a robust revenue provider, even in the education reform era.[36]

Advantages of Local School Policymaking

Numerous and conflicting positions express how well school politics meets the democratic ideal. The issue here is whether school politics is more democratic than control by federal or state authorities. Most citizens have a greater opportunity and chance of policy influence in their local district than they do with policymakers or administrators at the federal or state level. Local school policymakers serve fewer constituents than state officials and are much closer both geographically and psychologically. After all, it is longer and harder to get to the state capital.

Local board elections also provide a much more direct means to influence local policymakers than through a state legislator representing many areas. In the nation's thousands of small school districts, a significant proportion of the community knows at least one board member. Local media provide better information on education and can capture the citizen attention more effectively than reports from a distant state capital. All of this is not meant to claim that local school politics approaches the democratic ideal. Indeed, a Gallup poll revealed that 36 percent of a national sample of citizens knew "very little" or "nothing" about their local public schools.[37] But local school officials can better anticipate the zone of tolerance that local school constituencies permit than state policymakers.

Most states are too large and diverse for uniform policies to be effective in all areas. As Coombs puts it, in policy area after area, there exists "nested policy in which the states provide the general contours

and the local districts fill in with more specified policies."[38] This
condition creates a "functional tension" that tends to provide more
appropriate and adaptable policies than statewide specification.
There are large areas, however, like civil rights and equal opportunity, where local flexibility must be restricted. Yet most states, for
example, prescribe teacher certification requirements but leave hiring
and compensation issues to local districts.

The final argument for enhancing local discretion is based on the
linkage between political efficacy and public support of schools—
citizens will participate in politics more if they believe that they can
have an impact on policies. The local level offers the best opportunity
for efficacy; therefore, a lessening in local efficacy will lead to less
overall citizen participation in education policy. As Coombs stresses,

> a person is more likely to communicate his or her policy preference to officials
> when he or she perceives the probable impact of the communication on policy to
> be high . . . [If] local government decision making enhances citizen participation
> in school politics, it follows that citizen confidence in, and support of, the public
> school system are apt to be strengthened as well.[39]

The reasoning here is that people's satisfaction with the results of
collective decisions will be greater if they have taken part in making
those decisions. Consequently, less local control leads to more citizen
dissatisfaction. In California, for example, local parents are told that
the school board is too constrained to remedy their grievances. The
citizen is referred to a state office or in some cases a court order. This
kind of inaction could lead to alienation from the local public school.

Increasing Local Influence by Institutional Choice

How can one evaluate the arguments that Coombs has advanced
favoring redistributing power from higher levels to lower levels? One
useful concept called "institutional choice," focuses on the crucial
policy decision of which institution should be the decision maker. For
example, courts have been reluctant to delegate civil rights protection
to the institution of local school districts in Mississippi. Another type
of institutional choice is whether to place various functions in the
hands of markets (e.g., vouchers) or politics (e.g., school board
elections). The recent state reform movement has included an institutional choice to enhance the curricular and testing role of state
government.

Clune stresses that two general characteristics of available institutions are important: agreement on substantive goals and the capacity to achieve those goals. Substantive goals are crucial because of the need to insure support for a policy. Courts may be more supportive of civil rights than school boards, but its support must be buttressed by capacity. Courts cannot run school districts. So which institution should be chosen? A method for choosing can be called "comparative institutional advantage," which begins with distrust or criticism of a particular institution.

> Since no decision maker is perfect, the distrust directed at one decision maker must be carefully weighed against the advantages of that decision maker and both the advantages and disadvantages of alternative decision makers. In other words, although the logic of institutional choice typically begins with distrust, distrust itself proves nothing in the absence of a superior alternative. . . . The logic of comparative institutional advantage also implies the futility of seeking perfect or ideal implementation of a policy. . . . The real world offers a "least worst choice" of imperfect institutions.[40]

A problem with institutional choice analysis is the tendency to confuse predictive with normative applications. In education, predictive statements about outcomes from institutional choice are often unclear. For example, how much state control of curriculum will lead to how much decline in teacher professionalism? Or how does client control through vouchers lead to increased learning? The *rate* of substitution is equally unclear in terms of at what point will increased federal influence in education lead to a decline in the state role. It is possible to avoid zero-sum properties through various "win-win" scenarios, such as a state standardized curriculum that helps teachers communicate higher-order thinking and does not interfere with teacher professionalism or autonomy. In sum, institutional choice is complex, uncertain, and subject to continual political change. The balance of control in education will never be settled by scientific decision rules but is rather part of a series of evolving political bargains.

State Reforms and Local Organization: New Questions

Following the rush in the early 1980s to state reforms in schooling, in the late 1980s a revisionist research began appearing that raises questions about these reforms. Employing different data sets and methods, scholars by 1992 were questioning whether these reforms could actually be counterproductive.

Was state reform adopted with too little consultation involving educational professionals and with inadequate attention to research lessons?[41] The lack of consultation meant that state laws were designed to be administered effectively by professionals who had little input in their creation. Ignoring research lessons meant that the reforms rested on propositions about causal effects that might not work as presumed.

Does local autonomy itself affect the school's most important job—student achievement?[42] This question has rarely been pursued, but recently Chubb directed a Brookings Institution study that found such effects did indeed exist.[43] Studying over twenty-five thousand students in about one thousand public and private high schools—plus surveying principals and teachers in a sample of half these schools—Chubb measured the influence of different elements of school context and organization on school effectiveness. He concluded that in a four-year secondary program, the more effectively organized school (one element of which was local autonomy) was "worth at least a full year of additional achievement over attendance at an ineffectively organized school, all things being equal. Among other possible explanations, only student aptitude had a larger impact on learning than school organization."[44]

The influence of administrative superiors over schools was central to this connection. That is, the more problems that public schools had (student behavior, parental apathy), the more that outside authorities imposed remedial policies (requirements, monitoring). But then, this restriction of local autonomy would weaken effectiveness and hence student performance, thus kicking off another round of increased control. Required to comply, boards and administrators may respond by providing only procedural compliance and symbolic reform.

It is this warning of counterproductivity that is central to these scholars' recent review of reform efforts. Reformers respond to different values in the educational world—quality, choice, efficiency. They then urge a variety of programs to achieve these values—voucher plans, school site-based budgeting. However, another value—equity—is rarely addressed in this decade, either by reformers or their critics. As we saw in earlier chapters, an inherent tension exists among these four values that produces priority cycles.

The preceding sections point up the complexity of the seemingly simple proposition of local control of schooling. Values and actions on the local scene reflect the influence of diversity that affects all aspects of the political system and its policy outputs. As system and policy grow ever more complex, local control becomes less and less a real description. But in this change, much may have been lost for the citizen's role in democracy.

NOTES

1. David Easton, *A Framework for Political Analysis* (Englewood Cliffs, N.J.: Prentice-Hall, 1965), p. 114.
2. Ibid., pp. 132–33.
3. George S. Counts, *School and Society in Chicago* (New York: Harcourt, Brace, 1928).
4. L. Harmon Zeigler and M. Kent Jennings, *Governing American Schools* (North Scituate, Mass.: Duxbury, 1974), pp. 39–42. A similar finding exists for municipal councils.
5. For a review of this agency's functions, past and present, see Peter J. Cistone, ed., *Understanding School Boards* (Lexington, Mass.: Lexington Books, 1975).
6. Robert Bendiner, *The Politics of Schools* (New York: Harper & Row, 1969), p. 165.
7. Dale Mann, "Public Understanding and Education Decision-Making," *Educational Administration Quarterly* 10, no. 2 (1974): 1–18.
8. Michael W. Kirst, "Loss of Support for Public Secondary Schools: Some Causes and Solutions," *Daedalus* (September 1981), assembles the contrary evidence noted below.
9. For the poll data from both sources, see ibid.
10. See the evidence in Frederick M. Wirt, "Neoconservatism and National School Policy," *Educational Evaluation and Policy Analysis* 2, no. 6 (1980): 5–18, and Diane Ravitch, *The Revisionists Revised* (New York: Basic Books, 1978).
11. Frank W. Lutz and Laurence Iannaccone, eds., *Public Participation in Local School Districts* (Lexington, Mass.: Lexington Books, 1978).
12. Frank W. Lutz, "Methods and Conceptualizations of Political Power in Education," in *The Politics of Education*, 76th Yearbook of the National Society for the Study of Education (Chicago: University of Chicago Press, 1977), p. 32.
13. Frederick A. Rodgers, *The Black High School and Its Community* (Lexington, Mass.: Lexington Books, 1975).
14. Paul Peterson, "Urban Politics and Changing Schools: A Competitive View," and David W. Plank and Paul Peterson, "Does Urban Reform Imply Class Conflict?

The Case of Atlanta's Schools" (Papers under National Institute of Education contract, 1980).

15. Raymond E. Callahan, *Education and the Cult of Efficiency* (Chicago: University of Chicago Press, 1962).

16. David W. Minar, "The Community Basis of Conflict in School System Politics," *American Sociological Review* 31 (1966): 822–34; William L. Boyd, *Community Status and Conflict in Suburban School Politics*, (Beverly Hills, Calif.: Sage, 1975), and "Educational Policy-Making in Declining Suburban School Districts" (paper presented to the American Educational Research Association convention, 1978).

17. Zeigler and Jennings, *Governing American Schools*, Chap. 6.

18. Christine Rossell, "School Desegregation and Community Social Change," *Law and Contemporary Problems* 42 (1978): 133–83.

19. Emmett H. Buell, Jr., *School Desegregation and Defended Neighborhoods: The Boston Controversy* (Lexington, Mass.: Lexington Books, 1981).

20. Boyd, *Community Status.*

21. Carol Mullins, "School District Consolidation: Odds Are 2–1 It'll Get You," *American School Board Journal* 11 (1973): 160.

22. James W. Guthrie, "Public Control of Public Schools," *Public Affairs Report* (Berkeley: University of California, Institute of Governmental Studies, 1974), p. 2.

23. See note 17.

24. Leigh Stelzer, "Institutionalizing Conflict Response: The Case of Schoolboards," *Social Science Quarterly* 55, no. 2 (1974).

25. Frederick Wirt and Leslie Christovich, "Administrators' Perceptions of Changing Power Contexts: Superintendents and City Managers," *Education Administration Quarterly* (1989 forthcoming).

26. Keith Goldhammer, *The School Board* (New York: Center for Applied Research, 1964).

27. Frederick M. Wirt et al., *On the City's Rim: Politics and Policy in Suburbia* (Lexington, Mass.: Heath, 1972), pp. 161–66.

28. For an introduction to these concepts in an educational context, see Dale Mann, *Policy Decision-Making in Education* (New York: Teachers College Press, 1975).

29. Paul E. Peterson, *School Politics Chicago Style* (Chicago: University of Chicago Press, 1976), pp. 134–35.

30. William L. Boyd, "The Public, the Professionals, and Educational Policy-Making: Who Governs?" *Teachers College Record* 77 (1976): 556–58.

31. Jacqueline Danzberger et al., *Improving Grass Roots Leadership* (Washington, D.C.: Institute for Educational Leadership), p. iv.

32. Ibid., pp. 37–41.

33. Allan Odden and Beverly Anderson, "How Successful State Education Improvement Works," *Phi Delta Kappan* (April 1986): 582–585.

34. The remainder of this section is adapted from Lila Carol et al., "School Boards: The Forgotten Players on the Education Team," *Phi Delta Kappan* (September 1987): 53–59.

35. Fred S. Coombs, "The Effects of Increased State Control on Local School District Governance" (paper presented to the annual meeting of the American Educational Research Association, Washington, D.C., 1987).

36. Allan Odden, "The Economics of Financing Education Excellence" (paper presented to the annual meeting of American Educational Research Association, Washington, D.C.).

37. George H. Gallup, "18th Annual Gallup Poll of the Public's Attitudes Toward the Public Schools," *Phi Delta Kappan* (September 1986): 51.

38. Coombs, "Increased State Control," p. 15.

39. Ibid., p. 17.

40. William H. Clune, "Institutional Choice as a Theoretical Framework for Research on Educational Policy," Center for Policy Research in Education (Newark, N.J.: Rutgers University, 1987), p. 4.

41. William Chance, *The Best of Education* (Chicago: McArthur Foundation, 1986).

42. Coombs, "Increased State Control."

43. John Chubb, "The Dilemma of Public School Improvement" (Paper presented to the Spoor Dialogues on Leadership Program at Dartmouth College, 1987). An enlarged version of this study, with supporting data and analysis, is found in John Chubb and Terry Moe, *Politics, Markets and School Performance* (Washington, D.C.: Brookings Institution, 1988).

44. Chubb, "The Dilemma," p. 15.

7

The Local Conversion Process: Superintendents, Administrators, and Teachers

THE DECISIONAL CONTEXT

Within the decisional system of schools, the superintendents and principals provide professional leadership and advice to the school board, while also managing the personnel and resources that allow instruction to proceed. In reality, leadership and management are not separate activities, although they can be separated analytically. In this chapter we explore the role of these leaders in local decision making as part of the withinputs of the school's political system.

The Professional as Decision Maker

If the community is only occasionally active and the board has strong limitations, school professionals should retain a greater influence on policy issues. Professional educators have their resources, too. They define choices, produce research, provide specific recommendations, and shape the formal agenda. Using these resources, professionals generate pressures and information that can affect, if not

175

determine, the board's deliberations and decisions. In Easton's framework, the school superintendent and staff provide withinputs to the school board and the bureaucracy. Many specific policy issues, however, may never reach the school board if the superintendent and staff act under broad discretion from the school board. Consequently, both board and superintendent are authorities seeking to gain support from the community through the use of appropriate outputs in the form of budget, curriculum, teacher selection, and so on.

The professional staff does operate under certain constraints, however. They must anticipate reactions of board members to their actions because the board does have the basic power to fire them.[1] They also know that the ultimate power of a provoked electorate is to remove them by changing the board, as noted earlier. It is also likely that the superintendent would act in keeping with the school board's wishes on many issues even *without* the threat of job loss. It is natural to assume that board members would hire a person whose values were similar to their own. An example of this is the low rate of turnover in smaller districts, which tend to be more homogeneous in their values.[2] In effect, the board's impact on specific decisions may be more indirect than direct, but it is nevertheless real. The superintendent operates with considerable latitude as long as he or she stays within the board's ideological zone of tolerance.

A major research question during the 1970s was whether superintendents molded school boards into suppliant agents by professional control of policymaking. One way this was thought to occur was the socialization of the new board member to professional values. A two-suburb study rooted in the 1960s argued that this was the case, and a six-suburb sample in one state about the same time confirmed the finding. Community elites closest to the school professionals deferred more to their judgments and values than elites more removed. But a large sample of Canadian board members during the 1970s sharply challenged whether the process existed, much less had an effect.[3]

The question about who controlled whom received much national attention among educational administrators with the publication of the Zeigler and Jennings study of eighty-eight school districts.[4] The authors focused on whether democratic principles were being served in the interaction between board and superintendent; their answer was an emphatic "No," although numerous qualifying conditions were given. In summary, they found:

1. Board demands on and opposition to the superintendent increase and board victories decrease as one moves from small town to suburb to city school district.
2. Superintendent interaction with the board is positively related to board opposition to her or him in city and suburban sites, but much less so in rural locales.
3. The superintendent's socialization of board members reduces board opposition in both urban and small-town places, but both interaction and socialization effects have limited association with board victories against the superintendent in smaller districts, although high association exists in urban districts.

This represents considerable evidence that board behavior with the professional is sharply affected by district size. These findings support the thesis that a more diverse urban social context generates more potential conflict over school decisions and is more likely to place the board in opposition to the superintendent. But due to the board's own divisiveness, it is less likely to overcome the superintendent. Ironically, then, Zeigler and Jennings found that effective opposition to professional influence by the board occurred in small districts with their limited political conflict and consensual elite board. Urban boards, on the other hand, were more contentious but had only limited effect against professional power.

Yet, the recent political turbulence has turned the board more from "spokesman *for* the superintendent *to* the community," as Zeigler and Jennings conclude, that is, more activist agencies responding to such demands for change. As other studies demonstrate,[5] these new currents raise the consciousness of policymakers to the sharpness of the issue and so alter their behavior; this is more the case for board members than for administrators. In all the research reported here, the distinction between urban board behavior and values and those in other locales—while sharper on some issues and in some contexts than others—can be seen to work against board dominance by the professional.

But an immediate and powerful critique of this finding of superintendent dominance arose. Boyd pointed out that administrator control over the board was highly contingent on other matters.[6] It varied with the kind of policy at issue and with the size and homogeneity of the district. Administrative power is increasingly limited by new constituencies and government rulings, as noted previously. Criticism

of the undemocratic and unresponsive nature of this professional
control in education assumes that it is worse than in other local policy
areas. But the fragmentation of delivery systems for local transportation, welfare, or pollution control makes citizen access to any of these
a feat only slightly easier than the labors of Hercules. At least a citizen
knows where to go to register a complaint against the local school,
although few choose to do so.[7] School officials may seem less responsive because their greater accessibility, compared to other services,
makes them more "public." But an early 1970s study of nine major
cities and six public agencies found that education ranked highest on
responsiveness and innovation compared to the others (except for the
War on Poverty agencies especially designed to maximize client
input).[8]

In all this, Boyd noted, one factor of the board-administrator
relation not tapped in research is the force of what political scientists
term the "law of anticipated reaction." This is the capacity of the
administrator to estimate the limits within which she or he could act
without board concern—the "zone of tolerance" in organizational
theory. In other words, superintendents inhibit their own behavior
based on knowing the controls these boards may exert. Subtle and
hard to measure, this influence is still a reality that superintendents
will detail in endless anecdotes. We will question that control in a
later section.

THE PROFESSIONAL AS REPRESENTATIVE

Much research has put the professional at odds with the community,[9] the antihero of school democracy; but it is instructive to
consider an alternative perspective. This views the professional role as
being a representative of something other than the profession.

To begin with, many of the participatory trends set out in this book
have challenged other professions besides education. A "revolt of the
client" appears not only in education but also in law, medicine,
among the clergy, and in other areas. This is not only happening here
but in other English-speaking nations as well.[10] A consequence of this
tension between the professional and a mistrustful client is that
training schools have begun to redefine the professional role so that
graduates are more sensitive to citizen needs. One aspect of this in

schools of education is the growing attention to defining the "political" role that the educator must play. The traditional apolitical myth still holds for many, but future school administrators are often being taught that they operate in a web of external demands to which they must respond and balance in some fashion.[11]

Along these lines, Cuban's clinical study of how social and political forces reshape superintendent roles in our big cities reaches some significant conclusions.[12] Role definitions change under external challenges by pressure groups, as with school consolidation around World War I and the urban crisis of the last two decades. One consequence of this is increased turnover in these positions; in the early 1970s, twenty-two out of twenty-five urban superintendents were replaced. Another obvious outcome is that old role concepts become outmoded. Under political turbulence, adopting the role of "negotiator-statesman" is more effective than any notion of being a neutral technician. The first role sees conflict as inevitable in human affairs and regards interest group demands as legitimate, to be dealt with and reconciled as part of the job. The superintendent is not just a leaf floating helplessly on the flood of turbulent politics. Yet note how far this role brings us from that of the school administrator as an omnipotent, insensitive figure that many critics posit. We can see in the actual careers of many superintendents—for example, the late Marcus Foster of the Oakland, California, schools—that one achieves success in some instances while yielding to insuperable organizational and resource obstacles in others.[13]

We can go a step further in reviewing the role of school administrator so that he or she is not stolidly unresponsive to the community but still acts to represent it. This approach requires defining democracy not as some plebiscite on a range of issues but as a system in which administrative agents act in the interest of those represented ("substantive representation"[14]). In a range of districts, Mann found many principals who defined their role in primarily these terms ("trustee"). A minority went further and claimed their role was to act only as the community required ("delegate"); a scattering played mixed roles depending on the occasion ("politicos"). Mann urged the trustee role as a desirable norm, so long as the administrator used specified techniques for encouraging community involvement.[15]

We can see this variable representative role when principals act differently. As one superintendent in a West Coast suburb put it:

In some schools, changing the location of a bicycle rack will cause parents to call the principal. In other schools, we can cut the school day from seven periods to six periods without neighborhood reaction.

Principals also act differently toward the central administrative office, depending on the presence or absence of neighborhood groups other than parents. Principals can see themselves as neighborhood emissaries. Some neighborhoods generate strong demands on them; others make minimal or no demands. Thus the evidence is that the school site context helps shape this representational role.

GOVERNING STRUCTURES AND EFFECTIVE SCHOOLS

The impact of administrators in school site operation remains unclear despite the assumed importance of the superintendency and the bureaucracy. Bridges discovered that less than a handful of studies had investigated the superintendent's effect on the schools; hence, "nothing of consequence is known about the occupants of this role."[16] Part of the difficulty in sorting out the superintendent's impact is because the local school bureaucracy has expanded substantially in the past twenty-five years. Some of the causes include the growth of federal and state categorical programs, increased court and legal activity, expansion of collective bargaining, more aggressive community interest groups, and increases in functions that schools perform, such as environmental and bilingual education. These causes are individually analyzed in various chapters throughout this book, but one overall result has been a proliferation in central office subunits and a more complex administrative structure. What is this structure of administration like and how does it relate to school effectiveness?

CHANGING SCHOOL GOVERNANCE STRUCTURES

One result of the debate over how local school policy is made has been structural changes. As noted, the present structure that excludes school boards from city council jurisdiction is an adaptation to the machine era's governance structure. School consolidation represents another structural accommodation to changes in educational policymaking following the great population shifts around World Wars I and II. These structural changes had policy consequences. Thus, at the end of almost a century of the nonpartisan reform effort, a sixty-seven-city study showed that such reforms, independent of a district's economic and environmental characteristics, played a part in school expenditures.[17] The direction of the effect was negative; that is, the more reform elements existed in the school governance, such as nonpartisanship and independence from the mayor, the less it spent. But the more that school governance featured the older political structures—ward elections and so on—the more schools were open to influence from nonprofessional groups.

In recent decades the push for structural changes has been termed "community control." The first edition of this book paid much attention to this drive in its formative stages. Now, two decades later, many of its supporters have faded, though some changes occurred. Community control seeks to create several subsystems within one school system, relocating decision making from the center to several new community-based school boards of lay members.[18] Particularly favored by minority groups who lacked influence on central administrators, this new concept envisioned a neighborhood board able to remove personnel hired by the old centralized board and having complete discretion to reallocate budget priorities. Of course, little support for this existed among school professionals.

Decentralization, on the other hand, was supported by teachers, principals, and administrators who found the present centralized system cumbersome. They complained they could not get supplies and personnel from the central office and were prevented by overall regulations from making needed curricula and teaching reforms. They assumed that better education would be possible if more locally based, professional educators had more decision-making power. In effect, field administrators would gain authority from central administrators, something like an army command situation. Under community control, however, lay board members and citizens (particularly minorities) would gain more influence than when—as at present—they confront all the professionals as well as citywide voting constituencies. Looking at these two trends in structural changes, there has been little community control but widespread decentralization in big city schools throughout the 1970s.[19]

The increasing complexity of school policymaking tends to provide more influence to those who control detailed information and analyses of policy alternatives. The control of information highlights the role of the school bureaucracy vis-à-vis the superintendent. At this point, research in rural districts has not progressed enough to differentiate the influence of the superintendent from her or his own staff. However, we do know a lot about this pattern in the urban schools. There, the central office staff has accumulated so much decision-making authority, in such areas as curriculum, personnel assignment, and facilities, that the roles of outlying district administrators and building principals are restricted. Under present conditions, the principal is too involved with day-to-day management of the school to participate effectively in broad policymaking. District superintendents, in turn, are primarily concerned with assuring that policies set down by central headquarters are followed by the schools in their districts. The superintendent's impact in part comes from an orchestrating or choreographing role that develops a sense of mission for the bureaucracy and establishes a particular climate.[20]

Top officials at the central office are traditionally chosen from within the system by the superintendent or superintendent's committee. In some districts the board must ratify his or her recommendations, but a new superintendent cannot always bring in a new team of top administrators. Few incumbents are removed or fired from the district. The superintendent may not be able to implement policies through his or her administrative officers. For example, Rogers concluded that during the school desegregation program in New York, the board and superintendent policies were emasculated by the contradictory or evasive directives and actions of certain line administrative officers.[21] In fact, the central office might make official policy statements, but the operation of the school system was so highly decentralized that various bureaucrats ignored the central desegregation policy and went off in conflicting directions.

Influence Within the School System

A major debate surrounds the relative policy autonomy that school sites should have compared to the central office. Schemes to deemphasize the central office have gone through several phases and variations.[22]

In the 1960s, the focus was on school-site budgeting, and increased amounts of unrestricted funds were provided to the school building level. In most school districts, only very small amounts (less than 3 percent per pupil) are earmarked for flexible site decision making. This flexibility has been broadened to include the ability to trade off teachers for aides and to change the standard, centrally determined, personnel formulas. Indeed, school districts typically use allocation formulas for each school based on the number of pupils. Some states like California have directed unrestricted aid to the school sites from state school improvement programs.

Then the question becomes, Who should control such flexible school site resources? Four viewpoints have been advanced.

1. Under the concept of the principal as a site manager, the principal should control these resources and be held accountable for the success of the school. Success can be measured through school site performance reports that encompass pupil attainment measures, as well as the allocation choices the principal made. This view of the principal as the site manager was reinforced by the school effectiveness literature's focus on strong site leadership.
2. Parents should control site policy because they are the consumers and care most deeply about policies at schools their children attend. Parents are less interested in central district policies that have no easily discernible impact on their children. The American philosophy of lay control implies that parent school site councils should deliberate and decide on school level policy.
3. Teachers should form a school-site senate and allocate funds and personnel as well as decide instructional issues. Teachers cannot be held accountable for pupil performance if they do not control resource allocations but must instead follow standardized instructional procedures. School-site policymaking by teachers would also enhance the professional image and self-concept of teachers.
4. None of these rationales is sufficiently compelling that it should be the norm. Consequently, a school-site council should have "parity" of membership among teachers, administration, and

parents so that they must reach an agreement through bargaining and coalitions. At the high school level, students may be included. All factions deserve a place at the table, and the best arguments should prevail.

While this school-site control debate has been intellectually stimulating, few districts have permitted much school-site flexibility. The push for increased teacher professionalism, however, may change this control pattern in the 1990s.

SCHOOL REFORM: ADULT GAMES AND CHILDREN GAMES*

Another and more serious problem exists with site-based management (SBM) reforms. A striking omission from studies of these reforms is evidence that it affected school productivity by increasing student achievement. In the local education associations (LEAs) with the longest experience with SBM, while it changed processes and structures, there was little change in academic achievement in New York City[23] or Salt Lake City.[24] Recent research surveys of that American experience are similarly negative in reporting improvements.[25]

Those curious null findings support the thesis that much of this turbulence seems like an "adult game" that appears regularly in democratic policy conflict. Such games are a struggle over power to decide key and highly political goals, namely

1. what *symbols* will dominate among policymaking actors, often a form of "symbolic politics";[26] thus, reforms will increase educational and economic "productivity";

---

*This section is from Frederick Wirt, "Policy Origins and Policy Games," in *Restructuring School Management*, edited by Grant Harman, Hedley Beare, and George F. Berkeley (Canberra, Australia: The Australian College of Education, 1991), pp. 38-42. Reprinted with permission of The Australian College of Education.

2. how public *resources* will be allocated among these actors, both vertically (the American states' revenue-supplementing) as well as horizontally (allocation of funds within an American SBM school);

3. what *structure* for decision making will control both the symbol and resource sides of the policy struggle; thus, both decentralized as well as centralized reforms are about desirable decisional systems; and

4. which *historical forces* will influence these policy games; thus history is but another form of adult influence created by preceding generations that shapes the adult game today.

Fundamentally then, this set of interactions is basically political because it is a struggle for power to decide dominant symbols, to secure resources, to employ facilitative structures, and to express historical influences. If politics is, in Harold Lasswell's classic formulation, "the study of who gets what, when, and how," then these reforms clearly share those political qualities.

However, these interactions should be distinguished from "children games," namely, those that focus on what happens to students in the learning environment. The essence of this game is not overtly centered on power, hence it is not overtly political. Rather it focuses on leading children to learn, hence it is primarily educational. This kind of game

1. centers on the curriculum and instructional aspects of the educational profession; and

2. commences, operates, and concludes with an evaluation mode to determine whether these efforts actually do increase learning.

This evaluation component of the children game is central to how it is played, and its absence distinguishes it from the adult game of policymaking. It is evaluation that historically built a complex testing and measurement concern into an established field of pedagogy. Evaluation has also recently and widely demonstrated the inability of schools to increase achievement. But evaluation is a sword that cuts two ways.

Any reform arising out of the adult game must also be judged for how the learning environment is altered and how that produces, in turn, improved achievement.

The cold truth is that there is no convincing evidence that these reforms have played the children game successfully. Reports provided to date of achievement improvements, of reduced drop-outs, or of teacher and parent happiness in SBM systems are not convincing.[27] The ghost of *post hoc ergo propter hoc* haunts such reports. That is, because a reform preceded a change, the reform caused the change. Indeed, the fullest review of the literature of SBM effects[28] is highly critical that any effects are attributable to this structural change. Too little attention is paid to such findings and to the need for evaluation in the adult game.

For evidence of reform effects to be convincing, the evaluation mode should be featured prominently in the design, initiation, organization, and implementation of reforms like SBM. Knowing at the earliest stage that the children game is being played on this kind of field will, like Samuel Johnson's aphorism on hanging, wonderfully focus the attention of the players in the adult game. Furthermore, such evaluation must incorporate designs so that we can be sure that other causes are not confounding the alleged reform effects. These designs would involve

1. pre- and post-tests of the same student cohort;
2. comparison with other cohorts not undergoing the reform;
3. longitudinal studies; and
4. contextual analysis of the potential effects of *other* factors than just reform.

Given the political passion for SBM in some circles (but not widely adopted by 1992), it is unlikely that politicos will want to undertake such evaluation of their handiwork. Nor are the dissatisfied citizens likely to understand the matter, preferring rather to think that "something is now being done." But businessmen should have a concern for evaluation of these reforms because they believe that they will benefit from them. Scholars and educational practitioners should adopt this evaluative mode of analysis when they confront any school reform— and do so from the beginning.

Clearly then, the adult game of SBM dominates. But it is not too late to think about evaluation that sets in from the first design of SBM reforms, pursues comparative and contextual analysis through time, and concludes with the basic research and policy question of any public service—"So what?" Yet everywhere it is still an adult game, in which its players are asking: "It was good for me—was it good for you?" But at some point someone must begin to ask: "Was it good for the children?"

Fragmented Centralization

The growth of federal and state categorical programs has led to a fragmented centralization—no single office or program brings together separate categories and integrates them in a consistent way. Instead, numerous separate special controls and funding subsystems exist, each with its own specific purposes. Consequently, one finds separate local education coordinators for compensatory, special, bilingual, vocational, and environmental education, for desegregation, and so on. Sometimes these coordinators report through the state government to Washington; others report directly to the federal level. The federal system is fragmented not only by funding sources but also by its organizational or reporting structures. Some federal or state funding sources bypass intermediate levels of government and go directly to a particular school. Not even the greater shift to bloc grants during the Reagan administration could unify this fragmentation; the special programs noted above still retained their separate funding.

Each level of the educational system has to maintain administrative linkage not only with higher levels but also with horizontal groups. Principals negotiate with parents and the central office. The local director of compensatory education deals with a local parent advisory committee, and the state office of compensatory education is charged with enforcing federal regulations. When these horizontal and vertical organizational relationships are multiplied rapidly, the complex interactions can result in administrative overload and inconsistent policies. As Meyer observes:

> Consider the practical situation of a school principal or superintendent. The state will provide extra funds for a special program for handicapped students. The

federal government will provide further funds if there is no special program (i.e., for mainstreaming). The parents insist that funds be managed equitably within the school and district; but both state and federal governments provide special funds which must be spent only within a few schools, or even for a few students within a school.

What is the administrator to do? The answer is simple: have a differentiated subunit for each funding or authority program, let these subunits report as best they can in conformity with requirements, avoid having the subunits brought in contact with each other (so as to avoid explicit conflict or inconsistency), and remain in ignorance of the exact content of the various programs, reports, and budgets.[29]

All of these problems are magnified in large school districts that receive forty or more categorical programs and have eighty separate sources of income. For example, the state of California has over twenty large categorical programs of its own.

Fragmented centralization implies that the school-site impact of categorical programs will be nonuniform, cumulative, and primarily indirect. Indeed, the major federal categories do not attempt to prescribe teaching methodologies or curriculum. Few of the rules in these categorical programs specify and control the teacher's actual work processes. Consequently, it is increasingly difficult to pinpoint the precise policy outputs that result from this web of organizational complexity. Moreover, the superintendent and board are not clear how effective their central policy directives will be. Each organizational subunit can play constituencies off against each other. The special education director can blame undesirable components of the program on state requirements or the mandated parent advisory committee. The state department of education can increase its influence over local education agencies by claiming that federal coercion is responsible for the new pressures.

The historic pattern of educational leadership has changed to rely more on negotiations and bargaining with a multitude of internal and external subunits. The building principal is confronted with more duties and role expectations. Formal controls from the top are mostly heavily exercised in areas of budget, personnel, scheduling, and pupil behavior. During periods of resource decline, competition for scarce funds grows intense. Local authorities discover that they cannot reduce the number of administrators as rapidly as that of teachers due to external influences that require local project directors.

In a survey of how the principal's job has changed over five years, the respondents sound like superintendents—more constrained by rules, more subject to public scrutiny, and less in control of their own schedules. Principals get ahead by successfully decoding the desires of the upper bureaucracy. Crowson posits four laws: "avoid adverse publicity, do it on your own, produce, and don't embarrass the boss."[30] Three specific activities increased the most: paperwork (in part caused by special programs), consultation with parents, and coping with students' noninstructional needs. Principals are confronted with a loosely coupled hierarchy, but they also need to maintain credibility and trust with top-level administrators. Interestingly, collective bargaining contracts take more of the principal's time, but contracts can be modified to fit unusual school-site conditions. This flexibility depends on the particular relationship between the teachers and the principal. This confirms earlier studies which found that each school neighborhood had distinctive policies, depending on such things as the principal, community economic structure, and history of local activism.

Organization and Effective Schools

How do these organizational characteristics relate to the school's prime task—academic achievement? Scholars of education have long known that a relationship exists between schools' internal organization and student learning; in fact, the professional model of school organization was imposed decades ago to improve just such effectiveness in schooling. A very recent and truly major study of this relationship by Chubb points out the special contribution to learning that arises from organizational patterns.[31] While analysts have noted the limited effect the formal organization of schools has on learning (as in the first Coleman Report), Chubb argues that these studies lack data on the informal organization and its effects. He employed a national sample of over twenty-five thousand students to link high-quality data on schools and students; these data were supplemented with administrator-teacher studies of informal organization. He then traced potential effects on school performance statistically to school environment, the organization and working of the schools, and student background.

Some findings are striking:

1. High- and low-performance schools are *not* distinguished either by their formal structure (except for more graduation requirements and using academic tracks) or by classroom practices, including writing requirements. A bit more influence on achievement was traced to more time on homework, more discipline, and less routine in classrooms. "From good schools to bad, instructional activities evidence a predictable—and disappointing—sameness."

2. Familiar differences did emerge, however, in the student body (better schools have more affluent families, fewer blacks and poor).

3. The most striking influence on achievement, however, was found in a particular type of organization. Here, goals were diverse and more clearly articulated, academic excellence was emphasized, and leadership was important (e.g., principals were less motivated to seek higher office, had more experience teaching, secured more teacher confidence, and had "a vision of what the school should accomplish").

4. The leadership of this organizational style was not authoritarian but more democratic; that is, there was more teacher involvement and cooperation between them and principals, and authority was more often delegated to the classroom. Thus, "the distinction is between a team and a hierarchy. It is the team approach that works best in the educational enterprise."

But does this difference really matter? When effects on student achievement were sought, school organization contributed more than parental influence, school resources, and peer pressures. Only student aptitude has a bit more effect on achievement than organization does. Cumulatively, "attendance at an effectively organized school is worth at least a full year of additional achievement over attendance at an ineffectively organized school, all things being equal."

This work highlights one aspect of the shift from the superintendent as autocrat, engaged in "top-down" leadership, to the one currently discussed, "bottom-up" leadership. This clash in theories of leadership must confuse the superintendent caught in the new politics of education. Unintended consequences of top-down leadership have wrecked many professionals' careers in the last quarter-century. As

Cuban noted recently, many and more complex tools of management and leadership are needed to do the job. Cuban's analysis of how superintendents spend their time stresses the large amounts of verbal interactions with many people for a short period of time. Little time exists for reflection, and a lot of time is spent on the persuasion and discussion that are the essence of a political role in building internal coalitions of subunits. A review of how principals spend their time found the same priorities of communicating and monitoring in order to generate consensus or strike compromises.[32]

SUPERINTENDENTS, POLICY PRESSURES, AND CONFLICT MANAGEMENT

In this section, we wish to explore the kinds of pressure on superintendents. In Chapter 1, Figure 1.1, all the issue demands from new core constituences were pictured as impacting first on the school board, which then focused them on the superintendent. How does this person act when political shot and shell explode around the school? First we provide superintendents' own perceptions of high-pressure milieu and their judgment of its effect, then examine one of the pressure issues—retrenchment decision making—and finally conceptualize the new roles and skills they must learn in order to manage this conflict.

Evidence of Pressure

The presence of pressure shows up indirectly in the turnover figures among superintendents. Cuban's summary of this measure in the twenty-five biggest cities shows that this rate was 8 percent in the 1950s, 12 percent in the 1960s, 16 percent in the 1970s, and in the first half of the 1980s, lower than the peak of 1965–1979.[33] Nevertheless, in the 1980s, New York, Chicago, Cleveland, Boston, Seattle, and Denver each had three superintendents in less than five years! The problem was a conflict in their roles as manager, teacher, and politician.

What specifically was creating this job stress? A comparative study of hundreds of school administrators in Oregon and Tennessee before and after 1980 found the prime pressure was trying to adapt to new state and federal organizational rules and policies.[34] The second largest stress came from trying to get public backing for school programs, and the third, from involvement in collective bargaining. Note that all these stress sources are also aspects of the job becoming ever more political; that is, all three sources affect the emerging political tasks of the position. However, there are costs to administrators for learning a new political role. A 1981 study of over 270 administrators in the West found that half had some psychological or physiological stress-related illness, including ulcers, cardiovascular problems, and so on. This group, too, cited as reasons for such illness, in order, teacher negotiations, community pressures, and school finances in general and specifically.[35]

We can identify some sources of this stress in particular groups. Wirt and Christovich asked a national sample of superintendents how many and from which specific groups had they experienced pressures and was this pressure significantly greater than earlier in their careers? Also, did these pressures reduce the acceptance of their policy recommendations by school boards or citizens in general? Table 7.1 summarizes the answers.

Almost 60 percent recorded that four or more groups had increased their demands (a figure, incidentally, larger than that reported for city managers and planning directors in the same study). Was this greater pressure coming from citizens recently encouraged to increase their influence in school decision making? Using three different ways of defining "citizens," Table 7.1 reports that this particular group pressure is not much different from that of traditional and official groups; one suspects the high percentage for "lay opinion" might have been professional deference to the democratic image. The point is that, aside from elected local officials (e.g., school boards), all groups were increasing their demands. The highest reported increase in pressure was coming from teachers. Complementing these data was an open-ended question about what aspect had most changed since starting their careers; the answer was overwhelmingly "politics," often written with an exclamation mark.

Does this mean that increased group pressure had weakened acceptance of the superintendent's policy judgments? Quite the contrary. One-half reported an *increased* acceptance of those judgments by board and citizens; only 12 and 7 percent, respectively, reported that their acceptance had declined. One might think the answer to such

Table 7.1
Superintendents' Perceptions of Group Pressures

1. From how many groups have you perceived increasing demands?

8	7	6	5	4	3	2	1	0	N
5.8[1]	3.3	20.8	12.5	20.0	15.8	11.7	7.5	2.5	131

[1]That is, 5.8 percent perceived that all eight groups had increased demands on them; 3.3 percent perceived seven groups, and so on.

2. Which groups in particular have increased demands?

Group	Percent Replying "More" and "Much More" Demands Perceived*
Traditional:	
Business	48
Labor	62
Citizen:	
Clientele	52
Minorities	50
Lay opinion	61
Officials	
Elected local	34
State	50
Federal	54

*More than one choice was possible.

Source: Frederick Wirt and Leslie Christovich, "Administrators' Perceptions of Policy Influence: Conflict Management Styles and Roles." *Educational Administration Quarterly* (1989).

influence would vary with the kind of community. However, regression analysis reported no significant relationship among urban-suburban-nonmetropolitan areas, different population sizes, or other socioeconomic measures of communities. Unlike the findings of Jennings and Zeigler's 1960s data discussed earlier, community context did not affect the volume of group pressure or the influence of professionals on policymaking in the early 1980s. One might infer from the two data sets that as group pressure on this office expanded so, too, did the need for conflict management techniques of this professional. One technique is the socialization of board members to superintendents' view of problems, already noted. An indirect indicator of this particular influence shows up in the similarity between rankings of school problems by board members and superintendents, reported in Chapter 6.

But because not all superintendents can win all the time, one cost of the job is undoubtedly professional stress, reflected in the shortened tenure in big-city schools and the pervasive illnesses they reported. Yet the findings support two ideas usually seen as contradictory, namely, that the superintendent is "beleaguered" but also dominates school decision making. The reality may well be that this professional fits both descriptions but pays considerable costs for both activities.

The Case of Declining Enrollments

We can get a feeling for the reality of these ideas by focusing on a recent and difficult school problem, the need for retrenchment. This arises over consolidation of schools or restriction of certain educational services. As Boyd pointed out in a symposium on the issue:

> At the heart of the politics and management of declining public services is the question of who will bear the immediate and long-term costs of cutbacks in these services . . . Who *loses* what, when, and how is now often the central question. . . . There is wide agreement among analysts that politics, policymaking, and management in decline differ significantly from their characteristics under growth conditions. . . .
>
> Retrenchment entails a fundamental shift from *distributive* to *redistributive* politics. . . . Participation is intensified. . . . It is complicated by considerations of equity and entitlement. . . . Morale plummets. . . . Organizations cannot be cut back simply by reversing the sequence of developments by which they grew. . . . Systematic planning and analysis become essential.[36]

As others in this symposium noted,[37] no simple solution to the problem of retrenchment emerges. Decision making based on the rational or the compromise models may not work when those who lose a school or service regard it as vital to the quality of their life. Typically, such cutback decisions are not primarily evaluated for their impact on children. Closings may affect poor or minority children more severely; often their buildings are longest in use, hence most deteriorated and so an easy target for closing. Also, cutting services is rarely uniform; the first impact is on school programs that have the smallest or weakest constituency in the community, such as art and music—rarely is it varsity sports.

Parents of schools to be closed usually lose to the superintendent and staff who present powerful arguments of economic efficiency to the school board. Often, state law also provides incentives for district consolidation under some population formula. But local opposition can coalesce into a statewide battle against consolidation, as occurred in Illinois in the mid-1980s; the Illinois law was finally modified out of existence. Amid such conflict, however, superintendents get fired. A study of fifty-six cases of turnover in districts with falling enrollment found it possible actually to predict when turnover would occur.[38] The key explanatory variables were political (i.e., bad relations of superintendent with board and community), regardless of the type of city or local educational quality.

These results agree with Iannaccone and Lutz's dissatisfaction theory of democracy discussed earlier. That is, administrators can operate with minimum community concern until an issue reflecting popular dissatisfaction with professional decisions arises. Moreover, we agree with Boyd that retrenchment generates a new politics of education.[39] This politics is characterized by more intense policy conflict, by administrators learning new retrenchment and conflict management techniques, and by the fewer families with children in public schools pitted against other taxpayers who resent expenditures from which they do not benefit. Whether it is the big-city milieu— where single-issue or district-oriented board members insist on power sharing[40]—or smaller districts that face school closing, a new policy-making environment for superintendents emerges. Rather than executive leadership, this new context requires the professional to act in a representative, coalition-building way—actions well known to "politicians" in government. Caught as they are between old role definitions and new demands, no wonder superintendents have suffered more turnover and illness.

ROLE, STYLE, AND CONFLICT MANAGEMENT

The account to this point suggests that professionals are not simply reflexive responders to the demographic and political structures of their communities. We now will try to describe the varieties of superintendent behavior, especially as it exists today amidst so much educational change.

A Dynamic Model of Superintendent Response to Change

Much of what any executive does, whether in public or private organizations, involves managing routines, namely, implementing past decisions about allocated resources. Each profession provides training in such routine management (budgeting, personnel, planning, dissemination), and its practitioners fill their early careers with these tasks. But even routine management is not without its potential for conflict. The fight each year to get more personnel lines out of budget sessions is a typical example. This routine conflict has become so standardized that it looks like a dramatic play, as Meltsner demonstrated in the politics of city revenue.[41] But such conflict over routines still operates within bounds set by authority (e.g., deadlines), by reality (e.g., revenue limitations), and by the compromise principle (nobody gets everything, nobody gets nothing, everybody gets something.)

Our interest, though, is in how superintendents manage the conflict that comes from the outside and from groups not usually active in policymaking. Dealing with the latter is what we will term "conflict management." The subject is important both for administrative theory and for practitioners seeking to cope with conflict. In theoretical terms, our concerns are with two questions: What variation exists in the generic roles and styles of conflict management, and how does one explain that variation? For the practitioner, the research question is different. How can managing conflict advance one's district goals and personal objectives, such as survival and career enhancement?

The questions have some grounding in professional concerns, as is evident from reports of superintendent dissatisfaction and turnover rates. A 1982 survey by the American Association of School Administrators reported the same dissatisfaction. Tenure had dropped one full year (to 5.6 years) over the last decade; many were leaving the profession; and one-quarter would prefer working in another field (compared to 12 percent in 1972).[42] Understanding conflict management in theoretical terms requires us first to agree that the focus of analysis is the relationship of these officials to their administrative environments. We suggest that the basic paradigm in this relationship can be set in a central proposition:

> *Change* generates *demands* in *policymaking arenas* to which *superintendents respond* with *differing roles and styles* of conflict management.

We will provide some ideas about each of these emphasized terms.

THE INFLUENCE OF CHANGE

Several kinds of change in the decision-making environment of the school's political system can generate new demands. These in turn result in conflict with which the superintendent must deal.

Population Alteration: Changing the Players

Change in the social composition of the population has been a constant in urban history, everywhere transforming political, economic, and social institutions and programs. Recent transformations, stemming from the growth of minority and poor populations in the biggest cities, have had a major impact on city resources that cover the high-cost problems of welfare, crime, and education. It is also evident that the suburban exodus after World War II transformed politics on the city's rim from rural quiescence to conflict brought on by the upwardly mobile over better services.[43] In school districts, a politics of succession between newcomers and oldtimers emerged. The conflict was fueled by the former's dissatisfaction, which led to their triumph in board elections and superintendent turnover that we already portrayed. In short, changing the players means changing the game and thus changing its distribution of rewards.

The sources of these grand transformations in school politics lie with population growth or decline. Growth has curious effects on social structures and their performance. For example, an arithmetical growth of population inevitably brings on a geometrical increase in demands for services, both in quantitative and qualitative terms. A familiar case in the city manager's world is that as population grows the ratio of police to citizens increases. Another example is suburbanites flooding the urban fringe who did not want simply more traditional, but mediocre, school services. On the other hand, population decline has different effects on urban services and their administrators, as we have noted in our discussion of school closings.

The major point is that change in the population and its social mix has consequences for the administrative environment of superintendents. It generates new demands and pressures, and hence conflict, for the superintendent.

Fiscal Context: Living with Boom or Bust

Recent decades have witnessed a riches to rags story for schools and superintendents. That cycle is currently affecting even the Southwest, which in the early 1980s rode high on an energy-driven prosperity that other regions could only envy—until its recent slump.[44] Once again we see events in the national environment—and even abroad—creating conditions that affect the local world of superintendents. Prosperity makes for easy leadership, whether as president or superintendent. Recessions, though, make all leaders look bad. But in either case, local conflict is generated.

However, even when prosperity grows and superintendents hit it rich, conflict can still develop. As property values inflate, paying the property tax (the main source of school revenue) becomes ever more burdensome. The "tax revolt" in the late 1970s arose from just this problem. Also, while addressing problems of equity, the appearance of federal riches in the form of categorical and bloc grants over the last quarter-century has also created conflict. Bigger cities fell into greater fiscal dependency on federal grants that often carried requirements that altered the local policymaking context. Under the stimuli of such programs, public participation was enlarged,[45] minority and poor gained influence on the urban power structure,[46] and consequently public demands on urban delivery systems altered. More significantly, these grants bought state and local officials into local systems (see Table 7.1); state and federal intervention was the most reported problem among superintendents and city managers in the 1980s.[47]

In short, prosperity introduces conflict to superintendents in the form of new games of distributive and regulatory policies. Conversely, when recession tightens local budgets, superintendents face another conflictual game—redistributive policies—that we described earlier. Consequently, changes in the national economy send waves into the local economy and political system that generate conflict over distributive, regulatory, and redistributive actions of the superintendents.

The Elected: Living with Political Masters

National policy currents also affect superintendents' interaction with their political masters. Indicative of this is the survey by the American Association of School Administrators cited earlier that found a significant number of superintendents changing jobs due to the presence of newly elected boards of education. Another change in context came from the federal presence. New federal requirements for public participation in urban policymaking in the Great Society era and later changed the political context of both elected and appointed officials, stimulating new debates over programs and personnel.

Over time, the policy process of many communities moved beyond protest to adopt new features, such as newly politicized minority cadres, altered power structures, sensitized superintendents and bureaucrats, and new kinds of public policy. Such protests and elections, personnel and programs, everywhere characterize the school district most often studied—the big city and its "urban school chiefs under fire."[48] Fewer studies focused on other places, such as suburbs, but these reports also presented scenes of roiling conflict. Whether the issue has been desegregation, finance reform, accountability, student rights, handicapped or bilingual education, teacher power, or curriculum, school districts have found that this fragmented set of conflicts becomes focused on the school board, superintendents, and principals. These currents of conflict are captured in the model of Figure 1.1 earlier. How have these changes impacted on local policymaking, the next concept in our dynamic model?

THE ARENAS OF POLICYMAKING

The way that local governance is organized has consequences for which groups will get access and services. Accordingly, variations in how policymaking arenas are organized act as mediating variables between the forces of external change and the superintendent's environment.

Regular Players of the Game: Different Lineups and Scores

In the urban policy process, much attention is given to the interaction of interest groups, legislatures, bureaucracies, and executives who constitute regular players in the local policy game.[49] How these actors manage conflict can exert an independent influence on decision making, a point we expand on later. Superintendents face conflict within their own organizations, either downward with their staff or outward with community groups. Amid this array of actors who affect conflict management, some major research issues require analysis. The central question is understanding how externally invoked change systematically affects the actors and superintendents. But other questions are suggested.

The reaction to change moves superintendents in stages from *reflexive resistance* (i.e., if change were needed, we would have already done it) to *damage control* (i.e., let's reduce the effects of external change) to *intense conflict* (i.e., they can't do that!) to a final *conflict resolution* and *acceptance of changes* within the educational system (i.e., we can live with this). Also, it is not clear how large a part of the superintendents' actions involve both episodic and routine conflict. If conflict is extensive (i.e., like being pecked to death by ducks), superintendents' time for professional matters, such as planning and oversight, is reduced. In short, the superintendent exists in a political web of relationships with the local actors, all coping with external changes that create conflict locally.

The Structure of Policy Arenas: Different Fields and Games

The organizing of the field on which such conflict is played out can influence the process. An axiom of social science is that organization is not value free, that different forms of organization reflect different values. Early in this century reformers understood this axiom when their middle-class zeal overthrew the party-dominated forms of nominations and elections. The proposition was put precisely a quarter-century ago by Schattschneider:

> All forms of political organization have a bias in favor of the exploitation of some kinds of conflict and the suppression of others because organization is the mobilization of bias. Some issues are organized into politics while others are organized out.[50]

Consequently, now-familiar research finds that reformed governments featuring nonpartisan election on a citywide basis show striking policy differences from partisan governments. For example, the reformed governments spend less for many services and give civil rights groups less favorable policies than do the second type. The unreformed type facilitate access to voting and representation by working and lower classes—and racial minorities—while the reformed type do the same for the middle class.[51] This is the meaning of the "mobilization of bias."

Superintendents usually preside over reformed governments, which has meant more openness to middle-class interests—just as Progressive reforms early in this century had in mind. Against this middle-class context in the 1960s, new challenges appeared to that class from federal policies that supported the interests of poor, working-class, and some middle-class groups. Thus the bias of local structure confronted the bias of external policies. In the process, superintendents' conflict management over these external redistributive and regulatory policies was influenced by different structures of governance. For example, a study of school boards found that election by district produced much different board policies than election citywide. But this kind of analysis has yet to show what different structures mean for superintendents.

SUPERINTENDENT ROLES AND CONFLICT MANAGEMENT

Differences in roles and styles among superintendents provide another way of understanding conflict management in the face of change. Crowson's review of the research expressed some of the dilemmas this way:

> A job that self-report surveys discover to be increasingly tension-filled and declining in attractiveness nevertheless finds its role incumbents expressing confidence in their abilities, with a sense that they are very much "up" to their job challenges. A role that is growing in reputation as a high-conflict part of public officialdom is simultaneously described as much less burdened by conflict than the comparable job of city manager. A position known for its visibility and beck and call responsiveness to school board and community is nevertheless described as a position that at its core is more heavily focused *inward* toward management of the school district and its professionals.[52]

The Significance of Role

At the center of most analyses of social structure has been the
concept of the individual performing functional activities, or roles,
learned through socialization. *Role* refers to expectations of one's
behavior by significant others within the relevant social structure.
Professional schools are one relevant structure for superintendents,
and they also spend much time learning the roles expected of instructional leaders by the community. Of course, roles have changed
throughout this century; educational administration has shown an
increasing role shift from neutral technician, or manager, to a power-
sharing, active advocate of programs.

Conflict, Roles, and Values

Role also implies behavior in the pursuit of significant values, but
one problem in much writing about superintendents is the unstated
assumption that they pursue all values with equal strength. Can they
strive equally for quality, equity, efficiency, or citizen choice? That
seems unlikely in practice because personal resources are finite. But
certain values are so vital to the administrator that she or he would
expend more resources on these than on others. Also, this variation in
value emphasis implies a range of values that will vary among
superintendents, although they share some values (e.g., job security).
In this range of important values, the administrator will fight harder
for some, even when faced with adverse community pressure. Moreover, not all superintendent interactions with the community are
conflictual, so the degree of conflict provides another variable in
studying the superintendent context of community conflict. In short,
superintendents will pursue their values differently given different
degrees of community conflict.

We can structure this interaction of superintendent values and
community conflict by typologizing them into potential role models.
Table 7.2 ranges degrees of community conflict against degrees of
superintendent value intensity; from this we can infer different role
behaviors. We estimate from the research literature that these executives have relatively few occasions where the Beseiged role behavior
takes place, but there are many occasions for the Overseer of Routines
role; in the other two cases the frequency is indeterminant. Included

Table 7.2
A Typology of Community Conflict and Superintendent Value

Superintendent Value Intensity	Community Conflict	
	High	Low
High:	BESEIGED PROFESSIONAL	DOMINANT PROFESSIONAL
Outcome	Win or lose	Win
Frequency	Limited	Unknown
Low:	COMPLIANT IMPLEMENTER	OVERSEER OF ROUTINES
Outcome	Win	Win
Frequency	Unknown	Extensive

in the Overseer of Routines role are the tasks of routine management and intraorganizational conflict noted earlier. We believe that much professional training takes place in this area, but that much less training is provided for conflict management.[53]

What role behavior is likely when community conflict is high? When the superintendent's values are intensely engaged—the Beseiged case—he or she will have one of at least four orientations to conflict management: competing, accommodating, collaborating, or compromising.[54] Each is a way of perceiving information and responding to demands. Zeigler and associates' review of superintendents and city managers found the former were characterized by collaboration/competition and the latter by accommodation/competition; but both adopted technocratic/rational, rather than political, strategies.[55] We will examine such strategies shortly.

Again in Table 7.2, when community conflict is low and superintendent value intensity is high, the model of the Professional Dominant arises. Here, the superintendent dominates policymaking out of a professional orientation of "managing" the service provided to citizens. This role type characterizes the period before challenge rises and conflict ensues.[56] But when the community is highly conflictual and superintendent values are not intense, the latter can play another role. Assisting the community to devise and administer a program, this Compliant Implementer role behavior implies that no major challenge to professional standards or no fear of job security exists.

Viewing the professional in this situational fashion provides a fuller understanding of role behavior. The typology also makes the point that no role is dominant; rather a number of roles exist that the superintendent may select as conditions warrant. Further, this view prompts us to look at different policy contexts where conflict may or may not exist. The point is that these roles are like a collection of hats; the superintendent may choose one to fit the situation. Of course, the typology does not provide a precise measure of these two intensity qualities associated with superintendent value and community conflict. But its use encourages thinking in scalar terms about important features of the administrative environment when either routine or episodical conflict exists.

SUPERINTENDENT STYLES AND CONFLICT MANAGEMENT

Another personal aspect of the superintendent is *style*, or the quality of one's individuality expressed in action. Style is distinguished from role because it is a matter of choice rooted in individual emotions and judgments, while role is more narrowly confined to actions one was socialized to in professional training and experience. Style is little studied in the scholarship of professionals of any kind, although significant anecdotes imply how different styles operate. Yet studying style is important because the situational roles noted above permit individualization within each role in dealing with routine and conflict management.

A Typology of Conflict Styles

Conflict styles are few because individuals in conflict tend to fit into a few patterns of behavior. Different styles are all versions of the "fight-flight" or Hirschman's "exit-voice-apathy" characterization of how individuals act when confronted by situations inimical to their interests. That is, when confronted, one may actively oppose others, leave the scene of the confrontation, or loyally stay on the scene but

Table 7.3

A Typology of Community Conflict and Superintendent Styles

Superintendent Style	Community Conflict	
	High	*Low*
Avoid	Presider	Delegator
Mediate	Compromiser	Facilitator
Fight	Assertive	Professional

not act. We label these three styles in the face of conflict Fight, Avoid, and Mediate. The first two are familiar. The mediating style is a third possibility when those vested with authority must face conflicting groups; this is not a style available to citizens amidst their conflict. Mediation style can involve such strategies as accommodation, collaboration, and compromise. A comparison of city managers and school superintendents found that superintendents experience less conflict but feel more politically beleaguered because they expect to make decisions based on their expertise rather than on political negotiation.[57]

How does this range of styles interact with a range of intensity in community conflict? A typology of these ranges is set out in Table 7.3. If the professional's characteristic style of conflict management is Avoid, then when high community conflict occurs, he or she will seek only to preside over, but not to direct or oppose, the conflict. This includes not taking stands, assuring that rules of procedure are followed, and, in effect, deflecting the decision to the authoritative action of the school board. But when conflict is low, the Avoid style will delegate authority to other professionals within the organization and subsequently approve their decisions.

If the superintendent's style is more inclined to Mediate, greater conflict produces two different roles. Amid high community conflict, she or he will seek conflict resolution through compromise; note that this style enables one's own policy values to be incorporated into the final result to some degree. When conflict is low, however, the Mediate style has a propensity to act as facilitator, a "first among equals" style of assisting other professionals to do their job while assuring that the general direction of the organization is maintained.

The Fight style of conflict management is the most dramatic, the

subject of stories about "beleagured" professionals whose norms have
been challenged. This is most evident when community conflict is
high, and the superintendent style becomes assertive, taking the lead
in mobilizing group support and building coalitions to deal with
problems of change. By competing with other groups, but accommodating where politically feasible, assertive styles differ dramatically
from the presider style. When conflict is low, though, the Fight style
involves the kind of administrative leadership that training schools
and textbooks urge, the style that has created the modern service
bureaucracies. This includes thinking in terms of the "one best
system." [58]

REFLECTIONS ON CONFLICT BEHAVIOR IN URBAN PROFESSIONS

Research into these diverse superintendent styles and roles amid a
shifting world of conflict can move our conceptualizations from a
narrow or monolithic view of their behavior. That is, we are likely to
find if we studied diaries that professionals would shift among these
behaviors. Which role or style the person selects in a given case may
well involve cost-benefit calculations about getting the job done,
advancing professional goals, and enhancing one's career.

The growing fragmentation of the managerial, political, and educational tasks that superintendents perform is implied in these styles
and roles. The distinction between administrator and leader that runs
through them has been reinforced by superintendents' training and
experience. A leading text in educational administration draws the
distinction that typically applies to all superintendents:

> In sum, the professional administrator is likely to view his or her role as that of one
> who finds out what consumers want from the schools and who delivers educational
> services accordingly. The educational leader, by contrast, is very much concerned
> with the issues of purpose and direction. [59]

The administrative function exists in all but the Beseiged role of Table
7.2 and the presider and delegator styles of Table 7.3. All other roles
and styles in these tables describe the leader. The latter is usually
characterized by strong professional values and proactive behavior;

the former is portrayed as having uncertain attachment to profession values and a reactive stance amid conflict.

Research Prospects

Though we can apply broad questions to these role and style concepts that need empirical evaluation, we can only raise general questions here. What are the conditions under which shift will occur in role and style or under which the role or style is successfully carried out? What does "success" mean in these contexts? What are the skills most useful in both behaviors? Do these skills include: articulating professional goals, brokering them amid group pressures including those from political masters, strategizing plans drawn from valid concepts of the political territory, using professional knowledge, and so on? Finally, does the professionals' training in the universities provide as relevant skills and styles as they do for other professional roles?

We leave such research questions with the understanding noted throughout our analysis, namely, the superintendent is not a pure type because individuals vary and the context of conflict is not static. We see these administrators driven by professional values amid a turbulent administrative environment that is roiled by currents of change arising from outside the organization's boundaries. Often he or she is struggling to do more than simply manage routines, but rather to lead within a context of increasing power-sharing.

THE TEACHER AS A POLITICAL ACTOR

No group has increased its influence on policy in recent decades as much as teachers. The timid rabbits of thirty years ago are today's ravening tigers in the jungle of school systems. Unionism has produced this change, of course, and consequently made teachers a major political actor.

Teacher Politics

Grimshaw's study of Chicago schools made a strong argument that a total system transformation in who rules local schools has occurred as a result of teacher unions.[60] Those schools were first governed by a political machine rule, then by a reform rule (which meant a professional education bureaucracy); they are now governed by union rule. These three models differ in structure, process, and actors. However, the contemporary union rule is characterized by a crucial political quality—lack of control by elected officials; not even the late Mayor Daley could cope with teacher union demands. Thus, a continuing question of the democratic polity is, What if Grimshaw is correct in saying, "Union rule bears hallmarks of an enduring form of urban government"?

Certainly their size alone (2,740,000) enables organized teachers to be a local pressure group regularly confronting the district board and superintendent every few years. Every autumn, teacher strikes in major cities become a staple news item along with the closing days of the baseball season. Nor are these features found only in big cities. As collective bargaining became ever more authorized by state laws, medium and small communities experienced the unprecedented—a teachers' strike. The results can dramatically rearrange traditional power within the school system. For example, in 1987 the small town of Homer, Illinois, underwent a year-long teacher strike (longest in state history) when the local board was intransigent in the face of strikers' demands. This militancy was not always the case, because as recently as the mid-1960s a majority of teachers opposed collective bargaining or the endorsement of political candidates. Note that two-thirds of our teachers are women who were successfully discouraged from union or political activities by male administrators. Also, some teachers believed that collective bargaining and political campaign activities were "unprofessional."

As of 1986, however, thirty-two states had some form of collective bargaining statute covering teachers. Even states without collective bargaining laws have some locals with longstanding collective bargaining agreements (e.g., Texas and Mississippi). As a result, by 1980 more than 1.5 million instructional staff, or 65 percent of all full-time and part-time professionals, belonged to an employee organization. In short, collective bargaining is now an accepted part of school governance.

We can attribute much of the rapid increase in collective bargaining between 1965 and 1975 to the rivalry for members between the National Education Association (NEA) and the American Federation

Table 7.4
Teacher Strikes in the United States

Year	Number of Strikes	Number of Teachers Involved
1965	5	1,720
1975	218	182,300
1982	68	29,858
1987	39	not available

Source: Wall Street Journal, 21 September 1987.

of Teachers (AFT) discussed in Chapter 4. Initially neither the NEA or AFT would endorse strikes; it took until 1973 for the strike to become official NEA policy. Recently, the incidence of strikes has been declining to the lowest number in twenty years as evidenced by Table 7.4.

The recent decline in strikes is in part caused by the large increases in teacher salaries galvanized by the post-1983 education reform movement and the recovery from the economic recession in 1980–82. When teacher salaries are rising rapidly, less need or incentive to strike exists. Figure 7.1 demonstrates the gains that teachers made in 1980–87 relative to all workers.

The Impact of Teacher Contracts

The outcome of collective bargaining is a written and time-bound agreement covering wages, hours, and conditions of employment. As well as involving the specifics of the contract, major disputes can occur over the scope of bargaining and grievance procedures. The negotiated contract, however, is not felt by teachers until it is implemented in the work setting. At the school site, the board's contract language must be interpreted to apply to specific circumstances. This means that the site principal, teachers, and union building representative must become very familiar with the contract's term. Yet even familiarity does not forestall many disputes about specific teaching arrangements. These disputes can lead to grievances whose settlement can clarify the contract.

Thus teacher influence varies by district and site. Teachers at

Figure 7.1
The Rewards of Teaching

Average annual earnings of teachers and all U.S. workers in constant 1987 dollars
(In thousands of dollars)

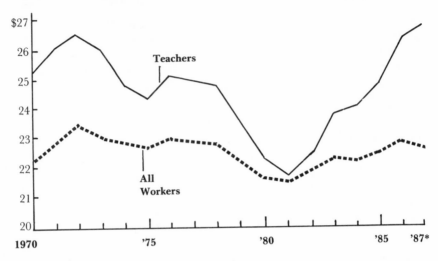

*The 1987 figure for all workers is estimated

Source: Wall Street Journal, 21 September 1987 (Original source: *American Federation of Teachers*).

school sites sometimes permit exceptions to the district contract if they believe specific school conditions warrant them. Teacher unions have had the most difficulty enforcing such contract provisions as pupil discipline, building maintenance, and security because grievance procedures were less effective. On the other hand, seniority and teacher transfer clauses were the most highly implemented. The unions' long-run influence, however, may come more from influencing decisions at state and federal levels that then percolate down to the local school system. As close students of this subject point out, there are serious potentials for rearranging traditional school governance by teacher lobbying in state capitals.[61] The NEA has a much stronger presence at the state level because the AFT has primarily big-city members.

What happens to administrator authority, particularly among principals, when contracts filter down through the loosely coupled school system? A major study found that while some provisions tightly limit this professional's freedom of action, others get redefined to fit the requirements at the school site level. That is, "such factors as teacher interests, educational consequences, administrative leadership, and staff allegiance were balanced and counterbalanced."[62] How the principal works with the contract also affects teachers' respect for them. Teachers want the contract respected, but the contract also allows for the principal's interpretation if she or he is seen as seeking a good school, whether authoritarian or democratic in leadership style. In short, having standards and expecting much of teachers earns principals a tolerance and even respect from teachers in interpreting the contract; for teachers, a good school is more important than union membership, close observance of a contract, or running the schools. This is because, as one administrator observed, "'Teachers like to be part of a winning team.'"[63]

Yet the ultimate effect of collective bargaining may not be as great as was once thought. Johnson stresses that the effects of collective bargaining are deep and pervasive but not so extreme nor uniform as critics often suggest.

> Collective bargaining has not been shown to have increased teachers' commitment to their work or enhanced their standing as professionals, but neither has it destroyed the schools. Caricatures of straitjacketed principals, Kafkaesque school bureaucracies, or schools under seige by militant teachers scarcely represent the experiences of these sample districts. Overall, the organizational effects of collective bargaining appear to be both moderate and manageable.
>
> This is not to suggest, though, that labor relations practices look the same in all districts of all schools. In fact, negotiations, contract language, and administrative practices are remarkably diverse.[64]

Understanding these consequences is confused by the diverse practices that have emerged in local systems. No single factor accounts for this diversity in local labor practices, but certain important variables included the history of local labor practices, the local political culture, and—most important—the people at the center of negotiations and contract management. In California, the same districts have strikes or acrimonious labor disputes near the expiration of every contract. Some of this is caused by personalities, styles, and relationships, and some is caused by a long and bitter history of labor-management relations. However, in other districts, both sides prefer cooperation over a long period of time. No simple predictive model can account for these factors, and the diverse outcomes are similar to the range in outcomes from federal grant programs discussed in Chapter 12.

But it is clear that collective bargaining has increased the complexity of the principal's job because he or she cannot apply the contract in a routine and standard manner. Moreover, there are some overall impacts of bargaining as summarized by Cresswell and Murphy:

1. The breakdown of the unitary command structure and its replacement by a multilateral bargaining system, or, in some cases, by a bilateral system.
2. The introduction of new participants into school decision making, including labor professionals (both advocates and neutral third parties), organized and unorganized citizens, and elected officials outside of education.
3. The movement of the locus of decision making to central offices within school systems and to locations outside of school systems, including legislatures, courts, and public administrative agencies.
4. The broadening scope of issues that fall into the labor relations arena—both issues raised during formal negotiations and those joined to the collective bargaining process during the administration of contracts.
5. The changing nature of managerial work, since there is evidence that school administrators face different types of issues, new constituents, different managerial roles, and new criteria for success in their jobs.[65]

These constraints on the principal's role, when viewed in light of what happens to the contract at the site level reviewed earlier, suggest a complex concept of this professional's tasks. The constraints also point to a centralization of decision making within the total school system. But the local development points to a decentralization of interpretation by the principal. Both developments in collective bargaining mean that the professional at this level, as well as those at higher levels, must increasingly work within a power-sharing context where educational leadership is still possible but under much more complex requirements.

Issues in Collective Bargaining

Other issues than the administrator's role arise over collective bargaining. At the outset a major issue was direct citizen participation in the bargaining process. Educators have adopted the private industry model for bargaining, but several groups assert this is inappropriate. In private industry only two parties, labor and management, are at the bargaining table. However, parent advocates pushed for bargaining in open meetings with public observers or even a place for parents at the bargaining table. Nine states enacted public participation with the hope that it would dampen expenditure increases for salaries and personnel. Whatever the philosophical merits of these arguments, the public has not shown much interest.

Despite the significant effect of collective bargaining on school costs and tax rates, the general public shows little sustained interest in teacher bargaining except during times of crisis. Citizens may simply assume that their elected representatives on school boards take an active part in negotiations, but we have seen that that this rarely happens. In any case, community participation advocates appear to lead a phantom army. However, general public attitudes toward organized labor and collective bargaining do affect the very broad parameters of contracts, probably through election of sympathetic board members who then appoint like-minded school executives.[66]

Another improvement in collective bargaining might be accomplished through a merger of two rival unions. It is alleged that their rivalry leads to increased and unnecessary union truculence. But despite frequent attempts by top union leadership to merge, no visible progress has occurred except in a handful of large cities. The NEA still has a huge numerical majority over the AFT (1.6 million to 500,000) and sees little need to compromise, particularly when its tactics are virtually indistinguishable from the AFT's. The NEA claims that it provides militant collective bargaining while being untainted from affiliation with "unprofessional" unions in the AFL-CIO.

A major new issue fueled by the educational excellence movement is the control of teacher certification. Teachers are certified by the states, but the Carnegie Corporation has advocated a national professional standards board.[67] Originally the concept was to have the national board recognize experienced teachers who could meet unusually high standards. Recently, discussion of national certification of new teachers has increased.

Teacher unions' reactions to such reform can be inferred from their work with states. They have sought control of the state certification boards for years and have succeeded in several states. They have also cut back the influence of the universities and administrators by achieving more members on these state licensing boards. The unions believe a true profession must control the entry of its own members and not cede this prerogative to others, such as universities. Moreover, union contributions to state legislators have given them influence that universities cannot match. The AFT has supported a national board while the NEA has been more cautious.

The Carnegie task force also proposed "lead teachers" who would share some of the principal's responsibilities in the instructional and teacher evaluation areas. This enlarged role in administration for teachers has engendered resistance from some administrator and school board groups. A crucial issue in the 1990s will be whether the private bargaining model is modified and adapted to the particular circumstances of public education. None of the alternative concepts has engendered much support, and labor-management bargaining seems embedded in the American public school culture.

By the middle 1980s, teacher shortages had appeared in several parts of the nation due to greater enrollments and large-scale retirements. This helped trigger a rethinking of the professional basis for a teaching career. Professionals like lawyers and doctors have more control over all aspects of their careers than teachers. The legacy of the turn-of-the-century reformers was the industrial model with male administrators presiding over a largely transient female labor force. But collective bargaining was a first step in changing this power relationship. It is uncertain whether any more major conceptual shifts in teacher power will take place soon.

Teachers as Political Brokers in the Classroom

There is also an entirely different way to view the teacher's political role, and this occurs when we turn from their outward relationship with school authorities to their inward relationship with their students. We have seen in Chapter 3 one aspect of this relationship in the teachers' role in political learning. But even in such a seemingly value-free subject as elementary level mathematics, the teacher is not simply an implementer of educational policy. As scholars presenting this new perspective have concluded:

> In this semi-autonomous role, teachers are better understood as political brokers than as implementers. They enjoy considerable discretion, being influenced by their own notions of what schooling ought to be as well as persuaded by external pressures. . . . This view represents a middle ground in the classic sociological contrast between professional autonomy and bureaucratic subordination. It pictures teachers as more or less rational decision-makers who take higher-level policies and other pressures into consideration in their calculation of benefits and costs.[68]

In a real sense—by allocating public resources in such matters as choosing which students get what kind of curriculum content—the teacher takes on a political role. This action parallels the similar political role of board and administrative decisions. Thus decisions in elementary math about what will be taught, to whom, and for how long are matters that teachers usually decide. Some pressures, however, also come from students (e.g., what has worked with them in the past predisposes its reuse) and from external sources. Externally, a varied urban environment with its ambiguous messages about instruction is much more likely to free the teacher to make such decisions compared to a small, homogeneous rural setting. Centralized versus decentralized state requirements—for example, statewide text adoption by the state board—are another kind of external factor affecting teacher discretion. But even within the school organization itself, Hawley and others have pointed to factors of organizational rigidity or receptivity that create expectations in teachers about how they are to use power.[69]

Much of the preceding suggests an organizational structure for schooling that is characterized by "loose coupling." This is the tendency of educational organizations to disconnect policies from outcomes, means from ends, and structure or rules from actual activity.[70] Such a nonstructure puts the teacher's behavior beyond the control of the formal authorities, who themselves have no chain of command with straight lines and precise directions for teaching policy. Within such disjointed relationships, one would not expect program innovations originating outside the local unit to have much impact. A survey of the history of classroom reforms finds there are lasting results only if the changes are structural, create new clientele, and are easily monitored.[71] Vocational education and driver training are good examples of this. But attempts to change classroom pedagogy have largely been unsuccessful because they lack these essential characteristics.

Much of this political quality is typified in the education reform policies that present particularly difficult dilemmas for teachers and their unions. Policymakers have been adamant about linking additional benefits to teachers with the creation of a more performance-based profession. Several state governors, for example, propose testing new teachers, using student tests in evaluating teachers, uniform accountability reporting systems, and performance-based compensation. But most teachers would be uncomfortable with a system that allocates benefits uniformly on the basis of seniority and educational attainment.[72] Consequently, if teacher unions embrace the reform movement they may lose the support of rank-and-file members. But if the teacher unions oppose "reform" and "professionalism," they will lose public support and alienate many top policymakers. Gradually, the NEA unions have moved from opposing certain key reform proposals to accommodating and modifying them. The AFT has been quicker to lead in shaping the initial version of the reforms.

Ironically, a national study of local teacher organizations concluded that reform policies were quite peripheral to their local mission and interests. Consequently, opposition was unnecessary, and so there was little need to depart from the traditional collective bargaining model.[73] The rank-and-file teachers expect unions to obtain material benefits such as higher salaries and better working conditions, but they are not particularly interested in such "professional" strategies as teacher participation in school-site decision making or performance-based compensation. This rank-and-file viewpoint is particularly troublesome for union leaders who endorse the reforms because the same national study concluded that between 1980 and 1985 there were very few improvements in teachers' working conditions. An analysis of union contracts found major strides in the attainment of noncompensation items between 1970 and 1980 but little progress since 1980. For example, teacher organizations were unable to include the exclusion of disruptive students, maximum class size, restrictions on involuntary transfer of teachers among schools, or a school level instructional policy committee.[74] Given this lack of progress on "bread and butter" items, the grass-roots endorsement of teacher reforms at the building level is highly problematic. Thus the role of teachers in local governance is much more than just trade-union politics. We need more knowledge of the classroom as a significant screen between external influences and the student and of the teacher as a political agent within the classroom or of teachers' responses to external efforts to shape their behavior to meet the public's wishes. Then we will better understand how teachers function as a local actor in the conversion of private needs into public policy, which is essentially a political process.

NOTES

1. William L. Boyd, "The Public, the Professionals, and Educational Policy-Making: Who Governs?" *Teachers College Record* 77 (1976): 556–58.

2. Based on several censuses of administrators conducted by Paul Salmon, American Association of School Administrators, Washington, D.C., mimeographed.

3. The sources, in order, are: Norman D. Kerr, "The School Board as an Agency of Legitimation," *Sociology of Education* 38 (1964): 34–59; Michael P. Smith, "Elite Theory and Policy Analysis: The Politics of Education in Suburbia," *Journal of Politics* 36 (1974): 1006–32; Peter J. Cistone, "The Socialization of School Board Members," *Educational Administration Quarterly* 13, no. 2 (1977): 19–33.

4. L. Harmon Zeigler and M. Kent Jennings, *Governing American Schools* (North Scituate, Mass.: Duxbury, 1974), pp. 39–42, Pt. III.

5. Leigh Seltzer, "Institutionalizing Conflict Response: The Case of School-Boards," *Social Science Quarterly* 55, no. 2 (1974).

6. Boyd, "The Public, the Professionals, and Educational Policymaking."

7. M. Kent Jennings, "Parental Grievances and School Politics," *Public Opinion Quarterly* 32 (1968): 363–78.

8. Roland L. Warren, S. M. Rose, and A. F. Bergunder, *The Structure of Urban Reform* (Lexington, Mass.: Heath, 1974).

9. David Rogers, *110 Livingston Street* (New York: Random House, 1968).

10. Frederick M. Wirt, "Professionalism and Political Conflict: A Developmental Model," *Journal of Public Policy* 1 (1981): 83–112.

11. For example, Thomas J. Sergiovanni, Martin Burlingame, Fred Coombs, and Paul Thurston, *Educational Governance and Administration* (Englewood Cliffs, N.J.: Prentice-Hall, 1980).

12. Larry Cuban, *Urban School Chiefs Under Fire* (Chicago: University of Chicago Press, 1976).

13. Jesse J. McCorry, *Marcus Foster and the Oakland Public Schools* (Berkeley: University of California Press, 1978).

14. The seminal theoretical work is Hanna F. Pitkin, *The Concept of Representation* (Berkeley: University of California Press, 1967).

15. Dale Mann, *The Politics of Administrative Representation* (Lexington, Mass.: Lexington Books, 1976).

16. Edwin Bridges, "Research on the School Administrator: The State of the Art," *Educational Administration Quarterly* 18, no. 3 (1982) 12–33. See also Robert Crowson, "The Local School Superintendency," *Educational Administration Quarterly* 23, no. 3 (Summer 1987): 80–101.

17. Brett Hawkins et al., "Good Government Reformism and School Spending in Cities," in *The Polity of the School*, F. Wirt, ed. (Lexington, Mass.: Lexington Books, 1975), Chap. 2.

18. Henry Levin, ed., *Community Control of Schools* (Washington, D.C.: Brookings Institution, 1972).

19. A six-city comparison is in George R. La Noue and Bruce L. Smith, *The Politics of School Decentralization* (Lexington, Mass.: Lexington Books, 1973).

20. Dale Mann, *The Politics of Administrative Representation* (Lexington, Mass.: Lexington Books, 1976).

21. For a good case, see Rogers, *110 Livingston Street*.

22. See John Meyer, "The Impact of Centralization" (Stanford: Institute of Educational Finance and Governance, 1979). See also James Guthrie, "School Based Management: The Next Needed Education Reform," *Phi Delta Kappa* 68 (Dec. 1986): 305–9.

23. D. Rogers and N. Chung, *110 Livingston Street Revisited* (New York: New York University Press, 1983); M. Gittell, M. Berube, F. Gottfried, M. Guttentag, and A. Spier, *Local Control in Education* (New York: Praeger, 1973).

24. Betty Malen and Rodney Ogawa, Professional Patron Influence on Site-based Government Councils: A Confronting Case Study," *Educational Evaluation and Policy Analysis* 10 (1988): 251–270.

25. Betty Malen, Rodney Ogawa, and J. Kranz, "What Do We Know about Site-Based Management: A Case Study of the Literature—A Call for Research," in *Choice and Control in American Education*, volume 2, edited by W. Cune and John Witte (New York: Falmer, 1990), pp. 289–342; A. Bryk, V. Lee, and J. Smith, "High School Organization and Its Effects on Teachers and Students: An Interpretive Summary of the Research," *Choice and Control in American Education*, volume 1 (New York: Falmer, 1990), see pages 152–154.

26. M. Edelman, *The Symbolic Uses of Politics* (Urbana: University of Illinois Press, 1967).

27. Carl Glickman, "Pushing School Reform to a New Edge: The Seven Ironies of School Empowerment," *Phi Delta Kappan* 72 (1990): 63–75.

28. Malen, Ogawa, and Kranz, "What Do We Know about Site-Based Management."

29. Meyer, "Impact of Centralization," pp. 16–17.

30. Robert Crowson and Van Cleve Morris, "Administrative Control in Large City Schools," *Educational Administration Quarterly* 21, no. 4 (1985): 51–70; Paul Hill et al., *The Effects of Federal Education Programs on School Principals* (Santa Monica, Calif.: Rand, 1980). For analysis of school site politics, see Harry Z. Summerfeld, *The Neighborhood-based Politics of Education* (Columbus, Ohio: Charles E. Merrill, 1971).

31. John Chubb, "The Dilemma of Public School Improvement," (paper presented to the Spoor Dialogues on Leadership Program at Darmouth College, May 4, 1987). Following citations are from this source.

32. Larry Cuban, "Transforming the Frog into a Prince: Effective Schools Research, Policy, and Practice at the District Level." *Harvard Education Review* 54 (1984): 129–51. The study of principals is in Martin Burlingame, "Using a Political Model to Examine Principals' Work," *Peabody Journal of Education* 63, no. 1 (Fall 1986): 120–29.

33. Larry Cuban, "Conflict and Leadership in the Superintendency," *Phi Delta Kappa* 67, no. 1 (1985): 28–30.

34. Jack Brimm, "What Stresses School Administrators," *Theory into Practice* 22 (1983): 64–69.

35. Cited in Brimm, "What Stresses School Administrators."

36. William Boyd, "Afterword: The Management and Consequences of Decline," *Education and Urban Society* no. 15,(1983): 255–56.

37. Boyd, *Education and Urban Society* 15, no. 2 (1983): 255–56.

38. Michael Berger, "Predicting Succession under Conditions of Enrollment Decline," *Education Administration Quarterly* 20, no. 2 (1984): 93–107.

39. Boyd, "Afterword," 256–57.

40. Gordon Cawelti, "Guess What? Big City Superintendents Say Their School Boards Are Splendid," *American School Board Journal* 169 (1982): 33–35; James Cibulka, "Explaining the Problem: A Comparison of Closings in Ten U.S. Cities," *Education and Urban Society* 15 (1983): 165–74.

41. Arnold Meltsner, *The Politics of City Revenue.* (Berkeley: University of California Press, 1971).

42. *Champaign News-Gazette*, 9 January 1983, A-3.

43. Frederick Wirt, Benjamin Walter, Francine Rabinovitz, and Deborah Hensler, *On the City's Rim.* (Lexington, Mass.: Heath, 1972).

44. James Guthrie, "The United States of America: The Educational Policy Consequences of an Economically Uncertain Future," in *Education, Recession and the World Village*, F. Wirt and G. Harman, eds. (Philadelphia: Falmer, 1986).

45. Stuart Langton, ed., *Citizen Participation in America.* (Lexington, Mass.: Lexington, 1978).

46. Rufus Browning, Dale Marshall, and David Tabb, *Protest Is Not Enough.* (Berkeley: University of California Press, 1984).

47. Harmon Zeigler, Ellen Kehoe, and Jane Reisman, *City Managers and School Superintendents.* (New York: Praeger, 1985).

48. Cuban, *Urban School Chiefs.*

49. Charles Jones, *Governing Urban America* (Boston: Little, Brown, 1983).

50. E. E. Schattschneider, *The Semisovereign People* (New York: Holt, Rinehart and Winston, 1960), p. 71.

51. This rich literature is reviewed in Jones, *Governing Urban America*, pp. 256–60.

52. Crowson and Morris, "Administrative Control."

53. Zeigler et al., *City Managers.*

54. Kenneth Thomas and Ralph Kilmann, *Conflict Mode Instrument* (Tuxedo, N.Y.: Xicom, 1974).

55. Zeigler et al., *City Managers*, pp. 121–26.

56. The stages of profession-laity conflict are explored in Frederick Wirt, "Professionalism and Political Conflict."

57. Zeigler et al., *City Managers*.

58. David Tyack, *The One Best System* (Cambridge: Harvard University Press, 1974).

59. Thomas Sergiovanni, et al., *Educational Governance and Administration* (Englewood Cliffs, N.J.: Prentice-Hall, 1980), p. 17.

60. William J. Grimshaw, *Union Rule in the Schools* (Lexington, Mass.: Lexington Books, 1979).

61. James Guthrie and Patricia Craig, *Teachers and Politics* (Bloomington, Ind.: Phi Delta Kappa, 1973).

62. Susan Moore Johnson, *Teacher Unions in Schools* (Philadelphia: Temple University Press), pp. 162–63.

63. Ibid., p. 163.

64. Ibid., pp. 164–65.

65. Anthony M. Cresswell and Michael Murphy, *Teachers, Unions, and Collective Bargaining in Public Education* (Berkeley: McCutchan, 1980), pp. 386–87.

66. Lorraine McDonnell and Anthony Pascal, *Organized Teachers in American Schools* (Santa Monica, Calif.: The Rand Corp., 1979), pp. 87–88.

67. Carnegie Corporation, *A Nation Prepared: Teachers for the 21st Century* (New York: Carnegie, 1986).

68. John Schwille et al., "Teachers as Policy Brokers in the Content of Elementary School Mathematics" (paper prepared for the NIE Conference on Teaching and Educational Policy, February 1981), p. r, and John Schwille, Andrew Porter, and Michael Gant, "Content Decision-Making and the Politics of Education," *Educational Administration Quarterly* 16 (1980): 21–40.

69. Willis D. Hawley, "Dealing with Organizational Rigidity in Public Schools: A Theoretical Perspective," in *The Polity of the School*, Wirt, Chap. 11; Willis D. Hawley, "Horses Before Carts: Developing Adaptive Schools and the Limits of Innovation," in *Political Science and School Politics: The Princes & the Pundits*, Samuel K. Gove and Frederick M. Wirt, eds. (Lexington, Mass.: Lexington Books, 1976), Chap. 1; D. C. Lortie, "The Balance of Control and Autonomy in Elementary School Teaching," in *The Semi-Professions and Their Organization*, Amitai Etzioni, ed. (New York: Free Press, 1969); and Alan Peshkin, *Growing Up American* (Chicago: University of Chicago Press, 1979).

70. Karl Weick, "Educational Organizations as Loosely Coupled Systems," *Administrative Science Quarterly* 21 (1976): 1–19.

71. Michael Kirst and Gail Meister, "Turbulence in American Secondary Schools: What Reforms Last?" *Curriculum Inquiry* 15, no. 1 (Spring 1985): 169–86.

72. Lorraine McDonnell and Anthony Pascal, *Teacher Unions and Education Reform* (Santa Monica: The Rand Corp., 1987), p. 3.

73. McDonnell and Pascal, *Teacher Unions*, p. 5.

74. McDonnell and Pascal, *Teacher Unions*, pp. 6–8.

8

Referenda in the Conversion Process

Numerous channels carrying demand inputs pour into the miniature political system that the schools form. A previous chapter explored one of these—electoral inputs—that provide for collective demands, even when participants are comparatively few. Another and separate input channel, explored in a later chapter, is litigation. Yet a third input channel is the referendum by which citizens vote directly on such school policy matters as budgets, bonds, or levies. In broader terms, the referendum is a device for registering the extent of public support for schools. Unhappiness with excessive spending, insensitive teachers, lack of student discipline, objectionable curriculum, or even the losing football team can all generate lack of support. Simply voting "no" is a convenient way of expressing this dissatisfaction. Of course, happiness with other facets of school policy can motivate a "yes" vote. Given the convenience of this device for voters, then, school boards and administrators have to pay attention to this potential support. In short, they must become "political" by seeking to mobilize group support within the community for what they see as necessary funding.

In recent decades, school authorities have found that this support is drying up. Whether because parents were increasingly unhappy with schools or squeezed by galloping inflation or whether there are simply fewer parents with children in the public schools, referenda have not

221

gained the public support they once did. This development is another part of the current political turbulence that fills the schools. In this chapter, we examine this phenomenon in order to show how such demands can actually make policy, that is, convert demands into public allocation of resources and values. The analysis will show practical consequences for administrators who must adopt political strategies, like those other actors who struggle for resources and values in the public arena.

BACKGROUND AND SIGNIFICANCE

By the end of the nineteenth century, many Americans were disgusted with their government. Legislative excesses in the American states had brought restraints and an expansion of governors' capacities to balance off corrupt assemblies. But as the century closed, neither political office received much praise. Moreover, political parties were everywhere seen as corrupt links between legislature and executive; the judiciary was equally tainted; and the beneficiaries of this degradation—in an era of rampant capitalism—were not only politicians but businessmen.

The political movement of Progressivism reacted against this union of private and public greed. Reformers felt that more democracy must be a part of the operations of the political system, and citizens should have more control over the corrupters of the political and economic weal. To achieve these purposes, the initiative, referendum, and recall—among other devices—were adopted in many American states. It is hard to realize now how radical these practices were once regarded. In our own time they have "become quaint; one thought of them, as one remembered Teddy Roosevelt's teeth, in a haze of mezzotint sentimentality."

The promise of referendum control by citizens, however, has not been matched by reality, for little evidence shows that they balanced interest-group power in state politics. The problem is that not many citizens consider them important enough to use. Aside from the occasional controversial issue that precipitates large turnout, most referenda attract far less than a majority of registered voters. Yet the promise is not completely hollow. One reality that policymakers have to keep in mind is that these devices *can* be resorted to if their actions become too offensive. Earlier advocates spoke of this power as "a shotgun behind the door"; today, political scientists speak of their potential for creating "anticipated reactions" in officials who will then ostensibly curb their excesses in anticipation of what the public will accept. The same idea applies to educational administrators' "zone of tolerance."[1]

However, the use of referenda to pass budgets, levies, and bonds in education did not arise from progressives. As Hamilton and Cohen point out, school referenda were the handiwork of *conservatives* seeking to *prevent* passage of bond issues and to keep property tax rates down by state law. To obtain taxes and expenditures above the state limits, these laws made school referenda required, often to be voted on only by property owners and requiring extraordinary majorities to pass. Conservatives thought that few such efforts would succeed, given these barriers, but that is not what happened. The unintended consequences of this reform were that local revenue sources dried up and pressures escalated on the state to bail out the locals. Around 1900, this process generated pressures for new state taxes and led to the widespread adoption of the sales tax and new grant and taxing arrangements for the local schools. This occurred again in the educational finance politics of the 1970s. Consequently, "the tax limitation schemes begat fiscal policy centralization and a web of state-local fiscal relationships and interdependence."[2] In addition, local districts regularly turned to the use of referenda to overcome the legal limitations imposed by the states.

In two respects the referendum is more significant for education than for other areas of public policy. It is the necessary device for securing financial support of schools in all states except Alabama, Hawaii, and Indiana; however, certain districts are exempt in fourteen other states. Also, this device may be viewed as a conversion process that bypasses the school board and authoritatively allocates values, a direct policymaking process. Passage or defeat of a measure on the ballot definitely allocates school system resources, in the form of levies and bond issues. The act of voting for or against—or not at all—links the individual citizen to the school in a direct and intimate way that is unparalleled for other major public policies.

The relationship can take several forms, however. Sweeping support of what school professionals offer citizens indicates close correspondence between the preferences of the two. Ostensibly that condition arises when school authorities carefully anticipate the limits of the public's demands; beyond this point officials believe that public support will drop off. Alternatively, public support may be closely divided but still large enough to provide a majority; this reflects community cleavage over policy issues. Here the school authorities have less room in which to anticipate the public's acceptable limits. A third possible relationship is when school authorities are defeated on the referenda they urge; here their anticipatory wisdom was poor. Consequent adjustments will vary depending on the size of the defeat. A narrow loss is worth another referendum effort, while a large defeat indicates considerable rearrangement of the school policies that the referenda funds were to support.

The Taxpayer Revolt

These conceptual distinctions are well illustrated by voting patterns for bond issues in recent decades. Figure 8.1 traces these dynamics over the turbulent years featured throughout this book. Here we can see the wave of nonsupport for local school financing in bond approval rates over three decades, reflected in the proportion of successful referenda and their dollar value. The figure displays massive shifts in both measures, signaling the volatile political world of changing educational needs. The early 1960s witnessed the greatest input of support, when the last baby boom students and a reaction against Russian space developments generated demands for capital construction. About 75 percent of both referenda and dollars requested were approved then. Soon, though, both support figures fell off dramatically until 1970 (success rates dropped to 41–45 percent). Next, amid the OPEC oil crisis and school expansion in the Sunbelt states, another cycle of success and failure followed until 1976. For these twenty years, success in both measures were extremely parallel; the rank order coefficient of the two curves is about .9.

But in the decade after 1976, these two measures of system response to educational needs drastically split, going in opposite directions; the coefficient changes to $-.7$. The number of bond elections (noted beneath the graphs of Figure 8.1) fell after 1977 from 831 to 332 in 1982 and rose again about 60 percent over the next five years. However, the number of these offerings was unrelated to the success rate, which fell ever lower, ending at 35 percent in 1985 and 1986. But

Figure 8.1
Three Decades of School Bond Approval, 1957–1986

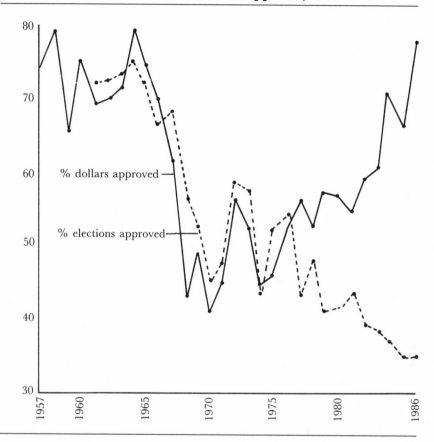

Source: Annual Reports, National Center for Educational Statistics, 1957–1976; combined report 1977–1986 (August, 1987).

surprisingly, the amount of money successfully approved increased just as steeply, from 45 to 77 percent! That increase paralleled an increase from 1983–1986 in the absolute dollar amount submitted for approval (from $1.8 to $5.2 billion).[3] One could interpret these graphs better if regional figures were available (the dollar increase may be related to school expansion in the Sunbelt), or if we knew the data for levies and budget elections.

But the record in Figure 8.1 of public response to school financial needs over thirty years points to voter dissatisfaction and the uncertainty surrounding the political system of local boards and superintendents. Imagine the difficulty these authorities have in estimating what the voters will accept; later we will explore what they actually learned from such defeat. For the total system, however, changing the dollar amount submitted to voters did not improve either the success rate or the dollar amount approved over the entire three decades. Of course, these are aggregate figures for a total political system of educational authority; they mask the variations caused by regional and community context.[4] The recent increase in the amount of dollars could be explained by several factors, including recent enrollment increases, concern about foreign competition, or specific state and local issues.

Until the 1970s, one could lament the surprisingly limited study of school referenda. After all, school districts were, until quite recently, by far the most numerous unit of governance in the country. The devouring force of consolidation noted earlier is starkly portrayed in the disappearance of 86 percent of these districts in just a third of a century. Today, only one school district remains where once seven existed. But about the time the voter revolt against referenda appeared, a spate of research and rethinking emerged. One major volume has evaluated the field so as to construct a propositional inventory of what the research showed; another tested these propositions in several ways.[5]

LINKAGES AMONG VOTERS, TURNOUT, AND SUCCESS IN SCHOOL REFERENDA

When a citizen votes aye or nay on a secret ballot for a school budget, levy, or bond issue, no one is there to inquire what she or he has in mind. Yet this is an important query, both for school authorities, who need to finely tune their public support if they are to mobilize sufficient financial resources, and for scholars interested in the conceptual ties of the act of voting to its reasons and results. The importance for the authorities has long been known; many professionals regret the time required to go about with a tin cup among the citizens, as they see it. Practical advice on the voter linkage has abounded for years—some based on singular, anecdotal evidence but some based on research.[6]

When scholars started to study these linkages, an extensive but complex body of knowledge emerged, which we will sketch out here. First it is important to discuss the underlying concepts about this linkage and then fill in with some of the strongest evidence. Figure 8.2 outlines the basic paradigm of this research effort and details some of its components.

The primary concept of these linkages is a model, namely: (1) present policy events within the school system are affected by (2) previous voting outcomes on school referenda, (3) which in turn were a consequence of the turnout, and (4) the turnout was a product of characteristics of the voters, their district, or both, and (5) this action can be explained in several ways.

We can begin at the left side of the model. There has been much research on which particular *voter* characteristics are associated with a larger turnout or with voting for or against a referendum. These characteristics are usually measured by social and attitudinal qualities (status, ethnicity, ideology, attitudes toward schools). Partial theories rooted in the individual voter's motivations are offered as attempted explanations for these associations. The explanation could be economic; that is, one votes for a referendum if what one gains is more than what the tax will cost or votes against it if one will lose more. There are also explanations based on whether the individual is oriented more to self or community. Explanations can also be based on psychological motivations, particularly the degree to which the voters are alienated from society or schools.

Another cluster of characteristics thought to be associated with good turnout and support are traced to *district* qualities. Districts differ in their demands for educational services, as measured by economic resources of the population or by the proportion of school-age children. Explanation is then derived from quantitative analysis of these environmental attributes and can involve testing the proposition that high demand will increase voter turnout or tax support. Or districts can be analyzed by such matters as qualifications for voting, size of the vote needed for referenda success, conditions under which financial matters may or must be submitted, and so on. These enable one to explore political explanations, such as rational decision making. Finally, the degree of political turbulence in a district and the qualities

Figure 8.2
Model of Research into Financial Referenda

Voter Characteristics: →	Individual-Level Explanations →	Turnout →	Voting Outcome →	Subsequent Policy Events
Variable – status – ethnicity – ideology – school attitudes	Economic—optimization Ethos—other-regarding Psychological—alienation	Percent of eligibles Social composition	Size of support Social composition of yeas and nays	Future frequency of referenda Results of future referenda Amount of funds in future referenda Board turnover Superintendent turnover Board policy (program changes)
District Characteristics: Demand levels: resources school age cohort Structural requirements: – voting – majority submission Amount of politicization	System-Level Explanations Environmental—macroanalysis Political access—legitimation Community conflict			

of that history are district attributes that enable one to use community conflict theory as explanations.

These independent variables are much more detailed than the dependent variables whose explanation is sought. Thus, turnout is usually measured by the proportion of eligible adults that actually votes and their social composition. Then the voting outcome is usually measured by the proportion of those voting for the referendum and by their social composition. Less studied but a logical next step would be to measure what happens after the votes are counted. This would indicate the consequences that follow from passage or failure of a referendum—what happens thereafter to future referenda (frequency, funding, results of votes), to the school authorities themselves, or to school policies?

We now turn to flesh out details of this model of individuals, communities, and referenda outputs.

WHO VOTES AND WHY?

Research rather consistently paints a picture of those who turn out and support school referenda and those who do neither. This is crucial information for school authorities who must spend time estimating where their support comes from. It is also significant for those testing ideas about citizen inputs to the political system of the schools. We only outline the main findings here because the literature is now fairly extensive and much of it is reinforcing.[7]

One quality of referendum voters has changed dramatically during the 1970s—they are no longer restricted to being taxpayers. In 1970, the Supreme Court struck down that requirement in the fourteen states that still required it.[8] The Court concluded that nontaxpayers were quite affected by such elections; also, that the practice rested on a false assumption that only taxpayers pay property taxes when in fact renters pay them indirectly to landlords and commercial stores. Thus a practice that was widespread for all kinds of voting when our republic began finally vanished from our electoral system.

The Influence of Status

The largest volume of research has traditionally fastened on the status of those who turn out and those who support referenda. One clear finding about this cohort always appears—they are predominantly drawn from the middle and upper strata of the community. Attributes of this status can be measured by income, occupation, or education, but all show much the same thing: a descending cascade of turnout and support from upper to lower statuses. Table 8.1 displays this characteristic, using education as a status measure as employed in nine studies from 1958 to 1970. Singly or combined, these status variables account for most of the variation in voting behavior and are therefore predictors of unusual power. Parental status and religious affiliation are also strong indicators; for example, parents and Protestants are much more likely supporters than nonparents and Roman Catholics.[9] Yet status accounts for much more of the differences between protagonists in school referenda.

Note that little evidence demonstrates that voters actually see themselves in such status terms. Rather, each group sees itself and its opponents as groups motivated by self-interest. One study found that economic explanations permeated both sides. Proponents saw themselves as parents seeking to benefit their children, and the opponents (elderly, retirees, those on fixed income) sought to escape the economic bite of more taxes. The opposition, however, saw a different group context, although still economically motivated. They regarded themselves as homeowners and taxpayers (not opponents of children's welfare), while they felt the supporters (teachers and schoolpeople) were only seeking to improve their lot economically.[10]

Note that these studies of status and voting results rest on data from 1970 or before. Given the political turbulence of the 1970s in the schools, has anything changed in these relationships? Reviews of that decade found little change in such items as higher support for referenda among the younger, richer, and better educated voters. But evidence showed that people in professional and managerial occupations had become stronger supporters than those in other occupations.[11]

Influence of Ethnicity

Other factors confound the influence of status. For example, ethnicity has significance in distinguishing among referenda voters; that is, within each income level, ethnic identity sorts out supporters and opponents. The scholarly revisionism of the 1960s found that alleged ethnic assimilation had not taken place. In Glazer and Moynihan's

Table 8.1

Percent Referenda Support by Education Level, Selected Studies, 1958–70

Years of School	Bowling Green, Ohio 1966	Youngstown, Ohio 1968	Birmingham, Michigan 1961	Corning, New York 1957	Ithaca, New York 1958	Okemos, Michigan 1958	Austintown, Ohio 1970	State of Washington 1970
1–8	30	38						41
9–11	40	48	35	23	43	32	24	46
12	49	56					45	50
13–15	57							53
16+	88	71	53	31	69	63	73	79

Source: Howard D. Hamilton and Sylvan Cohen, *Policy Making by Plebiscite: School Referenda* (Lexington, Mass.: Lexington Books, D.C. Heath and Company. Copyright 1974, D.C. Heath and Company), p. 180. Reprinted by permission of the publisher.

words, "The point about the melting pot is that it did not happen."[12] Thus in Chicago among those of the same status (low-income and middle-income voters), Irish and Polish voters were less supportive of a tax issue than were black voters. Others noted the curious partnership of the poorest black and wealthiest white precincts in giving high support for many school issues, including finances.[13]

The blacks' main problem has been relatively low turnout in such elections, even though they support tax referenda more than urban whites do.[14] Explaining voting behavior solely based on economics would have large numbers of the poorer blacks turning out to support such referenda, for these measures tax others to provide black children with greater educational resources. But clearly this is not the case when so few of this group actually turn out to vote. The political use of black votes to secure control of urban school systems has rarely been studied; Cleveland blacks were capable of withholding their supporting votes from a school system slow to desegregate.[15] The use of votes by black and Hispanic groups to control and direct the big-city schools needs more comparative study, as they increasingly constitute the majority in many urban districts. Do status divisions within these groups differentiate views about education policy as they occur among whites? Do the two groups share similar policy views, or does ethnicity drive them apart?

It would be an error to conceive of whites as a unified voting group. A survey designed to sort out the tie between ethnicity and referenda in the 1960s found quite different degrees of support among those of British versus European ancestry. Moreover, even when controlling for such powerful influences as status and parental type, this distinction did not disappear. In short, "Ethnicity was distinctly more potent than social class or parentage."[16]

Ethnicity may well have a distinct influence on referenda voting when the voting takes place in the absence of political parties. Indeed, the significance of ethnicity for referenda voting may actually arise from this very absence of party, for it is the party that, in other matters, provides cues to citizens on how to vote. In the absence of such cues, ethnicity may be employed by the voter instead, with one result being an increased social cleavage within districts. This is possible with school referenda, especially so as ethnic groups seem to differ on their views of the purposes of education and to receive different benefits from school resources within the same city.[17]

The Influence of Ideology

There are suggestions that in special school elections the voters may develop and use an ideology or ethos centered around the school as an institution in the society. Thus, ethnicity may be one of the ways that people are socialized to a particular perception of the function and value of schooling. This approach was central to an effort by Banfield and Wilson to contrast two opposed sets of attitudes about government and public issues. One ethos ("public regarding") centered on an Anglo-Saxon Protestant group life, which emphasized belief in "the interest of the whole," public obligation, rule by the most qualified, and a government that is honest, impartial, and efficient. The other ethos ("private regarding") centered on immigrant groups and on lower-class and working-class citizens. Private-regarding groups focused more on private interests of family and personal loyalties rather than on the community at large; politics was seen as an individual or family competition for advantage; and the party machine was the central way of governance in contrast to the nonpartisan governance of the public-regarding groups. While this overall concept has been strongly challenged, it has been applied to school politics once, focusing on school referenda attitudes. In a small Ohio town, scholars found results that matched well other big-city studies that had used ecological data. Here again is another possibility for valuable research.

Private versus public orientation to referenda is found in how people vote their economic interests. Figure 8.3 suggests four types of votes and orientations to community or personal interests. Voters with or without schoolchildren who voted against a school levy could be regarded as having a personal orientation. They may have decided that the cost of the levy was greater than what their children would gain, thereby ignoring any general (or public) commitment to the schools at large. Conversely, nonparents voting for the levy could be evidence of a community orientation; some such commitment to the community at large must explain why they agree to tax themselves. In several polls, these personal and community types were found to be about equal in strength, each ranging from 15 to 25 percent of voters. But when other mixed types were thrown in, about half the voters were, in Banfield and Wilson's terms, private-regarding and another one-quarter public-regarding.[18] Clearly, self-interest looms large as a

Figure 8.3
Personal and Community Orientations to Voting in School Referenda

Direction of vote	Voter Motives With Children in Public Schools	Without Children in Public Schools
For	Mixed	Community
Against	Personal	Personal

Community = Has first commitment to community, second consideration for economic costs of referendum, and consequently reasons in voting:

Community benefits > personal costs
Personal = Has first commitment to self-family-ethnic group, second consideration to community, and consequently reasons in voting:

Personal costs > community/personal benefits
Mixed = Motives may be either personal or community benefit as primary consideration, but not both, and consequently reasons in voting:
Indeterminate

motivation for voting, and it lies behind the decreasing public support for schools, as we have ever fewer adults with children in public schools. This is only the latest example of a long history of Americans satisfying their self-interest.[19]

INFLUENCE OF ATTITUDES TOWARD SCHOOLS

Clearly, an intervening factor can be the voter's perceptions and sense of worth about educational institutions. Evidence suggests that the more children one has in schools and the greater the personal contact one has with school officials, the greater the credibility extended to schoolpeople. Parents with children in school but who lacked contact with school officials did not support a tax levy very much. In short, what the school system communicates to its public can generate support, and without this, potential supporters will fall away.[20]

Another perspective on schools that could influence the vote is the voters' predisposition to regard public expenditures as a "good thing" or to believe that government taxes are "bad things" by themselves, regardless of the particular referendum in question. One study found these lines to be firmly drawn among substantial numbers of opposing voters. As the authors perceptively noted of these gross attitudes, "They . . . may be the principal devices used by voters for simplifying the problem, i.e., for coping with the information problem and reducing the decision-making burden."[21] But again little research has tried to trace the fixed constellations of attitudes that voters use for steering the turbulent seas of school politics.

It may be difficult for advocates of public education to realize that there are voters with an engrained bias against supporting school finances. However, elections are channels for funneling many kinds of attitudes, and one with great relevance for schools is "alienation." This is the sense of being ignored by a society thought to be controlled by a conspiracy of persons quite different from one's self. Researchers have found alienation to be significant in referenda on fluoridation, metropolitan government reform, and open housing, so it should not be surprising to find it present among those voting against school referenda. We must not exaggerate the proportion of alienated people nor underestimate its role in defeating such measures. After all, if one believes no channels to the powerful are open or that they ignore one's wishes about public policy, the referendum device is well adapted to striking back at the "they" who are thought to run roughshod over "us." And striking back means a negative vote, as the only other alternative—voting yes—would please "them." Yet we might understand this attitude better as reinforcing other motives for opposition. Thus alienation and referenda opposition are correlated, but they are also inversely correlated with social status.[22]

This discussion of voter characteristics linked to school referenda points both to continuities and divergences. Scholars are clearly moving beyond the once-traditional research focus on only status correlates of districts or voters themselves. The fuzziness of the findings to date, as well as the danger of "ecological fallacy,"* require that future work should fasten on attitudinal and ideological maps of these voters. How voters see schools—obviously these are diverse

---

*Ecological fallacy is inferring the attitudes of individuals from gross demographic characteristics of the place where they live.

perceptions—and how they feel about schools need to be related to basic values about one's self, the political system, and society in general. We are far from any general knowledge about the *origins* of either these underlying or manifest attitudes and perceptions. Such knowledge would be particularly useful for school authorities trying to determine what their public will accept in taxes. Knowing how to communicate and present educational programs to the public is of little avail if they are not accompanied by an understanding of what voters feel and think about education in general.[23] By the late 1980s, polls were showing that Americans were liking their schools somewhat more. But in reality, among our national institutions, schools had been *least* hit by public distrust in the previous two decades. The national branches of government, major companies, medicine, and the press had all been much more distrusted. Indeed, as Piele reported, "Despite all the outcry about school 'failures,' public confidence in those responsible for education ran ahead of all other institutional leaders except doctors."[24]

But this general goodwill about schools may be less important in policymaking by referenda than the fact of a changing demography of voters. As Figure 8.3 suggests, fewer public school parents today mean fewer people motivated to vote for referenda for either personal or community reasons. Rather, the new context of greatest importance for referenda is the increasing number of citizens without children in the public schools. These are both young and old, as well as private school parents, who, by the logic of Figure 8.3, will not vote for the taxes to support public schools. The results must be the erosion of the once stable and continuing base of public acceptance of referenda policy.

WHAT DIFFERENCE DOES THE DISTRICT MAKE?

As Figure 8.2 hinted, besides individual influences, public input on decision making can be enhanced or inhibited by the unique qualities of the district involved. Sometimes termed "structural," these are attributes of the organizational life and community behavior of a given locale. Researchers have studied these attributes more because information on this aspect of school referenda is readily available.

Environmental Factors

The resources in a community's environment, measured by census variables, have been explored for their alleged effects on referenda results. We know certain important environmental influences are at work. Simple district size is not highly predictive.[25] Rather the way social life is structured inside the district is what counts. The preceding chapter related how a community's structuring of the politics affecting board elections could shape outcomes. That is, high-status suburbs do this differently than low-status suburbs, a finding suggestive of the personal and community distinction noted above. Thus higher-status districts will more often tax themselves.[26] This situation represents the intersect of social, economic, and political factors. Parceling out these factors among twenty-two New York districts, Figure 8.4 traces the effects of size, wealth, and employment on operating expenditures. Also, the relationship of expenditures to political mobilization (voter turnout) and political dissent (contested seats) is positively correlated with school budget election defeats. We see evidence here that supports the findings of Zeigler and Jennings in Chapter 6: Greater politicization of school politics characterizes metropolitan rather than other districts.

Political Factors: Structures

Another structural factor of a district is how it organizes school board selections and terms of office. The first edition of this book set out the qualities associated with successful referenda, as determined in a major study by Carter and Sutthoff during the 1950s.[27] Success depended very much on whether it was a bond or a tax election under study; few types of political structures were associated with success in both types, and none consistently. As this massive study was set in a much more tranquil era of school elections, even less association is likely to exist today between these structures and referenda outcomes. Indeed, pursuit of this possible linkage disappeared from the research field by the late 1970s, but research is still necessary.

What other district characteristics are relevant to election outcomes? Both earlier and more recent studies have consistently found that a district's past record of success or failure is the best predictor of its present behavior. That is, what a district has done it will do. This

Figure 8.4
Social, Economic, and Political Linkages to Referenda Defeats, New York Districts, 1965–1973

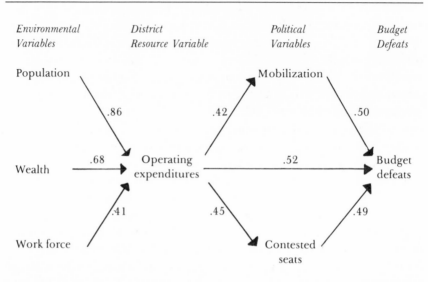

Source: Leigh Stelzer, "Public School Financing: A Theory of Popular Budget Decisions" (Paper delivered at Southwestern Political Science Association, 1974), p. 12.

finding implies that the divisions between school supporters and opponents—for whatever reasons—become fixed over time, including their stances on referenda. It is another matter, however, if that district's composition alters, as last chapter's discussion of the dissatisfaction theory of democracy set out. While Figure 8.1 points to an overall shift in district voting on referenda, some lag must occur between this national trend and what happens in districts with records of either rarely or regularly passing referenda.

Political Factors: Strategy and Conflict

Research has increasingly shown that some overtly political qualities of districts affect referenda. Although boards and administrators have long acted as if their efforts to mobilize referenda support were not political—in keeping with the traditional myth of the profession[28]—this strategic repertoire can hardly be denied its political qualities. These strategies have been set out in earlier textbooks for the fledgling superintendent, as well as by scholars urging the professional to use even more sophisticated techniques in analyzing the political process. If Democratic or Republican candidates for any office engaged in these techniques, we would instantly recognize the situation as typical voter mobilization, hence as being "political." However, the fact that school professionals engage in the same act does not change its essential quality despite the euphemism of "nonpolitical." School constituencies no longer accept a definition of such behavior as being nonpolitical, for often they are themselves deeply enmeshed in the politics of schools. Americans today still ask for the white or dark meat of a turkey dinner, using the same euphemisms Victorians of a century ago adopted in order to avoid speaking such words as "breast" and "leg." But, the meat is still the same, then and now, and so is the political quality of school professionals' strategies to mobilize referenda support.

We will not detail the strategic lore of winning school referenda; there is an enormous literature detailing anecdotes of this kind. But we do question whether much of that lore any longer applies to the current political turbulence. All of it rested on certain assumptions about the linkages between authorities and voters, that is, a low-visibility and low-conflict school politics. Little of the lore took into account the possibility that strategies would vary, given the differing social compositions of communities. But as Minar and Boyd have shown for the period when school politics was heating up, superintendents must adopt different "conflict management" styles in working-class and middle-class suburbs.[29] And, as shown in the preceding chapter, the size of the district (and the accompanying differences in heterogeneity) have major consequences for the political interaction of board and superintendent and for these authorities and the voters.

What is the value of traditional strategic lore when, as Cuban found, metropolitan superintendents were recently being replaced at a very high rate;[30] or when school officials in Youngstown, Ohio, sought to pass a referendum seven times within a thirty-month period, including three within six months?[31] What is its value when curriculum dissidents dynamited the school's central offices in Kanawa County, West Virginia, in the early 1970s, or flooded school boards with criticism of "secular humanism" in the 1980s?

Care must be taken that the training of school authorities does not assume far too much about the steady-state nature of American communities, for what we have seen in the last two decades is a persistent conflictual context. Coleman's classic essay on such conflict fully applies to school issues.[32] That is, school policy consists of a set of events that touch important aspects of the community and that citizens know they can do something about. In the process, conflict develops in a regular fashion. Thus the specific issue that starts the conflict becomes a general issue; new and different issues emerge from this, which in turn generate disagreements that escalate into hostility. These developments cause to surface latent community cleavages— class, race, generations—that have little to do with the original referendum issue. Then this upheaval in turn draws in groups usually uninvolved who are not really school supporters—for example, the alienated voters who regularly vote against incumbents or policy issues.

Consequently, referenda tell us much about the presence or absence of stress within a community. Comparative analysis of stress need not rely on case studies detailing actors and actions. One rough macromeasure of stress has been found in the size of voter turnout for referenda. Much evidence has shown that, traditionally, the greater the turnout the less chance of passage.[33] Yet evidence drawn from the more tumultuous 1970s suggests that this has become less certain. Increased turnout currently points to those groups who are not usually school supporters or are alienated, but who enter into the decisional context and vote down referenda.[34]

A macromeasure that indicates community stress more directly is the relationship between the size of the tax or levy increase sought and the degree of voting support for it. The first edition of this book presented data on California tax elections in the late 1960s that substantiated this association. Thus, of the referenda designed to *lower* the tax rate (N = 9), 78 percent passed; 97 percent of those also passed that sought the *same* rate (N = 79); but only 44 percent passed that sought an *increase* (N = 504). Also, as the size of the tax being sought increased, the proportion of successes fell off, from sixty cents or less tax in increase (48 percent successful) to sixty-one to eighty cents (38 percent) to over eighty-one cents (33 percent). Research elsewhere supports the negative relationship between size of levy increase and referenda success.[35]

Probably the macromeasure most directly tapping community conflict over schools is the size of the vote supporting a referendum. When support is in the range of 45 to 55 percent, the district must be much more sharply divided over school policy than when support exceeds 55 percent. By itself such analysis is insufficient to portray the complexities of such conflict, as Boyd's suburban studies demonstrate.[36] Narrow support seems an indirect measure of high community cleavage, that stressful environment which, in Easton's concepts, the political system works to avoid or accommodate.

Referenda Strategies: Learning from Defeat

The only significant attention in recent years paid to the role of referenda in local decision making arises from the Romer and Rosenthal econometric studies in Oregon and New York.[37] Their theoretical concern was to see how sensitive this political process was to local feelings. Several findings, greatly simplified, are significant.

District leaders would seek higher budgets when they could issue threats about what cuts meant, including closing a school. They would not let voters know about state aid of the flat-grant type but would advise them of the matching grant type. The latter required that new local monies be raised to receive additional state grants, an inducement offered voters to support the local referenda budget.

But if the referendum was defeated, then what? In response, districts pursued two basic strategies. Some adopted a "forget it!" strategy. One version emerged in core cities that refused another referendum but instead relied only on an increase in state aid in its expenditure base. Another version of this strategy was simple—shut down. In May 1987, however, a constitutional amendment was adopted by Oregon voters, redefining a district's ability to rely on its previous spending; that may affect both strategies.

In subsequent studies, Romer and associates reported on a second and more familiar strategy—"hit the voters again!" or, "budgeting by a sequence of referenda." Conventional wisdom held that after a first defeat of a budget, officials would reduce its size, resubmit it to referenda; then if that failed, reduce it even lower and resubmit; and so on until the referendum met approval. In practice, this did not appear to be the case. Rather, while budgets were often reduced, these cuts were small, and many budgets were not changed at all prior to resubmission and subsequent approval. That is, budget cutting and subsequent approval seemed unrelated. However, this form of analysis does not explore the effect that referenda failure has on school support groups; they may be stimulated to work harder in subsequent elections. These scholars do, though, report a curious pattern; some places more consistently defeat referenda than others. This suggests the presence of a permanent cohort of nay-sayers large enough to undermine any fiscal adjustment to the currents of educational change.

District size has some effects on this decision-making process. Smaller districts usually have higher turnouts; in bigger units, many voters act like "free riders," leaving others, especially professionals, to benefit them. However, larger districts more often defeat referenda than do smaller units. That result may arise because the more varied constituencies of larger units, facing large budget proposals, can find many small things to criticize in the budget. This suggests a process that also works to defeat popular adoption of state constitutions—accumulating small disaffections into a majority opposition.

THE LOCAL CONVERSION PROCESS IN TRANSITION

This chapter has pointed to the dual interest in referenda—by the practitioner who must rely on them in many states for continued sustenance, and by the scholar of democratic politics. School officials do not like the device, although they express little of that feeling publicly, but no evidence suggests that it will be abolished any time soon.[38] Despite the picture of public referenda rejection presented here, we must not underestimate the influence of the professional. Whether due to skilled conflict management, wise anticipation of reactions, or convincing definitions of public policy, school authorities have traditionally kept disruptive public inputs to their system to a minimum. But recently, escalating conflict has threatened this control and the system's persistence. Low-key community relations used to be the norm. Then, the decisional forum withdrew somewhere into the crevices of the professionals' world; supporters both inside and outside the system were maintained and reinforced; and a closed world of policymaking existed for a select few. There was only a limited citizen control over schools, exceeded only occasionally by episodic events.

But even these spasms did not often touch major policy, focusing rather on peripheral and specific issues.

In that context, one sees much of systems analysis and democratic theory in operation. As Minar concluded, "There is reason to believe that the reduction of public conflict is something of an ideal toward which school systems tend."[39] Here we see signs of system persistence, of coping with threatened stress by shaping the required referenda inputs, and of forestalling eruptive demands. All this is done to anticipate community demands. The result is an output reflecting both public and professional needs and wants.

We also see in this earlier period the conflict of majoritarian and minoritarian values raised in an earlier chapter. Although the rhetoric of majority rule is strong in our school districts, the reality has actually been minority decision making, as confirmed by referenda turnout in all but a few communities. That condition arose from the predominant influence of the school professionals who moved the system toward goals that they—and not often the community—defined. Board members' ties to the community were tenuous and ambiguous, while their control over the bureaucracy was limited and general. At best boards were adjudicators at the margins of school policy. When groups not satisfied with this minority control sought changes through official channels, they often found the professionals' control unassailable.

Yet the recent turbulence must have some effects on this traditional system maintenance, such as those items listed in Figure 8.2 under Subsequent Policy Events. We have seen in previous chapters how there have been board and superintendent turnovers and major policy changes of some persistence. Further, in the decline of the total number of referenda offered, Figure 8.1 shows the desperate efforts of school authorities to anticipate the voters' zone of tolerance in the 1970s. Yet another challenge to traditional authorities in this country has been litigation against school policies. Between the 1960s and 1970s, the volume of legal challenges against bond and tax referenda decisions tripled; recall and malpractice suits, while few, grew even more (although they were rarely successful).[40]

The presence of increasingly institutionalized sets of new actors at the local school level requires adaptation, and often new training, in administrative roles as well.[41] Training administrators has shifted somewhat from an emphasis on organizational theory as explaining their decisional environment to an emphasis on political context.[42] Certainly the superintendent today needs to understand much more than just the old notion of keeping the referenda campaign low key in order to win. Partial theories of what goes on in voters' minds in these elections abound, as we have shown. The professional needs to know much more about the politics of decision making, and for this, one must grasp other political theories—rational, incremental, implementation, and so on.[43]

Finally, whatever new role the professional adopts within this current turbulence, he and she will have participated in the most recent skirmish of our historic clash between participatory and meritocratic values. That clash reflects the ongoing tension between majoritarian and minoritarian impulses in a complex society, which we discussed in the chapter on pressure groups. James Madison, Alexis de Tocqueville, or Lord Bryce, brought back to life and observing the events discussed in these last two chapters, would understand quite well what they meant. These observers and many others have grasped the basic underlying dynamic of American politics and policymaking. That is the tension generated by a nation of diverse groups seeking to realize their values through the subsystems of society, including the political.

In one slice of time, the meritocratic impulse may seem totally dominant; pre-1960 writing about educational administration partakes of this quality. More recently, though, one can see the triumph of the participatory impulse in the success of new school constituencies. Yet in the 1980s, a return to "excellence" in schooling reflects once again the meritocratic impulse. Somewhere between the two may be long periods of accommodation to new and successful demands on the educational policy system. Professionals in many areas have learned to adapt when compelled by such clientele pressures, but the process[44] does not end at any of these stages.

If the nature of school governance seems more unstructured today because of this flux of actors and events at the local level, the new forces generated outside the district are just as perturbing. What the state and national governments and allied interest groups have done is to create another new—often highly constricting—set of inputs into the local political system. It is to the state influences that we next turn.

NOTES

1. On Progressivism and the quotation, see Eric F. Goldman, *Rendezvous with Destiny* (New York: Vintage books, 1956), p. 338. For origins and results of direct legislation, see William Munro, ed., *The Initiative, Referendum and Recall* (New York: Macmillan, 1913), and Joseph G. LaPalombara and Charles B. Hagan, "Direct Legislation: An Appraisal and a Suggestion," *American Political Science Review* 45 (1951): 400–21. On zone of tolerance, see William Boyd, "The Public, the Professionals, and Educational Policy Making: Who Governs?: *Teachers College Record* 77 (1976): 556–58.

2. Howard D. Hamilton and Sylvan H. Cohen, *Policy Making by Plebiscite: School Referenda* (Lexington, Mass.: Lexington Books, 1974), pp. 3–6.

3. National Center for Educational Statistics, U.S. Department of Education (August 1987), p. 22.

4. For a regional analysis, see Hamilton and Cohen, *Policy Making*, pp. 180 ff.

5. The volumes are Philip K. Piele and John S. Hall, *Budgets, Bonds, and Ballots* (Lexington, Mass.: Lexington Books, 1973) and Hamilton and Cohen, *Policy Making*. An updating through 1980 is found in Philip Piele, "Public Support for Public Schools: The Past, the Future, and the Federal Role," *Teachers College Record* 84 (1983): 690–707.

6. For example, Michael Y. Nunnery and Ralph B. Kimbrough, *Politics, Power, Polls, and School Elections* (Berkeley: McCutchan, 1971).

7. Piele and Hall, *Budgets, Bonds, and Ballots*, provides the major review of this research.

8. *Phoenix* v. *Kolodziewski*, 399 U.S. 204 (1970).

9. Hamilton and Cohen, *Policy Making*, p. 213.

10. For this innovative conceptualization, see Hamilton and Cohen, *Policy Making*, pp. 197–202.

11. Piele, "Public Support for Public Schools"; Philip K. Piele, "Voting Behavior in Local School Financial Referenda: An Update of Some Earlier Propositions," (Private manuscript, 1980).

12. Nathan Glazer and Daniel P. Moynihan, *Beyond the Melting Pot* (Cambridge, Mass.: MIT Press), p. 290.

13. James Q. Wilson and Edward C. Banfield, "Public Regardingness as a Value Premise in Voting Behavior," *American Political Science Review* 58 (1964): 883; Piele and Hall, *Budgets, Bonds, and Ballots*, pp. 105–7.

14. For Detroit data to this effect, see first edition of this book at page 103. Piele's manuscript (see note 11 above) reported that no change had been found in black support.

15. Louis Masotti, "Patterns of White and Nonwhite School Referenda Participation and Support: Cleveland, 1960–1964," in *Educating an Urban Population*, Marilyn Gittel, ed. (Beverly Hills, Calif.: Sage, 1967), pp. 253, 255.

16. Hamilton and Cohen, *Policy Making*, pp. 207–8.

17. Gerald Pomper, "Ethnic and Group Voting in Nonpartisan Municipal Elections," *Public Opinion Quarterly* 30 (1966); J. Leiper Freeman, "Local Party Systems:

Theoretical Considerations and a Case Analysis," *American Journal of Sociology* 64 (1958): 282–89. On ethnic attitudes towards schools, see Glazer and Moynihan, *Beyond the Melting Pot*. On differential ethnic benefits from one school system, see Dianne Pinderhughes, *Race and Ethnicity in Chicago Politics* (Champaign: University of Illinois Press, 1987).

18. Wilson and Banfield, "Public Regardingness."

19. Hamilton and Cohen, *Policy Making*, pp. 209–11; on economic motivations and status, see Piele and Hall, *Budgets, Bonds, and Ballots*, pp. 113–14, 143–46; on decreasing public support and demography, see Michael Kirst and Walter Garms, "The Political Environment of School Finance Policy in the 1980s," in *School Finance Policies and Practices*, James Guthrie, ed. (Cambridge, Mass.: Ballinger, 1980).

20. For example, Thomas A. McCain and Victor D. Wall, Jr., "A Communication Perspective of a School-Bond Failure," *Education Administration Quarterly* 12, no. 2 (1974): 1–17; for a review of this aspect, see Piele and Hall, *Budgets, Bonds, and Ballots*, pp. 83–91, 130–34.

21. Hamilton and Cohen, *Policy Making*, p. 211.

22. See discussion of alienation research in Hamilton and Cohen, *Policy Making*, pp.202–5, and Piele and Hall, *Budgets, Bonds, and Ballots*, pp. 128–30.

23. Nunnery and Kimbrough, *Politics, Power, Polls*.

24. Piele, "Public Support for Public Schools," pp. 690–950.

25. Piele and Hall, *Budgets, Bonds, and Ballots*, p. 75.

26. David W. Minar, "The Community Basis of Conflict in School System Politics," *American Sociological Review* 31 (1966): 822–34; William L. Boyd, *Community Status and Conflict in Suburban School Politics* (Beverly Hills, Calif.: Sage, 1976).

27. Richard F. Carter and John Sutthoff, *Communities and Their Schools* (Stanford: Institute for Communication Research, 1960), Chap. 4; these are summarized in the first edition of this book at page 99. See also Piele and Hall, *Budgets, Bonds, and Ballots*, pp. 75–77.

28. Robert H. Salisbury, "Schools and Politics in the Big City," *Harvard Educational Review* 37 (1967): 408–24.

29. Minar, "Community Basis of Conflict"; Boyd, *Community Status and Conflict*.

30. Larry Cuban, *Urban School Chiefs Under Fire* (Chicago: University of Chicago Press, 1976), Chap. 6.

31. For an account, see Hamilton and Cohen, *Policy Making*, pp. 164–67.

32. James S. Coleman, *Community Conflict* (Glencoe, Ill.: Free Press, 1957); for research using this framework, see Hamilton and Cohen, *Policy Making*, Chap. 7, and Piele and Hall, *Budgets, Bonds, and Ballots*, Chap. 4.

33. Piele and Hall, *Budgets, Bonds and Ballots*, Chap. 4.

34. Piele, "Public Support for Public Schools," pp. 690–95.

35. Calculated from the first edition of this book at page 105, Table 6.6. Supporting research is reviewed in Piele, "Public Support for Public Schools," p. 692.

36. Boyd, *Community Status and Conflict*.

37. The importance of this line of inquiry for empirical theory and administrative practice should be explored in other states with different political cultures and economic bases. See Thomas Romer and Howard Rosenthal, "Bureaucrats vs. Voters: On Political Economy of Resource Allocation by Direct Democracy," *Quar-*

terly Journal of Economics 93 (1979): 563–87; "An Institutional Theory of the Effect of Intergovernmental Grants," *National Tax Journal* 33 (1980): 451–58; "Median Voters or Budget Maximizers: Evidence from School Expenditure Referenda," *Economic Inquiry* 20 (1982): 556–78; "Voting and Spending: Some Empirical Relationships in the Political Economy of Local Public Finance," in *Local Provision of Public Services*, G. Zodrow, ed. (New York: Academic Press, 1983). See also Thomas Romer, Howard Rosenthal, and Krishna Ladha, "If At First You Don't Succeed: Budgeting by a Sequence of Referenda," in *Public Finance and the Quest for Efficiency*, H. Hanush, ed. (Detroit: Wayne State University Press, 1984).

38. Hamilton and Cohen, *Policy Making*, pp. 271–73.

39. Minar, "Community Basis of Conflict," p. 825.

40. Piele, "Public Support for Public Schools," pp. 696–97.

41. Cuban, *Urban School Chiefs Under Fire*, App. 2.

42. For a review of this shift, see Norman Boyan, "Follow the Leader: Commentary on Research in Educational Administration," *Educational Researcher* 12 (1981): 6–13. For an analysis of the recent contributions of social science to administrators' knowledge and training, see the essays in Glenn L. Immegart and William L. Boyd, eds., *Problem Finding in Educational Administration* (Lexington, Mass.: Heath, 1979), and Jack Culbertson et al., *Preparing Educational Leaders for the Seventies* (Columbus, Ohio: University Council for Educational Administration, 1969).

43. Dale Mann, *Policy Decision-Making in Education* (New York: Teachers College Press, 1975); Paul E. Peterson, *School Politics Chicago Style* (Chicago: University of Chicago Press, 1976); and on the referendum, see sources in n. 37.

44. Frederick M. Wirt, "Professionalism and Political Conflict: A Developmental Model," *Journal of Public Policy* 1 (1981): 61–93.

9

The State
Conversion Process

INTRODUCTION

Variety and Individualism

If variety is the spice of life, educational decision making in the fifty American states is a veritable spice cabinet. The situation is reminiscent of Kipling's aphorism that there are a thousand ways to worship God, and they are all correct. This variety is the key to understanding much about the basic value of individualism in the American system. We need not rely merely on assertions about this variety. Figure 9.1 sets forth the patterns of selecting and staffing administrative positions for education in the fifty states. Not only are there differences between the state board and chief administrator in such matters, but also within either office. Moreover, the ranges are impressive in board members' terms, size, and employees.

Such variety reflects a pluralism of views on how to express the taproot value of individualism. That value has been reflected through a prism of diverse historical experiences (the impact of losing versus winning the Civil War), different natural resources (the poverty of the South versus the richness of the North), demographic mixes (rural homogeneity versus urban heterogeneity), and so on. Through this tangle of past and present, the creation of institutions had to take

249

Figure 9.1
Chief State School Officer (CSSO) and State Board of Education
(SBE) Selection Patterns and Possibilities.

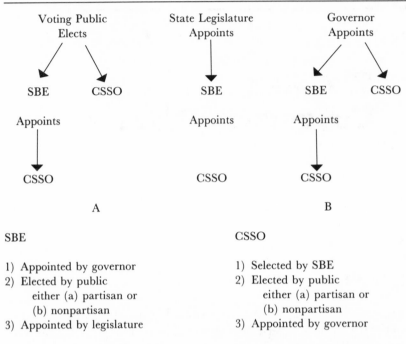

A

B

SBE

1) Appointed by governor
2) Elected by public
   either (a) partisan or
   (b) nonpartisan
3) Appointed by legislature

CSSO

1) Selected by SBE
2) Elected by public
   either (a) partisan or
   (b) nonpartisan
3) Appointed by governor

The only combination which presently does not exist is A3/B3

Source: James W. Guthrie and Rodney Reed, *Educational Administration and Policy* (Englewood Cliffs, N.J.: Prentice-Hall, 1986), p. 36.

various forms. The very basis of democratic life—the political institutions of party, pressure group, and voting—took different forms from
region to region as a result of these combinations of events, resources,
and population.[1] We should not be surprised, then, that the evolution
of educational institutions took different forms as well. For one thing,
ideas about how to organize and provide schooling were affected by
varied historical experiences. As we will see, the New England states'
violent opposition to George III instilled in them a fear of state-
centralized services, including schools, which remains today. On the
other hand, the states of the Confederacy were so devastated by the
Union troops' destruction that county institutions were wiped out.

State control and moneys had to be provided in large amounts, then and ever since.

Even the precise meaning of something that all states agreed to in principle—compulsory schooling—was affected by an intervening individualism. Massachusetts was the first state requiring school attendance in 1852. By 1900, thirty-five states had so acted, but the last state, Mississippi, did not adopt such legislation until 1918.[2] In short, it took two-thirds of a century to institutionalize acceptance of even an idea that had wide popular support. Today, though, it is not clear what the meaning of this service is; differing political, economic, sociological, and organizational explanations abound.[3] Underlying this variety is a long-standing thirst for education. From its beginnings, schooling has been thought to serve major purposes. But then and now, education was a means of salvation, whether of the soul or one's economic future.

However, just exactly how the goal was to be achieved was never easily agreed upon. A century ago conflict emerged over establishing free public education, racial equity, popular control, moral purpose, and financial support—just as there has in our time. The continuity of issues is surprising.[4] This is because laypersons and professionals alike recognized that schools taught moral, political, and social lessons, and consequently groups differed on what they felt these lessons should be.

Professional Dominance and Recent Challenge

This atmosphere of conflict was diluted for many decades until after World War II. This dilution occurred because, as noted earlier, professionals were able to convince citizens that they alone possessed the scientifically based, value-free knowledge necessary to provide the "best" education. Such an apolitical myth was highly useful to schoolpeople who could use it to keep politicians off their preserve. Professionals and their elected school boards consequently assumed the authority for making educational decisions relatively free from local and state officials, despite lip service to democracy.[5] Beginning in the 1950s, this immunity from the participatory impulse of democracy disappeared under attacks from many constituencies.[6] Within the web of federalism, constituencies defeated by the professional structure on one level could turn to higher levels to compel changes in local resources, structures, and policy services. State and federal legislatures and courts echoed with demands as pressure groups mobilized into national coalitions. Rarely has the federal structure shown its sensitivity to the multifaceted public demands so well as in this area.

In the process, the state took on a new, expanded role in education. As we shall see, the legislatures in particular became the center of such policymaking, but administrative agencies also intruded in the daily work of local education authorities (LEA) to implement the new changes. Interventions took the forms of mandating minimum and required services, rearranging tax and spending requirements, specifying new curricula, redefining the qualifications of the professionals, and so on. The analysis that follows sketches the patterns of these changes that have given the state role a new vigor in educational decision making. Much remains in flux, and the dust has not yet settled enough to reveal a clear picture of the state role. What is evident, however, is that the state is everywhere more active in school policymaking and services—and in many other policy areas as well. We see in this transformation a new way in which Americans work out the diverse meanings of their individualism.

SOCIOECONOMIC DIMENSIONS OF VARIETY

Multiple Responses to Systematic Problems

Understanding a state's politics of education requires a grasp of its societal background. In the case of the fifty American states, such a demonstration quickly overloads even eager students in the field because of the varied and many dimensions for categorizing or evaluating units of government. The fifty states and their sixteen thousand LEAs vary along all the traditional dimensions of demography—age composition; size of school age population; parents' education, occupation, and income; economic resources; and so on to form an almost endless list. Districts run from the behemoth, with a million students in New York City, to a rural hamlet with a dozen in the graduating class. Economics range from extremely wealthy suburbs to poor farm villages. Their resources vary just as much, from a multiple-building high school in a California suburb to a one-room schoolhouse on the Nebraska prairie.

This variety means that the total school system will adjust differently to impinging nationwide events. No such thing as state education policy exists; what does exist are differential state responses to common external and internal events. For example, a decreasing birthrate develops due to changes in contraceptive methods, new roles for women in the economy, more working married women in an inflationary economy, and new values about deferred child rearing. As a result, fewer children attend schools. Nationally, from 1969 to 1985, the enrollments in elementary school dropped from 36.8 to 31.7 million and in secondary schools from 15.7 to 13.3 million. Yet the reactions of various school systems differ by locality because some districts are growing, others are holding steady, and still others are declining. In another example, the state reaction to the excellence movement varies enormously. Some states enact omnibus bills with extensive state mandates. Other states do little and leave what few programs they do enact to local discretion. Table 9.1 shows how many of the forty recommendations in the *A Nation at Risk* report were adopted in the first two years after its publication. The data reflect a heavy response in the South (and California as well), which suggests that those states used the reform publicity to push changes that would move them toward national standards.

The Dimension of School Finances

School financing is another useful illustration of variety in local implementation, for money plays such a large part in the American politics of education. Schools have traditionally been heavily financed by local taxes, with the states providing only a small share and the federal government the tiny remainder. That commonality aside, though, almost total diversity characterizes school financing. Each state's contribution has varied with its own resources, traditions, and values, as well as with the general economic effects of wars and recessions. While the overall state share has increased between 1900 and 1981 from about 20 to 50 percent, variations among the states are huge. Thus in 1981, Hawaii, rooted in a royal tradition of centralism,

Table 9.1
Number of Reforms Adopted by State Legislatures

Number Adopted	Number States	States
0–4	17	Alaska, Ga., Md., Mass., Mont., Nev., N.H., N.M., N.Dak., Ohio, Oreg., Pa., R.I., S.Dak., Utah, Vt., Wyo.
5–9	16	Ala., Colo., Del., Hawaii, Ind., Ill., Iowa, Kans., Mich., Minn., Mo., N.J., N.Y., Va., W.Va., Wisc.
10–14	9	Ariz., Conn., Ky., La., Maine, Nebr., Okla., Tex., Wash.,
15–19	6	Ark., Calif., Ind., Miss., N.C., Tenn.
20 or more	2	Fla., S.C.

Source: Doh Shinn and Jack Van Der Slik, "Legislative Efforts to Improve the Quality of Public Education in The American States: A Comparative Analysis" (paper presented to the annual convention of the American Political Science Assn., New Orleans, 1985), p. 36.

provided 92 percent, while New Hampshire provided about 7 percent. The National Education Association reported that in 1987 the current operating expenditure per pupil varied from $6,299 in New York to $2,455 in Utah, with the national average at $3,970.[7] This interstate differential means that a Utah child got only $1 of state money for schooling compared with $2.56 for a New York child. Characteristically, the poorer states were in the Confederacy, a curious sign of the Civil War's lingering effects. The wealthier states cluster among the industrial and small states of the East Coast and Great Lakes.

Though greater disparities exist among the LEAs within each state, much stability still shows up in the ways states react to local needs.[8] Relatively rich and poor states remain very much the same over long periods of time; thus, the amounts of state aid or the patterns of other policies demonstrate little shift exists in these states' *relative* standings on such matters.[9] For example, from 1900 to 1966, state standings are highly correlated on such matters as the proportion of state support (rho = 0.60). In shorter periods, even higher stability is disclosed; for example, average teacher salaries between the very dynamic years of

1963 and 1973 showed almost no shift in these states' rankings (rho = 0.90). (The reasons will be explored later.) Thus, the pattern is one of both stability and variety among the American states. No conceivable socioeconomic dimension exists on which the states do not show such variation. Even the constitutional position of education in these states reveals pluralism.

POLITICAL BACKGROUND

Education and Constitutionalism

The authority for public education in the United States does not stem from our national Constitution but rather is a "reserved" power remaining in the states.[10] This arises from the Tenth Amendment, which reserves to the states those powers neither expressly given the national government nor denied the state government. The national Constitution has never mentioned education, and until very recently, federal action for education had remained limited.

If authority for public education is the state's, most have not exercised it directly until recent decades. The relative role of state and local levels is expressed in the familiar saying, "Education is a state authority locally administered." That is, everywhere except Hawaii (where there is *no* local authority), the state constitutions expressly indicate that the LEA is an agent of the state. But for most of the last century, states have used this authority only for setting broad goals and general guidelines—and for providing some money in support. In those decades, schooling was primarily in the hands of a huge number of LEAs (127,000 in 1931, now consolidated to about 16,000). Such initial decentralization has meant that schooling was multifaceted beyond comprehension, reflecting a varied society.

Then and now, LEAs govern different spans of education. Where once the rural township was common, covering all grades, we can now find districts that cover only elementary or only secondary schooling (or both), as well as separate vocational or special education schools (for gifted students or for mentally or physically handicapped students). Above these levels, the state's legal authority is vested in education committees of the legislature, the legislature as a whole, a chief state school officer, a state board of education, a state agency for higher education, a state department of education, and a governor.

We will return shortly to examine their political roles in educational policymaking. Then, add to this list the voters themselves, who in some states directly participate in policymaking by use of referenda. Often there is a quasi-official agency, the state university's school of education, which certifies the credentials of the professions by setting out course requirements (commonly fixed in the state constitution itself). The nineteenth-century reform wars, which removed the political party from school policymaking, ended up enmeshed in peace treaties of state constitutions and laws. These schools of education thereafter ensured that victory by certifying the competence of the professional novitiate seeking entry.[11]

Growth in State Responsibilities

The shift in the state role has been drastic, and the rate of involvement has increased dramatically. The original thirteen state constitutions made no mention of education. Today all states refer to education, sometimes briefly (Connecticut's schools rested on three paragraphs until well into this century) and sometimes at length (for example, Michigan's 1964 revision). State involvement started at the end of the last century, with school reforms that introduced more professionalism. The authorization of LEAs and the limitation on their taxing appeared everywhere at that time. Consolidation also emerged pervasively around World War I. By 1925, one-third of the states already had state supervision set out in detailed, minimum standards for such matters as local sites, buildings, lighting, heating, outdoor and indoor equipment (including even the size of a globe), academic and professional qualifications of teachers, length and kinds of courses, requirements for hygiene, and community relations programs.[12]

One significant example of this centralizing process is the number of states requiring a university degree to teach. In 1900 no state required a degree for elementary teaching, and only two did so for secondary education. By 1920 the figures were still only zero and ten; but by 1940 they were ten and forty; by 1965 all states required a degree for secondary, and forty-five required it for elementary teaching. In 1986 a survey of the state's role in educational standards provided innumerable examples of this growth in state function.[13]

All states do certain things, such as keeping records on pupils, for example, but only a few states do other things, such as guidance and counseling. A clearer picture of this variation emerges when we consider these differing policies as reflecting the "system maintenance" capacities that professions use to control the functions they deem most vital.[14] A later chapter will show that on such matters, all the states maintain very strong control.

In other words, the *potential* for state intervention in local schools, once remote but always possible, has today become a pervasive reality. This constitutional position does not, however, exhaust the political aspects of schools. We may now turn to more direct evidence of schools' political nature.

Increasing State Control over the LEA

Just as no political action takes place without different effects on different groups' values, educational policymaking is contentious because some win and some lose. Recall that in Chapter 1 we noted that politics is not only conflict over the distribution of resources, but also and more basically conflict over the distribution of group values. This concept leads us to expect that the basic interactions among schools, political system, and society are about who and what is to be valued in the educational process. So schools are caught up in a competition for resources, status, and value satisfaction like other institutions of our society. In previous chapters, we have seen this concept working in the *local* politics of education.

Central to this situation is the value of local control discussed in Chapter 6, a value that permits individualism to take the manifold forms so characteristic of American education. State control—constitutionally given—has worked in tension with this passion for local control.[15] Controls take several forms: service minimums that the LEA cannot fall below; encouragement of LEAs to exceed minimums (for example, by cost-sharing a new goal); organizational requirements; emphasis on efficiency methods, and so on. Such controls assume that the state can provide equality better than the LEA through standardizing instruction and resources. Advocates of local control assert, however, that greater payoffs will flow from a more flexible, hence more decentralized, system of schooling.

Thus the state-local clash has been between two major values— equity versus freedom of choice (as discussed in Chapter 4). More recently, states have introduced a third value—efficiency—by placing more controls over planning, budgeting, evaluation, and so on. The best assessment of this competition is that today equity and efficiency are more stressed by state action, but choice has been reduced. We can see this in the recent dramatic increase of state control in such areas as the state role in education finance, state requirements for accountability, state programs for children with special needs, and state efforts to increase local academic standards.

This capsule account highlights the point generally accepted by students of education, namely, that local control as a value and operational fact has declined.[16] In this process, other values have gained prominence. If concern for equality could not be met by independent LEAs pursuing their separate ways, it was thought that state mandating of equal education programs backed by state resources could do so. Reducing racially based educational inequalities beginning in the mid-1950s, restructuring fiscal relations to reduce resource inequities in the late 1960s, providing more for handicapped children in the mid-1970s, increasing academic standards in the 1980s—all involve state and federal governments dictating the meaning of school equity. Also by 1992, concern over academic standards had heightened interest in more efficient schools. Thus the pursuit of quality and efficiency have once more overridden local choice. But President Bush featured choice in the 1992 elections and will try to reverse this recent trend in priority among values.

CONSENSUS AND DIVERSITY IN STATE POLICY SYSTEMS

The fifty states are not fifty unique laboratories of schooling policy. Rather, distinct clusters of behavior prevail so that state policy is a matter of limited patterns. Indeed, many areas share a common agreement on policy for schooling. It is this mixture of consensus that characterizes other institutions and policies in American federalism. Both these qualities are evident in the education policy systems of the states.

Policy Values Among the States

We start with Easton's view that the function of the political system is to authoritatively allocate values and resources. Consequently, understanding what values are sought in education policy is a first task in grappling with the diversity of American federalism. The important values here are basic instrumental values, those used to pursue an even more fundamental political value. These instrumental values are four—quality, efficiency, equity, and choice—according to a recent analysis of values in education policy in six states by Mitchell, Marshall, and Wirt.[17] (Quality and equity are often also called excellence and equality.) The Mitchell et al. explanation will set the background for understanding how policymakers use public resources to realize values. We use these definitions here, set out briefly in Table 9.2.

These values are not pursued randomly in policymaking within any state; rather, they follow a natural, logical sequence as policy elites try to meet educational challenges. Quality is the first value sought in any era of education policy when the political will arises to improve an educational service for a constituency (student, staff, administrator, etc.). Horace Mann's initial drive for free public education is a classic example, as is raising course requirements for graduation in the 1980s. But to implement these policies, it is necessary to devise other policies that are rooted in the value of efficiency, by using resources effectively measured in economic or control terms.

Next in the policy sequence, equity goals arise when experience shows that a gap has developed between desired standards and actual conditions for specific groups. This gap generates calls for using additional resources to bring the group up to standards. Finally, one policy value operates at all stages of the process—choice. A democratic nation provides many opportunities for citizens to select options, and the policy area of education is no exception. Citizens may choose quality standards, efficient means of implementation, or gap-closing equity measures. The prevalence of the elected school board is a familiar and pervasive example of this choice value, as are financial referenda and—less evident—local curricular biases and parental advisory councils.

This brief exposition highlights two points often skimped in understanding policymaking. First, policymakers pursue some fundamental political value through selecting other, more instrumental values, as Table 9.2 indicates. Moreover, such instrumental values can be defined in ways that permit scholars a view of their presence and effect. Consequently values are not fragile clouds floating over the

Table 9.2
Definitions of Basic Policy Values and School Policy Linkages

---

CHOICE

Legislated options for local constituencies in making decisions.
  Example: Choice of textbooks.
Instrumental to realize basic democratic value of popular sovereignty, that is,
citizens' legitimate authority over officials' policy actions.

EFFICIENCY

Either:
  Economic mode, minimizing costs while maximizing gains.
  Example: pupil-teacher ratio.
Or:
  Accountability mode, means by which superiors oversee and hence control
  subordinates' use of power.
  Example: Publicizing stages of budgetary process.
Instrumental to basic organizational value, namely, responsibility of
power-wielders to those who authorize it.

EQUITY

Equalizing or redistributing public resources to meet morally and societally
defined human needs.
  Example: Compensatory or handicapped education.
Instrumental to basic liberal value, namely, the worth of every individual and
society's responsibility to realize that worth.

QUALITY

Use of public resources to match professionally determined standards of excellence,
proficiency, or ability.
  Example: Certification of teachers.
Instrumental to the basic social value that education is crucial for the future
citizen's life chances.

Source: Abstracted from Frederick Wirt, Douglas Mitchell, and Catherine Marshall, "Analyzing Values in State Policy Systems," *Educational Evaluation and Policy Analysis*, Fall 1988.

policy scene, barely connected to what goes on below. Rather, they
are clearly understood (although not always articulated) motivators
of citizen and policymaker alike, who seek public resources in policy
for the purpose of enhancing their fundamental values.

Policy Preferences Among the States

Some of these qualities are evident among state education policy-makers in government and interest groups in a 1980s study of six states by Mitchell and colleagues.[18] What were the common and diverse policy elements of such state policy elites?

First, despite differences among the states, much consensus existed about the relative importance of seven basic *domains*, or broad areas of education policy. Finance policy was everywhere seen as most import-ant; then, personnel, student testing, and school program policies followed in importance; the governance and curriculum materials policies were ranked next; and finally, buildings and facilities policies were of least interest. These priorities cascaded in parallel fashion among the states, with minor variations. Second, in the 1980s, state policymakers were pushing for greater state action in all domains but especially in personnel, finance, governance, and buildings. Third, much agreement also prevailed about specific *programs* within each policy domain in all but governance, as listed in Table 9.3. That is, among the six states, policy elites reported that these programs were receiving the most attention by their legislatures compared to other alternatives. But beyond such commonalities, considerable variation still existed among these states in both policy domain and program, especially governance, finance, and testing.

Table 9.3
High Agreement on Education Policy Programs Among Policy Elites of Six States, 1982–83

Domain	Specific Programs
Finance	Equalization
	Establishing overall funding level
Personnel	Preservice certification and training
Student testing	Specifying format or content of required tests
School program	Setting higher standards for graduation
Curricular materials	Specifying scope and sequence of instruction
Buildings and facilities	Remediation of identified architectural problems
Governance	None

Source: Douglas Mitchell, Frederick Wirt, and Catherine Marshall, "Building a Taxonomy of State Education Policies," *Peabody Journal of Education* 62–4 (1985): 7–47.

This snapshot of state policy structure in the mid-1980s may alter over time. The 1960s and 1970s had exhibited a greater policy emphasis among all fifty states on the value of equity, namely, redistributing public resources to close the gap between standards and achievement for the poor and ethnic minorities. In the 1980s, though, as inflation and the Reagan administration's withdrawal from equity programs combined to drive the states to seek greater resources, more policy emphasis was then placed on efficiency and quality as end values in education.[19] The emphasis shifted to constraining educational goals and to improving the services provided. In the future, though, with a different economy and political leadership, a restructuring of these value priorities is certain.

In any period, however, a state's policy structure will result from both national and state influences, one example of the confluence of central and peripheral influences within any modern nation. In short, a current of ideas about policy preferences will swirl through America from time to time, generated by new political movements, emerging perceived needs, or changes in the economy. Illustrative of such national reforms in education policy have been the concern for educating the poor after 1965, the crunch on school funding stimulated by the energy crisis after 1973, the Reagan administration's devolution, and the states' curriculum and testing reforms after 1980.

A second component of a state's policy structure stems from influences special to that state, that is peripheral preferences. We already noted how past events had produced a political cultural outlook on the issue of state versus local control of schooling. This peripheral influence can affect specific education policies as well. It takes only a little knowledge of American education to realize that citizens in California and Mississippi provide different resources, view their leaders' role differently, and expect different qualities of education. Does this cultural explanation affect what state policymakers see and do in their respective worlds?

Political Culture and State Policy Choices

These differing peripheral influences will reflect *political culture*, that is, "the set of acts, beliefs, and sentiments which give order and meaning to a political process and which provide the underlying assumptions and rules that govern behavior in the political system. It

encompasses both the political issues and the operating norms. . . . [20]
These "acts, beliefs . . . assumptions and rules" are not infinite in
number among the fifty states, rather they group into clusters. Daniel
Elazar has developed three distinctive state political cultures with
consequent differences in state political behavior.[21]

1. Traditionalistic culture (TPC): Government's main function is
maintaining traditional patterns, being responsive to a governing
elite, with partisanship subordinated to personal ties.

2. Individualistic culture (IPC): Government is a marketplace that
responds to demands, favors economic development, and relies on the
political party as the vehicle for satisfying individual needs.

3. Moralistic culture (MPC): Government is the means for achieving the good community or commonwealth through positive government action, social and economic regulations are legitimate, parties
are downplayed, and bureaucracy is viewed positively as an agent of
the people.

Recent analysis shows that state education policymakers believe
that the citizens of their own states possess distinctive "beliefs and
sentiments" about the political system.[22] Thus views about government's role, political parties, elections, bureaucracy, and politics in
general that those in one state hold will cluster out from those held in
another state; this occurs in ways that fit the historically based
designation of the three cultures by Elazar. Figure 9.2 reveals the
education policy elites' perceptions of their citizens' political views.
Their answers clustered in such a way that Wisconsin anchors one
end of the horizontal axis of a moralistic-individualistic continuum,
with Illinois anchoring the other end. California and Pennsylvania
also fall on the continuum in the direction that their cultural origins
would place them. While this dimension accounted for most of the
variation in answers (81 percent), another dimension (the vertical
axis in Figure 9.2) helped distinguish the traditionalistic culture of
Arizona and West Virginia that opposed the other cultural dimension. In short, policy elites perceived their constituents' political
culture in the same way that historical evidence had suggested.

But what difference in education policy do these cultural differences
make? Because democratic leaders reflect citizen values—no matter
how roughly—these elite perceptions of constituencies should be
linked to distinctive education policies. The policy domains and
programs actually did fit the cultural perceptions of these elites

Figure 9.2
State Centroids of Political Culture on Two Functions

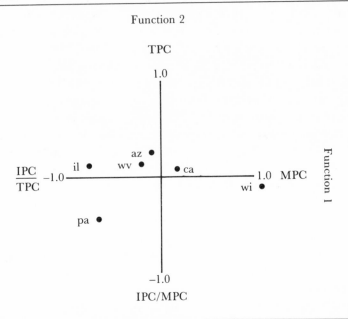

Function 2

TPC

1.0

IPC/TPC −1.0	il ● wv ● az ● ● ca 1.0 MPC

Function 1

wi ●

pa ●

−1.0
IPC/MPC

Source: Douglas Mitchell, Catherine Marshall, and Frederick Wirt, *Culture and Education Policy in the American State* (Falmer 1989), Chap. 5.

among six states. A statistical analysis of 33 program types within the seven policy domains (see Table 9.3) found that predictions were met in 24 programs for all three cultures, and another five programs matched the most polar cultures (moralistic versus individualistic); ultimately only four programs failed to fit cultural clusters. Some of the even broader policy domains—defining school programs and preparing curricular materials—demonstrated high, even significant, correlations. Such findings strengthen the belief that political cultures work even amid multiple, detailed program choices characteristic of the American states.

None of this analysis tells us what the best programs are though; that was not its purpose. But we now know that the policies that states use result from both national currents of reform as well as from local influences. The latter reflect variations in how policymakers and their constituents think of the political system and want the system to act.

History thus shapes contemporary policy actions through socialization to "beliefs and sentiments" that differ among the states and regions.

The Role of Washington and the States

The federal government has had no direct constitutional responsibility in education, but since 1965 it has found ways to take an enhanced role. Between 1862 and 1963, Congress considered federal aid to education thirty-six times but always rejected it. There were thirty-five federal laws prior to 1965 providing national resources in support of education, but rarely did funds go directly from Washington to the LEA's general budget. The Elementary and Secondary Act of 1965 (ESEA) changed that; in the next ten years, thirty-eight new education laws appeared. By 1974, some fifty-two programs had been funded for about $6 billion, covering about 7 percent of all school costs. This legislative effort was designed to cause LEAs to develop needed programs, yet the effects of this stimulus has been diffused—reform is adopted only if the local people welcome it.[23]

Federal funds entering the states are affected by state political cultures. If Washington's money was tightly tied—in amounts and objects of expenditures—to a formula, the money got on target. But if it was given to states without clear objectives or subsequent oversight, state legislatures used federal money the way they did their own. A six-state study found such moneys going disproportionately to rural and suburban areas—which also had more votes in the state legislature—than to central cities where the biggest educational problems existed.[24] Thus state policy systems are not simply captives of Washington. The Reagan administration had been successful in deregulating and consolidating several major federal programs, which increased the influence of the states even more. Reagan's policies have assumed that the states have the motivation and capacity to mount new programs without prior federal grant stimulus. Consequently, the Reagan administration used rhetoric rather than federal funds to promote academic standards.

School desegregation has been a more publicized federal effort, which we develop more fully in Chapter 11. This reform movement stemmed from the classic Supreme Court decision of *Brown* v. *Topeka Board of Education*, but in the intervening decades, this policy has followed a tortuous path. In the first ten years after *Brown*, nothing happened in the South where the greatest school segregation existed. In the next decade, and after the 1964 Civil Rights Act and 1965 ESEA, federal courts consistently overturned all dual-school systems resting on state law. The courts also began to tackle the difficult problem of Northern segregation rooted in privately segregated housing.[25] Much of segregation in the South had disappeared under strong federal pressures; where Washington was strong, segregation vanished.[26] But in the North, segregation has grown so that many central cities in metropolitan areas were mostly black or Hispanic by 1979. Desegregating the entire metropolis (was possible (Florida pioneered successfully),[27] but the Supreme Court drew a line at this remedy (*Milliken* v. *Bradley*, 1974). For the next fifteen years, Congress and presidents withdrew support for desegregation, and the Reagan and Bush administrations even sided with the challenged districts. By 1992, the Supreme Court declared many districts desegregated and ended forced bussing.

POLICY INFLUENCE AT THE STATE CAPITOL

Policymaking engages representatives of formal government agencies, special interests mobilized as groups, and the public in general. The process is mainly centered around routine decisions, the incremental changes in the vast body of past policy decisions already in existence. But this flow of incremental action is disrupted every so often by the sudden call for innovative policy change, involving new uses of public resources to achieve old educational values of quality, efficiency, equity, and choice. The last quarter-century has known much more innovation on all levels of government, arising from the political turbulence discussed throughout this book.

Amid such change, how have the state policymakers acted? Is it a case of fifty sets of policymakers doing fifty different things? We find that the process is more patterned than this because some commonalities are evident in each state. For example, the same set of official actors operate in each state; they have similar influence on policymaking; and all these actors must deal with limited assumptions about policy ventures as they do their job. We turn to review the influence of these actors and their outlook on the policy process for education.

Patterns of Influence among Policy Actors

A recent six-state study by Marshall, Mitchell, and Wirt found that educational policy elites ranked one another's influence with surprising consistency.[28] In Table 9.4 we see the composite ranking for eighteen types of policy influentials; the result is a picture of concentric circles of influence.

The Insiders have constitutional authority in making laws; these are the powerful legislators or the legislature as a whole. This finding confirms other research on the central influence of legislators in state policymaking. Next in influence are the Near Circle, school professionals (especially teachers) and specialists in the executive branch (especially the chief state school officer or CSSO). Next are outer circles more removed from pervasive influence. The Far Circle is influential but not vital to policymaking; among these, the state board is most prominent. Yet other actors have little if any influence. For example, Sometime Players are the pressure groups for local boards and administrators who are sometimes heard on special issues. The Forgotten Players, like courts, may affect only one state; an example is the powerful impact that West Virginia's supreme court had in altering local school financing in the state. But in the policy worlds surveyed here, many of this last cluster did not even come into view.

The ranking of each type of policy elite varies among the states. A state board can have no influence if it does not exist (Wisconsin), and the usually high influence of the CSSO was low in Illinois—just before he was replaced. In Arizona, the often low-ranking state board and local board associations rated well; the governor, well-regarded elsewhere for policy influence on education, was rated poorly here when he had to work with a legislature controlled by the other party. Illinois and West Virginia had many differences from the six-state average ranking, although California matched the average ratings quite closely.

Most important in this analysis is the rough agreement among state policy actors on the crucial importance of the legislative branch. This finding means that informal influence matches constitutional authority, a condition that adds to the legitimacy of the policy process. While regularity and differences showed among the rankings, "the regularity speaks to the impact of institutionalizing democratic practices across the nation. The differences speak to the distinctive impact on policy

Table 9.4
Ranking of Policy Influentials: All Six States

Cluster	6–state Rank	Policy Group
Insiders {	1	Individual members of the legislature
	2	Legislators as a whole
Near Circle {	3	Chief state school officer
	4	All education interest groups combined
	5	Teacher organizations
	6	Governor and executive staff
	7	Legislators staff
Far Circle {	8	State Board of Education*
	9	Others**
Sometime Players {	10	School Boards Association
	11	State Administrator Association
Other Forgotten Players {	12	Courts
	13	Federal policy mandates
	14	Noneducator interest groups
	15	Lay groups
	16	Education researcher organizations
	17	Referenda
	18	Producers of educational materials

* Based on Arizona, Illinois, West Virginia, and California. Wisconsin has no state board of education.
** "Others" includes, for example, Illinois' School Problems Commission and West Virginia's School Service Personnel Association.

Source: Douglas Mitchell, Catherine Marshall, and Frederick Wirt, *Culture and Education Policy in the American State*, (Falmer, 1989), chap. 2.

services and decisional systems made by state political cultures and the culture of each state capitol."[29]

Rules of the Game of Policymaking

Remarkable uniformity prevails in the lawmaking procedure of the fifty states because they are rooted in the British and colonial traditions. But just how that uniform procedure is perceived and conducted depends very much on the different perceptual screens that different actors bring to lawmaking. In the words of Catherine Marshall and associates, "These perceptions related to the expected behaviors, rituals, and judgments about feasible policy options. This perceptual screen we term the assumptive worlds of policymakers."[30] No printed manual of these perceptions exists in each state. Rather, these assumptive worlds emerge from the words and stories of policymakers when they informally discuss the persons and processes of their world.

This instructive use of qualitative data to build a grounded theory suggests that hidden within the operations of policymakers is a set of questions about their work to which they give answers in experience. How questions are answered often varies, but the basic questions remain the same:

1. Who must, and who has the right to, *initiate policy action?* Experience reveals that actors' answers focus especially on the roles of the legislature (as noted above) and others in the policy elite. In each state, the elite easily reveal who has this authority in their anecdotes and responses to influence scales.

2. What are the *unacceptable policy initiatives?* Again, experience shows that they are ideas that: trample on group, regional, or big-city interests; lead to refusal of agencies or citizens to obey; clash with existing practices; challenge dominant economic interests; or promote unorthodox values. Even limited inquiry among the elite will provide agreed-on accounts of what policy ideas won't fly.

3. What are the *appropriate policy actions?* Experience again points to such rules as: to get along, go along; carry out informal rituals that will recognize and define the boundaries of power; mobilize everyone who can benefit from a proposed policy; don't let friendship block policy action; utilize policy issue networks within and across the states; and so on.[31]

As a concept, then, assumptive worlds are derived from answers to fundamental questions arising everywhere in policymaking; of course, a particular state culture will contribute a distinctive cast to these answers rooted in its own history. Moreover, these culturally shaped answers are imposed on new actors entering the state's educational policy world, a classic form of political socialization.

These general propositions are illuminated by the assumptions surrounding higher education policy in two states, West Virginia and California. The former has treated this policy passively; indeed, in mid-1987 some of its state colleges had to close early due to reduced state funding. California, on the other hand, prepares this policy the way that other nations go to war—with full resources, vigor, leadership, and high expectations. Consequently, the two sets of policymakers treat the issue differently because their states' assumptions about important policy ideas vary.

Behind these assumptive worlds lie attributes of political culture discussed earlier in this chapter. West Virginia's elite-based and traditionalistic culture has consistently constrained the expansion of education, until its own supreme court compelled otherwise. California's open-society and moralistic culture has spurred an expansion of school resources in the search for the best education. In either state, though, such attitudes about the acceptable policy ideas have a dual effect; they keep the policy environment predictable, and they help policymakers build group cohesion that can produce policy outputs.

Such aspects of influence and assumptions attending the making of education policy reveal patterns for understanding it, despite the profusion and ambiguity of fifty state arenas. Broad expectations are widespread about which people have policy authority and how they should act amid policy conflict. State variations in these expectations do exist, though, due to varying histories and emphases in education values. Yet the common patterns among states do provide clarity, not confusion, to the policy system of American federalism. And it is the patterns that enable theory building in social science to thrive.

STATE-LEVEL INTEREST GROUPS

Among the many factors that could influence a state's policy system, major ones are variations in party competition, party cohesion in the legislature, and the socioeconomic context.[32] Zeigler and van Dalen found two basic mixes of these factors among the American states. One pattern consists of strong lobbies, weak legislative parties, and a population that is low on urbanism, income, and industrialism. In the second pattern, lobbies are weak to moderate in influence, parties are competitive, and the economy is urban and industrial.[33]

Patterns of Interest Groups

What emerges from these two concepts is not one pressure pattern among the states but four. The first is an *alliance of dominant groups*, much like the strong-lobby syndrome noted above; the Southern states are a good example of this. Second, a *single dominant interest* pattern emerges in states with undiversified economies, two-party competition, and some legislative cohesion; the roles of a copper corporation in Montana or oil companies in Texas are examples.

Third, a pattern of *conflict between two dominant groups* is visible where a diversified economic base generates differences that the two-party system expresses, for example, auto manufacturers versus auto trade unions in Michigan. Fourth, a *triumph of many interests* appears where lobbies can freely interact in a legislature unbounded by party control; thus in California, a highly diversified economy generates multiple interest and shifting legislative coalitions.[34] Clearly, lobbying overrepresents the business and professional strata of society; about three in five registered state lobbyists act for corporations or trade groups.

The chief lobby for education, though, has been the professional, particularly teachers. Chapter 4 sketched this lobby's evolution in the National Education Association (NEA) as an umbrella organization for teachers, principals, superintendents, school board members, and others.[35] We also noted that, beginning in the 1950s, events led to a more militant teacher movement, climaxing in successful collective bargaining drives in most states. This focus on the interest of only one of its constituents—teachers—weakened the cohesion of the NEA, which then took a more aggressive stance similar to its challenger, the American Federation of Teachers. As competition for shrinking financial resources grew in the 1970s, the unitary myth, which once bound different kinds of professionals, dispersed. No longer did teacher and administrator believe that they shared a unity in the goal of educating the young.

In contemporary school lobbying in the legislature, we must once again resort to diverse models of action. Iannaccone's highly influential typology of school lobbies is valuable here.[36] He conceptualizes the linkages between the lobbies and the legislature in four forms.

The *locally based disparate* linkage emphasizes local schoolpeople making contact with their state legislators; local legislators and professionals are the major interactors. Second, the *statewide monolithic* coalitions can form among state-level school interests who then speak with one voice to the legislature; here, differences among interests are resolved before proposals are put to the lawmakers. Third, in the *statewide fragmented* type, state interests fail to unify, and so they press their separate needs upon the legislature. Finally, the *statewide syndical* coalition is institutionalized directly in a government body, which resolves group interests before presenting them to the lawmakers.

The attributes of these types are sketched in Table 9.5. In each, the style of politics varies, as do such qualities as: the lobby's power to prevent or initiate legislation, the legislators' reactions, the focus of adjusting interest group conflicts, and the qualities of information available to these groups. Moreover, Iannaccone saw these types as part of a developmental model. That is, (a) school lobbies began as locally based disparate, then (b) evolved into statewide monoliths as professionals saw their common interests, but then (c) altered into statewide fragments when their conflicting interests grew in importance, and finally, (d) statewide syndicalism could emerge if lawmakers tired of this conflict. By the 1970s the splintered education groups sought more collaboration through coalitions around unrestricted increases in state aid.

Changes in Lobby Types

What best describes the lobby type that exists in the fifty states? In research up to the mid-1960s, Iannaccone found that the statewide monolith was most prevalent. But a decade later, Aufderheide's study of twelve states reported a major shift to the statewide fragmented type in nine of these states.[37] These were the more Northern industrialized systems, which shared a common history of a collapse of the old NEA umbrella that once protected the statewide monolith. Coalitions of schoolpeople had formerly written education law in their private councils and then issued an agreed proposal to the legislature, which accepted it because education was hard to be against and would reap the legislators little reward to oppose it. But in a few decades this pattern had been broken by growing conflicts of interests between education and by the increased interest and capacity of legislatures and governors to initiate their own policies.

What the twelve-state study also revealed was a system more

Table 9.5

A Typology of State Education Interest Groups

Attributes	Local Disparate	Statewide Monolithic	Statewide Fragmented	Statewide Syndical
Elite types	Squirearchy	Oligarchy	Polyarchy	Synarchy
Political styles	Entrepreneurial	Cooptational	Competitive	Coalitional
Lobby power:				
Prevention	Yes	Yes	Yes and no	Yes
Initiation	No	Yes	Yes and no	Yes
Legislator sentiment	Warm, paternal to teachers	Warm, undifferentiated	Differentiated: critical of administrators, warm to teachers	Warm, not critical
Focus of interest accommodation	Legislature	Apex of the monolith	Legislature	The group of syndics
Information:				
Quantity	Small	Large	Very large	Large
Nature	Unscientific	Precise, predictable	Scientific, but not predictable	Precise and predictable
Control	Personal	Monopolistic	Competitive	Monopolistic

Source: Abstracted from Laurence Iannaccone, *Politics in Education* (New York: Center for Applied Research in Education, 1967), Chap. 3.

complex than even Iannaccone's typology suggested. Added complexity came from those centrifugal forces that were making the school legislatures' policy systems everywhere more pluralistic and open. Indeed, the nature of the policy process seemed to vary with the issue in focus. This openness was a major shift from earlier decades when professionals kept policymaking a closed shop.[38]

When school lobbies sought success in the legislature, what were their resources and strategies? They possessed numbers, money, (teachers), and high status (administrators and school boards). They transformed these resources into power by different means. All used professional staffs, but teachers relied more on their campaign money and votes, while administrators and school boards relied more on their information resources and local legislator contacts. Unlike the other two, teachers were much more likely to campaign, transforming their prime resource of size directly into votes. This electoral activity marks a sharp break with teachers' traditional apolitical stance.

As a result of such uses of power, school lobbies were seen by their own leaders and legislators as among the most powerful pressure groups in the state. Legislators gave highest marks to the teacher associations, while administrators received the worst. They found: teacher associations generally the more effective of the school lobbies and administrators the more efficient (obtaining the most for their fewer numbers and less money); the smaller teacher federations inconsistent; labor-management relations the dominant issue of such politics; and former school coalitions increasingly crippled by splits over the issue. So long as schooling issues were regarded as "educational," school boards and administrators were more influential because they could rely on their higher status to be heard. But when teacher groups changed the criteria for deciding issues from the professional to the "political," the teachers benefited from their greater numbers and money.

The pressure group matrix that emerges from this research, then, is one of open access, multiple participants, and shifting coalitions of school groups. We should also find that the transition from a state-wide monolithic to a statewide, fragmented system would enhance the role of the state legislature.

Interest Groups and Enrollment Decline

Public education is in most, if not all, states the largest single budget item. Current trends of increases in academic and teacher certification standards, and in state general funds have also increased the influence of state governments in educational politics. States have responded to these conditions with enhanced legislative involvement and expanded professional staffs in both the legislative and executive branches.

No longer can unified educational interest groups count on the state's docile accession to their demands as they once could. Internal divisions could not be contained. For example, school boards realized that the costs of maintaining unity would exceed the benefits to be gained from a more independent and skeptical state government. Accordingly, they splintered. In addition to the old-line groups, flourishing on their own in this period of plenty for education, federal and state categorical programs inspired the proliferation of new single-focus interest groups. It became truly a time for the "triumph of many interests" noted earlier.

In at least one state, Illinois, the highly conflictual splintering of educational interest groups generated such an array of competing demands that the state felt compelled to resurrect the old monolithic structure in a new guise. The Illinois School Problems Commission—a formal body composed of the primary educational interests and state executive and legislative officials—embodied Iannaccone's statewide syndical model. It achieved internal consensus, thus freeing the legislature from the time-consuming task of arbitrating conflicts, but it generated other internal divisions; by the mid-1970s, it broke apart. No other syndical organization has arisen in another state.

It seems clear that contemporary conditions surpass Iannaccone's framework. He and later analysts did not account for the increased state assumption and proliferation of special focus groups. The assumption enhances cooperation by school boards and teacher unions at the state level. The proliferation militates against it because so many more groups must coalesce. The fragmentation model of interest groups in Table 9.5 acts against efforts to augment state general aid, while the locally based model is clearly anachronistic. Also, the monolith model is truly lost due to deep-seated labor-management conflicts and to general aid versus categorical program conflicts; the syndical model appears as a transient aberration during the 1960s in Illinois, unattainable elsewhere. To be sure, we are indebted to Iannaccone for prompting students to think more systematically about a dynamic and complex phenomenon, but it is necessary to update this concept of state educational politics. As Boyd found in Pennsylvania, a marked shift in environmental conditions was associated with a major change in the strategies of interest groups. A dramatic shift from conflict to collaboration occurred in order to better confront a skeptical governor and the lack of effectiveness that fragmentation had caused. We can call this the statewide general-aid collective.[39]

Specific State Educational Interest Groups

Our review of Iannaccone's developmental construct suggested the diminished authority of state education lobbies. However, an alternative tool for differentiating among these lobbies is to divide them, as Boyd does, into "general focus" and "special focus" groups.[40] The former—typified by teacher, administrator, and school board organizations—are broad based and must, therefore, represent the full spectrum of educational interests. Given their size and resources, they are often assumed "to have more political clout than they actually have." Their resources are scattered over a wide range of issues and political levels, associations of locally based organizations. Despite formal procedures and often sophisticated state leadership, power is essentially decentralized. They are "characterized by a strong 'bottom-up' flow of power wherein there is a continuous and taxing necessity of building coalitions among significantly autonomous locals." This is especially true of the management associations, whose independent-minded membership is reluctant to cede authority to state executives. Consistent with Olson's interest group theory of collective action discussed in Chapter 4, the costs of organizing large-member groups are high, while group cohesion around specific policy goals is low.

In contrast, the small-member group with a single "special focus" finds it easier to reach optimal effectiveness and outmaneuver the larger associations. Special focus groups fall into two kinds. One is functional, such as those representing special education, and the other is geographic, such as the big-city school district. Because of their narrow interests and concentrated power bases, these organizations are becoming increasingly influential in state politics.

The functional type generally pays attention to the source of its special funding, often the federal level and then the state administrative unit that dispenses those funds. A typical arrangement involves only a few governmental officials, as most state policy actors never enter the narrow realm of the special interest. For example, in Michigan the directors of the respective special and compensatory education units within the state department were reported to be among the most powerful individuals in state educational politics. They are able to mobilize the highly motivated and frequently volatile constituents and practitioners who support the causes of handicapped and compensatory education.[41]

In fact, these interest groups, or the significant individuals within them, often have served as part of the formal governing apparatus for their programs, such as the Title I ESEA Advisory Committee. A specialized version of Iannaccone's syndical arrangement, this overlap between special interest advocacy and formal function constitutes the "institutional interest group." These entities perform formal political or social functions while simultaneously pursuing their own interests.

The highly effective, geographically based, special interests are even better embodiments of the institutional interest group. Here school districts in a given locale form natural alliances with other local and state government agencies, and they employ other groups to augment their gains in the allocation process. Their greatest resource is their direct link to legislative delegations, which in the case of a large city, such as New York, Chicago, or Los Angeles, can have enormous influence. With these descriptive concepts in mind, we can now delineate individual groups, beginning with the broadly based interests.

The State Teachers Association. Teachers affiliated with the NEA remain a strong, if not the strongest, group in most states. Although weakened by the growth of the rival AFT and the expulsion of school administrators, local associations possess a powerful resource advantage over other groups. Due to sheer numbers, the money from dues used for political action, and sophisticated staffing, they remain, according to one analysis, "giants by comparison."[42]

This glowing assessment of the associations' influence must be tempered by the fact that we cannot measure power by a simple aggregation of membership, money, and information. Internal cohesion is crucial to effective mobilization of those resources. For example, the Michigan Education Association (MEA), although much larger than many others, is so internally divided over local political strategies that it cannot muster much influence at the state level. MEA's power is thus more apparent than real; local rivalry with the AFT has certainly contributed to this ineffectiveness.

The State Teachers Federation. Although growing rapidly in most urban areas, the AFT affiliates have a tendency to bypass state-level lobbying in favor of local militancy. This underdeveloped and inconsistent state influence does not apply in California, though. There, the federation's strong labor stances in the 1970s pushed rival NEA locals into more militant postures; the latter no longer characterizes itself as a purely professional association. Between 1965 and the late 1980s the proportion of teachers in the AFT versus the NEA remained stable. NEA controls teachers in 87 percent of the LEAs with students over 1,000; the AFT controls 13 percent.

Classified School Employees Associations. The nonprofessionals who work in schools are usually ignored by commentators on state educational interest groups. That neglect stems from their relatively recent emergence in state politics and their lack of a substantive focus. They are labor unions whose sole objective is the protection of their membership's financial interests. Classified employees include custodians, secretaries, and food service personnel. Until the recent jump in state authority, these people have been able to rely on local collective bargaining strength. Their sheer numbers and financial resources give them considerable potential clout at the state level; thus they became a factor in school finance policymaking.

The State School Board Association. Members of the State School Boards Association find themselves pitted against the teachers in an effort to hold the lid on salaries. Increasingly in the 1970s, local school boards—confronted with the politically, economically, and legally complex realities of collective bargaining—came to rely in varying degrees on the data and expertise that the state association could muster. At the state level, policymakers view school board groups as deserving respect and empathy because they represent locally elected officials who, in turn, unselfishly represent the interest of the public.[43] This status and prima facie credibility is augmented by small but generally efficient lobbying staffs funded by the highest membership dues of all the education groups.

The State School Administrators Association. School administrators often try to be "a bridge over troubled waters" for school principals, business officials, superintendents, personnel managers, and other administrators. Once firmly entrenched at the peak of most state teachers associations, the administrators became exiled by teacher militancy, and administrator groups find themselves allied with the school board groups in order to provide some semblance of balance vis-à-vis the teachers. Legislators accord administrator groups respect as representatives of educational leadership in their districts. In fact, engaging in face-to-face contact with legislators in their home districts is a prevalent political strategy. This is reversion, born of necessity, to tradition, a locally based, disparate, interest-group politics. But this predilection for going it alone can hamper the group's lobbying efforts. The administrators pay high dues, second only to the school board's, and maintain an effective lobbying staff.

Other Groups. In addition, there are categorical interests and associations of geographically based groups too numerous to mention that can be powerful players in state educational politics. They have their champions in the legislatures, either individuals with pet interests or constituency links or, in the case of programs for the disadvantaged, the black and Chicano caucuses. Their bureaucratic home bases have a vested interest in sustaining and adding to the programs, and they often have recourse to the threat of judicial intervention. In short, many special focus groups have clout disproportionate to their numbers.

The PTA. Associations representing nonprofessional or lay persons interested in education, while locally oriented, have both state and national organizations. The National Congress of Parents and Teachers is not only the largest of these groups but also the largest volunteer organization in the United States. Its strength is felt primarily at the local level where it actively pursues solutions to specific problems at specific schools. At the state level, its influence diminishes due to the heterogeneity of its membership and the lack of any method for maintaining internal discipline.

Labeled "good government groups," the PTA and its allies, the League of Women Voters (LWV) and the American Association of University Women (AAUW), are occasionally granted formal representation on advisory committees and asked to join educational coalitions. They generally restrict themselves to monitoring policy developments and providing lay support for professionals' recommendations. The professionals who gain the most from PTA activism are the administrators. Others tend to regard them as useful friends when they agree but a not a very bothersome enemy in the event of conflict. As we saw in Chapter 4, though, many participants obtain psychological rewards from their involvement.

The LWV and AAUW exist to promote much broader social improvements. State branches may have a specialist in education, but they tend not to posit controversial views, preferring to provide general support for public education as an ongoing social good.

Lobbying Strategies

Whatever their type, groups are more than just structures of interests. They appear most clearly as dynamic parts of the policy process, from the emergence of issues through implementation and evaluation. We can see this dynamic quality in case studies of single-issue conflicts, such as that over creationism in textbooks, but little systematic knowledge emerges from this kind of understanding. We can portray the interaction more fully by focusing on the lobbying strategies that education interest groups use.

Both personal experience and research suggest that lobbying strategies in the states parallel those at the national level. Partisanship is risky in competitive two-party situations except where party identification of interests is a given. Thus management and labor tend to support the Republican and Democratic parties, respectively. Timely campaign contributions sprinkled across party lines, however, is an effective means of obtaining access and occasionally influencing a vote. However, individual lawmakers do not want to become obligated or "owned" over the long haul. In general, campaign contributions are of much lower volume in state politics than at the national level, "although a little money goes a longer way at the state level."[44] Volunteers and endorsements in association newsletters are also popular tactics, especially in large membership labor groups. In heavily unionized states, the labor organizations can take on the entire job of running a campaign. The mass public relations pressure tactic, more prevalent in national politics, is usually too expensive and too complicated for state education interest groups.

Direct contact with state legislators is easier, cheaper, and still more effective. Consequently, most education lobbying strategies are fundamentally low key; they emphasize expertise, professionalism, and honesty. Lobbyists prefer to work within the conventional mode; they are, after all, representatives of the dominant social interests and have a corresponding commitment to maintain the status quo. If the moderate approach fails in a particular instance, contributions of money and election workers to specific legislators may help. Another step often adopted before "all-out-war" is cooperative lobbying and coalition building.

State Coalition Concepts

In large part, politics involves fashioning coalitions of influence in an attempt to determine what values government will authoritatively implement. Different individuals and groups bring various interests and objectives to state educational policy forums. Amid this tangle, an essential quality of a state education leader is to build political coalitions.

The coalition view of state decision making envisions any decision is possible if enough support for it exists among interest groups. In order to secure support, various trade-offs are undertaken. Policy proposals are modified to include (or exclude) items of concern to key potential supporters; agreements are made to trade support on other or future state policies for backing on a current issue; and third parties are encouraged to intervene. In short, coalitions are formed by horse trading until an acceptable policy is reached.

Riker has developed several theories on coalitions that can be validated in state education lobbying.[45] He contends that the growth of coalitions depends on the ability of leaders to attract followers by offering "side payments." These include anything that has value for possible coalition members, including money or promises on policy. Sometimes coalition leaders have a stock of side payments in their hands as working capital when they begin negotiations. As they dispense promises, they use this capital, which presumably will be replenished from the future gains of a winning coalition. More typically, in our judgment, education leaders operate on credit; that is, they promise rewards with the understanding that they will honor their promises only if successful.

Leaders and followers are differentiated according to whether they offer or receive side payments. A leader rarely has enough resources to pay everybody. Also, excess members of a winning coalition cost something to acquire, and they lessen the gains. Thus at some point in the process of making side payments, the leader decides that all has been paid out that is worth winning. But as some factions are still left out, the attempts to form a coalition generate opposition that could result in an opposing coalition.

Riker enumerated various kinds of side payments, which can be illustrated from education lobbying.

1. *The threat of reprisal.* This side payment consists of a promise not to carry out the threat, so the follower simply gains an escape from prospective misfortune. For example, a governor can threaten to campaign against an elected state superintendent of schools.
2. *Payment of objects that can be converted to money.* One example is appointing a major financial backer of a key legislator to a position in the state education department.
3. *Promises on policy.* A leader accepts an amendment to her or his bill that brings the support of the state teachers' association, but modifies the policy thrust of the bill.
4. *Promises about subsequent decisions.* The speaker of the assembly can promise to support an agricultural bill if rural interests will vote for an income tax dedicated to education.
5. *Payments of emotional satisfaction.* Some legislators will follow the educational decisions of a charismatic governor.

These strategies involve lobbyists in subtle considerations, for the possibilities in any single policy conflict are numerous. The ways these considerations can be combined in practice are particularly complex. Such analysis requires making judgments and answering strategic questions.

Is there a winning coalition? Is the goal to be achieved by a winning coalition unique? Is anything (for example, a particular legislative provision) clearly excluded? Would the possibilities (for example, more school finance reform) be changed by expanding the coalition slightly? It follows that in some situations several potentially winning coalitions exist. Consequently, there is a role for leadership in constructing a particular coalition and thereby limiting the policy options and goals. It is this matrix of lobbies that the state legislatures face.

State Legislatures

With exceptions, the following characterizes American state legislatures:[46]

1. Primarily political, not value-free, institutions.
2. Recently subject to more demands.
3. Recently taking on a more professional cast, for example, more and better staff.
4. Better apportioned as a result of Supreme Court actions that resulted in an increased voice for urban and suburban interests, an advantage to Democrats, and more responsiveness to new needs.
5. Often recruited to office by political parties, but the turnover rate high and the influence of the party on legislative votes varying widely with state tradition.
6. Electoral competition for seats limited.
7. The general public evaluating them negatively (mostly for wasting time), but they are very responsive ("congruent") to public wishes on controversial issues.
8. Some policies are innovative (usually controversial), but many are incremental (for example, budgets), but, as noted earlier, reforms are adopted in different degrees.
9. Subject to influence from external and internal sources (committees, caucuses, governors, lobbies, experts, and so on), but the influence of the legislators is still prime.
10. Pressure groups everywhere influential, but one group's

influence varies from state to state (most often mentioned: bankers, trade unions, teachers, manufacturers, farmers, doctors, and utilities).

Observers agree that the legislative role in school policymaking has recently changed. Education was once of limited interest to legislators, but of late they have taken a strong hand in finance reform and minimum competence testing.[47] In particular, lawmakers are now more involved in the distribution of state revenue, both its proportion and uses. The reasons for this change reflect other changes.[48] That is, because legislatures are now more representative and better staffed, groups can turn to a body ready and willing to act; and as their sessions became longer, they were readier longer. Legislatures are also developing closer ties with other state school agencies, exchanging ideas about program possibilities.

Explanation of the legislature's role in school policymaking is confounded by three vigorous research traditions.[49] The *institutional* approach (the oldest) focuses upon the internal structure of the legislature. The *process* approach examines the dynamic interaction between structure and outside environment, for example, correlations among environmental characteristics of states, their policies, and legislative votes. The *behavioral* approach (the most recent) explores legislators' interactions within the body itself. As a consequence of these different approaches, what we know is much like the three blind persons who described an elephant in terms of the particular part each touched. However, great variation in both stable and dynamic elements are found in legislatures from state to state. Education is currently a popular arena for legislators because of its size and visibility. Ideas spread rapidly across states through interstate organizations like the National Conference of State Legislators and the Education Commission of the States.

American Governors

Head of state and of party, the American governor has had to weave these two roles together to be effective.[50] But the recent increase in demands on all states has brought this office under greater cross-pressures. Service demands continue to increase, but so do demands to stabilize taxes that would pay for the services. The social welfare needs of the central cities are opposed by suburban and nonmetropolitan legislators who are less responsive to those needs. Most observers would agree that beneath the federal level the governor is the most important agent in American policymaking. This fact emerges in many individual studies of policymaking, even though it runs counter to recent macrolevel analyses that stress the primacy of the state's environment (especially economic factors) rather than the political context in determining state policies.[51]

What is the significance of the governor for education policy? The limited research of this role prior to the 1970s generally found it minimal, "most often nonexistent, and when it does exist it appears sporadically, reflecting the idiosyncratic character of particular governors and/or educational crises in specific states."[52] When the first truly comparative analysis of these figures appeared in the early 1970s, it found a much wider range of behavior across the states and the stages of policymaking.[53] As policymaking progresses, the governor's influence declines. Governors are most active in defining educational issues before their authorization and least active in having a decisive effect on policy enactment. But again, the spread expresses the usual American style—a wide range of possibilities. But the academic and teacher quality reforms of the 1980s produced a new activism on the part of governors.

Strong gubernatorial leadership emerges in particular kinds of states. These are the larger industrialized states with highly effective legislatures and a moralistic political culture that emphasizes policy reform. However, governors from the South were very active in initiating the 1983–87 reforms featuring higher academic standards. The governors of South Carolina, Tennessee, Florida, Virginia, Georgia, Arkansas, Texas, and North Carolina made national news with their comprehensive ideas. The governor is also most likely to be involved and powerful in certain issues, particularly where a traditional policy climate exists of supporting education by creating much state revenue: Connecticut, Florida, New York, and California.[54] The weaker governors appear in locally oriented policy cultures: Nebraska, Colorado, and New Hampshire. Recently, governors in several states have advocated tax increases to improve education, citing the international competition of the 1980s.

Further, this office is becoming more politicized over educational policy, as are other agencies of government. In 1986 three of four governors focused on education in their campaigns. Their particular interest was in school finance, most favoring its expansion. This is a clear sign of the new pressures for more state aid to schools and the counterpressure against too high taxes, already noted. Even traditionally weak governors had initiated education policies in 1983–87, and all had expanded their staffs of education experts. The National Governors Association also doubled its education staff in Washington.

As with interest groups and legislatures, the governor's office fails to provide regular leadership for the development of educational policy in the American states. Some do so, of course, but only on limited issues and episodically. Like Sherlock Holme's nonbarking dog, the systematic importance of this office is that it does not consistently do the expected. It is doubtful that governors in the future can provide as much focus on education policy innovation as they did from 1983 to 1992.

THE IMPLEMENTERS OF STATE SCHOOL POLICY

The initiation and authorization of major school policy do not complete the policy process, for laws are not self-executing. The implementation stage in state school policy involves three agencies: the state school board (SBE), the chief state school officer (CSSO), and the state education agency (SEA). The diversity of these authorities has already been suggested in Tables 9.1 and 9.2, so again our focus is on patterns of behavior.[55]

The State Board of Education and Chief State School Officer

School policy implementation has been spread among these three agencies, with the SBE and CSSO responsible for oversight and innovation and the SEA for daily administration. The linkage between the SBE and CSSO is complex because their methods of appointment and authority are so diverse. They may be independent (elected, appointed, or a mix), or the SBE may choose the CSSO. Some SBEs only issue regulations, while others have operating responsibilities (vocational schools, state colleges, or universities). Rarely, however, are such broad responsibilities unified in a single office (except the New York Board of Regents).[56]

SBEs are usually appointed by the governor and the CSSO by the SBE, but the linkage is not ministerial. The selection methods of the SBEs seem to have consequences for their policy behavior. That is, elective bodies are designed to be open to more conflict, while appointed bodies respond to their appointers. That is the case with the SBEs, where 69 percent of those appointed reported little internal disagreement compared with 42 percent of those elected.[57]

Whatever their origins, these actors have differing influence. One observer reported that SBEs are "only marginal policy actors in the legislative arena and are largely overshadowed by the CSSO in state education."[58] Elected SBEs appear to have more influence with the CSSO and legislature, for they can speak with independent power. But recall that few SBEs are elected, and their elections are rarely competitive, visible, or draw many voters; one observer called such elections "nonevents." In the main, then, the SBE is a weak policy actor, primarily because of its inability to hire or remove the CSSO who has major constitutional oversight of state education. The SBE is also often poorly staffed or organized to operate effectively and often lacks political lines to the legislature and governor. They seem to wander about in the wilderness while the battle is being fought on a plain somewhere else.

The CSSOs, however, know where the action is and are often in the thick of it. SBEs look to them for leadership and information in policy conflict and seldom oppose them. But the CSSO is not a strong office with the legislature unless it is elected and has a big staff and formal powers, and unless the party life of the state is weak and the economy poor. The same office can be used for quite different policy concerns by different occupants. Thus in California in the 1970s categorical programs for the disadvantaged were a priority, but in 1988 curriculum content in academic subjects became the priority. By 1980 the CSSOs, through better interstate coordination and national networks, were becoming even stronger. However, the impact of state political culture helps shape the role and impact of all state administrators.

The element of political culture that most affects state policymaking is the strength of local control norms. Both the role SEAs play in state education policy and their capacity to assist local districts largely depend on the support they receive from general government and whether the political culture sanctions an active presence in local jurisdictions. This finding suggests that state political culture, in effect, preordains SEA roles and that SEAs in states with a strong local control ethos will always play a less active role and have less capacity than their counterparts in states where a strong central government is seen as legitimate.[59]

The State Education Agency

The daily job of implementing state policy goals rests in the hands of anonymous bureaucrats in the SEA. When the century opened, these agencies were tiny, but then succeeding waves of school reform policies were left with the SEAs to administer, and so they expanded greatly.

Today, SEAs supervise a vast array of federal and state programs, either through direct administration (for example, state schools for the blind) or through overseeing state guidelines. Their compliance techniques include requiring and reviewing a torrent of reports from the LEAs; enforcing mandated levels of service (for example, curriculum); assisting LEAs in designing and staffing newly required programs; providing continuing career education for professionals; and so on.[60] In a larger perspective, they were given the task of institutionalizing the professional model of the schools that states adopted over the last century. Programs that fell to them sought the "Americanization" of immigrants, vocational training for farm and city work, upgraded language and math training, improved resources for educating disadvantaged and minority children, and on and on in an almost unending list.

A comparative study in the 1970s provides a rare look at several hundred top members of this invisible bureaucracy in twelve states.[61] They appear primarily to be "locals," that is, born, educated, recruited, and serving mostly in their own states. These qualities generated in them a distinct parochialism in defining good education and proper state-local relations. Some were more rural in origin; others were more experienced and educated; a few were mobile types who had worked in several states. Little discernible relationship, however, showed up between different types and their states' political, social, and economic environments. It seems as though the local political culture does not differentiate much among professional bureaucrats, who may well be more responsive to the nationwide norms of their profession instead.

Specialists in little niches of expertise, SEAs constitute a complex of daily spear carriers for curriculum, finance and accounting, administration, personnel, and many other matters. Their political influence may be the most subtle, that of inertia defending the status quo. Their role in innovation and its implementation is one of the many unstudied aspects of the educational policy system, but it appears to be increasing because of state initiatives concerning testing, teacher quality, and local academic standards.

The SEAs sometimes find themselves in political disputes with governors and legislators. For example, McDonnell and McLaughlin found:

> Even in states where education enjoys the active support of general government, this support does not extend to federal programs for special needs students (administered by the SEAs). . . . Governors and legislators are generally opposed to categorical funding, and except for handicapped students, those representing special needs students command little visibility or political influence. . . . The governor and the state legislature believe that these programs should be subordinated to more general goals, such as increased competency in basic skills for all students.[62]

State Political Parties

In democracies numbers count, as do organizations of voters. The chief organization is the political party, so its role in shaping any public policy must be looked at. After all, the institutions reviewed above are products of electoral impulses diffracted through political parties in times past. And the epitome of individualism is not merely voting for officeholders but speaking directly on policy matters through the initiative and referendum.

A surprisingly little studied aspect of school policymaking is the role of political party. Available reports show that parties differ on school policymaking, although no consistent pattern in this difference emerges. Some of these studies are of single states in which the party is seen as a significant agent affecting policymaking.[63] State legislatures are frequently quite partisan, such as the 1987 California case where a Republican governor preserved his budget through straight party-line votes. A recent analysis of the link between parties and the adoption of school reforms from the study entitled *A Nation at Risk* provides a rare chance to trace statistically the influence of parties. Findings show that adoption rates were little associated with the degree of party competition, but adoption had occurred much more often in states where parties had usually not taken policy stands (e.g., the South). In the main, though, party factors were not significant. Yet we still have no fifty-state comparison using such process-oriented studies. One four-state study of legislatures and school policymaking, examining parties as only one factor, found the familiar variety. Thus Republicans supported increasing state taxes for schooling more than Democrats did in Massachusetts and North Carolina (two quite different wings of the Democratic party, incidentally), but less than Democrats did in Oregon and Utah. Even this association between party and policy was influenced more if the legislator came from a competitive district and was a party leader.[64]

Evolution of State Education Politics

Several impressions remain from the preceding overview. Variety is of course the hallmark of state school policymaking, but, perhaps more important, some commonalities also emerge. First, until the 1960s, state school policy had been left mostly to professionals and their lay cohorts, constituting what could be termed Low Conflict politics. Pressure groups concocted policy recommendations that legislatures accepted with little debate; governors were usually not involved in the process; SBEs and their active managers, the CSSOs, made major policy and oversaw its administration, while the SEAs took charge of the daily operations of the states' schools. Political parties played a minor or no role in many states, and even where they did, recent events have made them act much alike. So in the Low Conflict mode of educational policymaking, the stages of initiation, formulation of alternatives, authorization, and implementation were primarily in the hands of the professionals themselves or their supporters. It was a game played by few with the rules set by the players.

A second commonality is that this general situation has altered dramatically since 1965 as the states entered a High Conflict mode. Political turbulence from different lay groups has stimulated elected state officials to take more direct interest in school policymaking. Governors and legislators have been goaded by widespread popular discontent with school taxes and with purported teaching failures. These officials everywhere have moved to take education under their budgetary control. School policy is no longer regarded as being apolitical by these policymakers or as having little political return for them. Rather, they now see it simply as one of a number of policies that must be held more accountable and administered on tighter funds to match the efficiency mood of the 1980s.

Another development underlying recent turbulence is a third commonality. This has been the challenges to traditional definitions of how school policy should be decided, policy services delivered, and schools financed and in what amounts. Much of this has involved a shift in defining and financing policy objectives to the state level, accompanied by the opening up of state policymaking once handled by professionals. This means not only a larger role for laity—although that is still episodic and affects only a few issues—but it also points to the fragmentation of school professionals themselves. Also it points to the increased roles that legislatures and governors play in school decisions.

A fourth commonality has only been hinted at: the degree to which a state's school policymaking is shaped by distinctive beliefs based on historical decisions or events. Thus it seems that contemporary forces are diffracted by the prisms of state political culture. If ESEA funded expanding the state education bureaucracies, not all states dealt with this stimulus the same way.[65] All might use the money to add staff—some dynamics of bureaucracy are eternal—but whether and where they then led the state's educational program development depended very much on the state's political culture. New York, already a national leader, simply got better; a second state might do nothing because it always had, but a third might seize the federal funds in order to improve the quality of its education. Whether for this or other programs for dispersing federal aid to education, states use traditional ways of operating to reallocate resources, and these ways reflect customary ways of defining such basic political values as individualism. We noted earlier that the way state versus local control is defined depends upon the state's political culture, rather like dam gates built in earlier eras to regulate the flow of power between the two units. Thus the past provides a common influence among the fifty states, but, like streams down a mountainside, the influence takes different courses.

That is quite a different picture from the closed system noted by observers in previous years. Hence, contemporary research must also share this tentative condition, echoing the professionals' cry that,

CHAPTER 9

"The times they are a-changing." In these respects, the American public school and school decision making are in a transition unknown since the reform effort to extricate schools from party control late in the nineteenth century. Everywhere there is talk about the crisis in education, about more public support for effective schools, about reaching for new decision-making techniques, and about emerging redefinitions of teachers' role vis-à-vis administration. These currents also characterized the reform era of a century ago that resulted in a much better system of education. Few then could visualize the nature of the result, much argument over state policy occurred, and there is also no agreement today.

NOTES

1. An excellent review of this regional variety and its political consequences is found in Daniel Elazar, *American Federalism: A View from the States* (New York: Crowell, 1984).

2. George Collins, "Constitutional and Legal Basis for State Action," in *Education in the States: Nationwide Development since 1900,* Edgar Fuller and Jim Pearson, eds. (Washington: National Education Association, Washington, 1969), pp. 29–30.

3. For a review of five interpretations, see David Tyack, "Ways of Seeing: An Essay on the History of Compulsive Schooling," *Harvard Educational Review* 46 (1976): 355–89. Also useful is Michael S. Katz, *A History of Compulsory Education Laws* (Bloomington, Ind.: Phi Delta Kappa Educational Foundation, 1976).

4. See Michael S. Katz, *School Reforms: Past and Present* (Boston: Little Brown & Co., 1971).

5. For a full description of this process, see Raymond E. Callahan, *Education in the Cult of Efficiency* (Chicago: University of Chicago Press, 1962).

6. Frederick M. Wirt, "Political Turbulence and Administrative Authority in the Schools," in *The New Urban Politics*, Louis Masotti and Robert Lineberry, eds. (Cambridge, Mass.: Ballinger, 1976), Chap. 3.

7. National Center for Education Statistics, *Digest of Education Statistics 1980* (Washington: Government Printing Office, 1980), p. 78.

8. Ellis Katz, *Education Policymaking 1977–1978: A Snapshot from the States* (Washington: Institute for Educational Leadership, 1978).

9. The definitive review of these events, policies, and results is Walter Garms, James Guthrie, and Lawrence Pierce, *School Finance: The Economics and Politics of Federalism* (Englewood Cliffs, N.J.: Prentice-Hall, 1988). For a valuable introduction to current issues, see James Guthrie, ed., *School Finance in the 1980's* (Cambridge, Mass.: Ballinger, 1980).

10. An authoritative review of the following constitutional aspects of schooling law is Tyll van Geel, *Authority to Control the School Program* (Lexington, Mass.: Lexington Books, 1976).

11. This development is analyzed in the influential Callahan, *Cult of Efficiency* and in Lawrence Cremin, *The Transformation of the School: Progressivism in American Education, 1876–1957* (New York: Vintage Books, 1964).

12. A useful set of essays on many of these developments since 1900 is found in Fuller and Pearson, *Education in the States.* A more recent catalogue of state education requirements for each of the fifty states is found in National Institute of Education, Department of Health, Education and Welfare, *State Legal Standards for the Provision of Public Education* (Washington D.C.: National Institute of Education, 1978).

13. Margaret Goerty, *State Educational Standards* (Princeton: Educational Testing Service, 1986).

14. Frederick M. Wirt, "State Policy Culture and State Decentralization," in *Politics of Education,* Jay Scribner, ed. (Chicago: Yearbook of the National Society for the Study of Education, 1977), pp. 164–87. A brief statement is in Frederick M. Wirt, "What State Laws Say about Local Control," *Phi Delta Kappan* 59 (1978): 517–20.

15. See Michael Kirst, "The State Role in Regulation of Local School Districts," in *Government in the Classroom,* Mary Williams, ed. (New York: Academy of Political Science, Columbia University, 1979), pp. 45–56.

16. Ibid., p. 11. For a recent update, see William Chance, *The Best of Education* (Chicago: McArthur Foundation, 1987).

17. Douglas Mitchell, Catherine Marshall, and Frederick Wirt, *Culture and Education Policy in the American State* (Falmer, 1989).

18. Douglas Mitchell et al., "Building a Taxonomy of State Education Policies," *Peabody Journal of Education* 62, no. 4 (1985): 7–47.

19. David Clark and Terry Astuto, *The Significance and Permanence of Changes in Federal Educational Policy 1980–1988* (Bloomington, Ind.: Policy Studies Center of the University Council for Educational Administration, University of Indiana, 1986).

20. Lucius Pye, "Political Culture," in *International Encyclopedia of the Social Sciences,* Vol. 12 (New York: Crowell, Collier and Macmillan, 1968), p. 218.

21. Daniel Elazar, *American Federalism.*

22. Mitchell et al., *Culture and Education Policy,* Chap. 5.

23. Paul Berman and Milbrey McLaughlin, *Federal Programs Supporting Education Change* (Santa Monica, Calif.: Rand, 1975) Vol. IV, R-1584/4HEW; and the special issue of *Teachers College Record* 77, "Making Change Happen" (February 1976).

24. Joel Berke and Michael Kirst, *Federal Aid to Education* (Lexington, Mass.: Heath, 1976).

25. The fullest analysis of these developments is Gary Orfield, *Must We Bus? Segregated Schools and National Policy* (Brookings Institution, Washington, D.C., 1978).

26. Harrell Rodgers and Charles Bullock, *Coercion to Compliance* (Lexington, Mass.: Heath, 1976).

27. Everett Cataldo et al., *School Desegregation Policy: Compliance, Avoidance, and the Metropolitan Remedy* (Lexington, Mass.: Heath, 1978).

28. Marshall et al., *Culture and Education Policy,* Chap. 2.

29. Catherine Marshall, Douglas Mitchell, and Frederick Wirt, "Influence, Power, and Policy Making," *Peabody Journal of Education* 62, no. 1 (1985), p. 88.

30. Ibid., "Assumptive Worlds of Education Policy Makers," *Peabody Journal of Education* 62, no. 4 (1985): 90–115; citation is at p. 90.

31. Michael Kirst, Gail Meister, and Stephen R. Rowley, "Policy Issue Networks: Their Influence on State Policymaking," *Policy Studies Journal* 13, no. 2 (December 1984): 247–64.

32. The following is drawn from Harmon Zeigler and Henrick van Dalen, "Interest Groups in State Politics," in *Politics in the American States: A Comparative Analysis*, Herbert Jacob and Kenneth Vines, eds. (Boston: Little, Brown & Co., 1976), Chap. 3.

33. Ibid., 134.

34. Ibid., pp. 95–109 characterize and detail these types. For a fuller elaboration based on four states, see Harmon Zeigler and Michael Baer, *Lobbying, Interaction and Influence in American State Legislatures* (Belmont, Calif.: Wadsworth, 1969).

35. For a brief history, see J. Howard Goold, "The Organized Teaching Profession," in Pearson and Fuller, *Education in the States*, Chap. 14; and Lorraine McDonnell and Anthony Pascal, "National Trends in Teaching Collective Bargaining," *Education and Urban Society* 11 (1979): 129–51.

36. The following is drawn from Laurence Iannaccone, *Politics in Education* (New York: Center for Applied Research in Education, 1967), Chap. 3.

37. J. Alan Aufderheide, "Educational Interest Groups and the State Legislature," in *State Policy Making for the Public Schools: A Comparative Analysis*, Roald Campbell and Tim Mazzoni, Jr., eds. (Berkeley: McCutchan, 1976), p. 201.

38. See the review of Iannaccone's typology using twelve-state data in Raphael Nystrand, "State Education Policy Systems," in Campbell and Mazzoni, *State Policy Making*, Chap. 7. Nystrand's analysis may not have fully tested this typology, according to some critics.

39. Michael Kirst and Stephen Sommers, "Collective Action Among California Educational Interest Groups: A Logical Response to Proposition 13," *Education and Urban Society* 13, no. 2 (1981): 235–56.

40. William Boyd, "Interest Groups and the Changing Environment" (paper presented to the American Educational Research Association, Washington D.C., 1987).

41. Kirst and Sommers, "Collective Action," p. 256.

42. Aufderheide, "Educational Interest Groups," p. 213.

43. Ibid., p. 209.

44. Zeigler and van Dalen, "Interest Groups," p. 147.

45. William H. Riker, *The Theory of Political Coalitions* (New Haven, Conn.: Yale University Press, 1962).

46. For a useful introduction to this literature, see Samuel Patterson, "American State Legislatures and Public Policy," in Jacob and Vines, *Politics*, Chap. 4. The major survey is Malcolm Jewell and Samuel Patterson, *The Legislative Process in the United States*, 2d ed. (New York: Random House, 1973).

47. Nicholas Masters, Robert Salisbury, and Thomas Eliot, *State Politics and the*

Public Schools (New York: Knopf, 1964): Jerome T. Murphy, "The Paradox of State Government Reform," in *Educational Policymaking*, 1978 Yearbook of the National Society for the Study of Education, Milbrey McLaughlin, ed. (Chicago: University of Chicago Press, 1978).

48. Ellis Katz, *Education Policymaking*, pp. 40–41.

49. A major review and addition to this scholarship is Douglas E. Mitchell, *Shaping Legislative Decisions: Education Policy and the Social Sciences* (Lexington, Mass.: Lexington Books, 1978).

50. The following draws on Sarah Morehouse, "The Governor as Political Leader," in Jacob and Vines, *Politics in the American States*, Chap. 5. An invaluable exploration of this office is Thad Beyle and J. Oliver Williams, *The American Governor in Behavioral Perspective* (New York: Harper & Row, 1972).

51. The seminal work is Thomas Dye, *Politics, Economics, and the Public* (Chicago: Rand McNally, 1966).

52. Iannaccone, *Politics in Education*, p. 44.

53. Edward Hines, "Governors and Educational Policy Making," in Campbell and Mazzoni, *State Policy Making*, Chap. 4.

54. An excellent analysis is Mike Milstein and Robert Jennings, *Educational Policy Making and the State Legislature: The New York Experience* (New York: Praeger, 1973).

55. A full catalogue of these authorities is Sam Harris, *State Departments of Education, State Boards of Education, and Chief State School Officers* (Washington, D.C.: United States Government Printing Office, 1973).

56. For their history and variety, see Lerus Winget, Edgar Fuller, and Terrel Bell, "State Departments of Education," in Fuller and Pearson, *Education in the States*, Chap. 2. For New York, see Milstein and Jennings, *Educational Policy Making*.

57. Fuller and Pearson, "State Departments of Education," *Education in the States*, p. 83.

58. On the "nonevent," see a major challenge to the once-popular notion of the SBE influence, Gerald Sroufe, "State School Board Members and the State Education Policy System," *Planning and Changing* 2 (April 1971): 16–17. For a twelve-state review of the SBE, see Roald Campbell, "The Chief State School Officer as a Policy Actor," in Campbell and Mazzoni, *State Policy Making*, Chap. 3. For suggestions on how to improve state boards, see Michael Cohen, "State Boards in an Era of Reform," *Phi Delta Kappan* 69, no. 1 (September 1987): 60–64.

59. Lorraine M. McDonnell and Milbrey W. McLaughlin, *Education Policy and the Role of the States* (Santa Monica, Calif.: Rand, 1982), p. 79.

60. Almost all the comparative chapters of Fuller and Pearson, *Education in the States*, detail these SEA functions. Especially useful for understanding the different kinds of authority under which SEAs operate are Chapters 8, 10, and 13.

61. Drawn from Gary Branson, "The Characteristics of Upper Level Administrators in Departments of Education" (unpublished part of the Campbell and Mazzoni study, mimeo).

62. McDonnell and McLaughlin, *Education Policy*, p. 73.

63. Zeigler and Baer, *Lobbying*, pp. 143, 146, 149.

64. Doh Shinn and Jack Van Der Slik, "Legislative Efforts to Improve the Quality

of Public Education in the American States: A Comparative Analysis" (paper presented to the annual conference of the American Political Science Association, New Orleans, 1985).

65. Jerome Murphy, *State Education Agencies and Discretionary Funds* (Lexington, Mass.: Lexington Books, 1974); Mike Milstein, *Impact and Response* (New York: Teachers College Press, 1976).

10

The State Role
in Education
Policy Innovation

SYSTEMS ANALYSIS AND AMERICAN FEDERALISM

Systems analysis has provided a framework for organizing the information from thousands of diverse local districts about education policy and politics. The same concept enables us to search for patterns of behavior among the fifty states of the Union. Each state can be conceived as a miniature political system, receiving and processing a flow of inputs arising from unmet needs over resources and values within the state's environment. The result is the education policy system of each state. But systems analysis does more by encouraging the analyst to look not for just fifty sets of policy behaviors but for similarities as well as differences among the fifty.

Earlier we noted how the concept of political culture served to shake down into roughly three patterns of policy behavior. We will see in this chapter how surges of national attention to particular policy needs create a standardization of that behavior. The states have undergone successive waves of reform, often generated by professionals, that left behind patterns of policy action that are somewhat similar from Hawaii to Maine. In the last quarter century, the federal government has been a major stimulant of such pervasive policy change as it interacted with each state to pursue federal goals. But in the 1980s, due to a weakening of the federal stimulus under the

Reagan administration, the states turned into laboratories of innovation, although again we will find striking similarities existing alongside differences.

In larger perspective, then, a federal system, with its typical division of formal authority among central and peripheral governments, introduces a new dimension for understanding the political system of American education. Federalism also provides another framework for understanding how group conflict gets raised and responded to across the variety of our people.

HISTORICAL BACKGROUND

Under the United States Constitution, education is a power reserved to the states. In turn, state constitutions charge the state legislatures with responsibility for establishing and maintaining a system of free public schools that are locally operated. Local control has been a hallmark of American education, distinguishing us from most other Western nations. But an unprecedented growth of state influence over local education has taken place since the 1960s, which will be the focus of this chapter.

States show different historical patterns of control over local policies of such matters as curriculum, personnel finances, and teaching, but all states established minumum standards for local school operations. Presumably the state's general welfare required a basic educational opportunity for all children. Consequently, states require a minimum number of days at school, certain courses of study, and standards for teacher certification. Most states also require localities to levy a minimum tax and guarantee a base level of expenditures. There has been an urban-rural distinction to this state role. Earlier in this century, states began upgrading the standards of rural schools, but the cities received less attention because their expenditures and property wealth were already the highest in the state. Indeed, Chicago, New York, and Philadelphia had special statutes that exempted them from major areas of state control. Decades later, in the 1970s, state school finance reforms created special provisions for the core cities, but then the rationale was based on high fiscal stress.

A principal reason for state intervention is that only the state can ensure equality and standardization of instruction and resources. This rationale is contested by local control advocates, who contend that flexibility is needed to adjust to diverse circumstances and local preferences. Local control advocates stress that no proven educational technology is optimal for all conditions. This dispute over state versus local control really centers on two values—equal treatment and freedom of local choice. The traditional compromise has been state minimums with local options to exceed the minimums, but this compromise was challenged by school finance reformers in the 1970s because state minimums were inadequate or were substantially exceeded by localities with extraordinary taxable property.

Some Causes for the Growth of State Influence

Some of the major policy areas that show the dramatic increase of state influence in the last two decades are state administration of federal categorical grants, the state role in education finance, state requirements for educational accountability, state specifications and programs for children with special needs, and state efforts to increase academic standards. Substantive changes have become possible in large part due to an increase in the institutional capacity of states to intervene in local affairs. Thus most state legislatures have added staff and research capacity, and they also now meet annually or for more extended sessions than in earlier years. Legislative staff increased by 130 percent between 1968 and 1974.[1] During the 1970s, the states also diversified their tax sources and expanded their fiscal capacities.

The capacity of state education agencies (SEAs) to intercede in local school policy has also mushroomed in the last twenty years. Ironically, the federal government created the impetus for this expansion. The Elementary and Secondary Education Act of 1965 and its subsequent amendments required state agencies to approve local projects for federal funds in such areas as education for disadvantaged, handicapped, bilingual, and migrant children and for educational innovation. In each of these federal programs, 1 percent of the funds were earmarked for state administration. Moreover, Title V of ESEA provided general support for state administrative resources, with some priority given to state planning and evaluation. By 1972 three-fourths of the SEA staffs had been in their jobs for less than three years. All the expansion in California's SEA from 1964 to 1970 was financed by federal funds. In 1972, 70 percent of the funding for the state education agency in Texas came from federal aid. New staff capacity was available for SEA administrators or state boards that wanted to take a more activist role in local education.² The 1983 academic reform era galvanized a significant increase in state testing and curricular experts. State staff has increased to implement new teacher policies including career ladders.

Another factor is the increased confusion among and decreased respect for traditional supporters of local control. Thus local control advocates—such as teachers' unions, school boards, and school administrator associations—feud among themselves and provide a vacuum that state control activists can exploit. As we have seen, these education groups cannot agree on common policies with their old allies such as parent organizations. The loss of public confidence in professional educators and the decline of achievement scores also cause many legislators to feel that local school employees should no longer be given so much discretion.

In addition to all this, a key structural change in the growth and diversification of state tax sources has developed. From 1960 to 1979, eleven states adopted a personal income tax, nine a corporate income tax, and ten a general sales tax. Thirty-seven states used all three of these revenue sources in 1979 compared with just nineteen in 1960. State income taxes provided 35 percent of all tax revenue in 1978 compared to 19 percent in 1969. This diversification of the revenue systems provided the states with a capacity to increase services that was further enhanced by numerous tax increases to fund reforms after 1983. The favorite tax to increase was the sales tax, either through rate increases or extension of the sales tax base to services. Even states with slow economic growth raised the sales tax from 1983 to 1986, including Arkansas, South Carolina, and New Mexico.

RECENT STATE EDUCATIONAL REFORMS: APPRAISAL AND THE FUTURE*

Crisis is a constant in American education. Scholars, university educators, businesspeople, and legislators regularly find major problems with elementary and secondary schools and propose

*This section is based on research conducted by Michael Kirst, of Stanford University, and William Firestone and Susan Fuhrman, of Rutgers University, on behalf of the Center for Policy Research in Education (CPRE), which is funded by the U.S. Department of Education. It was published earlier in *Educational Policy*, Vol. 5, No. 3, September 1991, pp. 233–250, and reprinted with the permission of Corwin Press.

substantial reforms to solve these problems. Until mid-century, the preferred approach to galvanizing action was a symbolic one relying on the commission report or other authoritative pronouncement by respected sources. The Report of the Committee of Ten in 1893, *The Cardinal Principles of Secondary Education* in 1918, and *The American High School Today* in 1959 were followed by *A Nation at Risk* in 1983. Since the 1950s, governmental action has become more prevalent and includes National Science Foundation grants for curriculum development, court action to effect desegregation, and Title I and Chapter I and other federal programs to improve educational opportunity.

Two things are notable about these reform efforts. First, the agendas for reform fluctuate dramatically. While the Committee of Ten sought to standardize secondary education for precollegiate students, *The Cardinal Principles* was geared to students who would take jobs directly after school.[3] The 1950s' reforms were aimed at the future scientific leaders, whereas the 1960s' reforms stressed equity for children of all races and achievement levels. Many reform reports in the 1970s recommended humanizing education; those of the 1980s stressed tightening standards.[4]

Second, the reformers' targets are rarely met in practice. Review of a century of national commission reports suggests that commissions make strong dramatic gestures to call attention to problems but give ambiguous recommendations and too little attention to implementation problems. As a result, the impact on school and classroom life is meager.[5] Similarly, the most frequently cited study of the implementation of federal legislation highlights "mutual adaptation," whereby external requirements are adapted to local conditions.[6] While it is possible, albeit with great difficulty, for court-ordered desegregation to change who goes to which school, it is more difficult to change what goes on when they get there.

The reform efforts of the 1980s were characterized by national commission reports and state legislative and executive action. The commission reports, such as *A Nation at Risk*,[7] established a series of targets and directions for change. State action provided the mandates, incentives, and resources to ensure local action. Actual changes in practice, of course, took place at the local level.

Commission Report and Reform Targets

Of the twenty-nine books and reports issued in and around 1983, *A Nation at Risk* had the most lasting significance. In the succeeding five years, three themes emerged from efforts to reform American education:

1. Emphasis was placed on *increased academic content* through a curriculum more focused on major academic areas. The exemplar report for this theme was *A Nation at Risk* itself. The preferred vehicles for providing access to more content were increased course requirements, increased student testing, the establishment of curriculum standards, and the alignment of curriculum frameworks, tests, and textbooks.

2. *Teacher professionalization* was introduced by *A Nation at Risk*, which stressed changes in licensure requirements and compensation to recruit and retain the best. By 1986, the emphasis had shifted to "restructuring" education to give teachers a greater role in such decisions as hiring, staff evaluation, and curriculum. A substantial redistribution of authority was envisioned by *A Nation Prepared* and *Tomorrow's Teachers*, among others.[8]

3. A reprise of the *equity* theme, which was given passing attention in *A Nation at Risk*, was the central concern in *An Imperiled Generation: Saving Urban Schools*.[9] There were fewer clear action recommendations in this area, but the interest in measuring and reducing the dropout rate, providing services for at-risk youths, expanding early childhood education, and attending to urban schools reflected this concern.

State Reforms

The same five-year period saw a level of state policy activity in education unprecedented since the formation of the common school system. The federally funded Center for Policy Research in Education's (CPRE) tracking of state educational reform suggested seven conclusions about this activity.

1. States were most responsive to providing more academic content and to those aspects of professionalization dealing with changes in certification and compensation.

The effort to provide more academic content was substantial across the nation. All six states in the CPRE sample increased their high school graduation requirements, as did the majority of other states in the nation. Student testing requirements also increased substantially. Some states, like Pennsylvania, introduced statewide mandatory testing for the first time; others, like Georgia and Florida, expanded existing programs. California was notable for its efforts to coordinate state-mandated tests, state textbook adoption, and curriculum standards in order to move instruction to a higher cognitive level. By contrast, a few recommended reforms were not so popular, the most striking being the suggestion to increase the school year to 200 or even 220 days. While thirty-seven states considered such action and nine actually took action, none lengthened the number of student contact days beyond 180.[10] Other suggestions that received relatively little state attention were to (a) lengthen the school day, (b) upgrade the elementary curriculum, and (c) change homework policies.

The most pervasive changes in teacher policy were those that modified certification requirements and increased teacher salaries. Entrance requirements were also increased; however, it is not clear how these would hold up if teacher shortages become more severe. Arizona, Florida, and California are among the twenty-seven states that set a minimum grade point average for entering teachers, and forty-six states require some kind of certification test. At the same time, the proliferation of alternative routes to certification created the possibility of decline in the role played by teachers' colleges in training educators. Over twenty states offered some alternative route to certification that allowed individuals with a liberal arts background to go into teaching. Along with changes in entrance requirements came changes in incentives. Teachers' salaries increased 22 percent in real terms between 1980 and 1988, with most of the growth occurring between 1983 and 1988.[11] While not quite back to earlier levels, they still grew faster than those for the average worker.[12]

Reforms to restructure the organization of instruction or revise decision-making roles within schools received less attention. Until recently, the most discussed reforms aimed at enhancing the teaching profession were merit pay and career ladder programs. By 1991, twenty-five states had or were planning such efforts.[13] Florida and Tennessee were among the few to try implementing such programs on a massive basis. Florida rescinded its program, and Tennessee's program has been heavily modified. Some of the programs that continue have led to only minor changes in teaching roles, like California's mentor teacher program, or are being implemented on a limited basis, like Arizona's pilot career ladder, which affects only twenty-one of the over two hundred districts in the state. Although states continued to experiment with career ladders, they were doing so more carefully, often through pilot programs or with more intensive participation during planning. Much of the initiative in this area shifted from the state to the district level.[14] The concepts of career ladders and teacher merit pay have been mixed together in some states, like Virginia, causing some teacher resistance.

2. *States' responses to national reform targets reflected local political culture.*

In spite of the national press for reform, state context affected the process of passing reform, the kinds of reforms adopted, and the way they were implemented.[15] For instance, in the CPRE's six-state study, three that had a history of turning to large-scale policy fixes did so again. California's SB 813 of 1983 is in the tradition of its early childhood legislation of 1972, school finance reform in the same year, and school improvement program of 1979. Florida also has a history of major reforms that was repeated in 1983. As in earlier efforts, leadership came from the Speaker of the House and the Senate President. In this case, the governor was also a major player, but his experience had been in the legislature.

The states that lacked experience with comprehensive reform did not initiate it in the 1980s. Pennsylvania's reforms were organized by the governor and came about largely, as in the past, through state board action. Arizona has a history of modest legislative reforms like its pilot career program that affected very few districts.

The reform policy mechanisms also reflected state context. For instance, Georgia's state policymakers often distrusted the 187 county districts, especially the 117 with elected superintendents. This mistrust encouraged the state to rely heavily on mandates. California, in contrast, is very large and has a constitutional requirement that the state must pay for all mandated changes. As these could become prohibitively expensive, the state stressed incentives.

The implementation process itself often reflected state culture. For instance, in Arizona, the Republican legislature distrusted the executive, which was run by an elected Democratic chief state school officer. This partisan concern contributed to the decision by the two education committees to administer the pilot career ladder directly. Pennsylvania's legislature has a history of serving as a court of appeal for interest groups objecting to legislative action. Thus when the teacher association objected to newly mandated continuing professional development requirements, it turned to the House of Representatives.[16]

3. States tended to focus on the more manageable recommendations.

The most popular reform to come out of the 1980s was that of increasing graduation requirements. There was little direct cost to adding courses, although sometimes, teachers specializing in particular areas had to be added. Often, the courses added were very similar to those already on the books before the proliferation of electives in the 1970s. If not, teachers often had ideas about what they wanted to teach. Moreover, in many states, most district graduation requirements already met the increased state requirements. Finally, although there was some reallocation of opportunities from vocational to academic teachers to accommodate changed course requirements, no major redistribution occurred because all those affected were already at the same level.

The reforms that were not widely adopted had the opposite characteristics. Increasing the school day and year could be extremely expensive in terms of additional teacher salaries. Career ladders were also expensive, as they required adding to the salary pool to avoid divisiveness, and complex because creating fair and reliable assessment instruments strained existing technology. Finally, the introduction of neophyte and mentor teacher roles could lead to a major redistribution of authority both among teachers and between teachers and administrators. When states ventured into these more complex areas, they often constructed the reforms in ways that made them more manageable. For example, they began with pilot programs on a small scale.

Other reforms fell between the extremes. Three of the six states studied by the CPRE increased teacher salaries but only by raising minimums. All six states increased student testing, but most stayed within the existing technology. By the end of the decade, however, more states were developing tests of higher-order cognitive thinking and cutting back on the focus of testing basic skills. By 1991, every one of our six states had revamped its state testing program initially implemented in the 1980s.[17]

4. Most state reform packages lacked coherence.

Reforms designed as coherent packages should have greater impact. Each part will facilitate the other, and the set will send a more coordinated message to local educators. As a rule, such coherence was missing from the recent round of reforms. Specific provisions were rarely in conflict, but they were often unrelated, sending a barrage of signals to districts and requiring complex decisions about where to allocate time and money.

The lack of coherent reform provisions is typical of efforts of the past century. It reflects in part the inconsistent thinking behind some of the reforms. For instance, teaching reforms have been motivated by concerns about both quality and quantity of teachers. Yet some reforms, like tightening certification requirements designed to enhance the quality of the teaching force, could very well increase shortages. Similarly, policies such as alternative certification routes risk increasing the number of teachers but watering down the quality. Moreover, the compromises required to get omnibus legislation passed often encouraged the inclusion of specific provisions advocated by individual leaders and groups.

Where coherence increased it was because of the efforts of state leaders to integrate existing provisions rather than to create new ones. Thus California's state superintendent orchestrated existing requirements for student testing, state textbook selection, and state curriculum guides to place greater stress on higher-order cognitive thinking.

Policies to increase standards for teaching affected recruitment, certification, and professional development. Yet the notable thing about recruitment and training policies was their limited connection to curriculum and testing. Two state policies affected hiring. The first was the amount of state aid, which influenced salaries. There were dramatic increases in teacher salaries early in the decade.[18] By the end of the period, weakening fiscal conditions in several states and districts appeared to be slowing the rate of increases. Second, states were heavily involved through certification policies, which included a mix of tests and course requirements.

The big development in the 1980s was the expansion of teacher testing: forty-five states now do some form of teacher testing, usually at exit from the college teacher preparation program or before receiving certification. The most frequently used tests emphasize basic skills knowledge of the sort that might be asked of the general public, although the National Teacher Examination (NTE) includes a component on professional knowledge of teaching and provides for testing in specific subject area fields.[19] Because of their emphasis on basic skills, the usefulness of most tests is limited to ruling out fundamentally unprepared future teachers. Because the tests are generic, they are not clearly linked to state curriculum and testing policies.

A similar lack of coherence is apparent in governance. The major change in the 1980s was centralization of control at the state level. The changes in state curriculum, testing, and teacher policies described earlier here limited local discretion over what would be taught and by whom while mandating the ways in which progress would be assessed. Such centralization was partially limited by inconsistencies between policies and changes over time that either confused local educators or reduced requirements, thereby giving them more leeway.

However, the trend to centralize was limited by intentional efforts to bring additional actors—either parents or teachers—into the decision-making process. While efforts to enfranchise additional interests were usually locally initiated, there were a number of state efforts. For instance, some states started programs that required wider participation in local decision making. These included the school-parent councils in Georgia and the requirement that teachers participate in the design of local staff development programs mandated by Pennsylvania's Act 178.

In effect, both centralizing and decentralizing tendencies are progressing simultaneously. It is difficult to find any overarching pattern here, but a tendency toward moderation is apparent in the six states we followed most carefully. The most comprehensive and mandate-driven efforts, notably those in Florida and Georgia, progressively reduced their regulation from a peak reached in the mid-1980s when their omnibus reform bills passed. On the other hand, states that traditionally supported local control and employed incentives to persuade locals to take action became more aggressive in legislating reform. Minnesota and Arizona particularly have become more active in testing and curriculum development in the past few years.

5. States are continuing to work on reform, but there is no clear shift in direction from the first wave of reform to the second.

The rhetoric of reform portrays two waves: The first, from approximately 1982 to 1986, focused on standardization through minimum requirements for students and teacher certification; and the second, beginning about 1986, focuses on moving beyond standards to quality improvements designed at the school site. Designated the "restructuring" movement, the second wave is supposed to reorganize instruction to improve teaching and learning for understanding, more depth of content as compared to coverage, and more emphasis on higher-order thinking. It also has governance aspects, including school-site autonomy, shared decision making, enhanced roles for teachers and parents, and regulatory simplicity.[20]

Elements of the second wave are being put into practice in a number of district-level experiments and in several state programs that provide planning and implementation grants to schools and/or districts through a competitive process.[21] However, examination of state actions in the 1986–1990 period leads to the conclusion that states are continuing to enact policies that are more characteristic of the first wave. For example, Florida has twenty-nine school districts implementing the first steps of school-based management. Oklahoma passed a package of reform measures in 1990 similar to what many other states did from 1983 to 1986. Minnesota, whose 1985 and 1987 choice programs make it a pioneer in elements of the second-wave agenda, instituted a basic skills exam for teachers in 1987 more typical of the first wave. At this point, it is more accurate to think of the reform movement as a broad set of policy recommendations that states consider in a time frame reflecting their own needs and political culture rather than as a set of successive waves marked by major changes in direction.

6. The easy reforms that were adopted have stayed in place.

For the most part, the reforms adopted in the 1983–1985 period of extensive legislative and executive activity have been maintained. The biggest exception within the CPRE sample is Florida's master teacher program. Originally, just under $10 million was allocated to this program to give an annual bonus of $3,000 to qualifying teachers. However, the major teachers' association objected to a program that would reward some teachers over others. Because the program was rushed into place, the complex administrative demands of scheduling teacher tests and evaluations were not met. Applications were lost or disqualified on technicalities. The state's teacher of the year and runner-up to be the first teacher in space did not qualify. Although some of these problems were later rectified, the fairness of the program was never established, and it was repealed three years later.

7. *Expansion of the economy facilitated reform early in the decade but was not a complete explanation of it.*

The period from 1981 through 1984 was one of rapid economic expansion. Most of the more aggressive reform states benefited financially from this upturn and had more funds that could be committed to education. The economic expansion in some of the states studied by the CPRE contributed directly to reform in those states. Georgia's governor mounted a major reform effort while pledging not to raise taxes. Business interests in both Georgia and Florida lobbied hard for reform partly because new costs would be relatively small.

Yet economic factors alone do not explain the distribution of reform efforts. It is not surprising that among those states with weak economies, several did not participate in the reform movement. Yet a substantial number—including Arkansas, South Carolina, Tennessee, Texas, and West Virginia—did initiate reforms.

Whatever the cause, there was a significant increase (over 25 percent after inflation) in expenditures between 1983 and 1990.[22] However, states varied greatly in their increases for education, and the state share fell in twenty states, demonstrating that the local property tax is still alive and well.

It is unclear how much of the new money went for "reform" as against higher salaries and other expenditures that did not change curriculum, school structure, or other variables. Moreover, the definition of reform is unclear and difficult to calculate in terms of specific categories of expenditures devoted to reform.

Despite increases in state aid that far exceeded inflation, the property tax remains an important source of increased school revenues. The share of state revenue from sales and income taxes has risen at an uneven rate, whereas taxes on severance, gas, and cigarettes have declined since 1978.[23]

New ideas and concepts are needed to justify another large-scale increase in state aid. At this point, public concern and willingness to pay more taxes are not matched by consensus on new programs or approaches with high payoff for school improvement.

District Action in Response to State Initiatives

As might be expected, district response to state reforms varied widely. Nevertheless, three conclusions about district activity appear warranted from the data.

1. There was very little resistance to the reforms related to increased academic content. However, implementation of these reforms had some negative side effects.

Districts have demonstrated very little organized resistance to the current round of reforms, especially those having to do with curriculum intensification. There are a number of reasons for this positive response. First, in many cases, the reforms legitimated existing practices. That is, in several states, district requirements met or exceeded those newly established by the state. Second, even where state policy required changes, these were well within the capacity of local educators.[24] Finally, there was often widespread support for the changes introduced in the 1980s, unlike the more politically unpopular redistributive changes of the 1960s.

Efforts to raise standards for students met with mixed response. Many of the initiatives reflected an effort to "tighten up" without specifying what should be tightened up. A major example was the effort of some states to increase graduation requirements without specifying what the content of required courses should be. A number of states instituted no pass–no play rules, which bar students from participating in extracurricular activities unless they meet academic criteria. This sometimes produced coping strategies, like allowing students to register for easy courses. There were also reports of reduced participation in extracurricular activities. Other state initiatives included providing incentives for introducing middle schools or early childhood education programs and encouraging the introduction of course work in specific areas like drug education. None of these requirements encouraged systematic thinking about what should be taught, and some risk increasing the fragmentation of curriculum. By 1988, 73 percent of high schools had adopted stricter attendance policies, 69 percent used no pass–no play, and 97 percent enforced stricter student conduct policies.[25]

2. *Much of the progress on the restructuring agenda has resulted from district initiatives.*

While a few states, such as Washington, Arkansas, Maine, and Massachusetts, have initiated newer programs to encourage restructuring, these usually take the form of seed money for local experimentation. A great deal of the creative development is still being done by school districts. The earlier pioneers, like Rochester, New York; Miami, Florida; and Cincinnati, Ohio, are being joined by others, like Santa Fe, New Mexico. In addition, some smaller districts in the CPRE states are also experimenting with new strategies without the same level of publicity or state support. Elements of programs in these districts included provisions for site-based management, usually including teachers; shared decision making at the district level; and sometimes innovative approaches to inservice. Such experiments usually rest on the foundation of an unusually cooperative relationship between district administrators and the teachers' association.[26]

3. *Some districts are actively orchestrating various state policies around local priorities in order to achieve local priorities.*

Past research has shown how the local level typically minimizes responses to mandates and responds to grants with mutual accommodation rather than extensive change.[27] This pattern was found among the CPRE districts, as was another one: where the district exceeds the state requirements. One major urban district coordinates almost all state teacher policies to meet its prime objective of hiring large numbers of new teachers. Two districts in another state are using a merit schools program to support their own efforts to promote site-based management, and one is even putting in additional money. A fourth district is using state teacher policies to overcome teacher attrition problems encouraged by the competitive salaries offered in neighboring districts. At least six districts exceeded changes in graduation requirements mandated by the state.

One possible way to give more consistent signals is to link tests to financial incentives for teachers. While this strategy is extremely rare in American education, four of the six states in the CPRE study provided differential incentives to teachers. In three—Arizona, Florida, and Pennsylvania—these incentives are or were linked in part to test performance.

Whatever the mechanism involved, teachers reported that testing programs had a greater impact on their behavior in class than did curricular changes, especially changes involving increased course requirements.[28]

Looking to the Future of Reform

This review indicates that states have met with only modest success in achieving the educational goals expressed in *A Nation at Risk*. It is true that high school curricula are more academically oriented, standards for entering the teaching profession are more selective, teachers' salaries are higher, and state and local governments have boosted educational funding.

But there are still doubts about the rigor and challenge of some of the new courses in academic subjects, the impact of reform on at-risk students, the quality of teachers and teaching, and the equitable funding of schools. We still lack adequate indicators to measure the veracity of either of these concerns. Furthermore, several of the most highly touted reform proposals, such as the introduction of career ladders, have not been widely adopted.

These outcomes do not warrant despair. School reform is a long-term endeavor that requires many years of consistent effort. The graduation requirements for the classes of 1987, 1988, or 1989 are an example. Initially, the new requirements led to districts adapting higher-level academic courses for middle- and lower-achieving students. Over time, the new courses may become more rigorous. States such as California are initiating policies to upgrade curriculum. Professional associations are spearheading efforts to develop core curriculum components, elevate teacher standards, and heighten student and parent expectations. Districts and schools are taking steps to better prepare elementary and middle school students for more academic courses in high school. All this is to say that tests given in 1988 cannot measure the long-term effect of recent education reforms.

On the other hand, if reformers were as wrong-headed as some critics charge, there is little reason to expect the new policies will produce improvement, no matter how widely implemented or how much time they are given to show results. If the reforms are insensitive or detrimental to at-risk students, if they reduce rather than enhance minority access to teaching, and if they mistakenly assume that top-down directives induce productivity, it is unlikely that schools will improve in their wake.

Education improvement can occur regardless, or even in spite of, specific policy initiatives. Indeed, it is our opinion that renewed public commitment to education improves morale, promotes experimentation, and supports the efforts of everyone involved in the educational enterprise, including students and parents. The 1980s' reforms were characterized by such public interest and commitment.

No More New Waves. There is only one reform agenda: improving teaching and learning for all. Achieving this agenda encompasses a variety of policy approaches, including both the establishment of the more rigorous standards that characterized most state reforms between 1983 and 1987 and local school restructuring efforts. Rhetoric about moving from "Wave 1" to "Wave 2" of reform correctly acknowledges that standards alone cannot do the job—that standards set minimums but rarely inspire excellence; that mandates depend on local capacity for implementation and state capacity for enforcement, neither of which may exist; that collegial goal development and dedication is crucial to effective schooling; and that different kinds of policy problems require different kinds of solutions.

However, some Wave 2 rhetoric incorrectly, and in a politically unsophisticated way, implies that school-based problem solving means scrapping standards. On the contrary, standards are essential for expressing to educators and the public the expectations of state policymakers who are constitutionally responsible for education. Standards also establish the parameters for the accountability that the public receives in return for its substantial dedication of resources. They signify a commitment to a degree of educational uniformity in today's highly mobile society. Finally, they represent a commitment that no student's education will entirely depend on local decision making, especially if that results in inequitable treatment.

The reform agenda—improving teaching and learning for all— implies the need to move on several fronts at once. Improving curriculum, establishing new roles for teachers, and developing school-level structures to support teaching and learning are each pieces of the solution, not successive topics to be sequentially cycled through policy mechanisms.

In particular, we are convinced that much more work is needed in strengthening the curriculum through providing better teacher education and staff development programs and improving instruction and academic content. A major overhaul of the science curriculum, for example, could include strategies similar in scale to that of programs created in the 1960s by the National Science Foundation to improve curricula, texts, tests, and staff development.

Match Policies to Problems. Too often, policy solutions are not well suited to policy problems. Our examination of state reform tells us that some problems require several approaches. In the 1980s' reforms, policymakers raised graduation requirements to get high schools to emphasize academic instruction. But the graduation standards are a blunt instrument. Although they can lead students to take more academic courses, in the absence of other strategies such as upgraded curriculum frameworks and staff development, they are not likely to succeed. Similarly, policymakers have waived some regulations for schools experimenting with school-based management. However, without models of successful schooling, technical assistance, and staff development to help personnel implement the experimental programs, waiver offers are not likely to generate much interest.[29]

Another potential pitfall for policymakers is assuming that a particular policy response is the answer for all types of students. In general, students at the top two-thirds of the achievement band benefit from curricular intensification. More rigorous content enhances these students' academic achievement. However, students in the bottom one-third of the achievement band may need strategies beyond curricular intensification. Policies such as giving parents greater choices among schools and those promoting greater links between schools and potential employers might help these children. Analysts and policymakers also urge prompt attention to the entire range of school and social services for children and an overall attack on out-of-school influences that inhibit learning. National reports like *Investing in Our Children* by the Committee for Economic Development[30] highlight the need to improve and coordinate programs addressing children's health and psychological needs, child care, income support, and protective services. Schools cannot provide all these services, but they can do a better job of brokering them for individual children who are at risk. States could fund schools to hire case managers to bring these fragmented services together for individual children. Some chief state school officers have proposed developing the individualized teaching and learning plan (ITLP) for at-risk youths, much like the individualized education plan that pulls together services for physically handicapped children.

Our lowest achieving students are the most threatened by the impending changes in the labor market. According to the Department of Labor, the average level of education required to do the lowest level jobs is rising. There appears to be sufficient supplies of engineers, but other jobs that require more than repetitive low-skill operations go unfilled. Approaches such as the Job Corps or coordinated service delivery systems between public and private organizations could help at-risk youths acquire the skills necessary to do these jobs.

Coordinate Reform Policies. For states to attack the problems of schools simultaneously from several fronts, their policies must send coherent signals to local educators and boards. As noted in our discussions of the student standards and teacher policy reforms, many state policies are ambiguous and lack coordination.

Combinations of policy approaches hold particular promise for future reform. Some scholars have suggested that higher curriculum standards be incorporated into school restructuring efforts.[31] Under such a plan, the state would provide a broad but explicit curriculum framework to guide teachers in presenting content. Careful alignment of the content in state curriculum frameworks, tests, texts, and accreditation standards would assure additional coherence. State-funded in-depth staff development and preservice programs would provide even more reinforcement.

Restructuring comes in as teachers design and implement pedagogical strategies that comply with state curriculum frameworks and student standards but are also appropriate for the local contexts. Teachers could use strategies such as peer and cross-age tutoring, cooperative learning, and new student configurations.

Another combination, suggested by the National Governors' Association,[32] would combine restructuring with performance accountability. States would reduce some of their cumbersome rules and regulations and give schools more decision-making authority. In return for their greater autonomy, schools would agree to regularly evaluate and report their performance. Continued state deregulation would depend on the schools' making satisfactory progress on performance indicators. The scheme can be taken one step further by recognizing outstanding school performance with cash rewards. This proposal is especially compatible with "choice" strategies.

The most effective combinations will vary from state to state. But whatever the combination, it will need much more attention to coherence among its various pieces. For example, curriculum intensification can take place only if policymakers and educators at both elementary-secondary and post-secondary levels cooperate. The subject matter preparation of prospective teachers needs to be coordinated with state curriculum frameworks; otherwise, teacher preservice is a jumble of credits and courses. Similarly, staff development— offered by states, regional agencies, districts, teacher organizations, or universities—must be coordinated with curriculum revisions and new roles and responsibilities. This is especially true when both school restructuring and curriculum intensification are pursued simultaneously.

Implications of the Economic and Political Environment for Reform. Whether states continue to drive education reform may depend on the growth of the American economy and how this growth is distributed across the nation. The hefty per-pupil budget increases that financed the 1983–1990 reforms (over 29 percent after inflation) cannot continue indefinitely. School finance cycles correlate roughly with periods of economic growth and recession. Any slowdown in growth of the U.S. economy puts major new and costly reforms on hold, with state governments likely to allocate their resources to improving efficiency, developing performance incentives, and evaluating the 1983–1990 reforms.

As of late 1992, there was no clear consensus about the future directions of education reform. Education remains a priority issue for politicians, but they are searching for a specific set of initiatives similar in scope to the 1983–1986 reforms. Nonetheless, the low achievement of at-risk youths is viewed by many as a threat to the nation's economic competitiveness, and so the movement to make schools more responsive to the needs of these students is building momentum.

Enhancing the education of our most disadvantaged students is clearly an imperative, especially given the limits that the reforms of the early 1980s placed on this issue. State concern about at-risk youths has produced a few token dropout and preschool programs but nothing very substantial or widespread.[33]

Historically, significant political advances for disadvantaged children have emerged from upheavals in the economy and major social or political movements.[34] The depression of the 1930s galvanized huge federal efforts to relieve the suffering of the poor. The civil rights movement's success in the 1960s was crucial in creating a climate favorable to government programs for disadvantaged children. This concern may lead to government interventions to upgrade the skills of those individuals who do not have the minimum competencies for employment skills in our rapidly changing economy.

Understanding Innovation

Many unanswered questions still remain about the causes and processes of policy innovation. Polsby has divided recent federal innovations into two different types: (a) acute and (b) incubated.[35] In acute innovation the time lapse between when an idea first surfaces within the network of decision makers and its enactment is brief. Little time is spent on extensive search for alternative solutions or research about potential impact. Whoever comes to the right meeting or has the loudest voice and some hard data might carry the day. For example, after extensive documentary research, we are still not certain who put the key concept of "maximum feasible participation" into the poverty program of 1965.[36] The innovation process resembles the "organized anarchy" of decision theorists.[37] Innovations can come about even though no widespread view exists that there is a major problem. Lots of policy entrepreneurs with solutions are looking for problems. The minimum competency test for high school graduation is an example of an acute innovation.

A good example of an "incubated" innovation is the Elementary and Secondary Education Act of 1965 or the state school finance reforms of the 1970s. Incubated innovation takes place slowly and incrementally over several years. The specific ideas and solutions are often those of experts and entrepreneurs outside the inner circle of such policymakers as governors or legislative staffers. Politicians adopt the idea and then publicize and adapt it to the state political culture. The policy issue networks push from outside and inside the state to keep the innovation alive during periods of low interest.

Incubated innovation includes a careful canvass of alternatives and some sophisticated research. School finance reform involved simulation of numerous formulas as well as major conceptual alternatives such as full state assumption of all school costs. A crucial characteristic of incubated innovation is considerable controversy. This creates the time needed for alternative searching and simulation. School finance reform involved redistributing state aid from wealthy to poor districts. These winner and loser characteristics naturally engendered intense controversy. In contrast, minimum competency testing was not controversial and thus could be enacted quickly. Innovations with little controversy can be enacted too quickly—before enough research has been completed.

Both types of innovations fit into specific state political cultures and political routines that may accelerate, retard, and reshape them. States with little history of political innovation in education (New Hampshire) may react slowly. New governors or state legislative candidates, however, often need new ideas to enhance their electoral chances so they are receptive to both types of innovations at four-year intervals. But the political strategies for the two types are quite different.

> Type A innovation consists of letting sleeping dogs lie and slipping an initiative by as a side issue or nonissue; Type B consists of meeting opposition head-on and overcoming it.[38]

In either case the political system includes incentives to search for innovations. It was highly fashionable to be an "education governor" between 1983 and 1987, and state senates are classic incubators of policy initiatives. The policy issue networks stand ready to give credit to politicians who adopt their cause. The issue networks and the politicians need each other to reach their respective goals.

NOTES

1. Susan Fuhrman, "Increased State Capacity and Aid to the Disadvantaged" (paper prepared for the U.S. Department of Education, November 1986), p. 3.

2. Jerome Murphy, *State Education Agencies and Discretionary Funds* (Lexington, Mass.: Lexington Books, 1974).

3. Thomas James and David Tyack, "Learning from Past Efforts to Reform the High School," *Phi Delta Kappan* 6 (1983): 400–406.

4. H.A. Passow, "Tackling the Reform Reports of the 1980s," *Phi Delta Kappan* 66 (1984): 674–683.

5. R. Ginsberg and R.K. Wimpelberg, "Educational Change by Commission: Attempting 'Trickle down' Reform," *Educational Evaluation and Policy Analysis* 9 (1987): 355–358.

6. Paul Berman and Milbrey McLaughlin, *Federal Programs Supporting Educational Change* (Santa Monica, Calif.: RAND, 1975).

7. National Commission on Excellence in Education, *A Nation at Risk* (Washington, D.C.: U.S. Government Printing Office, 1983).

8. Carnegie Forum on Education and the Economy, *A Nation Prepared: Teachers for the 21st Century* (Hyattsville, Mary.: Carnegie Forum on Education and the Economy, 1985); Holmes Group, *Tomorrow's Teachers: A Report of the Holmes Group* (East Lansing, Mich.: Holmes Group, 1985).

9. Carnegie Foundation for the Advancement of Teaching, *An Imperiled Generation: Saving Urban Schools* (Princeton, N.J.: Carnegie Foundation for the Advancement of Teaching, 1986).

10. William Bennett, *American Education: Making It Work* (Washington, D.C.: U.S. Government Printing Office, 1988).

11. Allan Odden, *School Funding Changes: 1960 to 1988* (Los Angeles: University of Southern California Press, 1989).

12. Linda Darling-Hammond and B. Berry, *The Evolution of Teacher Policy*. A report prepared for the Center for Policy Research in Education (Santa Monica, Calif.: RAND, 1988).

13. L. Cornett, *Linking Performance to Rewards for Teachers, Principals, and Schools* (Atlanta: Southern Regional Education Board, 1991).

14. Ibid.

15. Susan Fuhrman, "State Politics and Education Reform," in *The Politics of Reform and School Administration*, Robert Crowson and Jane Hannaway, eds. (New York: Falmer, 1989), pp. 61–75.

16. Ibid.

17. William A. Firestone, "Continuity and Incrementalism After All: State Reforms in the 1980s," in *The Educational Reform Movement of the 1980s: Themes and Cases*, Joseph Murphy, ed. (Berkeley, Calif.: McCutchan, 1990), pp. 143–166.

18. Darling-Hammond and Berry, *Evolution of Teacher Policy*.

19. Martha M. McCarthy, "Teacher-Testing Programs," in Murphy, *Educational Reform Movement of the 1980s*.

20. Theodore Sizer, *Horace's Compromise: The Dilemma of the American High School* (Boston: Houghton Mifflin, 1984).

21. J.L. David, *Restructuring in Progress: Lessons from Pioneering Districts* (Washington, D.C.: National Governors' Association, 1989).

22. Allan Odden, *Conditions of Education in California* (Berkeley, Calif.: Policy Analysis for California Education, 1991).

23. Odden, *School Funding Changes*.

24. T. Timar and David Kirp, *Managing Educational Excellence* (Philadelphia: Falmer, 1988).

25. Educational Testing Service, *School Policy Changes: 1983 to 1988* (Princeton, N.J.: Educational Testing Service, 1989).

26. David, *Restructuring in Progress*.

27. Susan Fuhrman, William H. Clune, and Richard F. Elmore, "Research on Education Reform: Lessons on the Implementation of Policy, *Teachers College Record* 90 (1987): 355–358.

28. M.J. Shujaa, "Policy Failure in Urban Schools: How Teachers Respond to

Increased Accountability for Students," in *Going to School: The African-American Experience*, edited by K. Lomotey (Albany: State University of New York Press, 1990).

29. Fuhrman, "State Politics."

30. Committee for Economic Development, *Investing in Our Children* (New York: Committee for Economic Development, 1989).

31. Marshall S. Smith and Jennifer O'Day, "Systemic School Reform," in *The Politics of Curriculum and Testing*, edited by Susan Fuhrman and Betty Malen (Philadelphia: Falmer, 1991).

32. National Governors Association, *Time for Results*.

33. Lynn Olson, "States and the at Risk Issue," *Education Week* (September 21, 1988): 14.

34. Michael W. Kirst and Gail R. Meister, "Turbulence in American Secondary Schools: What Reforms Last? *Curriculum Inquiry* 15 (1985): 169–186.

35. Nelson Polsby, *Political Innovation in America* (New Haven, Conn.: Yale, 1984).

36. Daniel Patrick Moynihan, *Maximum Feasible Mis Understanding* (New York: Free Press, 1969), pp. 167–205.

37. Michael Cohen, James G. March, and Johan Olsen, " A Garbage Can Model of Organization Choice," *Administrative Science Quarterly* 17 (March 1972): 1–25.

38. Polsby, *Political Innovation*, p. 159.

11

The Courts as Policy Innovator and Implementer

SYSTEM ANALYSIS AND THE FEDERAL SYSTEM

System analysis has enabled us to understand the seeming confusion of a diverse federal system governing education. The concept of the political system as the object and source of both demands and policy provides a unifying pattern to a seeming confusion across the nation. We have noted unification in the roles of a few values, of interest groups that spread across districts and states, of professional norms that accompany the practitioner from the training school to the mission stations of local districts, and so on.

In the next two chapters we will view the role of two agencies of national government that also contribute to this unification, namely, the constitutional authority granted the federal government. In this chapter we will explore the special role of federal courts as they deal with innovation and implementation of major educational reforms over the last few decades. In matters where peripheral governments are at odds with the goals of Washington, the superior constitutional authority of the United States Supreme Court provides a distinctive unifying function. That is a useful social purpose that courts in all lands know—to resolve two-party conflict without recourse to violence.

The constitutional authority of another agency, the federal government, has grown enormously in the policy area of education. Just how that level works its will—if at all—with often recalcitrant state and local governments has been the subject of enormous study by scholars in the last two decades. Educational practitioners have also experienced what that has meant. But again, the federal government may be conceived as a political system seeking to impose its values—often equity—upon these other governments' resources.

In both the courts and other branches of the government, we can conceive of systems analysis as a way of understanding how group demands, often contradictory or in conflict with Washington or the Constitution, become regulated through the national political system. The processes of inputs, withinputs, and outputs noted earlier for local and state governments can be conceptualized at the national level also. As always, use of the concept enables the scholar and professional educator to find systematic patterns of policy behavior that help clarify what that system is doing.

COURTS AS A NEW POLICY AGENCY

The enlarged role that state and federal governments play in the local schools come in part from the judicial branch. Group after group, frustrated by school policies, have turned to the state and federal courts for relief. The courts became involved not merely in settling disputes, but circumstances also often compelled them to initiate policy solutions to school problems and then to oversee their implementation. This chapter surveys this dual judicial role of innovation and implementation that has affected all school districts in some ways.

At first thought, courts seem an unlikely adjunct of schools and an unlikely partner in policies. Yet the history of education has been shaped by important court decisions on the duties and responsibilities of school officials; though trivial, the right of students not to have their hair cut is only the latest of many such contributions. At a more significant level, the United States Supreme Court has been directly involved in the question of religion in our schools—Bible reading, required prayers, flag salutes, the transportation and other expenses of parochial students, the teaching of evolution, and "secular humanism" in textbooks. Court involvement can be as narrow as whether school lockers can be searched (they can) or as extensive as whether schools can be segregated by race (they cannot). School officials may react by massive noncompliance, as with the Bible and prayer decisions, but they find that being indifferent is very difficult.[1]

Court involvement in such matters surprises only those who view the bench as a political eunuch. Contemporary analysts of the judiciary look not only at its behavior but also at the values that this behavior reflects. Judges are political because they must choose between competing values brought before them in conflict. As early as 1840, Alexis de Tocqueville was noting that "scarcely any political question arises in the United States that is not resolved, sooner or later, into a judicial question." The reason for this is that when citizens differ in the political arena, a recourse for resolution may be the courtroom. The form and rules of judicial contests may differ from those in other sites, but they remain essentially political. That is because contenders are seeking the authority of the political system to justify and command the distribution of resources—such as rights and property—that each wants. The allocation of resources to citizens that follows from a court mandate is just as effective as legislation.[2]

What, then, are the relationships between the judiciary—part of the political system of the state—and the political system of the school? What are the constraints and strengths in this relationship? What are the accommodations and conflicts in the input, conversion, feedback, and outcome phases of the political process here? How does federalism filter the outcome? What values are reflected among participants? These are the questions we will pursue to illuminate the role of judges as policy initiators and implementers.

THE JUDICIARY AS A POLITICAL SUBSYSTEM

The judiciary is only one subsystem of the larger political system. Like other subsystems—legislatures, agencies, and executives—the judiciary's environment presents it with demands that become outputs and outcomes in time that can generate later inputs to the court. This process means that no distinct boundaries separate the judicial subsystem from the others. Instead, it interacts with legislative and executive subsystems continuously, as well as with private systems in the social environment.

The environment within which judges operate marches constantly into their chambers, sometimes unobtrusively and sometimes loudly, seeking the protection or enhancement of certain values. In an earlier chapter, we saw in state law the four basic educational values of quality, equity, choice, and efficiency. However, the judge is not free to make such value choices alone. A historical constitutional framework imposes certain constraints, and these traditional forces also shape who is made a judge and what he or she does. Professional canons have additional effect on who is selected or even considered; institutional traditions require procedures that shape the pace and division of labor. Further, the partisanship of extramural party life, which has affected a judge's recruitment and deliberations in our past, carries influence even today.[3] Moreover, changes in the social order outside judicial chambers bring changes inside to the courts' domain to its issues, structures, and attitudes.

The value conflict thrust into the court seeks authoritative allocation of resources to implement those values. For this reason, federal courts have a *manifest* function of resolving conflict within American federalism in accordance with special rules. Such decisions have an impact—not always favorable—on all branches of the national government and at all levels of the federal system. This conflict-resolution task also carries *latent* functions for the values underlying the conflict. Thus, the Supreme Court legitimizes national policies and the values they reflect and, conversely, illegitimizes others. Illustrative are the reinforcement given to desegregation and special education by favorable Court decisions in recent decades. The difficulty, of course, is for the Court to do this in such a way that support for the courts as an institution does not decrease, while their decisions are complied with.

Further, the Supreme Court must maintain some kind of balance with other national subsystems in order to reduce potential conflict among them. In the process, the judiciary provides signals to litigants, the general public, and political subsystems and their actors (including their own local courts) as to the policy and value outputs that it will reinforce. Issuing such signals is not the same as their acceptance, however. Throughout its history, the Court has had to balance itself carefully at key intersections of a nationally separated government, a federally divided nation, and a diverse population. Yet judicial policy-making has shown more consistency than one might expect. Whether at the trial or appellate level, distinguishable processes are commonly at work. There is initiation of controversies, accommodation among contestants via out-of-court settlement, persuasion of judge or jury, decision making, implementation of decisions, and so on.

All of this is understandable as a facet of systems analysis. Inputs for the judicial subsystem reflect environmental demands. Their form and presentation differ for this subsystem, though. The lobbyist gives way to the lawyer; buttonholing takes the form of law review articles; and publicity campaigns appear as litigants' briefs.[4] The demands on a court are presented formally, dealing with matters of logic and legal precedent; however, recent research has stressed the independent role of a judge's values in the decisional process. Outputs of courts result from the interplay of judicial values within the court procedures, with political consequences for the environment.[5] It is particularly when the issue is new or has new applications that the values of the bench exert an independent force in explaining judicial outcomes.

However such decisions are derived, they constitute outputs for society. They instruct a wide circle of citizens as to the value norms that the judicial subsystem seeks to impose on the environment. But what if no one notices or, if noticing, defies them or, if obeying, misinterprets them? When the Court confirms widely accepted social values, as with its nineteenth-century opposition to polygamy, then output and outcome are similar—compliance is very high. When, however, the Court innovates in a direction contrary to accepted norms, some gap between output and outcome is to be expected, and compliance will be less.

Despite the popular notion of a powerful Supreme Court, the conditions under which it can innovate are highly limited. Given a majority of justices favoring a change, a national majority in similar agreement, and the chances that the Court's decision would not hurt it in other policy areas, then successful innovation would occur. But these combinations have not often existed in our history. These constraints account for much of the inertia and procrastination that emergent demands in the American political system face. If the Court moves when conditions do not permit, considerable opposition will arise from other political subsystems.

The policy actions we analyze next will flesh out this concept of judiciary and educational innovation in the political system in recent decades. The difference that the courts have made is evident in the legal foundation of many educational services that is accompanied by a massive set of regulations. Furthermore, recent change in court decisions revolves around their shifting priorities for the values of equity, quality, choice, and efficiency.

LEGALIZATION AND REGULATION

The courts have been a major arena for the recently increased political turbulence around schools. Indeed, Kirp has added to the traditional three Rs of schooling a fourth—rules.[6] Government centralization of school policy has followed on the heels of courts establishing rules—that is, laws—that affect the schools.

Rights, Procedures, and School Policies

Legalization, as Kirp explains, involves "establishing a system of decision making committed to rules, trafficking in rights rather than preferences or interests, and justifying outcomes with reasons"; *regulation* involves "efforts of one level of government to control the behavior of another level."[7] These activities of courts, legislatures, and bureaucracies have promoted educational programs such as desegregation and compensatory, special, and bilingual education. Much of these efforts, however, have been subjected to heavy criticism from school professionals and lower governmental officials. It is important to remember that this policy movement has as its goal the pursuit of the value of equity in distributing school resources; opponents claim, however, that other values are being lost in the process.

Two central legal concepts have been developed to justify this legalization, Kirp notes. First, the concept of substantive rights has emerged, which advocated that students educationally disadvantaged by the prevailing distribution of resources had suffered a wrong inflicted on their constitutional rights. These rights were linked to the federal Constitution, particularly the equal protection clause of the Fourteenth Amendment. This process first appeared in *Brown* vs. *the Board of Education of Topeka* in 1954, which evoked the right of equity for black segregated students. But such a right could also be applied—and later was—to equity for handicapped, Hispanic, poor, and female students. Court decisions often stimulated major congressional action embodying equity rights, with applications to all school districts nationwide.[8] The most recent was a 1988 act of Congress mandating that discrimination in use of federal funds in one part of an institution—say, a university—could bar such funds for all other parts.

A second aspect of legalization was the emerging concept of due process in schooling; that is, students were held to have protections about how school policies were made and implemented. Due process procedures became fixed in federal law as a result of this judicial stimulus. Due process arose from protections in criminal law, rooted in the Magna Carta of 1215 A.D. and our own Fourteenth Amendment. The procedural protection spread by litigation in the 1960s to the policy areas of welfare and public employment and in 1975 to education in the Supreme Court decision of *Goss* v. *Lopez*. Congressional statutes then provided education for handicapped children with explicit procedural protections in the individual education program's required meetings, hearings, and appeals.[9] Court-based protections against arbitrary suspensions and dismissals have also created elaborate procedural safeguards that school administrators must follow. By 1980, in San Bernardino, California, for example, there were over six pages of rules for expelling a student.

Centralization and Regulations

As these new forms of legalization in education arose, implementing them meant issuing more and more regulations. Officials in Washington sought compliance through coercion, by means of detailed regulatory oversight, reports, and the threat of withdrawing federal funds. Meanwhile, behind this strategy lurked the potential citizen threat of litigation if particular children were treated inequitably. Also, because so many states subsequently incorporated these programs into their own statutes (sometimes under federal stimulus), state capitols sought compliance on their own by issuing even more regulations. Education was not the only policy area where this centralization occurred; in fact, education was impacted less than other areas. Analysis of the origins of mandates for twelve policy areas in the late 1970s found that states were issuing far more than were "the feds." The ratio of state to federal mandates was higher in seven of these twelve areas than in education; there were two state actions for every federal one.[10]

A central theme in this intergovernmental connection within the world of education, as Kirp notes, was for higher governments to seek more control than to provide assistance. Possibly this arose because legalization began in the experience with the highly contested desegregation, as discussed later. Here, there was enormous resistance at the district level that produced several successive rounds of litigation and even more federal control through regulations. Such regulatory growth would appear later in other local school programs when inequities were charged, and this time the states joined in Washington's control strategy.

The Politics of Legalization

Before examining legalization in detail, we need first to characterize certain general qualities of a basically political process. To begin with, even critics of the excesses of legalization recognize its success. As Kirp notes,

> It bears remarking that the promise of legalization has been greatly fulfilled. The history of America generally and of the public schools in particular may be told as a tale of progressive inclusion in the polity, and in that telling the forms and values of law have a central place.[11]

If the interests of certain groups have been advanced in the name of equity, the interests of yet others have not. Certainly the claim of educational professionals that they provide quality has been challenged, as we noted in our introduction. Further, the failure of states and local school boards to provide certain groups with access to decision making also brings into question their commitment to the democratic value of choice. Moreover, the costs—economic or otherwise—of regulations to the system of schooling have not been calculated against their alleged benefits. That is, the value of efficiency in various legal actions has not been much addressed.

Throughout the 1970s, this stream of criticism aimed at regulation joined that in other policy areas so that the Reagan administration made strong efforts to overturn many regulations. "Deregulation" was begun, but it is uncertain how successful this was in education. While federal education budgets were cut (as were those in many other policy areas), and thirty small categorical grants were combined into a bloc grant with few regulations, much of the regulations for bigger categorical programs still remained (compensatory, handicapped, and bilingual education). Also, while the Reagan administration withdrew from the plaintiff's side in desegregation cases, those cases continued nevertheless, and the Supreme Court continued its support of busing. Additionally, the Reagan-sponsored voucher system of school funding got nowhere in Congress, and the U.S. Department of Education was not abolished although its secretaries reduced some regulations and its Office of Civil Rights stopped requiring reports on the amount of segregation. Finally, the attempt of the Office of Management and the Budget to apply cost-benefit measurements to regulations in handicapped education was stalled.

The tenacity of this complex regulatory program in the field of education against an administration determined to eliminate it indicates the political strength that lies behind regulation. That strength arose from a network of pressure groups that defended special programs before often friendly congressional committees, and the courts were always available, too, as an option for asserting rights against unresponsive local administrators. Nor has deregulation had much success at the state level, where state affiliates of these same groups have closer contact and often greater strength with the formal agencies of state government.

Federal and state courts remain arenas for arriving at specific decisions that will implement earlier won constitutional victories. Reagan administration attempts not to enforce specific laws that grant either rights or entitlements have been blocked by uncooperative federal courts. Even an occasional innovation issued from the Supreme Court in the 1980s, such as preventing school districts from barring the children of illegal aliens (*Plyler* v. *Doe*, 1983). All this suggests that court decisions have provided a continuing stimulus to regulation as new developments arose in specialized fields of schooling.

The politics of legalization and regulation point to the primacy of legal rights in educational decisions and to the inherent conflict of basic educational rights, as pointed out in earlier chapters. This political process also demonstrates familiar qualities of American federalism. Groups frustrated at one level of government jump to higher levels and different decision-making branches—and often with considerable success. Central to that success, though, has been the recent establishment of the idea that legal rights inhere in students and their education.

We turn now to examine in more detail this general process with two examples of where courts have stimulated massive changes, namely, the federal courts in desegregation and the state courts in school finance.

INPUT AND CONVERSION IN DESEGREGATION

The Southern Experience

The 1954 case of *Brown* v. *the Board of Education of Topeka* represents both an ending and a beginning of the Court's view of the linkage between race and schools.[12] That case was a dramatic departure from six previous decades when the judiciary had accepted "separate but equal" education in the South. Hints of this judicial change of mind occurred during the 1930s and 1940s, as the Court insisted that "equal" must mean truly equal for the education of blacks—and it rarely did, of course.

The *Brown* case arose when a private party, the National Association for the Advancement of Colored People (NAACP), acted for its members' children. The NAACP sought a declaration that segregation violated the "equal protection of the laws" clause of the Fourteenth Amendment, no matter how equal the facilities provided were. Joining the NAACP in supportive legal briefs were nineteen other groups (for example, the ACLU, CIO, and the U.S. Solicitor General). In May 1954, the court's lengthy deliberation yielded the historic opinion that the doctrine of "separate but equal" had no place in public education. Yet how was this turnaround to be implemented? On this question, the Court heard arguments for yet another year, finally deciding only that "all deliberate speed" should be employed to abolish the dual school system. Private accounts indicate that the Court members were badly torn over remedies; some wanted immediate compliance, others wanted it done a grade at a time, and still others wanted it left totally to the states. The resulting vague formula was the only compromise that Chief Justice Earl Warren could contrive to present a unanimous face to the nation.

Without judicial guidelines, the Southern states did very little except to resist, which the first edition of this book detailed. After a decade the outcome was almost no change in the deep South but some in the border states. However, public opinion had moved to a greater acceptance of the concept in the North but not in the South.

This stalemate changed dramatically in the 1960s due to a combination of new laws on civil rights and education and the strong enforcement of desegregation by President Lyndon Johnson's administration.[13] Also, after a decade of silence, the Supreme Court started blocking Southern evasions, eventually upholding the use of busing if it were the only policy that made desegregation possible. From the mid-1960s through the 1970s, then, even when later presidents withdrew active support for this change, the courts in Washington and the local districts heard individual suits against many Southern school systems and with rare exception upheld black plaintiffs.

By 1980 in the South, despite a trickle of white children into private "Christian" academies to avoid desegregation, the totally segregated school district or school site was a rarity. Even as early as 1972, the percentage of black students in predominantly white schools had risen to 44 percent from 18 percent in 1968, while in the North segregation actually rose. When federal administrative action was joined to judicial pressure, the results were impressive. One study of thirty-three Georgia districts found that the only successful federal strategy for desegregation was "coercion to compliance," that is, the threat to withhold federal school funds.[14]

By the end of the 1970s, many changes were evident in the South. For example, a dramatic change showed up in the opinion polls from whites who had once objected to integrated education. Where most desegregation had taken place, white parent opposition to integrating their children in schools with either a few or majority blacks declined sharply.[15] But repeatedly, whites, by majorities as large as 75 to 80 percent, objected to busing as a way to do the job—even though this became the only successful way of doing it. Typically, in the same election Florida voters opposed busing but supported desegregation, both by large majorities.[16]

The Northern Experience

Outside the South in recent years, another picture has emerged because as segregation diminished in the South it increased elsewhere. Typically, segregation for blacks and Hispanics became least in the Southeast, but greatest in the Northeast and North Central regions.[17] Central cities in the North increasingly became islands of minorities in a sea of white suburbanites. City after city in the Northeast became majority black, first in pupils and then in adults. The courts were an active agent in this region. Through changes in presidential administrations and membership on the bench, the Supreme Court unanimously overturned vestiges of legal desegregation, although they wavered on how to define its other forms.[18]

Just as after the *Brown* decision, when the Southern school systems did not comply, so also in the North the middle-sized and large cities used a variety of devices to resist compliance. When such matters entered federal courts on challenge, however, school systems were found using different methods to maintain segregation. Table 11.1 presents the court findings in twenty-six northern sites; it reveals how far the courts had moved from simply striking down legal segregation laws.

There was variation around the country in the effort it took to desegregate. Most school districts have so few minorities that desegregation was easy; most districts in the Northwest were of this kind. Elsewhere, some states had problems with only a single city, and some of these desegregated relatively easily—Denver, Omaha, Minneapolis-Saint Paul, Las Vegas. Indeed, "most of the thirty-three states outside the southern and border state regions [had] either negligible segregation problems or ones that [were] manageable without basic change."[19] Finally, it is in the largest Northern cities that the conditions for desegregation have become worse and will continue to do so in the 1990s. "White flight" has emptied many of these cities of whites, and even "black flight" appears in Newark, Chicago, and San Francisco; the great middle-class hegira to the suburbs has no respect for color.

Desegregation Methods: Busing and Metropolitan Plans

Amid the flood of litigation surrounding the Northern struggles, several principles have emerged.[20] Removing unconstitutional segregation is the district authorities' inescapable responsibility. Also, segregation in a significant area of a city establishes the presumption that the entire school system is unconstitutionally segregated. Further, as one means to determine racial effects, the plaintiffs and judges can use such information as site selection, boundary lines, and other matters that have been board policy. Finally, metropolitan desegregation is not suitable to deal with the problems of the central city (except in Wilmington, Delaware); on a countywide basis, however, Florida has shown that this is an effective remedy.[21] As the composition of the Court changed with the more conservative appointments made by Presidents Nixon and Reagan, a majority came to accept the view that it was not necessarily evidence of discrimination when school board policies *resulted* in segregation. Rather, it had to be shown that this result was the *intent* of school officials—a much more difficult proposition to prove, although not impossible.

Yet much to the disappointment of conservatives on this matter—including recent presidents—the Court has continued to uphold the busing remedy when intent was demonstrated. "Busing" had become a symbol of deeply held opposing views among the general public. But it was a symbol unrelated to a reality when half of all American students bus to school, segregated academies bus most of their own children, many pupils can be moved with only minor adjustments in the busing schedule, and other evidences that busing is not what the contention is about. Supporters see busing as a means to achieve the value of choice; opponents see it denying them the value of choice—and doubt that it provides their children with quality education. However, busing supporters see opponents as more concerned about racial fears than about educational results ("It's not the bus, it's us!").[22] There is a curious, little-noted effect of metropolitan busing; more residential integration takes place *after* busing and busing itself decreases. Charlotte, North Carolina, became one-third more integrated racially, and therefore had to bus less, over a ten-year period.[23]

This brief review of court-initiated desegregation demonstrates the judiciary's potential for policy influence and the environment of value conflict in which it works. Despite the possibility for resolving the conflict in busing and metropolitan plans, the changing demography of American cities and continuing white resistance make further progress unlikely in the biggest cities during the 1990s.

Table 11.1

Discrimination Found by Federal Courts in Northern School Desegregation Cases, 1956–76

School District

Type of discrimination found by courts	Benton Harbor	Boston	Buffalo	Cincinnati	Cleveland	Dayton	Denver	Detroit	Gary	Grand Rapids	Hillsboro	Indianapolis	Kalamazoo	Kansas City	Las Vegas	Manhasset	Minneapolis	New Rochelle	Omaha	Oxnard	Pasadena	Pittsburg	Pontiac	San Francisco	Phoenix—South Holland	Springfield
Discriminatory drawing or alteration of attendance zones	—	X	X	—	X	—	X	X	—	—	X	X	X	—	—	X	X	X	X	X	X	—	X	X	X	—
Discriminatory location of new schools	—	X	X	—	X	—	X	—	—	—	—	X	X	—	X	—	X	—	X	X	X	—	X	X	X	—
Discriminatory expansion of existing schools (such as enlarging minority schools rather than transferring minority students to nearby white schools with available space)	—	X	—	—	X	—	X	—	—	—	—	X	—	—	X	—	X	—	—	X	X	—	—	X	—	—
School board's failure to relieve overcrowding at white schools by transferring white students to nearby minority schools with available space	—	X	X	—	X	—	—	—	—	X	—	X	—	—	X	—	X	—	—	X	X	—	—	—	—	—
Discriminatory hiring of teachers and administrators	X	X	X	—	—	—	X	X	—	—	—	X	—	—	X	—	—	—	—	X	X	—	X	—	X	—
Discriminatory assignment of teachers and administrators	—	X	X	—	X	—	—	—	—	X	—	—	X	—	—	—	X	—	X	X	X	—	X	X	—	—
Discriminatory promotion of teachers and administrators	X	X	X	—	X	—	—	—	—	X	—	X	—	—	—	X	X	—	X	X	X	—	X	X	—	—
School board's perpetuation or exacerbation of school segregation by its strict adherence to neighborhood school policy *after* segregated school system had developed	—	—	X	—	—	—	—	—	—	—	—	—	—	—	X	X	X	X	—	X	X	—	—	X	—	X

School board's failure to adopt a proposed integration plan or to implement previously adopted plans

School board's adoption of "open enrollment" or "free transfer" policies, with the effect of allowing whites to transfer out of black schools without producing a significant movement of blacks to white schools or whites to black schools

School segregation de facto rather than the result of state action

Source: Center for National Policy Review, Catholic University Law School, "Why Must Northern School Systems Desegregate? A Summary of Federal Court Findings in Recent Cases" (Washington, D.C., January 1977; processed); cited in Gary Orfield, *Must We Bus?* (Washington, D.C.: Brookings Institution, 1978).

THE COURTS AND FINANCE REFORM

Earlier in this book we pointed out that a major aspect of the new school turbulence is found in efforts to reform the basis of school financing. As with desegregation, the judiciary played a key role in stimulating this effort by formulating a general constitutional wrong and calling for a change in school policy. Unlike desegregation, though, most of this effort has been a product of the *states'* highest courts, not of the United States Supreme Court. By a narrow five to four majority in 1974, the Supreme Court refused to claim a constitutional safeguard against finance schemes that discriminated between rich and poor school districts. But note that school finances engage three of the four major educational values—equity, quality, and efficiency. And if public school critics got their way with school vouchers, there would also be a choice value. Finance is also the issue most engaging legislators in six states analyzed in an earlier chapter. The issue is always current, controversial, and relevant to most everything that schools do.

School finance reform began in California as a result of the stimulus of the pressure group reform network cited earlier.[24] That state's supreme court declared a new principle, in *Serrano* v. *Priest*, that the "quality of public education may not be a function of the wealth of . . . a pupil's parents and neighbors." Because financing schemes had to possess "fiscal neutrality," and California's did not, it offended the equal protection clause of the federal and state constitutions and so would have to undertake reform. This approach spread, as the state legislatures across the land faced challenges in over half the states. By the early 1980s, several dozen states had made changes, some minor but others major, to meet this new standard. In certain states, the route of the referendum was attempted, but it was much less effective than legislative action. While the Supreme Court's refusal to join their state brethren in this reform halted matters for awhile during the mid-1970s, the pace soon picked up again.

More inequities than just those traceable to taxable wealth came under attack. Complex state financial support formulas were introduced to adjust for city cost overburdens and for special kinds of educational needs afflicting handicapped, vocational, and other educationally needy children.[25] The degree of technicality now contemplated in adjudication generates serious problems. The courts are involved in areas that scholars know less about—how to adjust for pupil needs in some precise way, control for uncontrollable costs of education, or compensate for the high costs in big cities. It was much easier when the task was only to devise formulas so that equal property tax effort resulted in equal amounts of local school revenue.

As noted in an earlier chapter, such changes also require additional state funds to increase spending in low-wealth districts. Political limitations also emerge out of the effort to sustain a reform coalition when each partner worries about getting its own slice of limited resources.[26] That need became even more pressing when the federal government, under presidents of both parties, was reluctant to increase its share of local school costs.

The initiative of the state courts thus generated a flurry of legislative actions, and both court and legislature were further stimulated by an elite of scholars and educational reformers. The reformers met with much success in many states, providing authorities with new knowledge and policy options, as noted earlier. If success is measured by the number of states addressing the problem of resource inequity, then the reform did well; at least half of the states made changes. But if success is measured by how much money actually got redistributed to improve the poor's schooling, the evidence is less certain. An intensive 1979 study of five states indeed found some changes in property tax imbalances, but some of the poorest districts had not closed the per-pupil spending gap with their high-property-wealth neighbors; in fact they may have lost ground.[27] Property tax rates, however, became more equalized among school districts. Certainly the 1970s reforms left behind a strong cohort of school finance reform specialists, possessed of inventive minds, knowledge, and other resources needed to continue fighting.

The finance reform litigators are now pursuing a second generation of lawsuits, claiming that state governments have not met the court requirements imposed in the 1970s. In New Jersey, for example, plaintiffs were in 1990 successful in asserting that the low-property-wealth districts or big cities have not received state aid sufficient to close the spending gap with wealthy suburbs and thereby neutralize the predominant effect of local property wealth on school spending. The *Serrano* case in California initiated in 1969 was still pending before the California Supreme Court in 1992 on yet another appeal based on the same reasoning as the 1969 case. The plaintiffs in California and

New Jersey acknowledge that each state has made some improvements in its finance formula, but has not met the standards set by the initial court orders. The continued attention that litigators paid to school finance equity re-emerged in the 1983–92 state reform era through several provisions in state aid formulas helping the lowest spending districts more. While finance equity was not a highly publicized issue, it played a role in orienting how the states distributed the large increases voted to enhance academic "excellence."

The debate can never be completely resolved until the courts have heard arguments based on all major educational values. To date, plaintiffs have featured equity as their key goal through equalized, per-pupil spending. Often the state defendants have countered with arguments based on quality and efficiency. For example, state defendants claim that no strong correlation exists between per-pupil expenditures and education achievement, that marginal increases in per-pupil spending are not strong determinants of educational outcomes. Also, defendants assert that waste and inefficiency occur in school spending, with too much money allocated to overhead costs that do not help teachers in the classroom. Voucher proponents contend, on the other hand, that choice should be the priority value by giving money directly to parents rather than school districts. Parents could then choose which school they wanted, rather than being assigned a school by a public authority. These differing viewpoints will never be reconciled, and the courts will be just one of the forums that the various contestants will use to advance their specific values.

ROLE OF THE JUDICIARY IN TRADITIONAL AND REFORM LITIGATION

These accounts of two major educational reforms in which the judiciary played a major part do not exhaust either the impact of this process or the reforms; the latter are much too extensive for any but the most superficial review. Rather, it is to the meaning of the courts in the political process that we now turn as they originate and implement public policy.

Judicial and Legislative Policy Functions Compared

It would help to understand first that far more similarities exist between what courts and legislatures do than is popularly known.[28]

Traditional litigation may seem to be very different from the action in sweaty legislative committee rooms or boisterous chambers, but the differences are in some part only matters of form. Also, some analysts have argued that reform litigation differs basically from traditional litigation, partaking more of the nature of legislation than do court decisions.[29] Table 11.2 brings these three policy processes together in comparison to demonstrate their policy equivalents.

The distinctions emerge clearly between, on the one hand, traditional litigation and, on the other, public law litigation and legislation. The first deals with only two interests, looks backward, provides relief for a revealed violation that is sharply defined and, finally, involves a policy actor (judge) who is passively unpartisan in the matter. But the other two, public litigation and legislation, possess quite different qualities. They deal with multiple interests and look to the future for a "solution" that will work; the relief sought must be modifiable and involve others; and the policy actors (judge, legislators) are partisan in the sense of being advocates. Of course, Table 11.2 skims over much that is complex, but it directs attention to the new role of courts in public policy.

The implementation of decisions made by these bodies also takes on other similarities. Table 11.3 sets out different tasks that courts and legislatures undertake when they seek to reform an institution, as demonstrated in the cases of racial discrimination and finance noted above. In either case, implementation breaks down any time even one of these tasks is not done. Note the problems that arise in just one of the tasks, for example, "setting intelligible standards." We have seen in the discrimination and finance cases that the highest courts—federal and state—failed in this task in their initial decrees. When there was no supportive coalition to seek fuller compliance in the state legislatures—as with desegregation—contending parties then had to go back to the courts to set standards drawn out of specific cases. Yet where there was support for the court decision, as with financial reform, parties in each state still had to work their way through the labyrinth of the legislative process, in which each member was vitally interested in the outcome for his or her district. But in the latter case, despite its legislative complexity, a much more precise set of standards—such as various formulas of tax reform—resulted in the early stages than was the case with desegregation.

Table 11.2

Structural Aspects of Traditional Litigation, Public Law Litigation, and Legislation

Structural Aspect	Traditional Litigation	Public Law Litigation	Legislation
Parties	Two, with mutually exclusive interests	Many with diverse interests—for example, amici in *Robinson v. Cahill*	Intervention by multiple interest groups is the rule
Fact-Finding	Retrospective and adjudicative (what happened, and so on)	Prospective and "functional"—what will work	Problem-solving approach is the norm
Relief	Coextensive with violation—nature of violation determines relief	Violation tells little about relief. New factors, like cost, enter in	Total pragmatism
	Relief closes transaction	Continuing jurisdiction, relief modifiable	Corrective amendments common
	Relief "nonintrusive," especially damages	Relief often entails running local governments	More detailed plans common
	Relief imposed and adjudicated (defendant has no role)	Formulation of decree involves negotiation, compromise	Social reform usually accommodates opposing interests
Decision Maker's Role	Judge is passive as to fact-finding, uninvolved with relief, no public identity	Judge must form court's position on facts, work out relief, and become identified with cause	Legislative fact-finding committees, work on specifics of bill, legislator identification with bill.

Source: William H. Clune with Robert E. Lindquist, "Understanding and Researching the Implementation of Education Laws: The Essential Characteristics of Implementation," Law, Governance, and Education Seminar, Institute for Research on Educational Finance and Governance, Stanford, February 1980, p. 31.

Table 11.3
Judicial and Legislative Implementation Tasks

Courts	Legislatures
Decree formulation: negotiations between plaintiffs and defendants, use of experts, concern with such factors as fiscal burden and personnel resentment, setting intelligible standards.	*Formation of legislation:* input from interested parties, expert testimony, budgetary role, setting intelligible standards.
Monitoring: retention of jurisdiction and compliance reports, need for master or special experts to serve as unbiased ally of courts.	*Administrative monitoring:* compliance data, field offices, inspections, and so on.
Dispute resolution: application of standards to new facts, differing interpretations of standards.	*Administrative dispute resolution:* negotiation when standards are unreasonable, appeal to administrative law judge, and so forth.
Enforcement: use of contempt power, brinkmanship, clarification of responsibilities, obtaining new resources, graduated sanctions.	*Enforcement:* continuum of harassment (extra reports, inspections), threatened fund cutoffs, actual cutoffs, and so on.

Source: Note, "Implementation Problems in Institutional Reform Litigation," *Harvard Law Review* 91 (December 1977): 428–63.

Judicial Strategies in the Policy Process

Why, then, should courts or legislatures be so vague? There are some major strategic advantages to ambiguity under certain circumstances. As van Geel noted about the Supreme Court on the desegregation cases:

> Ambiguity may be, in part, a tactic to minimize the anger caused by the opinion. An unclear opinion leaves people puzzled and, consequently, less angry. Ambiguity also leaves the Court more room to maneuver in the future, to change directions as practical requirements arise which recommended such a change. Finally, ambiguity might be marked up to judicial uncertainty regarding its proper role without scheme of government. . . . When doctrine is less clear, this leaves more room for the political process to have its way [as] choices can be left to the discretion of others.[30]

If there are policy change agents who are willing to seize on one aspect of the ambiguous goal that the court sets, as with finance reform, then the political process can be carried out. But what if judicial vagueness has no decisive public support so that the normal political processes are blocked? That actually occurred in the South for a decade after the *Brown* decision and thereafter in the North as Congress and presidents backed off from enforcing both court orders and national law.[31] Then the other tasks of implementation noted in Table 11.3—monitoring, dispute resolution, enforcement—fell into the laps of the judges. In this process, the highest court at first seeks to provide only broad guidelines, but these get more narrowly defined as more and more specific situations are brought to it on appeal. This means that the lower level judges become increasingly embroiled in the implementation of desegregation. As Buell's close study of the Boston case reveals, the monitoring judge can get involved in the innumerable minor details of school administration—boundary changes, personnel replacements, and so on—either because the local school system ignores the original order to desegregate or because it thoroughly resists the order.[32] As judges become increasingly faced by noncompliance with what to them is a constitutionally based order, they are compelled by their institutional responsibility to take on more of the implementation usually associated with administrative oversight.

AN EVALUATION OF JUDICIAL ACTION

Clearly, there are limits to what judges can do. Nor is it the case that judges should do nothing because no political support exists for correcting an unconstitutional situation. If this were the case, we could leave the interpretation of every law up to each citizen, an excellent formula for social anarchy and a major reason why we have rules of law in the first place. But in over three decades of judicial involvement in major policy reform and institutional changes, courts have been able to do some things better than others. As one concerned about the "limits of legalism," Kirp has noted that the federal government can indeed provide national standards of service and behavior and the funds to implement these; however, settlement of the standards' details is better attained by political agencies at all levels of government.[33] Yet, as desegregation demonstrates, what if those agencies not only do not act but actually also obstruct the national standard?

Judicial Activism and Its Effects

What are the consequences of judicial activism? Besides having direct effects upon groups of citizens (e.g., the Brown child in the 1954 case or Rodriguez in the San Antonio case), it can affect other governmental institutions as well. Note the earlier reference to the San Bernardino reforms, pursuant to state procedural law and Supreme Court requirements for expulsion. Or, in desegregation, there is what Orfield terms a "ratcheting" effect, in which one court's determination that a particular school practice is discriminatory becomes an input to federal agencies; they then incorporate it into their regulations, which can later be used in other courts as litigation arises. Or courts may affect one another more directly. State supreme courts have been found to influence one another mutually in public policy initiatives, a form of "horizontal federalism," for example, in school finance reform.[34]

For example, convoluted events in New Jersey over financial reform brought the state supreme court into conflict with the state legislature.[35] The latter's lack of guidelines for policy direction, as well as its mandate to correct the unconstitutional financing law, threw the politics of that state into greater conflict for eighteen months in 1974–1976. However, the results did establish standards that in turn set off challenges to such laws in other states, just as the California decision in the *Serrano* case in the late 1960s set off a round of challenges.[36] A close analysis of the New Jersey controversy by Lehne concluded that the results demonstrated that the judiciary's main role must be "agenda setting," not "decision making." That is, courts do their utmost when they raise policy issues that other government agencies must resolve but without the courts designating the actual process of solution.

Others have noted the broader policy roles of *state* supreme courts in our history. They have innovated in policymaking, complemented state legislative goals, elaborated the meaning of Supreme Court opinions, restricted the latter's opinions to protect their state's laws from invalidation, and lobbied in legislatures to maintain and develop their own judicial institution.[37] All of these actions have consequences for public policy—causing new policy issues to emerge, stimulating discussion of policy alternatives, authoritatively deciding the direction of new policies, and overseeing policy administration.

How is the judiciary—state or federal—capable of such policy influence? Their capacities are impressive because when undertaking implementation the judiciary possesses considerable authority, trust, and information. A judge is thus in a strategic position in policy conflict to assure that decisions are emphatically enforced. The judicial presence, as it were, changes the power quotient of the plaintiffs when court sanctions and information can be added to their side. Policy goals thus can more easily be put into effect. However, courts can also lag in such matters because they can misconceive and misapply knowledge. As critics of regulation insist, they can use sanctions that are too clumsy and are actually counterproductive.[38] Then, as is true of other governmental agencies who fail in their political tasks, the policy results will not meet plaintiffs' needs and so may generate distrust of the courts.[39]

The Judiciary in the World of School Policy

The judiciary has made its role much more evident in the arena of educational and other policies in the last two decades. When it *does not* act to define problems and needs, other agencies do so. When it *does* act, new distributions of resources and values usually emerge in educational policy. If both judicial inaction and action have policy consequences, then either condition makes the courts policy actors. When the Supreme Court sidesteps a decision on the equity value in the finance reform case, then other levels of government feel free to seek their own solutions. However, when that same Court voids legal segregation, it sets the scene for actions that effectively eliminate the practice a decade later. If, however, the Court is evasive in defining Northern segregation problems, then lower federal courts take on a much more active and determinative role.[40]

The judiciary, however, cannot do everything, as initial Southern rejection of the *Brown* decision demonstrated. Intervening between what the court seeks (outputs) and what eventuates (outcomes) are barriers of group resistance that reflect other values, popular ignorance, communication failure, information overload, and other confounding aspects of social and policy conflict. Even a court mandate does not bring total or quick acceptance; it does not provide sufficient resources for the resourceless, and it does not teach us how to resolve conflict or to live with ambiguity. Other persons and events must perform these tasks, even with a supportive judiciary. While the judiciary has been a major stimulus for educational innovation in the last quarter century, it has also met with obstruction, misunderstanding, and uncertainty. The court is thus in the position that Shakespeare described in *Henry IV*, when one character proclaims, "I can call spirits from the vasty deeps," and Hotspur responds, "Why, so can I, or so can any man, but will they come when you do call for them?"

The supreme courts of state and nation have been called upon from their "vasty deeps" by citizens afflicted by racial and fiscal discrimination. Despite some reservations about how much courts can do in policy innovation, both judicial friend and foe would agree that little would have been changed without positive judicial response to such calls. That agreement marks the significant potential for educational policy innovation and implementation that inheres in these judicial "spirits." Even on its own, the judiciary can at least create a national dialogue about the standards of education that we will provide our children. In this way, the unthinkable of yesterday becomes the convention of today. Creating this flexibility of mind is a function that the judiciary and good teachers share equally.

NOTES

1. The best recent review is David Kirp and Mark Yudof, eds., *Educational Policy and the Law* (Berkeley, Calif.: McCutchan, 1982). On compliance problems, see Milton R. Konvitz, *First Amendment Freedoms* (Ithaca: Cornell University Press, 1963), Pt. 1. For reactions to the decisions, see Frank J. Souraf, "*Zorach v. Clauson*: The Impact of a Supreme Court Decision," *American Political Science Review* 53 (1959): 777–91; Robert H. Birkby, "The Supreme Court and the Bible Belt: Tennessee Reaction to the 'Schempp' Decision," *Midwest Journal of Political Science* 10 (1966): 304–15; H. Frank Way, Jr., "Survey Research on Judicial Decisions: The Prayer and Bible Reading Cases," *Western Political Quarterly* 21 (1968): 189–205; and William K. Muir, Jr., *Prayer in the Public Schools* (Chicago: University of Chicago Press, 1967).

2. Seminal statements of this thesis are Benjamin Cardozo, *The Nature of the Judicial Process* (New Haven: Yale University Press, 1921); and, in the contemporary period, Jack W. Peltason, *Federal Courts in the Political Process* (New York: Random House, 1955).

3. By 1987 differences between federal judges appointed by Presidents Jimmy Carter and Ronald Reagan were clearly evident.

4. Clement R. Vose, *Caucasians Only* (Berkeley: University of California Press, 1959); and "Litigation as a Form of Pressure Group Activity," *Annals of the American Academy of Political and Social Science* 319 (1958): 22–25.

5. The behavioral school embodying this concept of values is illustrated in Glendon Schubert, *Constitutional Politics* (New York: Holt, Rinehart & Winston, 1960); and Glendon Schubert, ed., *Judicial Decision-Making* (New York: Free Press, 1963).

6. David Kirp, "Introduction: The Fourth R: Reading, Writing,'Rithmetic—and Rules," in *School Days, Rule Days*, David Kirp and Donald Jensen, eds. (Philadelphia: Falmer, 1986), p. 12. This book is a thorough, often critical, view of these developments but with a balanced sense of what they have produced that is beneficial.

7. Ibid.

8. For a full review of these leading decisions, see Kirp and Yudof, *Educational Policy and the Law.*

9. For a critical review of some aspects, see David Neal and David Kirp, "The Allure of Legalization Reconsidered: The Case of Special Education," in Kirp and Jensen, *School Days*, pp. 343–65.

10. Catherine Lovell and Charles Tobin, "The Mandating Issue," *Public Administration Review* 41 (1981): 321.

11. Kirp, "Introduction," p. 6.

12. Robert Kluger, *Simple Justice* (New York: Knopf, 1975) is an exhaustive account of this drama.

13. For a thorough coverage of the 1960s, see Gary Orfield, *The Reconstruction of Southern Education* (New York: Wiley, 1969). For the most comprehensive analysis of all phases of desegregation up to 1978, see Gary Orfield, *Must We Bus? Segregated Schools and National Policy* (Washington: Brookings Institution, 1978). The following account relies heavily upon these sources.

14. Harrell R. Rodgers, Jr., and Charles S. Bullock III, *Coercion to Compliance* (Lexington, Mass.: Lexington Books, 1976).

15. Orfield, *Must We Bus?*, p. 109.

16. Everett F. Cataldo, Michael W. Giles, and Douglas S. Gatlin, *School Desegregation Policy: Compliance, Avoidance, and the Metropolitan Remedy* (Lexington, Mass.: Lexington Books, 1978); "Policy Support within a Target Group: The Case of School Desegregation," *American Political Science Review* 72 (1978): 985–95.

17. United States Commission on Civil Rights, *Desegregation of the Nation's Public Schools: A Status Report* (Washington: Government Printing Office, 1979), pp. 20–21.

18. Tyll van Geel, "Racial Discrimination from Little Rock to Harvard," *University of Cincinnati Law Review* 49 (1980), and "School Desegregation Doctrine and the Performance of the Judiciary," *Educational Administration Quarterly* 16, no. 3 (1980): 60–81.

19. Orfield, *Must We Bus?*, pp. 66–67.

20. The fullest review is Tyll van Geel, *Authority to Control the School Program* (Lexington, Mass.: Lexington Books, 1976). For leading cases, see Kirp and Yudof, *Educational Policy and the Law.*

21. Cataldo, et al., *School Desegregation Policy.*

22. See the attitudinal evidence in John B. McConahay and Willis D. Hawley, "Is It the Buses or the Blacks?: Self-Interest versus Symbolic Racism as Predictors of Opposition to Busing in Louisville," Center for Policy Analysis, Duke University, 1977, and David O. Spears, Carl P. Hensler, and Leslie K. Speer, "Opposition to 'Busing': Self-Interest or Symbolic Racism?" *American Political Science Review* 73 (1979): 369–84.

23. A National Institute of Education study by Diana Pearce, Center for National Policy Review, Catholic University, November 1980. Two sets of seven paired cities were compared.

24. The following draws on: Donna E. Shalala and Mary F. Williams, "Political Perspectives on Recent Efforts to Reform School Finance," in *Political Science and School Politics,* Samuel K. Gove and Frederick M. Wirt, eds. (Lexington, Mass.: Lexington Books, 1976), Chap. 3; Joel S. Berke, *Answers to Inequity: An Analysis of the New School Finance* (Berkeley: McCutchan, 1974); Michael W. Kirst, "The New Politics of State Education Finance," *Phi Delta Kappan* 60 (1979): 427–32; Stephen J. Carroll and Rolla E. Park, *The Search for Equity in School Finance,* (Santa Monica, Calif.: Rand, 1979); Norman C. Thomas, "Equalizing Educational Opportunity Through School Finance Reform: A Review Assessment," *University of Cincinnati Law Review* 48 (1979): 255–319.

25. A thorough examination is found in Walter Garms, James Guthrie, and Lawrence Pierce, *School Finance: The Economics and Politics of Education* (Englewood Cliffs, N.J.: Prentice-Hall, 1987).

26. Michael W. Kirst, "Coalition Building for School Finance Reform: The Case of California," *Journal of Education Finance* 4 (Summer 1978): 29–45; Berke, *Answers to Inequity.*

27. Carroll and Park, *Search for Equity;* David L. Kirp, "School Desegregation and the Limits of Legalism," *Public Interest* 47 (1977): 122–28.

28. For different basic views on the policy function of courts, see Alexander Bickel, *The Supreme Court and the Idea of Progress* (New York: Harper & Row, 1970); Archibald Cox, *The Role of the Supreme Court in American Government.* For an understanding of the judiciary as an active policy agent, see Stephen Wasby et al., *Desegregation from Brown to Alexander: An Exploration of Supreme Court Strategies* (Carbondale, Ill.: Southern Illinois University Press, 1977).

29. Abrahm Chayes, "The Role of the Judge in Public Law Litigation," *Harvard Law Review* 89 (May 1976): 1281–1316. For actual commentary by judges involved in desegregation, see *Law and Contemporary Problems,* 39 (1975), 135–63.

30. van Geel, "School Desegregation Doctrine," p. 78.

31. Orfield, *Must We Bus?*, Pt. two.

32. See the details in Emmett H. Buell, Jr., *School Desegregation and Defended Neighborhoods: The Boston Controversy* (Lexington, Mass.: Lexington Books, 1981).

33. David L. Kirp, *Just Schools: The Idea of Racial Equality in American Education* (Berkeley: University of California Press, 1982); Donald L. Horowitz, *The Courts and Social Policy* (Washington: Brookings Institution, 1977).

The role of social science in such litigation is a new facet of the politics of litigation. See the articles in Ray C. Rist and Ronald J. Anson, eds., *Education, Social Science, and the Judicial Process* (New York: Teachers College Press, 1977), and empirical studies by Mark A. Chesler et al., "Interactions among Scientists, Attorneys and Judges in School Desegregation Litigation," Center for Research on Social Organization, University of Michigan, 1981.

34. A wide review of these roles is found in G. Alan Tarr and Mary C. Porter, "State Supreme Court Policymaking and Federalism"(paper presented to the American Political Science convention, August 1980).

35. Richard Lehne, *The Quest for Justice* (New York: Longman, 1978).

36. For a review of these interstate reactions, see Thomas, "Equalizing Educational Opportunity."

37. Tarr and Porter, "State Supreme Court Policymaking."

38. For education, see Kirp and Jensen, *School Days*.

39. William H. Clune with Robert E. Lindquist, "Understanding and Researching the Implementation of Educational Laws: The Essential Characteristics of Implementation" (paper presented at the Stanford Berkeley Seminar on Law, Governance, and Education, 1980), pp. 33–34. Compare the judge's role with that of the "fixer" in administration in Eugene Bardach, *The Implementation Game* (Berkeley: University of California Press, 1977).

40. On the active role of other federal courts, see Michael W. Combs, "Courts of Appeals and Northern School Desegregation: Questions, Answers, and Public Policy" (paper presented to the Midwest Political Science convention, April 1981).

12

Federal Education Politics*

The federal government has always been a junior partner to state and local agencies in financing and operating American schools.[1] The impacts of federal policies on the nation's classrooms, however, continue to fascinate researchers, policymakers, and the public. Interest and concern about this role intensified during the 1960s and 1970s, motivated in part by expanding expenditures as well as by the increasing directiveness of most new federal policies. Through the 1970s, the federal role emphasized securing extra services for traditionally underserved students, promoting innovation, and supporting research.

In the 1980s, the federal government's spending for elementary and secondary education has not kept pace either with inflation or with state and local support of schools. Relative to state and local levels, the U.S. Department of Education's share of elementary or secondary school expenditures dipped to 6.1 percent by the 1984–1985 school year, its lowest share in almost twenty years.[2] Also, the regulatory pressures from the federal government in education during the 1980s have subsided. Still, this decade has witnessed an unparalleled out-

*The authors gratefully acknowledge the contributions of Richard Jung to this chapter and the use of some copyrighted material owned by the University Council for Educational Administration.

349

pouring of research and commentary on a federal role that has exerted a substantial influence on elementary and secondary education.

THE EVOLUTION OF THE FEDERAL ROLE

In 1950, when the U.S. Office of Education (USOE) was transferred to the Federal Security Agency—forerunner to the Department of Health, Education, and Welfare (HEW)—it had a staff of three hundred to spend $40 million. Growth was slow and largely unrecognized. By 1963 forty-two departments, agencies, and bureaus of the government were involved in education to some degree. The Department of Defense and the Veterans Administration spent more on educational programs than the USOE and National Science Foundation combined. The Office of Education appointed personnel who were specialists and consultants in such areas as mathematics, libraries, school buses; these specialists identified primarily with the National Education Association (NEA). Grant programs operated through deference to state priorities and judgments. State administrators were regarded by USOE as colleagues who should have the maximum decision-making discretion permitted by categorical laws.

While the era of 1963–1972 brought dramatic increases in federal activity, the essential mode of delivering services for USOE remained the same. The differential funding route was the key mode, seeking bigger and bolder categorical programs and demonstration programs. The delivery system for these categories continued to stress the superior ability of state departments of education to review local projects. Indeed, the current collection of overlapping and complex categorical aids evolved as a mode of federal action that a number of otherwise dissenting educational interests could agree on.[3] It was not the result of any rational plan for federal intervention but rather an outcome of political bargaining and coalition formation. Former USOE head Harold Howe expressed its essence this way:

> Whatever its limitations, the categorical aid approach gives the states and local communities a great deal of leeway in designing educational programs to meet various needs. In essence, the Federal government says to the states (and cities) "Here is some money to solve this particular program; you figure out how to do it. . . ." But whatever the criticisms which can in justice be leveled against categorical aid to education, I believe that we must stick with it, rather than

electing general aid as an alternative. The postwar period has radically altered the demands we place on our schools; a purely local and state viewpoint of education cannot produce an educational system that will serve national interest in addition to more localized concerns.[4]

An incremental shift in the style of USOE administration also came with expanded categories. The traditional provision of specialized consultants and the employment of subject matter specialists were ended in favor of managers and generalists who had public administration rather than professional education backgrounds. As we will see shortly, these newer federal administrators have been more aggresive, creating a political backlash against federal regulation that Ronald Reagan was able to highlight in his 1980 campaign.

Modes of Federal Influence

There have been basically six alternative modes of federal action for public schools:

1. General aid: Provide no-strings aid to state and local education agencies or such minimal earmarks as teacher salaries. A modified form of general aid was proposed by President Reagan in 1981. He consolidated numerous categories into a single bloc grant for local education purposes. No general-aid bill has ever been approved by the Congress.
2. Stimulate through differential funding: Earmark categories of aid, provide financial incentives through matching grants, fund demonstration projects, and purchase specific services. This is the approach of Elementary and Secondary Education Act (ESEA).
3. Regulate: Legally specify behavior, impose standards, certify and license, enforce accountability procedures. The bilingual regulations proposed by the Carter administration (and rescinded by President Reagan) are a good example.
4. Discover knowledge and make it available: Have research performed, gather and make other statistical data available. The National Science Foundation performs the first function and the National Center for Education Statistics the second.
5. Provide services: Furnish technical assistance and consultants

in specialized areas or subjects. For example, the Office of
Civil Rights will advise school districts that are designing
voluntary desegregation plans.

6. Exert moral suasion: Develop vision and question assumptions
through publications and speeches by top officials. Thus President Reagan's Secretary of Education William Bennett advocated three C's—content, character, and choice—in numerous
speeches and articles in the popular media. This mode of
federal influence is termed "the bully pulpit" by the press.

The Reagan administration endorsed a tuition tax credit to reim-
burse parents who send their children to private schools. Although
various members of Congress have pushed this idea for decades, this
was the first time a president had endorsed it. While he was defeated,
federal aid to private schools will continue to be a major issue in
federal aid during the 1990s although vociferously and unanimously
opposed by public education interest groups.

Overall the Reagan administration promoted five other basic
changes in the federal educational policy in addition to assisting
private schools, moving:

1. from a prime concern with equity to more concern with quality, efficiency, and state and local freedom to choose;
2. from a larger and more influential federal role to a mitigated
federal role;
3. from mistrust of the motives and capacity of state and local
educators to a renewed faith in governing units outside of
Washington;
4. from categorical grants to more unrestricted types of financial
aid;
5. from detailed and prescriptive regulations to deregulation.

The Reagan administration made no progress on financial support
for private education but was able to implement a major policy shift
by diminishing the federal role as the initiator of change. As Chapter
10 demonstrated, state government became more prominent in policy
initiation. That result was only one of several major changes between
the Carter and Reagan administrations, as Table 12.1 point outs.
Table 12.2 summarizes in further detail the changes in federal education policy that occurred during Reagan's first term.

Table 12.1
Educational Agenda of the Reagan Administration 1985–88

Policy Preference	Supporting Actions (taken or proposed)
1. *Institutional Competition:* (breaking the monopoly of the public school to stimulate excellent performance)	−Tuition tax credits −Vouchers −School awards programs −"Wall chart": monitoring state educational achievements
2. *Individual Competition:* (recognizing excellence to stimulate excellence)	−Merit pay, career ladders for teachers −Academic fitness program −Awards to teachers and principals −Eligibility for post-secondary scholarships, fellowships, loans
3. *Performance Standards:* (increasing minimum standards for teachers and students)	−Increased credit requirements for high school graduation −Proficiency examinations in addition to course requirements −Competency tests for teachers −Modified admission and certification standards for teachers
4. *Focus on Content:* (emphasis on basics to ensure performance in critical instructional areas)	−Concentration on: traditional basics, the 3 Rs new basics, sciences, mathematics, computer skills −Scholarships for science and mathematics teachers −More required courses for college and vocational preparation −Funds for NSF and ED for science and mathematics education
5. *Parental Choice:* (parental control over what, where, and how their children learn)	−Tuition tax credits −Vouchers −Parental involvement in the schooling process −Parental involvement in determining curricular content
6. *Character:* (strengthening traditional values in schools)	−Discipline in the schools −Character education −School prayer −Work ethic

Reprinted with permission of Macmillan Publishing Company, a division of Macmillan, Inc., from David L. Clark and Terry A. Astuto, "The Implications for Educational Research of a Changing Federal Educational Policy," in *Higher Education Research and Public Policy*, Manuel J. Justiz and Lars G. Bjork, eds. © 1988 by American Council on Education and Macmillan Publishing Company.

Table 12.2

The Reagan First Term: Changes in Federal Educational Policy —
1981–84

Year	Hallmark	Actions	Effects
1981	Rescissions Reductions	• Cumulative education budget cuts of over 20 percent	• Establishing the expectations for less (diminution)
1982	Block grant	• Implementation of ECIA.	• Dismantling the categorical programs (disestablishment, decentralization)
	Deregula-tion	• Revocation of regulations	• Constraining ED from the design of educational interventions (disestablishment, decentralization)
		• Constraint of enforcement of regulations	• Moving accountability to the state level (deregulation, decentralization)
1983	Report of the National Commission on Excellence	• Publication of *A Nation at Risk*	• Moving from a focus on equity to excellence
		• Support for the design of career ladders for teachers and other forms of merit pay	• Focusing improvement strategies on adjusting standards (decentralization)
		• Encouragement of upward adjustment of standards	• Reducing the role of the educationist in school improvement
		• National Forum on Education	• Increasing educational policy activity at the state level (decentralization)
1984	Awards and Recognition	• Secondary School Recognition Program	• Developing consensus on direction of reform

• Academic Fitness Awards	• Highlighting reform already underway (disestablishment, decentralization)
• Excellent Private Schools Program	• Recognizing established performance
• National Distinguished Principals Program	

For two decades the equity value, that of promoting equal educational opportunity, had been the most pervasive theme of federal education policy. Indeed, the Reagan administration could not substitute choice or efficiency values as the major orientation of federal policy because the Democrats controlled Congress. The most obvious expression of equity is through numerous categorical grants targeted to students not adequately served by state and local programs (for example, disadvantaged, handicapped). The Reagan administration attempted to scale back aggressive federal activity in such areas. The interest groups that are the recipients of federal policy resisted and were able to form successful countercoalitions at both the federal and state level. The findings by Mosher et al. summarize the approach of the equity-oriented groups.

> The interest groups are also quite typical in their efforts to concentrate as much influence as possible, at the appropriate time, in a variety of policy arenas—the courts, particular state legislatures, the Congress, federal agencies, and so on. The accomplishments of the past decade indicate that they have all acquired a large degree of sophistication in political maneuvering.[5]

The last comment suggests that the objectives of categorical interests such as the handicapped may lose out temporarily at the federal level of government only to succeed at another.

Table 12.3

Federal Resources[1] by Department/Agency[2] for Programs that Improve the Education/Provide Services During the School Years

Department/ Agency[3]	Current $ in Millions			Change 1989–1991		
	FY 1989	FY 1990	FY 1991	Current Dollars %	Constant Dollars[4]	
					$ in Millions	%
Education	8,364	9,342	10,651	27%	1,472	16%
Agriculture	4,006	4,287	4,594	15%	198	4%
Labor	1,321	1,332	1,349	6%	−101	−4%
Defense	1,068	1,142	1,305	22%	133	11%
Interior	166	199	222	34%	40	22%
NSF	128	147	210	64%	70	49%
HHS	103	110	126	22%	13	11%
Energy	0	7	21	N/A	N/A	N/A
ACTION	19	19	19	0%	−2	−9%
NEH	12	12	15	25%	2	14%
NASA	6	7	13	117%	6	97%
NEA	5	5	5	0%	0	−9%
Smithsonian	3	3	3	0%	0	−9%
State	3	3	3	0%	0	−9%
EPA	0	1	1	N/A	N/A	N/A
TOTAL	15,203	16,616	18,537	22%	1,851	11%

[1]Figures rounded to nearest $1 million. Tables may not total due to rounding.
[2]Department/Agency contributing less than $1 million in FY 1991 not included.
[3]Complete Department/Agency titles are in Appendix D.
[4]In 1991 dollars; see Appendix B.
Source: Education Goals Panel, *Goals Report: 1991* (Washington, D.C.: NEGP, 1991).

An Overview of Federal Funding

The federal government provides support to education through numerous agencies (see Table 12.3). The creation of a Department of Education in 1980 was justified partly on the basis that it would consolidate more education programs in a single accountable department. But the interest groups resisted this and preferred to stay in separate agencies. Consequently, school lunch aid is still provided by the Department of Agriculture, and the National Science Foundation provides research and demonstration grants for secondary school science. Headstart is part of the Department of Health and Human Services even though it is designed to help the transition to public kindergarten. Several of the lobby groups with programs outside of the Education Department did not want their programs controlled by a department that would presumably be dominated by professional educators. Ironically, former Secretary of Education William Bennett was extremely critical of the National Education Association, so these fears were not wholly justified.

An unconsolidated budget obscures the numerous separate categorical programs described in Table 12.4. Since no one was sure what type of federal intervention would be effective in earlier years, the congressional view was to try almost any politically palatable program. President Reagan tried to reverse this trend through massive consolidation into two bloc grants—one for local education agencies (LEAs) and another for state education agencies (SEAs) but was only partially successful with Congress. The budget growth in recent years for most education categoricals has barely kept pace with inflation because the Reagan administration has recommended about a 25 percent cutback. Congress refused to go along with this but could not add much to the base.

The growth of federal education expenditures has made the secretary of education a highly visible and important leader. By contrast, the predecessors, the USOE commissioners from 1867 to 1963, are known to only a few historians. The secretary can use his or her cabinet position to command widespread media attention. Despite President Reagan's plan to downgrade the Department of Education to subcabinet status, his education secretaries have created large-scale public visibility for the department through their creative use of mass media and the "bully pulpit."

NATIONAL STRATEGIES FOR THE 1990s

The hallmark of U.S. education has been local and state control, but in the past few years there has been a dramatic increase in nationwide initiatives for education policy. These initiatives will take several years to become concrete, but by the end of the 1990s will have a major impact on states and localities across the United States. Given the slow economic growth in most states, there will be few resources for state education initiatives during most of the 1990s.[6] Consequently, the period 1991–1995 will contain a larger portion of nationwide initiatives than new state programs. State programs were the hallmark of the 1980s, when forty-four states passed large-scale reform packages. This new emphasis on nationwide initiatives will be a major contrast to what took place in the 1980s—state leadership peaked from 1983 to 1987, with a result of an increase in education expenditures of 30 percent in real terms for the decade.

The key concept is "nationwide" influence, as contrasted with "federal government" policies. Almost no one expects a large array of

Table 12.4

Major Federal Programs[1] that Improve Education/Provide Services During the School Years

| Program | Current $ in Millions[2] | | | Change 1989–1991 | | | Service Levels |
| | FY 1989 | FY 1990 | FY 1991 | Current Dollars % | Constant Dollars[3] | | |
					$ in Millions	%	
Chapter 1 (Education)	4,026	4,721	5,466	36%	1,048	24%	4,650,230 students grades 1–12 (88–89)
School Meals Programs (Agriculture)[4]	3,762	4,007	4,271	14%	142	3%	24.4 million lunches and 4.4 million breakfasts daily; 1.7 million summer meals; 183 million 1/2 pts. of milk (1991)
Special Ed. Basic State Grants (Education)	1,366	1,420	1,705	25%	206	14%	4,097,837 children served (1991)
Classroom Instruction (Defense)	845	885	998	18%	71	8%	191,955 students (Sept. 1990)
Jobs Corps (Labor)	326	353	381	17%	23	6%	27,459 16- and 17-yr.-olds completed program (7/89–6/90)
Impact Aid Grants (Education)	708	717	741	5%	–36	–5%	N/A
JTPA Summer Jobs (Labor)	709	700	683	–4%	–95	–12%	466,006, 14–17-yr.-olds (1990)
Vocational Ed. Basic State Grants (Education)	503	515	518	3%	–34	–6%	97% of all high school students enrolled in at least 1 course (1989)
Drug-free Schools (Education)	323	504	553	71%	199	56%	78% of nation's LEA receive program funds (1988–1989)
Chapter 2 (Education)	463	457	450	–3%	–58	–11%	99% of nation's schools received program funds (84–85)
JTPA II-A (Labor)	286	279	285	0%	–29	–9%	43,841, 14–15-yr.-olds (1989)
CN Commodities[4] (Agriculture)	183	218	259	42%	58	29%	N/A
Eisenhower Math/ Science (Education)	128	127	200	56%	60	42%	1/3 of all math/science teachers benefit annually
BIA Indian Schools (Interior)	162	170	192	19%	14	8%	40,841 students (1991)
Bilingual Education (Education)	100	103	109	9%	–1	–1%	281,322 students (1990)
Vocational Rehabilitation State Grants (Education)	116	122	131	13%	4	3%	4,690 served, under 18 yrs. old (1990)
Magnet Schools (Education)	114	113	110	–4%	–15	–12%	54 school districts in 25 states funded (1990)
Others[5]	1,084	1,205	1,485	37%	296	25%	N/A
TOTAL	15,203	16,616	18,537	22%	1,851	11%	N/A

[1]Program descriptions are in Appendix C. Complete Department/Agency titles are in Appendix D.
[2]Figures rounded to nearest $1 million. Tables may not total due to rounding.
[3]In 1991 dollars; see Appendix B.
[4]Obligations.
[5]Other federal programs that improve/provide services during the school years funded for less than $100 million in FY 1991.
Source: Education Goals Panel, Goals Report: 1991 (Washington, D.C.: NEGP, 1991).

mandated federal policies or a gigantic increase in federal aid, which currently provides only 5 percent of the total education expenditures. The federal government's role will be more indirect, through supporting research and development and reporting pupil outcomes. For example, by the end of the 1990s, the United States will *not* have a detailed national curriculum like France had in the 1930s, but it will have nationwide curriculum standards and subject matter frameworks. Currently, nationwide policy is all around us, including the Scholastic Aptitude Test (SAT), American College Test (ACT), school accreditation (e.g., North Central Association of Schools and Colleges), and such organizations as the Education Commission of the States, the College Board, and the National Collegiate Athletic Association (NCAA). These policy-setting organizations do not represent a specific group of education employees and have the legitimacy to recommend or administer nationwide policies. Unlike many foreign nations, the United States has a long tradition of voluntary, nonprofit, tax-exempt organizations that can administer policies such as the SAT or the NCAA. Some of these, such as school accreditation, became prominent before there was a major federal government role in education.

All of the major new influences are compatible with one another and reinforce the following six national education goals developed by President Bush and the nation's governors in 1989.

1. All children in America will start school ready to learn.
2. The high school graduation rate will increase to at least 90 percent.
3. American students will leave grades four, eight, and twelve having demonstrated competency in challenging subject matter including English, mathematics, science, history, and geography; and every school in America will ensure that all students learn to use their minds well, so that they may be prepared for responsible citizenship, further learning, and productive employment in our modern economy.
4. United States students will be first in the world in science and mathematics achievement.
5. Every adult in America will be literate and will possess the knowledge and skills necessary to compete in a global economy and exercise the rights and responsibilities of citizenship.
6. Every school in America will be free of drugs and violence and will offer a disciplined environment conducive to learning.

Many of the political developments in the 1990s arise from the perception about the alleged dismal status of K–12 education presented in the following points.

1. Current state and local standards for pupil achievement and teacher performance are not high enough, nor do they provide uniform pupil outcome data that is useful for interstate or local comparisons.

2. The commonly used multiple choice tests are excessively oriented to low-level basic skills that emphasize single right answers. The proclivity of LEAs is to choose commercial tests that do *not* adequately emphasize analysis, statistical inference, mathematics problem solving, hands-on science, synthesis, expository writing, and complex reading. Our current tests, such as the California Test of Basic Skills or the Stanford or Metropolitan achievement tests are not geared to the high curricular standards of our economic competitors in Europe and Asia. Since we are involved in worldwide economic competition, local control of tests and curriculum is a luxury the United States cannot afford.

3. Since the commonly used standardized multiple-choice tests are at such a low level, the parents and general public receive a "phony story" that exaggerates what U.S. pupils know and can do compared with students in other nations or with U.S. students in prior decades.

4. United States tests and exams often do not contain "high stakes" for the pupils who take them. Few employers look at high school transcripts of high school graduates, and state assessments are not used for college entrance.* The SAT is not aligned with the high school curriculum and alleges to measure "aptitude" rather than achievement in subjects like history and science.

A coalition of nationwide leaders (discussed in the next section) concludes from these points that national subject matter curricular standards are needed that meet world-class benchmarks. This coalition contends that a nationwide exam system should be developed and aligned to these world-class standards in five core subjects (En-

---

* Examples of state tests are the California Assessment Program, Illinois Goals Program, and the Connecticut Mastery Tests.

glish, mathematics, science, social studies, foreign languages). Moreover, the exam scores should be reported for individual students, and "high stakes" decisions based largely on student performance. Specifically, employers should utilize the national exams when hiring high school graduates, and universities should consider national exam scores as well as high school grades. These national initiatives should be a part of a state systemic reform strategy that revamps staff development and teacher training so that it is compatible with the national curricular standards.[7] For example, California had most of the elements of systemic reform by the late 1980s. But since then it has repealed its pupil assessment program and failed to invest adequately in staff development. Consequently, few teachers are able to implement California's curricular frameworks, which approach world-class standards.[8]

Specific Components of a Future Nationwide Strategy

Many groups of political and education leaders represent these national initiatives in education policy. We next discuss nine major groups and initiatives.

1. *National Education Goals Panel (NEGP)*. NEGP resulted from the 1989 Presidential Summit, and in 1991 included six members from the Bush administration and six governors to oversee progress toward the national goals. In 1992, the NEGP probably will be broadened to include representatives from Congress, education, and the public. Congressional members never participated after the 1989 summit and Congressional Democrats want education to broaden the structure and functions of NEGP. The National Governors' Association (NGA) has been very active in elaborating and measuring the national goals as well as in playing a major role in the annual reports on how well the United States is meeting the goals. National standards are implied in Goals 3 and 4:

- American students will leave grades four, eight, and twelve having demonstrated competency in challenging subject matter including English, mathematics, science, history, and geography; and every school in America will ensure that all students learn to use their minds well, so that they may be prepared for responsible citizenship, further learning, and productive employment in our modern economy.

• U.S. students will be first in the world in science and mathematics achievement.

2. *National Council for Education Standards and Testing (NCEST).* NCEST was created by Congress to decide the feasibility and desirability of national standards and assessments. NCEST has a thirty-member bipartisan board co-chaired by the same governors who are leaders in NEGP. The NCEST Board listed in Table 12.5 is a good example of the emerging national coalition pushing these nationwide initiatives. NCEST's final report in January 1992 advocated the establishment of national curriculum standards and exams, with heavy reliance on bottom-up initiatives from professional organizations like the National Council for Teachers of Mathematics (NCTM). NCEST is important because, unlike NEGP, it has Congressional authorization and participation, so it expands the coalition beyond the governors and the Bush administration. NCEST recommended that it be succeeded by a new entity, the National Education Standards and Assessment Council (NESAC), that would oversee and provide quality assurance for new standards and exams.

3. *New Standards Project (NSP).* NSP, co-directed by Marc Tucker of the National Center on Education and Economics and Lauren Resnick of the University of Pittsburgh, is funded by the Pew Memorial Trust and the MacArthur Foundation and is charged with building a national consensus for educational standards in five core subject areas (same as Goal 2). NSP is also working on designing exams that will be high stakes and compatible with national standards. The first subject area developed will probably be in mathematics and based on the NCTM standards, which many consider world-class quality.

4. *National Assessment of Educational Progress (NAEP).* Since the 1970s, NAEP has conducted periodic national assessments on student achievement in core subject areas. NAEP is funded by the federal government and is overseen by the U.S. Department of Education. The federal contractor is the Educational Testing Service, which supplies the NEGP with subject matter trends for its reports. NAEP is *not* based on curricular standards or frameworks that NEGP, NCEST, or NSP envisioned for the high stakes individual pupil exam. NAEP is not meant to guide classroom syllabi and therefore its long-run future in "world class high stakes" exams is uncertain. It will continue in the

Table 12.5
National Council on Education Standards and Testing

Co-Chairs

Governor Carroll A. Campbell, Jr.   Governor Roy Romer
South Carolina (R)   *Colorado (D)*

Members

Gordon Ambach, *Council of Chief State School Officers*
Eva L. Baker, *University of California, Los Angeles*
Brian L. Benzel, *Edmonds School District, Washington*
Mary Bicouvaris, *Hampton Roads Academy, Virginia*
U.S. Senator Jeff Bingaman, *Committee on Labor and Human Resources (D-New Mexico)*
Eve M. Bither, *Maine State Department of Education*
Iris Carl, *National Council of Teachers of Mathematics*
Lynne V. Cheney, *National Endowment for the Humanities*
State Senator Carols Cisneros, *New Mexico Senate*
Ramon C. Cortines, *San Francisco Unified School District*
Chester E. Finn, Jr., *Vanderbilt University*
Martha Fricke, *Ashland School Board, Nebraska, former President National School Boards
    Association*
Keith Geiger, *National Education Association*
U.S. Representative William Goodling, *Committee on Education and Labor (R-
    Pennsylvania)*
State Senator John Hainkel, *Louisiana Senate*
Sandra Hassan, *Beach Channel High School, New York*
U.S. Senator Orrin Hatch, *Committee on Labor and Human Resources (D-Utah)*
David Hornbeck, *David W. Hornbeck and Associates*
David Kearns, *U.S. Department of Education*
U.S. Representative Dale E. Kildee, *Committee on Education and Labor (D-Utah)*
Walter Massey, *National Science Foundation*
Edward L. Meyen, *University of Kansas*
Mark Musick, *Southern Regional Education Board*
Michael Nettles, *University of Tennessee*
Sally B. Pancrazio, *Illinois State University*
Roger B. Porter, *The White House*
Lauren Resnick, *University of Pittsburgh*
Roger Semerad, *RJR Nabisco*
Albert Shanker, *American Federation of Teachers*
Marshall S. Smith, *Stanford University*

short run as an overall measure of educational attainment at the
national and state level, but it will *not* be an exam each pupil takes.
NAEP will be used to compare state performance and provide impetus for specific state curricular reforms based on subsections of the
NAEP exam.

5. *U.S. Labor Department Secretary's Commission for Achieving Necessary Skills (SCANS)*. SCANS produced a report outlining the skills necessary for meeting the demands of the U.S. workplace. These workplace skills also provide guidance for pupil exams but are not entirely compatible with the concepts emphasized by NSP or NAEP. For example, SCANS stresses group work, oral communication, and interpersonal skills, but these skills are not featured now by NAEP or NSP. Groups skills are difficult to combine with individual high stakes exams.

6. *New American Schools Development Corporation (NASDC)*. NASDC is a board composed primarily of big U.S. businesses that will fund several "break-the-mold" school experiments. All grantees must address the world-class standards in the core subject areas specified in NEGP and NCEST. NASDC hopes to provide $200 million in privately funded school experiments between 1992 and 1996, but will definitely commit $25 million in 1992 design teams.

7. *America 2000*. This is President Bush's proposed strategy to improve U.S. education by the year 2000. It combines a series of federal, state, and private initiatives in order to meet the education goals. Most relevant to this analysis is the President's support for world-class standards, high-stakes testing, federal funding for break-the-mold schools developed by NASDC, and a continuation of NAEP.

8. *National Board for Professional Teaching Standards (NBPTS)*. NBPTS, based in Detriot, Michigan, has a sixty-three member board (two-thirds teachers) that will begin in 1994 to nationally certify teachers. NBPTS certification assessments will be based on the ability of teachers to teach the curriculum envisioned by the NSP and NAEP. NBPTS views certification as appropriate solely for teachers with five or more years of experience. State education agencies and local education agencies will be urged to reward teachers who pass NBPTS assessments. NBPTS assessments will be different from any current teacher evaluations and will feature the ability to adapt subject matter to diverse students (e.g., teach fractions to sixth graders). NBPTS assessments stress teachers' knowledge of their students and demonstrated ability to work with other teachers to improve local schools.

9. *Neighborhood Schools Improvement Act* (HR 3320 or S2, 102nd Congress). These bills provide $800 million in grants to states that are to be used for state systemic reform plans that implement the strategy embodied in the above initiatives. Specifically, HR 3320 says federal

aid shall be used to "develop innovative reform plans which include state achievement goals, a means for developing or adopting high-quality, challenging curricular frameworks and coordinated curricular materials, professional development strategies, and assessment instruments." HR 3320 has bipartisan Congressional support, but is opposed by the Bush administration because they view it as a primarily Democratic alternative to America 2000. Figure 12.1 presents most of the organizational structures that undergird the nationwide initiatives outlined above.

Implications for State and Local Policy

These nationwide efforts may not all achieve their intended outcomes or be as well integrated as the preceding descriptions imply. But it is quite likely that the general direction of these initiatives will result in new nationwide and state policies by the end of the decade.[9] Probably, the "national exam" will *not* be a single exam but rather an exam that state pupil assessment systems could be anchored to. Most likely is the impact of NBPTS, because it does not require development of the other initiatives as prerequisites. For example, all states will have to decide whether to recognize and reward NBPTS-certified teachers by 1994.

The developmental costs for these national efforts need not be borne by hard-pressed state budgets but might be covered by grants from foundations and businesses and by federal appropriations.

The political momentum behind these national efforts is impressive and growing. Opposition has focused on the alleged negative impacts, impracticality, and costs of national exams.[10] States need to monitor developments carefully, while keeping in mind that state curricular policy in the 1980s was quite similar to the orientation of these nationwide forces. For example, California's new state assessment includes revamped curricular frameworks and individual testing, and is compatible with the high-stakes pupil outcomes.

The political momentum for national changes is *not* solely top-down, but rather is coming from all directions, including business, professional associations (such as NCTM), universities, and LEAs. The parts can interlock (e.g., standards, curriculum frameworks, and exams), and state education needs to keep the interrelationships in mind rather than merely looking at the parts one at a time.

Political support for these initiatives is not solely linked to Presi-

Figure 12.1
Nationwide Initiatives in Education Reform

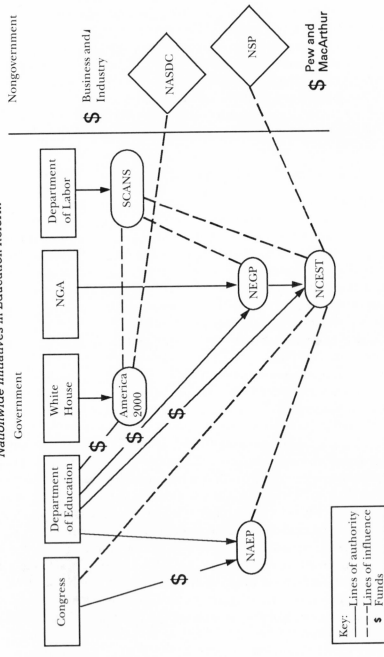

Source: *Basic Education* (No. 10, 1991), December 7, 1991, pp. 8-12.

dent Bush, and includes, for example, a significant number of Democratic governors, legislators, and Presidential candidates, such as Governor Clinton (D-Ark). The recommendations by NCEST in January 1992 for national standards and exams was supported by both teacher unions (NEA and AFT), as well as by the National School Boards Association. Resistance based on local control of schools appears to be crumbling, but the technical issues of designing national exams are formidable and costly.[11]

The biggest political disagreement concerns the federal role in U.S. education's meeting world-class standards and providing equity for all students. The view of most elected Republicans is that the federal role is limited to keeping score on progress toward the national goals and providing research and development. Many elected Democrats contend that the federal government should play a major role in funding state and local operations, especially for school readiness, finance equity, and the disadvantaged. After a protracted battle, the 1992 NCEST report concluded that all these functions are up to SEAs and LEAs. This political conflict over federal funding of school operations will continue as more federal funds are made available for reallocation from defense cuts.

These emerging nationwide policies imply revised concepts for school finance. During the past twenty-five years, school finance debates have been dominated by inputs such as pupil-teacher ratios and disparities in spending between state and school districts.[12] The national goals and assessments suggest it is time to focus school finance on pupil outcomes.

As the preceding section indicates, there is an emerging consensus on the macro strategy for how to accomplish major school change that produces quantum improvements in student learning and helps accomplish the nation's bold education goals:[13]

- Set clear student learning outcome goals.
- Have a high-quality curriculum program.
- Site base manage implementation, allowing teachers to have major influence and power over implementation.
- Have an assessment or monitoring system calibrated to world-class standards to indicate the degree to which objectives are being accomplished.
- Have a sharp-edged accountability system with rewards and sanctions.

SUMMARY AND IMPLICATIONS

The federal role in education has always been uncertain and subject to political controversy as well as the influence of broader social movements. Just as the approaches to implementing the elementary/secondary education programs emanating from the Great Society initiatives seemed to realize a growing national consensus, the federal government, under the leadership of a conservative political coalition, attempted to turn federal policy in a new direction, using a set of bully pulpit strategies instead of regulations to achieve its objectives. This chapter has reviewed some of the analytic tools available for researching the federal role in elementary and secondary education. It has also assessed a disparate, and often fugitive, literature on this federal role since the most recent research anthologies were published in the early 1980s.

This chapter highlights several important developments. First, state and local implementation of the more mature federally sponsored categorical programs had, by the early 1980s, often moved beyond the mutual adaptation stage generally portrayed in the research anthologies. The most recent national studies of these longer standing programs portray reduced or more circumscribed intergovernmental conflicts compared to earlier assessments, accustomed rather than new or adjusting relationships, more emphasis on program improvement rather than on a strict compliance orientation, and highly tailored programs customized to fit the contours of local circumstances and capacities.

Second, it is still to early to assess fully the state and local impacts of the streamlining of compensatory education requirements, the effects of the bloc grant, and the consequences of easing federal oversight across programmatic and regulatory strategies. The first wave of investigations were often undertaken by constituency groups that typically used exploratory case studies to examine the major programmatic reforms in ECIA. This initial surge of evaluations was then followed by a wave of large-scale national assessments on state and local responses to the new or revised federal programmatic strategies. These reported that even under Reagan-administration cutbacks or eliminations, programs with strong institutional and professional support at state-local levels successfully resisted cuts— and even thrived.

Third, the Reagan administration's qualitatively different use of the bully pulpit as a major, independent policy strategy has been inadequately examined. There is broad recognition of the widespread public and professional reactions to the publication of *A Nation at Risk*, the issuance of the wall chart comparing state resources and college entrance scores, and other moral suasion devices. Still, to date, most commentary on these strategies has little if any empirical base and has been more public relations filler than systematic assessment. A real possibility exists that the failure of recent reforms to rest on well-researched foundations may lead to overall failure—and more popular disenchantment.

Probably the greatest challenge for researchers of the federal role in elementary and secondary education will be to design and conduct systematic assessments of the origins and impacts of the modern use of the bully pulpit strategy. Only through such scholarship, and with the benefit of time's perspective, will the impacts of the Reagan administration's education policy be fully understood.

The past decade has produced a consensus on ways to improve the probability that federal intent will be implemented at the state and local levels. This consensus includes: (a) having a precise and feasible objective, (b) securing broad-based state and local political support for the intervention, (c) generating a sense of urgency for achieving the objectives, and (d) concealing the federal government's weaknesses in forcing the state and local units to comply.[14] The federal threat to recover funds by audits should be used sparingly because it is difficult to enforce through the courts. Federal administrators can build vertical networks of like-minded administrators in the state and local bureaucracies. We have seen how successful this is in vocational education and Chapter 1 funding. The key is to bring about a sharing of values within this vertical network. Elmore and McLaughlin summarize this way:

> The central paradox of policy implementation is that policies cannot succeed unless individuals and organizations take responsibility for their success, but if they had assumed that responsibility to begin with it may not have been necessary to have a policy. The paradox is instructive in two ways. It tells us that compliance is a necessary part of any implementation strategy, but that it is hardly ever a sufficient condition for success. Mobilization of the knowledge necessary to make a policy work depends on people accepting responsibility for their actions.[15]

The Federal Role: Retrospect and Prospect

The federal role in aggregate has passed through three stages:

1965–1972—an era of policy innovation and large-scale growth in numbers of discrete programs as well as dollars. The percentage of federal aid peaked at 9 percent of total school expenditures.

1973–1980—a period of consolidation and increased regulatory effectiveness. Implementation became more aligned with national objectives, and the federal percentage of the budget stabilized. Two Republican presidents and one Democratic president made no large-scale changes in the federal role.

1980–1992—a time of gradual devolution of responsibility to states and localities with an attendant decline in the federal budget share to its current level of 6 percent. The dominant federal innovation technique shifts from categorical programs to the bully pulpit.

Any three of these scenarios is possible in the post-1988 period. But the huge federal deficit left as a legacy of the Reagan administration makes a repeat of the expansive 1965–1972 era unlikely. The major causes of the deficit have been large increases in defense expenditures and cuts in federal taxes, neither of which will be reversed in the short term. The continued concern with economic growth and education's alleged key role in foreign competition makes it unlikely that further large-scale cutbacks will be a feature of the next administration. Most likely then is a gradual incremental growth with a steady state or slight percentage rise in the federal share. Initially, new programs will be linked with international trade enhancement.

All such predictions are hazardous. Only a few observers predicted the 1983 education "crisis" that spawned so much state legislation. The key factors in any change are often exogenous events that override such predictable variables as short-term demographics.

NOTES

1. For an overview, see Michael Timpane, ed., *The Federal Interest in Financing Education* (Cambridge, Mass.: Ballinger, 1979).

2. U.S. Department of Education, *The Fiscal Year 1987 Budget* (Washington D.C.: U.S. Department of Education, 1986).

3. James Sundquist, *Politics and Policy* (Washington, D.C.: Brookings Institution, 1968), pp. 155–221.

4. Harold Howe, "National Policy for American Education" (speech to the seventy-First Annual Convention of the National Congress of Parents and Teachers, Minneapolis, Minn., May 22, 1967).

5. Edith Mosher, Anne Hastings, and Jennings Wagoner, "Beyond the Breaking Point," *Educational Evaluation and Policy Analysis* 3, no. 1 (1981): 47.

6. Steve Gold, *Understanding School Budgets* (Washington, D.C.: U.S. Government Printing Office, 1992).

7. Marshall S. Smith and Jennifer O'Day, "Systemic School Reform," in *The Politics of Curriculum and Testing*, edited by Susan Fuhrman and Betty Malen (Philadelphia, Penn.: Falmer, 1991).

8. Policy Analysis for California Education (PACE), *Conditions of Education in California: 1990* (Berkeley, Calif.: PACE, 1991); David Cohen, "Revolution in One Classroom," in Fuhrman and Malen, *Politics of Curriculum.*

9. Marshall S. Smith, "A National Curriculum in the United States?" *Education Leadership* 49, no. 1 (1991): 74–81.

10. Theodore Sizer, "Educational Policy and the Essential School," *Horace* 6, no. 2 (Providence, R.I.: The Coalition of Essential Schools, Brown University, 1990).

11. Daniel Koretz, Statement on National Testing Before the U.S. House of Representatives, Subcommittee on Elementary/Secondary Education, February 19, 1992.

12. Allan Odden, "School Funding Changes in the 1980s, *Educational Policy* 4, no. 1 (1990): 33–47.

13. Business Roundtable, *Essential Elements of a Successful Education System* (Washington, D.C.: The Business Roundtable, 1991); National Governors' Association, *Educating America: State Strategies for Achieving the National Educational Goals* (Washington, D.C.: National Governors' Association, 1990); Thomas Peters and Robert Waterman, *In Search of Excellence* (New York: Harper and Row, 1982); The White House, *American 2000: An Education Strategy* (Washington, D.C.: The White House, 1991).

14. Lorraine M. McDonnell and Milbrey McLaughlin, *Education Policy and the Role of the States* (Santa Monica, Calif.: Rand, 1982).

15. Richard Elmore and Milbrey McLaughlin, "Strategic Choice in Federal Education Policy: The Compliance-Assistance Trade Off," in *Policymaking in Education*, Ann Lieberman and Milbrey McLaughlin, eds. (Chicago: University of Chicago Press, 1982), p. 175.

13

Systems Analysis, Research, and Educational Politics

In the course of exploring American schools during their current conflict and crisis, we became convinced of the soundness of the Chinese viewpoint that is expressed in their word for *crisis*. As stated at the book's beginning, the Chinese word *crisis* is composed of two symbols—one for danger and the other for opportunity. We have seen an abundance of both in moving over the terrain of educational governance, and it is a view certainly expressed by the practitioner. But as we near this journey's end, it is important to comprehend this field conceptually and suggest new research directions to enhance our understanding of educational politics. This chapter undertakes both tasks.

Easton's system analysis views the political system as engaged in "the authoritative allocation of resources and values" in order to alleviate crisis and conflict in the society. We have not used Easton's approach as "theory" because it does not itself predict; rather, we have used it as a "framework of analysis," to use Easton's designation. He believed that its "goal is not to undertake the validation of the statements [in the framework] or to demonstrate definitively the applications of such concepts."[1] We, on the other hand, have tried throughout this book to deal with validation and application because they help explain the politics of education.

Figure 13.1 sketches the social environment; support; group values; and local, state, and federal policy making subsystems that each chapter has had as its focus. Briefly, constant and stressful elements of the social environment generate both support for and demands on the political system of the schools. At one time, the educational policy process was handled primarily through the local policy system with access channels like board elections and power structures; with demand conversion processes like schools boards, superintendents, and referenda; and with policy implementation through administrators and teachers. But in recent decades, the state and federal policymaking systems—particularly the former—have intervened. As a result, new agencies of government and new pressure groups have played a major role in shaping new educational programs.This newness, however, still reflects a classic set of older values. These results then fed back into all government levels and private groups with consequences for both system support and the social environment.

SYSTEM SUPPORT AND POLITICAL SOCIALIZATION

The analysis begins with how support is built for the political system as an ongoing method of allocating resources and values. Support and demands are the two prime inputs into this system, and both interact. Creating such support is vital to sustaining the system when it is criticized for its response to demands. The creating and sustaining of support for the total political system apply as well to the political system of schools. Shifting the analytical focus from the system to the individual level, we can understand how support is created. For example, in Piagetian terms the developing child is subjected to socialization to create political support, with stages of ever-widening cognition, affect, and action. Back at the system level, many institutions contribute to building this broader support for the larger political system, including the schools. If civics training is characterized by blandness, it is because that quality helps school members defuse community criticism.

Research in political socialization halted over two decades ago as no new and interesting questions emerged following studies on the

Figure 13.1

A Sketch of System Analysis Components and Related Chapters

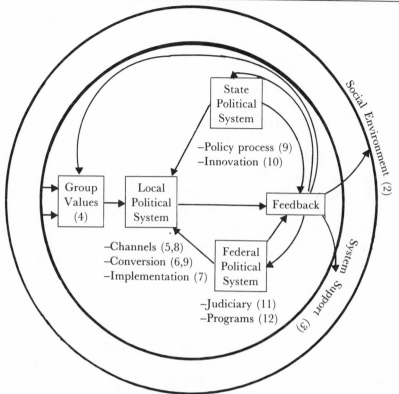

(Relevant chapter numbers in parentheses)

stages of political learning and the role of institutions in such learning. The period since has witnessed certain traumatic events on the national and world scene, but the impact of these events on political learning has so far gone largely unstudied. It has been an era of disjunction between what had been taught—the ideal—and what has occurred—assassinations, political malfeasance, war, and economic crisis.

Major research questions arise. Has this experiential learning affected socialization? Has television become a source of new political learning? Have real-world experiences and television foreshortened or altered civic instruction, bypassing Piaget's belief in stages of successive learning? We also need comparative study of the socialization process in order to comment on larger questions of citizen linkages to government. Finally, a need for major theories to guide such research questions is obvious. We suspect that these theories lie in anthropology's focus on modernization, in organizational theory's interest in institutional effects on role creation and maintenance, and in educational psychology's attention to the cognitive and affective development of the young.

DEMAND INPUTS: INTEREST GROUPS

Support alone is not the only input to governing. The more visible and dramatic element is the flow of demands into the political system. These inputs arise out of value conflict, and they influence policy outputs. Dissatisfactions break out over differences about basic values within the larger society. More specifically, educational policy arises over conflict among the values of quality, efficiency, equity, and choice, as they have developed sequentially in American history.

This conflict is transferred into the political system by interest groups that represent general and specific policy values. In the educational policy area, these groups have proliferated in recent decades as conflict has intensified. Even the professional groups have fragmented over divergent policy values, and other groups emerged that reflect differences about the directions and methods of education. But the numbers of such groups, and their effort to convert demand into output, are characteristic of the political turbulence of schools in conflict.

Research into this phase of systems analysis has been vigorous, partly because group pressure is so evident and dramatic—and effective. Our understanding of these developments has been helped by recent theories of political group action. For example, dissatisfaction theory has been fruitful in exploring how groups arise; networking concepts have helped us understand the resulting policy innovations. Economic and organizational theories suggest other research directions. For example, how are members moved to join interest groups and how are group leaders motivated to operate? These questions get some explanation in economic theories of individual self-interest. The study of educational interest groups could also benefit from the understanding that they operate, in Berry's term, in an "interest group society," with common features of organizational behavior. Those commonalities involve internal matters of who governs—organizational design, decisional processes, and dealing with change—all enmeshed in lobbyist and constituency connections.[2]

DEMAND INPUTS: CITIZEN CONTROL

Demand inputs to the political system are created by crises, gaps between needs and the resources to meet them. In dealing with crisis, those affected may turn to any of the social subsystems, including the political. Thus we can conceive of demand inputs as stimuli to the political system, triggering responses by political authorities.

Demand inputs take concrete form in several ways. A particularly vital way in a democratic system arises from voters; this mode of input is crucial to educational policymaking due to the tradition of local control. That principle has meant that voters select their own school boards, superintendents, budgets, and programs. But efforts to filter out such direct influence have occurred through nonpartisan reforms, community power structures, and school professionals promoting their own expertise as the only right way to make decisions.

The result has been limited citizen participation in all aspects of this decision making, although that is less true for higher-status citizens. Public dissatisfaction can still erupt, though, and usually does so episodically to transform both policy and policy process in school systems; this adaptation of systems to pressure is a rough approximation of local control. Also, recent redistributive trends in state and federal programs have had contradictory results for local groups. Traditionally powerful local groups have been compelled to meet external goals; at the same time, more educational opportunities arose for those usually inactive in school policymaking.

Research opportunities from these and other changes in the citizen's role in education policy suggest themselves. Yet voters studies are rare today, and community power studies ended in the early 1970s. Consequently, the impact on citizen participation of recent state and federal policy mandates, the private-school movement, desegregation, the "minoritization" of big city demography, and national economy influences remains unknown. Does local participation remain low and do closed systems remain active in the face of these external intrusions? We don't as yet know. Such research would require more than just one city and issue for analysis; comparative analysis is salutary for practitioners, policymakers, and social theorists.

INPUT CONVERSION: SCHOOL BOARDS

When demands move into the political system, they are sometimes ignored, but at other times they are converted into decisions about resources and values. We know these outputs as legislative laws and ordinances, bureaucratic regulations, and judicial decisions, as well as board resolutions and memos to staff from administrators. The political system of the local schools involves an outside intervention by state and local governments, which interact with local policymaking agents. These policy agents are school boards, superintendents, teachers, and voter referenda. The policy process they engage in make up the withinputs in a systems analysis of the politics of education.

Local conversion of education policy displays some constants over time, although episodic changes also emerge. These constants appear in the policy role of the local school boards when it is a closed model. For example, local policymaking has been characterized by the limited participation of voters in electing board members, and that fact shapes the nature of school policymaking. Conversely, a political system with heavy voter involvement must act differently than one where few voters are involved. Another constant in local demand conversion is that board membership has been dominated by middle and business classes since early in this century. A conversion system that hears only the views of those groups must reflect in its policy only a limited perspective. Thus, not all policy demands at the input stage are acted on, nor are they acted on at the same speed. Multiple sets of withinputs arise due to the nature of those who sit on these boards and their policies and social values. Another constant is the aura of rationality permeating this process when board members are all agreed on objectives.

But episodic inputs also arise to challenge this closed system of policymaking and make it more pluralistic. Challenge develops when new groups seek power and conflict with established objectives and methods of education. Then the board becomes an arena of struggle over the reallocation of these new values and resources. The past saw little of this model in local school politics. That is why the mid-1980s reforms of program and accountability took place at the state level, bypassing local boards and making them the agents for carrying out state mandates. This is not the first time or the first policy area where local dominance of a service institution had to be reformed by going up to the state level.

The once-moribund field of research into school-board behavior is now open to important research questions. Does the dissatisfaction theory of democracy apply on a large scale to the state reform movement? That is, did dissatisfaction with schools prior to the mid-1980s stimulate state leaders to action, or did those leaders see school reform as one way of dealing with a budget crunch through more efficiency and accountability? Also, given this development, how have reforms actually changed board behavior, including provision of resources for its own training, evaluation, and other activities? Further, have reforms altered the traditional class basis of board membership, and if so, do new boards produce different policy actions? And finally, is citizen control of public education enhanced (e.g., by stimulating voter involvement or group representation) or is it diminished (e.g., by state mandates for quality and efficiency)?

INPUT CONVERSION PROCESSES: SUPERINTENDENTS AND TEACHERS

Systems analysis views the political world in terms of institutions and groups, broad processes and interactions. But leadership—or the individual's role in influencing the system—is also key to understanding it. Little study of leadership appears in the Eastonian framework of analysis, though, except as it contributes to legitimacy and support of the political system. That is why we paid special attention to the leadership role of school administrators and to the influence of teacher groups in school policymaking.

We see schools' administrators as the key decision makers whose leadership role stems from the power of their expertise as professionals. In a context where community voices were few and faint, and where boards had limited policy initiatives, school administrators have filled a vacuum in policymaking and implementation. Research two decades ago found that superintendents in particular were dominating their boards in policy matters. Other literature found these professionals dominating even the administrivia of school operations.

This leadership role has altered in the last two decades, however, as the administrators' enviroment became increasingly politicized. The autocrat gave way to the negotiator and power dominance to power sharing; in the process, new leadership roles developed. Such changes also stimulated new demands in policymaking arenas; superintendents responded with more differentiated roles and styles. Meanwhile, teachers mobilized to confront board and administrators with new demands, usually over economic concerns. Because collective bargaining has always involved the power potential of the strike weapon, local school authorities have had to face it and the consequences in an expanded policymaking context. Indeed, as teachers more often got elected to boards, lines between board and teacher responsibilities blurred. But it was evident that teachers had become new actors in educational policymaking, at least on budgets and, increasingly, on curriculum and other program matters.

Given these recent constraints on administrators, we need to know much more about how they can exercise leadership. Just giving in to community demands from groups or boards does not fit any definition of leadership. At the other extreme, the autocrat of earlier times, operating with limited check and input on decisions, may be impossible now, although research should determine the kinds of communities where this role remains. Also, a comprehensive review of the training needs (including conflict management) for administrators under this changed context is important to inform schools of education and professional organizations of needed new competencies. As for teachers, research is needed on their roles in the legislatures during the federal decentralization and state reform efforts of the 1980s. Research should gauge their influence by using organizational theory of challenge and response, as well as pressure-group theory on the logic of collective action. These theories would also provide powerful analytical guides in studying teachers as they struggle to define a new role in local policymaking.

INPUT CONVERSION PROCESSES: REFERENDA

Inputs to policymaking in the political system come from the general population usually indirectly, for example, through elections and interest group activity. Rarely does the population vote directly on policy matters in any political system. Political systems are usually constructed to diffuse popular will except in democracies, and the popular will on a specific policy only prevails, even in a democracy, when it is strong, insistent, and continuous. But the local politics of education does provide the opportunity for such direct input on conversion, taking the form of the referendum on school taxes and budgets.

This device serves as a gross indicator of citizen satisfaction with the operation of the school system. The percentage and direction of response can reflect great support in times of system expansion or great disenchantment in times of system dissatisfaction. They perform as barometers of public attitudes. Participation is modified by voter characteristics and the community itself; that is, turnout and support differ because of such factors. Another perspective is to view referenda as a vehicle for mobilizing majority support. This perspective is a matter of intense interest to many superintendents, particularly in the last two decades of shrinking support for school budgets.

Explicit in much research is the theory that referenda decisions are a function of rational self-interest. That means that voters without children or with children in private schools are less likely to support public school finances, while those with children in public schools are more likely. Research in this public-choice mode needs to expand in two ways to augment this theory. Researchers need to introduce the role of voters' nonrational influences and to expand the notion of self-interest to the noneconomic qualities of community life. Furthermore, strategizing for the superintendents needs to be broadened to incorporate new data (e.g., voter polls) and new analytic methods. Finally, scholars of democratic theory and systems analysis could explore the evidence of referenda. Does it enhance a dissatisfaction theory of democracy or provide an ignored component of the Eastonian framework?

POLITICAL REGIMES: STATES IN AN ERA OF INNOVATION

The constitutional rules and procedures for authoritatively allocating resources and values is the "political regime" in systems analysis. It is the object of demand inputs that are then either converted into policy or rejected. How the regime is organized for this task reveals what groups and which values dominate that society at present. There are fifty regimes in the American states, and they demonstrate both variety and regularity in handling demands for educational policy. During the 1980s, however, these fifty acted almost like a single regime in responding to public dissatisfaction with schooling.

Popular unhappiness with schooling finances and academic achievement at the local level generated demands in all fifty states. These demands were stimulated and articulated by national coalitions. Consequently, reforms have filled the agenda of every state. Also, policy networks for different reforms spread their ideas across the nation to make an impact on the fifty states. These efforts pursued typical educational values of equity, quality or excellence, efficiency, and choice—although priorities shift among these values over time and among states. Presentation and adoption of the reforms were relatively rapid, and they affected similarly states with different political cultures, particularly in the areas of finance and testing or assessment.

The result of these reforms has been a centralization of state policy mandates over local schooling. During the last ten years, legislatures have become what their constitutions had always authorized, central arenas for educational policymaking and implementation. Other state institutions, like governors and CSSOs, have also grown in influence. In addition, the capacities and competencies of state agencies to perform this expansion have grown. In short, the American state regime, facing a popular crisis, has adjusted by assigning new mandates in more areas.

This enlargement of state functions has stimulated a spate of research, much of it comparative for at least samples of the states. Many of these studies have been descriptive, although some seek to explain variations in reform by such measures as state culture and economic resources. But no one has yet evaluated this entire research stream, although there are recent comparative analysis reports about implementation. In the 1980s scholars were moving toward comparative analysis in aspects of this change and were using the rigor called for by Burlingame and Geske.[3]

Comparative analysis will be crucial to examining the policy stage beyond adoption, namely, implementation. Reform adoptions may be systemic due to national currents of needs and references, but later, we need close analysis of how different configurations of power and value produce different implementation patterns, as our discussion of state accustomization to federal innovations suggested. Indeed, such studies could influence future reforms when another window of opportunity arises. However, a larger research question about democratic theory remains; does this era demonstrate the dissatisfaction theory of democracy? And if so, will a permanent cost be the loss of citizen control of their local schools, or is that value less important to citizens than was once the case?

THE NATIONAL CONVERSION SYSTEM: THE JUDICIAL AGENCY

The judiciary occupies a special place in all political systems due to prevalent disputes among individuals and groups over the allocation of resources and values. By constructing a set of principled reasons for their allocation decisions, courts both settle the instant controversy and defuse certain policy options. Such adjudication does not eliminate conflict, but it does regulate it to reduce stress on the political system as a whole. Acceptance of such decisions also carries values of equity and justice into the community. That role of the courts has been significant in American history because we have always been an extremely litigious society and because the U.S. Supreme Court holds unusual authority to resolve major disputes. This power is particularly useful in a federal system, with its inevitable differences in response to almost any policy question. As a result, the judiciary becomes a miniature subsystem within the larger political system.

Education policy has been affected by these systematic qualities of the judiciary. Many elements of curriculum, authority relationships, discipline, and so on in a long list have brought courts into school policymaking. Recently, courts have taken a leading role in educational policy innovation through the processes of legalization and regulation. These events, signaled by leading court cases, have shaped the distribution of school services and the composition of school personnel and student body. Criticism of legalization and regulation developed, though, and reached a crescendo in the 1980s, part of widespread criticism about overwhelming federal regulations in many aspects of society. But the courts have been reluctant to back away from their definition of rights and responsibilities. The most controversial federal event involved desegregation; in the states it was school finances. The final evaluation of these decisions has yet to be made in either case.

Research in this area has been voluminous, occasioned by the flood of court cases and studies of their impact on school practices or state-local policy systems. That is, analysis has focused on the substance of opinions and their influence. However, other research needs to be directed at the role of judges' personal values in opinions, the mediating effects of state and community on the implementation of judicial orders, the process by which legal opinions guide state legislative policymaking, and the role of state courts in shaping school policy. Clearly the judiciary as conversion agency will continue as a major partner in this policy field, and as such it deserves more attention from other than legal analysts.

THE NATIONAL CONVERSION SYSTEM: FEDERAL LEGISLATIVE AND EXECUTIVE AGENCIES

The federal role is buffeted by powerful crosscurrents that make it difficult for the conversion process to deliver many significant policy outcomes. On the one hand, education is a popular national issue, and presidential candidates feel they must talk about the federal role. But on the other hand, the federal budget deficit of the Reagan administration and its impact on the economy greatly constrain the money for any domestic initiatives.[4] The result seems to be specialized small-scale programs or demonstration grants, administered with a large dose of rhetoric from the federal bully pulpit on broader issues.

A major research issue will remain the effectiveness of the bully pulpit. Secretary Bennett has spoken out on everything from AIDS to the math curriculum. But do state and local educators act after such federal urging? For example, do direct appeals to the public by federal officials result in public pressure on school officials to follow the federal position? Can the bully pulpit achieve what federally funded demonstration grants might, in terms of spreading new concepts or practices?

Interest in the impact of the modest federal steps toward deregulation will continue. Has the removal of federal strings resulted in many new local policies, or do the federal programs continue to operate in a routinized fashion similar to the past? What do LEAs spend their federal bloc grants on, and does this allocation contain lessons for states that choose to consolidate their own categorical programs? We hear less complaining recently about federal red tape; is it possible that this will diminish as an issue, to be refocused on the state agencies?

Perhaps the major new area for federal policy is the linkage between federal education policy and international economic competitiveness. What can the federal government do to improve economic growth through specific education initiatives? Obvious areas such as more math and science suggest themselves, but what about education technology? What new education interest groups are spawned by the economic competitiveness issue? Existing interest groups seem satisfied with an incremental federal role rather than new concepts like international trade implications for education policy. These federal interest groups, largely organized around categorical grants, have been on the defensive for fourteen years, trying to protect the gains they made from 1965 through 1980. They have coalesced well around incremental funding increases for the existing federal melange of programs. An interesting research question would be to explore these federal interest group strategies and tactics with their linkages to electoral support of specific candidates. Perhaps the interest groups will find a way to capitalize on economic competitiveness and thereby modify the direction of the federal role.

CODA

This chapter attests to a theme implicit throughout this book. This is a dual, interacting notion, that research in the politics of education over schools in conflict is both very exciting to scholars and deeply important to practitioners. Crisis does mean danger, but it is also rife with opportunity for those who seize the moment to add to knowledge and to learn from that knowledge. We have sought to do both.

NOTES

1. David Easton, *A Systems Analysis of Political Life* (New York: Wiley, 1965), p. vii.

2. Jeffrey Berry, *The Interest Group Society* (Boston: Little, Brown & Co., 1984), especially Chapters 5, 6, 7.

3. Martin Burlingame and Terry Geske, "State Politics and Education: An Examination of Multiple Case Studies," *Educational Administration Quarterly* (June 1979): 101–21.

4. See Paul E. Peterson, "The New Politics of Deficits," in *The New Direction in American Politics,* John E. Chubb and Paul Peterson, eds. (Washington, D.C.: Brookings Institute, 1985), pp. 365–98.

Subject Index

America 2000, 364
American Association of School
  Administrators (AASA), 97,
  299
American Association of University
  Women (AAUW), 94, 102, 280
American College Test (ACT), 359
American education
  choice and, 2, 3, 83–86, 150, 184,
    257, 258–260
  efficiency and, 10, 82–86, 150,
    171, 258–260, 262
  equity and, 2, 14, 82–86, 150, 171,
    184, 257–260, 262
  quality of, 2, 15, 82–86, 150, 184,
    258–260, 262, 301, 360–361
American Federation of Teachers,
  18, 95–96, 208–210, 213–217,
  271, 277–278, 367
A Nation Prepared, 302
A Nation at Risk, 253, 289, 301, 302,
  311, 368
Apolitical education, myth of, 1–2, 4–
  9, 238–239, 251

Boyer, Ernest, 101
Brown v. Topeka Board of Education,
  10, 265, 330, 332, 342, 344

"Bully pulpit," 352
Bush administration, 2, 361, 364

Carnegie Foundation, 101
Carter Administration, 351–352
Carter, Jimmy, 96, 115, 127, 149
Center for Policy Research in
  Education (CPRE), 302–317
Changing political agenda, 2–5, 369
Chief State School Officer, 286–288
Civil Rights Act, 266
Collective bargaining, 208–217
Committee for Economic Develop-
  ment, 315
Common Cause, 90
Conflict, origin and values of, 77–87
Conlan, John, 102
Conversion process
  federal agencies and, 379–385
  judicial agency and, 383–384
  local, Chapters 6 and 7
  referenda in, Chapter 8
  school boards and, 378–379
  state, Chapter 9
  superintendents and teachers,
    379–380
  transition in, 242–244
"Core constituencies," 9–21

387

197, 201–207, 240
as decision maker, 134, 156, 164,
    175–178, 190–191
input conversion and, 379–380
as representative, 178–180
Systems analysis, Chapter 2
    courts and, 323–326
    federalism and, 297–298
    research and educational politics
        and, Chapter 13

Teacher
    as political actor, 207–217, 271,
        274, 277–278
    certification, 365, 367
    input conversion and, 379–380
    organizational power and, 17–19,
        94
    political socialization and, 58–60
    professionalization, 302, 303
    strikes, 18, 208

Textbook content, and political
    socialization, 57–58
Tinker v. The Des Moines School District,
    14
Tomorrow's Teachers, 302

United States Department of
    Education (USDE), 329, 349,
    364
United States Labor Department
    Secretary's Commission for
    Achieving Necessary Skills
    (SCANS), 364
United States Office of Education
    (USOE), 350–351
United States Supreme Court
    desegregation and, 330–335
    finance and, 336
    policy and, 322–326, 341, 344

Warren, Earl, 331

Author Index